# Socialism and the Diasporic 'Other'

A comparative study of Irish Catholic and Jewish radical and communal politics in East London, 1889–1912

*BW*

STUDIES IN LABOUR HISTORY 11

## Studies in Labour History

'...a series which will undoubtedly become an important force in re-invigorating the study of Labour History.' *English Historical Review*

Studies in Labour History provides reassessments of broad themes along with more detailed studies arising from the latest research in the field of labour and working-class history, both in Britain and throughout the world. Most books are single-authored but there are also volumes of essays focussed on key themes and issues, usually emerging from major conferences organized by the British Society for the Study of Labour History. The series includes studies of labour organizations, including international ones, where there is a need for new research or modern reassessment. It is also its objective to extend the breadth of labour history's gaze beyond conventionally organized workers, sometimes to workplace experiences in general, sometimes to industrial relations, but also to working-class lives beyond the immediate realm of work in households and communities.

# Socialism and the Diasporic 'Other'

A comparative study
of Irish Catholic and Jewish radical
and communal politics in East London,
1889–1912

Daniel Renshaw

LIVERPOOL UNIVERSITY PRESS

First published 2018 by
Liverpool University Press
4 Cambridge Street
Liverpool
L69 7ZU

This paperback edition first published 2021

British Library Cataloguing-in-Publication data
A British Library CIP record is available

ISBN 978-1-78694-122-0 cased
ISBN 978-1-80085-717-9 paperback

Typeset by Carnegie Book Production, Lancaster
Printed and bound by CPI Group (UK) Ltd, Croydon CR0 4YY

*This book is dedicated with all of my love to my wonderful wife Rose,
and to our son Joel.*

*And to the memory of my grandparents*

*Eric and Minnie Woodall
and George and Winifred Renshaw*

# Contents

# Acknowledgements

This book grew out of my PhD thesis, which I began work on in the autumn of 2011. Along the way, I have been helped immeasurably by the support, advice, and friendship of a very large number of people. First, I am grateful for the patience and love of my family. In particular, I wish to thank Phil and Cailine Woodall and Geoff and Irene Renshaw for putting me up (and putting up with me) whilst I was carrying out research further afield; Paddy and Mary Renshaw for the interest they showed in my work, and my sister Layla Renshaw and brother-in-law Patrick Coupar for their love and support. I am thankful too for the interest shown by my wife's family, Elizabeth Harland, Bob and Jane Harland, Kate Lund, and Sarah Harland. Most of all, thanks to Mum and Dad, for everything.

Throughout writing the thesis and book, I have had the support of the History Department and fellow doctoral students at the University of Reading. Thanks to everyone in the History Department for encouragement over the last seven years, and the admin team in the School of Humanities for holding everything together. Thanks to Jacqui Turner, Jeremy Burchardt, Elizabeth Matthew, Richard Blakemore, Helen Parish, Patrick Major, Ruth Salter, Max Hodgson, Jason Parry, Matt Broad, Tom Squire, Coleen Weedon, and everyone in the Department, past and present, for support, kindness, and advice. Special thanks to my PhD supervisors, Matt Worley, who has been variously personal tutor, supervisor, colleague, and friend for the last ten years, and Emily West, for her invaluable advice when the thesis was being re-written. Thanks too to my PhD examiners, David Stack and David Feldman, for their very helpful and detailed suggestions.

Thanks to the archivists across the country for being so generous with their time and advice – grateful thanks to Darren Treadwell at the People's History Museum; Dawn Waterman at the Board of Deputies of British Jews; Adrian Ailes at the National Archives; Susannah Rayner and Father Nicholas Schofield at the Westminster Diocesan Archives; Elizabeth Selby,

Alice Quine, and Jemima Jarman at the Jewish Museum; and the archivists at the LSE Special Collections, the London Metropolitan Archives, the Tower Hamlets Local History Library and Archives, the Warwick Modern Records Centre, the University of Southampton, the British Library, the University of Reading Library, and the Bodleian. Thanks also to Bronwen Walter, Tom Linehan, Ben Gidley, Giulia Ni Dhulchaointigh, and Francis King for advice and help. Thanks too for the AHRC which funded the PhD that formed the basis for this book. I would like to thank everyone at Liverpool University Press involved in the project from the genesis of the book proposal to its completion, and particularly Alison Welsby and Patrick Brereton, as well as Rachel Chamberlain at Carnegie Book Production. Thanks to Tom Hall, a good friend for the last twelve years. Cheers to everyone from Bulmershe days for still being great friends, twenty years on. Thanks to everyone at Wycliffe for love and support. And finally again, this is for Rose and Joel.

# Introduction

One late afternoon in London, at the end of the 1890s, the well-known socialist, novelist, and campaigner Robert Blatchford went for an excursion with friends from the centre of the metropolis into the neighbourhood of Whitechapel in the East End. For Blatchford, editor of the *Clarion* newspaper, the experience was a 'painful dream', or perhaps a nightmare.[1] 'Street after street, mile after mile, district after district ... and still the same dense streams of hurrying souls, each wrapped up in self – each with heart steeled and eyes hardened against all the tragedy, sorrow, anxiety, weariness, of all the rest.'[2] In an earlier chapter of the collection of essays, *Dismal England* (1899), the author made explicit at least one root cause of the profound dislocation that Blatchford, himself no stranger to poverty, experienced during his brief time in Whitechapel – the presence of the diasporic 'other':

> We entered the Ghetto. The children of the ghetto swarmed about us. They were swarthy, yet had in their faces the unwholesome pallor peculiar to London ... Jewish they all were, but of different nationalities: the prevailing language, my companion said, was Yiddish. It was a strange experience: within half an hour's walk of the City boundaries we were in a foreign country.[3]

Thus one leading figure in the socialist movement reported an encounter with the 'new' East End, an area in which it seemed that English had been displaced as the lingua franca of the streets, where an old (and in fact mythical) ethnic homogeneity had been succeeded by a disorientating cosmopolitanism.

---

[1] Robert Blatchford, 'A Transpontine Theatre', in *Dismal England* (London: Walter Scott Ltd, 1899), pp. 27–28.

[2] Blatchford, 'A Transpontine Theatre', pp. 28–29.

[3] Blatchford, 'The Children of the Ghetto', in *Dismal England*, p. 16.

The years between 1889 and 1912 were a key transitory stage in the evolution of the British left. The strikes of 1888–1889 heralded the birth of an aggressive and proactive socialist-led trade union movement that organised workers in unskilled occupations. This was followed by a coalescence of some of these forces in the early twentieth century around what would become the Labour Party. In turn there was a fragmentation in the explicitly Marxist left in 1911–1912, and by the end of the period a build-up of momentum in the workers' movement that would come to fruition after the First World War. This book considers the role that metropolitan socialism as a movement, as well as individual socialists and trade unionists, played in this arena of ethnic, religious, and class difference described by Blatchford above. It will examine the influence of radical politics in the lives and struggles of East End migrant groups in the late nineteenth and early twentieth centuries, between the great waves of industrial action of 1889 and 1911–1912. The text will approach this question by comparing the experiences of the two largest diasporic 'outsider' groups present in the East End during this period – the Jewish and Irish Catholic communities – and their interactions with late-Victorian and early twentieth-century radical politics.

First, this study will analyse the importance of both ethnicity and diasporic identity in the formation of socialist ideology and practice. Rather than a mere footnote in the history of radical politics to which socialist interactions with ethnic or religious minorities are often reduced, concepts of ethnic difference and socialist complicity in or rejection of 'othering' were crucial in the evolving socialist narrative. The struggles of the wider East End labour and trade union movements were viewed through the prism of ethnic, religious, and diasporic difference, with, as we shall see, whole groups being designated en masse as 'blacklegs' or 'good comrades', depending on the roles played by individuals in the industrial disputes of the period.

Difference, in particular the supposed propensity towards violence that it was suggested existed in migrant communities, was used to demarcate ideological positions, to define an 'English' social-democracy against 'alien' strands of socialist thought: anarchism, nihilism, communism, and syndicalism.[4] This relationship was often characterised by a lack of consistency and coherence. The late-Victorian left was not a 'broad church', but rather a number of competing places of worship, with different hymn sheets and liturgies. Indeed, even within the memberships of the various socialist organisations of the period operating in the capital, the Social Democratic Federation (SDF), its successors the Social Democratic Party (SDP) and the British Socialist Party (BSP), the Socialist League, the

---

[4] See Paul Ward, *Red Flag and Union Jack: Englishness, Patriotism and the British Left, 1881–1924* (Martlesham: Boydell Press, 1998).

Fabians, the Independent Labour Party (ILP), and the Labour Party, there was no consensus on the correct 'position' towards migrant communities.[5] The attitudes of the wider trade union-based labour movement towards ethnicity was if anything even more fragmented and confused, oscillating between professions of inter-ethnic solidarity and at times explicitly racist agitation, especially in port and docking communities.[6] The movement of the socialist and labour organisations towards their eventual position as defender and champion of the rights of minority working-class communities was not a simple or easy one, and was not inevitable.

Secondly, this book will contrast the agendas and structures of the metropolitan Jewish and Catholic religious and secular hierarchies in a comparative framework. It will discuss the relationships between the communal leaderships on the one hand – the Catholic Church, the Board of Deputies of British Jews (BoD), the United Synagogue, the Federation of Synagogues and the Jewish ecclesiastical law court the *Beth Din* – and working-class co-religionists and the socialist movement(s) on the other. What was the nature of the complex and reciprocal relationship between Catholic priest or Jewish rabbi and their congregations in East London? How did the differing leadership structures of the hierarchies, domestic and international, condition the response to working-class radicalism? Catholic and Jewish minorities, however impeccably 'respectable' the leaderships perceived themselves to be, remained partially excluded from a national narrative well into the twentieth century. In the following chapters we will consider the interplay of faith and ethnicity unique to these two groups that distinguished them from other religious minorities in late-Victorian Britain, and how the crucial factor of transnational affiliations and networks shaped the ways in which Jewish and Irish Catholic communities were perceived in wider society.[7] Catholicism and Judaism in Britain were portrayed in sectarian and antisemitic rhetoric as combining the powerlessness (and economic competition) of poor inner-city immigrant communities with transnational power, wealth, and elite influence, giving anti-immigrant or sectarian rhetoric against the Jewish or Catholic 'other' a peculiar potency.

Finally, this work will interpret Irish–Jewish relations and comparisons at a grass-roots level. It will examine the appeals of socialism, the success

---

[5] See Mark Bevir, *The Making of British Socialism* (Princeton, NJ: Princeton University Press, 2011); E.H. Hunt, *British Labour History, 1815–1914* (London: Weidenfeld & Nicolson 1981), p. 186.

[6] Laura Tabili, *'We Ask for British Justice': Workers and Racial Difference in Late Imperial Britain* (Ithaca, NY: Cornell University Press, 1994).

[7] See Paul Ward, *Britishness Since 1970* (Oxford: Routledge, 2004), p. 183 for discussion of the importance of religion in the perception of Irish, Jewish (and Muslim) communities settled in Britain.

of unionisation in immigrant neighbourhoods, the devolved nature of working-class minority worship in the East End, and the reaction to anti-migrant or anti-Catholic organisations active in the area. The diasporic groups encountered each other in differing contexts, from the workplace and places of worship to the school and the public house, and in the rough and ready arena of local East End politics.[8] It will address how Irish and Jewish minorities were placed by the socialist movement on the wider metropolitan class gradient, and the difficulties that were faced in trying to reconcile the complex and sometimes divergent socio-economic processes at work in migrant communities with the idealised image of a classic proletariat. Both Irish and Jewish East End communities shared a conditional, precarious (and shifting) 'white' status in the late-Victorian racial pyramid.[9] The following narrative will address the extent to which both groups were associated with political violence (Fenianism in the Irish case; anarchism and related political activities in the case of Jews). There was also, conversely, and at times simultaneously, a strong association with emasculation, a supposed Jewish 'weakness' and aversion to hard physical labour and an Irish 'infantilisation' (rooted in the colonial experience). This emasculation sat alongside gendered relations within the migrant communities that were predicated on demarcated roles for men and women and cultures of hyper-masculinity operating within the Irish and Jewish diasporas. How did class relations and communal authority function in the diasporic East End?

The recognition by historians of the rich potential that could be drawn from a comparative study of Irish and Jewish communal and radical politics in a metropolitan context is by no means recent, although few academics have acted upon this. The value of a comparative study involving Irish Catholics and Jews in the East End was noted in the early 1970s. In Bernard Gainer's groundbreaking study of the Jewish community and the 1905 Aliens Act, *The Alien Invasion* (1972), the author concludes by appealing for more detailed comparisons to be drawn between the Jewish community and other immigrant groups, and briefly outlines potential Irish/Jewish comparisons. Writing four years after the passing of the 1968 Race Relations Act and Enoch Powell's 'Rivers of Blood' speech, and during a period marked by

[8] Paul Thompson, *Socialists, Liberals and Labour: The Struggle for London, 1885–1914* (London: Routledge and Kegan Paul, 1967), p. 29.

[9] 'Introduction', Shearer West (ed.), *The Victorians and Race* (Aldershot: Ashgate Publishing, 1996), pp. 8–9 and Douglas A. Lorimer, *Colour, Class and the Victorians* (Leicester: Leicester University Press, 1978), pp. 14–15. See also Matthew Frye Jacobson, *Whiteness of a Different Color: European Immigrants and the Alchemy of Race* (Cambridge, Mass.: Harvard University Press, 1998), p. 6.

increased anti-immigrant agitation, Gainer argues for further discussion of parallels between past (and retrospectively celebrated) waves of migration and current arrivals from the New Commonwealth:

> The nature of the constant factors between often unwilling host and usually unwelcomed guest may be open to dispute, but the correlation among the cases of the Irish, East European Jews, and West Indians and Pakistanis, separate though they are by time and circumstance, show that some such factors exist, and certainly deserve further study.[10]

In the final paragraphs of the text Gainer considers in detail potential avenues of explicit comparison of Irish and Jewish populations, in particular the articulation of prejudice against both groups.[11]

However, despite Gainer outlining this territory for further detailed work on Irish–Jewish intersections and comparisons in a London-based context, this area continued to be neglected by academics working in the fields of migrant and minority history. Historians have largely concentrated on either intra-communal relations *within* diasporic communities or interactions between diasporic groups and the host society rather than with other diasporas in the same physical location. More than twenty years after the publication of *The Alien Invasion*, Hugh McLeod concluded a chapter in the collection of essays *Retrieved Riches* (1995), on working-class religion in the late-Victorian metropolis, by identifying a gap in the academic literature:

> Finally, I would plead for a more comparative approach to London's religious history … the histories of Christianity and Judaism in London have largely been written in isolation from one another, and in this paper I have continued this tradition. It must be hoped that more historians will attempt a broader religious history that embraces both communities, and strengthens our understanding of both by drawing comparisons between them.[12]

Twenty years on from this appeal, comparative discussion of Irish and Jewish communities, or comparisons between the progress and interactions of Catholicism and Judaism in the capital, are still few and far between, generally portrayed, to quote Nazneen Ahmed in an article on the inter-connections

---

[10] Bernard Gainer, *The Alien Invasion: The Origins of the Aliens Act of 1905* (London: Heinemann, 1972), p. 211. In John A. Garrard, *The English and Immigration, 1880–1910* (London: Oxford University Press, 1971), Garrard also draws connections between anti-Jewish prejudice and contemporary racism against black and Asian communities.

[11] Gainer, *Alien Invasion*, p. 213.

[12] Hugh McLeod, 'Working-Class Religion in Late-Victorian London: Booth's "Religious Influences" Revisited', in David Englander and Rosemary O'Day (eds), *Retrieved Riches: Social Investigation in Britain, 1840–1914* (Aldershot: Scolar Press, 1995), p. 282.

of Muslim diasporas and other faiths in the East End, as 'social worlds that pass each other by relatively untouched'.[13]

Nancy L. Green first made the case for the utility of comparative discussion of migrant groups and diaspora, and the different ways and different levels at which the comparative approach could be employed, in 1994.[14] There are now a number of comparative studies of different branches of the global Jewish diaspora, with historians comparing Jewish communities in London, New York, Amsterdam, Paris, Germany, and Scandinavia.[15] Similarly, a number of recent collections of essays on the Irish diaspora adopt a transnational perspective, comparing and contrasting Irish communities in North America, Argentina, India, South Africa, Australia, and New Zealand.[16] These do not address group interactions or comparisons with *other* diasporic populations, but focus on interactions *within* a particular diasporic transnational community. Historians of American immigration have discussed to a much greater degree interactions between different minority groups, particularly in urban areas such as New York; London on the other hand is surprisingly still relatively neglected ground.[17]

---

[13] Nazneen Ahmed, with Jane Garnett, Ben Gidley, Alana Harris and Michael Keith, 'Historicising Diaspora Spaces: Performing Faith, Race, and Place in London's East End', in Jane Garnett and Sondra L. Hausner (eds), *Religion in Diaspora: Cultures of Citizenship* (Basingstoke: Palgrave Macmillan, 2015), p. 55.

[14] Nancy L. Green, 'The Comparative Method and Poststructural Structuralism: New Perspectives for Migration Studies', *Journal of American Ethnic History*, Vol. 13, No. 4 (Summer 1994). See Donald M. MacRaild, 'Crossing Migrant Frontiers: Comparative Reflections on Irish Migrants in Britain and the United States in the Nineteenth Century', in Donald M. MacRaild (ed.), *The Great Famine and Beyond: Irish Migrants in Britain in the Nineteenth and Twentieth Centuries* (Dublin: Irish Academic Press, 2000), pp. 42–43.

[15] Selma Berrol, *East Side/East End: Eastern European Jews in London and New York, 1870–1920* (Westport, Conn.: Praeger Publishers, 1994); Andrew Godley, *Jewish Immigrant Entrepreneurship in New York and London, 1880–1914: Enterprise and Culture* (Basingstoke: Palgrave, 2001); Karin Hofmeester, *Jewish Workers and the Labour Movement: A Comparative Study of Amsterdam, London and Paris, 1870–1914* (Aldershot: Ashgate Publishing, 2004); and Tobias Brinkmann, *Points of Passage: Jewish Transmigrants from Eastern Europe to Scandinavia, Germany and Britain, 1880–1914* (New York: Berghahn Books, 2013).

[16] See Andy Bielenberg (ed.), *The Irish Diaspora* (Harlow: Pearson Education, 2000) for discussion of Irish diasporic identity in Boston, the American Deep South, Argentina, India and Europe and David T. Gleeson (ed.), *The Irish in the Atlantic World* (Columbia: University of South Carolina Press, 2010) for articles on the transatlantic aspects of Irish nationalism and republicanism.

[17] Ronald H. Bayor, *Neighbors in Conflict: The Irish, Germans, Jews and Italians of New York City, 1929–1941* (Baltimore, Md.: Johns Hopkins University Press, 1978). For a snapshot of Irish–Jewish relations in New York during the period under discussion, see Edward T. O'Donnell, 'Hibernians versus Hebrews? A New Look at the 1902 Jacob Joseph Funeral Riot', *Journal of the Gilded Age and Progressive Era*, Vol. 6, No. 2 (April 2007).

Two comparative East End studies that bypass ethnic and religious and indeed chronological boundaries are Anne Kershen's book, *Strangers, Aliens and Asians* (2005), and her chapter, 'The Migrant at Home in Spitalfields', in Burrell and Panayi's *Histories and Memories* (2006). Here, Kershen compares migrant groups that have shared common geographical space in different time periods. These three groups – seventeenth-century Huguenot religious refugees, Victorian Eastern European Jewish arrivals, and Bangladeshi migrants in the early 1970s – do not coexist or interact in a physical day-to-day sense. However, Kershen stresses the common ground, not just physical but spiritual and political, held by migrant groups arriving at different times. Kershen explores the complex migrant experience of what constitutes 'home' and how immigrant groups 'belong' in a particular area.[18] Kershen's book and chapter point the way to how a study of different minority groups sharing a common physical space could be approached.

A small number of texts exist that explicitly compare the Irish Catholic and Jewish diasporas in some detail. Catherine Jones, in a pioneering overview of the response of the British state to immigration, has examined side by side in some detail the nineteenth-century Irish and Jewish experiences of migrant settlement and their interactions with the British state and welfare provision.[19] George Bornstein has focused attention on the cultural and political conflations between transnational Irish and Jewish communities on both sides of the Atlantic and a third diasporic group, the descendants of the African slaves forcibly brought to North America. *Colors of Zion* (2011) stresses the positive elements of the shared suffering, cultural dislocation, and forced migration of the Irish, Jewish, and African diasporas.[20] Bornstein discusses at length the racialisation of Jewish and Irish populations in the nineteenth century and their inclusion in that category of European 'others' described by L.P. Curtis as 'white Negroes'.[21] William Rubinstein's 1996 work on British Jewry also compares in some detail the similarities and differences between the Catholic and Jewish experience in Victorian society. Rubinstein contends that in Britain antisemitism always ran a poor second

[18] Anne J. Kershen, *Strangers, Aliens and Asians: Huguenots, Jews and Bangladeshis in Spitalfields, 1660–2000* (Abingdon: Routledge, 2005) and Anne J. Kershen, 'The Migrant at Home in Spitalfields: Memory, Myth and Reality', in Kathy Burrell and Panikos Panayi (eds), *Histories and Memories: Migrants and their History in Britain* (London: Tauris Academic Studies, 2006).

[19] Catherine Jones, *Immigration and Social Policy in Britain* (Cambridge: Tavistock Publications, 1977).

[20] George Bornstein, *The Colors of Zion: Blacks, Jews and Irish from 1845 to 1945* (Cambridge, Mass.: Harvard University Press, 2011).

[21] L.P. Curtis, *Apes and Angels: The Irishman in Victorian Caricature* (Newton Abbot: David & Charles Ltd, 1971), pp. 13–14.

to anti-Catholic sectarianism, and that anti-Catholicism 'diverted much potential religious hostility' from the Jewish community.[22]

In the last thirty years there have been three detailed studies of Catholic–Jewish interactions located specifically in East London. In the final chapters of *London Jewry and London Politics* (1989), Geoffrey Alderman discusses at length, and in the context of local Labour Party organisations, the political relationship between Jewish and Irish constituencies in the inter-war period. This encompasses the common cause made during the First World War by Jewish radicals and Irish nationalists against the provisions of the Defence of the Realm Act (DORA) and the political alliances of the 1920s that in 1922 resulted in Jewish voters electing a Roman Catholic Labour MP in Whitechapel. He also considers the effects on communal relations of the rise of fascism in the 1930s.[23] This book was followed by Henry Srebrnik's *London Jews and British Communism* (1995), which offers a largely negative interpretation of inter-war Irish–Jewish intercommunal relations, both inside local Labour Party organisation and in the wider East End.[24]

The second extended piece of work to compare the social history of the Irish and Jewish East End is L.V. Marks's 1990 doctoral thesis, 'Irish and Jewish Women's Experience of Childbirth and Infant Care in East London, 1870–1939', and the monograph that followed it, *Working Wives and Working Mothers* (1990). Marks's work is primarily concerned with health care provision in the two communities, but, in discussing this, wider comparisons and contrasts between Irish and Jewish neighbours in East London emerge. Marks's chosen constituency, immigrant women, is, as Louise Raw writes in her history of the match-women's strike, an excluded and disenfranchised 'other' three times over, by virtue of gender, class, and ethnicity, and Marks writes of the common discrimination faced by both Irish and Jewish women.[25] Marks's thesis takes in the wider role of the

---

[22] W.D. Rubinstein, *A History of the Jews of the English-Speaking World: Great Britain* (Basingstoke: Macmillan, 1996), pp. 8 and 34.

[23] Geoffrey Alderman, *London Jewry and London Politics, 1889–1986* (London: Routledge, 1989), pp. 80 and 84.

[24] Henry Felix Srebrnik, *London Jews and British Communism, 1935–1945* (Ilford: Vallentine Mitchell, 1995), pp. 8–10, 29–30, 31–34. See also W.J. Fishman's chapter 'Allies in the Promised Land: Reflections on the Irish and Jews in the East End' in Anne J. Kershen, *London: The Promised Land? The Migrant Experience in a Capital City* (Aldershot: Avebury, 1997) pp. 46–48 for a positive socialist analysis of Irish-Jewish working class relations in East London.

[25] L.V. Marks, 'Irish and Jewish Women's Experience of Childbirth and Infant Care in East London, 1870–1939 (DPhil, University of Oxford, 1990); Lara Marks, *Working Wives and Working Mothers: A Comparative Study of Irish and Eastern European Jewish Married Women's Work and Motherhood in East London, 1870–1914* (London: PNL Press, 1990); Louise

family and kinship networks transplanted from Eastern Europe or rural Ireland to the East End, and the barrier of language felt by newcomers from both communities. She also considers the immense social pressures experienced by young Jewish and Irish women as a result of the expectations of the host society and socially conservative migrant communities.[26]

The third and most recent addition to the literature on East End relations and comparisons between the two communities is Bronwen Walter's 2010 article, 'Irish/Jewish Diasporic Intersections in the East End of London'. Walter's discussion of shared locations between Irish and Jewish neighbours sketches out in detail the lines along which a more extended comparison of the two communities could run. She establishes several key commonalities in the Irish and Jewish diasporic experiences. Walter points to the traumatic circumstances in which both Irish Catholics and Jews left their homelands to settle in Britain. She makes the important point that religious faith could be at times a divisive factor in relationships between the two communities, as well as a common factor in Jewish and Irish outsider status.[27] Walter also stresses the complex class and gender dynamics at work in Irish/Jewish intersections.[28] This book is intended to expand upon and reinterpret the existing discussion of interactions and comparisons between the two communities in the explicit context of radical political engagement between the great waves of industrial action that serve as bookends for this study.

Nineteenth-century East London in a national context was not unique in its poverty, its levels of disease and insanitary conditions, its mortality rates, or its slum housing, but the area was special for two reasons. First, there was a prevalence of sweated and casual trades: tailoring and boot-making, cabinet-making, and the docks and building sites. The nature of these trades, and the difficulties in organising casual labour, meant that socialism and the labour movement followed a different trajectory in the East End than it did in other industrialised areas of the country, for example, in Lancashire, Scotland, and South Wales, all of which possessed 'classic' proletariats and strong trade union and socialist organisations. Trade unionism and

---

Raw, *Striking A Light: The Bryant and May Matchwomen and their Place in History* (London: Continuum International Publishing Group, 2009), chapter 8.

[26] Marks, 'Irish and Jewish Women's Experience of Childbirth', pp. 72, 138–139.

[27] Bronwen Walter, 'Irish/Jewish Diasporic Intersections in the East End of London: Paradoxes and Shared Locations', in M. Prum (ed.), *La Place de l'autre* (Paris: L'Harmattan, 2010), p. 54.

[28] Walter, 'Irish/Jewish Diasporic Intersections' pp. 59–60. See also Bronwen Walter, 'Placing Irish Women Within and Beyond the British Empire: Contexts and Comparisons', in D.A.J. MacPherson and Mary J. Hickman (eds), *Women and Irish Diaspora Identities: Theories, Concepts and New Perspectives* (Manchester: Manchester University Press, 2014), pp. 135–138 in which this is expanded upon by Walter.

socialist organisation in the East End was structurally weaker than its robust northern counterparts.[29]

Mainstream politics in London also exhibited a different dynamic from the rest of the country. The year 1889 was not only marked by sustained industrial action in London's sweated industries but also by the first elections to the newly established London County Council (LCC).[30] The principal opposition in metropolitan political cut and thrust at a local level was between 'Progressives' and 'Moderates', designations which aligned to the national division of Liberals and Conservatives. For much of the period under discussion, therefore, explicitly socialist politics in the capital ran a poor third to the well-oiled Progressive and Moderate party-political machines. Indeed, it was not clear whether successful explicitly socialist politics, based around class antagonism, would take root in the East End, or, as seemed likely until 1906 at the earliest, be subsumed into a more general 'Lib.-Lab.' Progressive alliance.[31] Notable labour figures that will feature in the following account, principally John Burns in South London, very successfully sought and attained election and re-election under this wider 'Progressive' affiliation.[32] Whilst this study focuses principally on the interactions of explicitly *socialist* politics within the Irish Catholic and Jewish communities, it is important to note that communal politics in East London in the period was dominated by formidable Progressive/Liberal/Radical and Moderate/Conservative local organisations, which did not wholly yield to Labour until after the First World War, and to which the majority of politicised Jews and Irish Catholics who enjoyed the vote in the 1890s and 1900s subscribed to and supported.

Secondly, East London, partly but not solely because of its proximity to the docks where many migrants from the continent first arrived in Britain, was poly-cultural and poly-diasporic in a way that few other areas of Great Britain were during the 1889–1912 period. This differentiates East London from the smaller British towns, still largely mono-cultural. It also contrasts with cities

---

[29] John Saville, *The Labour Movement in Britain* (London: Faber and Faber, 1988), pp. 23–24.

[30] Ken Young, *Local Politics and the Rise of Party: The London Municipal Society and the Conservative Intervention in Local Elections, 1894–1963* (Leicester: Leicester University Press, 1975), pp. 38–39.

[31] Eugenio Biagini, *British Democracy and Irish Nationalism, 1876–1906* (Cambridge: Cambridge University Press, 2007), p. 314; David Dutton, *A History of the Liberal Party since 1900* (Basingstoke: Palgrave Macmillan, 2004) (republished 2013), p. 37. See John Shepherd 'Labour and Parliament: The Lib.-Labs. As the First Working Class MPs, 1885–1906', in Eugenio F. Biagini and Alastair J. Reid (eds), *Currents of Radicalism: Organised Labour and Party Politics in Britain, 1850–1914* (Cambridge: Cambridge University Press, 1991) for the evolution of the 'progressive alliance' in general and John Burns in particular.

[32] See Susan D. Pennybacker, *A Vision for London, 1889–1914: Labour, Everyday Life and the LCC Experiment* (London: Routledge, 1993), p. 103.

such as Glasgow and Manchester, and the northern mill towns, in which one predominant 'outsider' ethnic group, the Irish, interacted with a Protestant host population.[33] East London in the nineteenth century, and particularly after 1881, rather like Tiger Bay in Cardiff, and some areas of Liverpool, was an area where *multiple* diasporas and the host society interacted with each other in multiple contexts and combinations, one of the few areas of the United Kingdom that approached the poly-ethnic make-up of a city such as late nineteenth-century New York, with its 'Italian, German, French, African, Spanish, Bohemian, Russian, Scandinavian, Jewish, and Chinese colonies'.[34] Avtar Brah in *Cartographies of Diaspora* (1996) defined such an area of myriad cultural, religious, social, and political interactions as *diaspora space*:

> Diaspora space is the point at which boundaries of inclusion and exclusion, of belonging and otherness, of 'us' and 'them', are contested ... diaspora space as conceptual category is 'inhabited', not only by those who have migrated and their descendants, but equally by those who are constructed and represented as indigenous ... In the diaspora space called 'England', for example, African-Caribbean, Irish, Asian, Jewish and other diasporas intersect among themselves as well as with the entity constructed as 'Englishness', thoroughly re-inscribing it in the process.[35]

The boundaries of the East End of London have always been somewhat porous and uncertain. To quote Alan Palmer, 'No government would be so rash as to give the East End local administrative unity, not least because no one can draw its boundaries with definite precision on a map.'[36] Charles Booth's definition in the first volume on 'Poverty' in his social study of the late nineteenth-century metropolis, *Life and Labour of the People in London*, serves as a good rough model: 'Shoreditch, Bethnal Green, Whitechapel, St. George's-in-the-East, Stepney, Mile End Old Town and Poplar'. To this I will add the following areas also contained in the early nineteenth-century Tower Division of Middlesex (also known as Tower Hamlets): Bow, Spitalfields, Limehouse, and also suburban outposts rapidly being absorbed into

[33] Both Glasgow and Manchester (and Leeds) experienced Jewish settlement post-1881, but not to the same extent in numerical terms as East London.

[34] Jacob Riis, *How the Other Half Lives* (New York: Penguin Books, 1997) (originally published 1890), p. 21. See also Panikos Panayi, *An Immigration History of Britain: Multicultural Racism since 1800* (Harlow: Pearson Education, 2010), p. 117 on the multicultural histories of Cardiff and Liverpool.

[35] Avtar Brah, *Cartographies of Diaspora: Contesting Identities* (Oxford: Routledge, 1996), pp. 208–209.

[36] Alan Palmer, *The East End: Four Centuries of London Life* (London: John Murray, 1989), pp. xi and 3. See Paul Newland, *The Cultural Construction of London's East End: Urban Iconography, Modernity and the Spacialisation of Englishness* (Amsterdam: Rodopi, 2008), p. 17 on this ambiguity.

the East End in the 1890s such as West and East Ham and Canning Town. In his study, Booth lists Hackney, to the north, separately.[37] While centred on the neighbourhoods of East London, this discussion will sometimes stray as far south as Battersea and west to Hyde Park, and sometimes leave London and indeed the United Kingdom altogether. But the study is rooted in the streets, schools, workshops, and places of worship of the East End.

Irish and Jewish communities were only two of a number of diasporic groups settled in the streets of East London, from Welsh colonies in Whitechapel to a long-established 'Chinatown' in Limehouse. However, there were a number of factors that distinguished the two communities. In numerical terms, the Irish and the Jews were the largest minorities in the eastern part of the metropolis. Unlike other numerically significant European immigrant groups settled in London (for example, the large French and German communities), Irish and Eastern European Jewish migrants into the East End had arrived on English shores in traumatic circumstances which coloured future communal politics and interactions with the host society. They were also 'stateless', the Irish through British colonialism, the Jews through legalistic persecution in Russia and Poland, in a way that these other groups were not.[38] As was the case with smaller groups, such as the Chinese and Italians, both the Irish and Jews were associated in hostile anti-migrant discourse with inherent criminal inclinations and activities.[39] As was the case with the Italians, both were associated with adherence to an alien and perhaps antagonistic religious faith, carrying at the same time a dangerous strain of political radicalism.[40] Both communities, like the Chinese, were depicted as effeminised and emasculated as well as presenting a sexual threat.[41] However, the Italian population in England in this period was small, and the Chinese population miniscule compared with the Jewish and Irish Catholic communities. In

---

[37] Booth, *Life and Labour of the People in London*, First Series, *Poverty*, Vol. 1, *East, Central and South London* (London: Macmillan, 1902), p. 32.

[38] See Constance Bantman, *The French Anarchists in London: Exile and Transnationalism in the First Globalisation* (Liverpool: Liverpool University Press, 2013) for detailed discussion of French radical political refugees in the metropolis.

[39] Alan J. Lee, 'Aspects of the Working-Class Response to the Jews in Britain, 1880–1914', in Kenneth Lunn (ed.), *Hosts, Immigrants and Minorities: Historical Responses to Newcomers in British Society 1870–1914* (Folkstone, Kent: W.M. Dawson and Sons, 1980), p. 114.

[40] Booth, *Life and Labour of the People in London*, Third Series, *Religious Influences*, Vol. 2, *London North of the Thames: The Inner Ring* (London: Macmillan, 1902), p. 141. See also Lucio Sponza, 'Italian Immigrants in Britain: Perspectives and Self-Perceptions', in Burrell and Panayi, *Histories and Memories* for discussion of Italian Catholicism and radical activity in the capital.

[41] For discussion of race-based sexual angst against non-white minority groups, see Sascha Auerbach, *Race, Law and the 'Chinese Puzzle' in Imperial Britain* (New York: Palgrave Macmillan, 2009), pp. 158–159.

the 1891 census, the Chinese-born population of England and Wales was estimated at 582.[42] In the same year, the Italian-born population of England and Wales was identified as being 9,909, while the Irish-born population of England and Wales was 458,315 (not taking into account second- and third-generation Irish Catholics born on the mainland). This was a decline from the highpoint of Irish settlement – 601,634 in 1861.[43] The Jewish population at the turn of the twentieth century has been estimated at around 150,000 to 200,000, with a claim made in a volume of Charles Booth's *Life and Labour of the People in London* of a Jewish community of some 60,000 to 70,000 living in the East End in the early 1890s.[44]

Both of the communities contained a powerful current of nationalism that, in the Jewish case, would increasingly come to prominence in the inter-war period, but that for Irish East-Enders influenced domestic concerns prior to 1914. Finally, and importantly for the purposes of this study, both Irish and Jewish East-Enders were heavily involved in the strike actions of 1889 and 1911–1912, and socialist attempts to radicalise East End migrant groups focused largely on these two communities.

In comparing the Irish and Jewish communities and their interactions with socialism, this study employs both individualising and universalising comparative approaches, the former demonstrating the differences in the Jewish/Irish Catholic diasporic experience in the East End and the latter the similarities between the two communities. This book aims to be symmetrical in its scope, giving equal weight to both communities and their communal hierarchies. In doing so it will follow on from Neil Evans's 1988 appeal for 'rigorous and empirically grounded' comparisons – breaking national histories down into 'the building blocks of regional and national distinctiveness within the British State'.[45] Stefan Berger, discussing the utility of drawing comparisons in labour history in particular, writes about comparing labour movements in a transnational context, but his words could equally be applied to studying different cultural or ethnic groups interacting within the same national movement:

---

[42] Gregor Benton and Edmund Gomez, *The Chinese in Britain, 1800–Present: Economy, Transnationalism, Identity* (Basingstoke: Palgrave Macmillan, 2008), p. 51.

[43] Lucio Sponza, *Italian Immigrants in Nineteenth-Century Britain: Realities and Images* (Leicester: Leicester University Press, 1988), p. 322; Donald M. MacRaild, *Irish Migrants in Modern Britain, 1750–1922* (Basingstoke: Macmillan, 1999), p. 43.

[44] Panikos Panayi, *Immigration, Ethnicity and Racism, 1815–1945* (Manchester: Manchester University Press, 1994), p. 51; H. Llewellyn Smith in Booth, *Life and Labour of the People in London*, First Series, *Poverty*, Vol. 3, *Blocks of Buildings, Schools and Immigration* (London: Macmillan, 1902), pp. 106–107.

[45] Neil Evans, 'Debate: British History: Past, Present – and Future', *Past and Present* Vol. 119, Issue 1 (1988), p. 197.

If comparative labour history has to reach out beyond organisation and ideology to experience and perception, it also cannot be carried out without taking into account the international dimension. National labour movements, just like national societies, did not develop in isolation from each other ... Especially in the early days of socialism individuals played a crucial role as mediators between two or more different cultures and societies, facilitating such cultural transfer and allowing for the reception of ideas originally developed in different national and social contexts.[46]

These socialist 'mediators'– Eleanor Marx, Woolf Wess, Annie Besant, Rudolph Rocker, Theodore Rothstein, Robert Dell, Ben Tillett, and others – 'go-betweens' of a sort between the organised left and the East End migrant communities, will have a crucial part to play in the following narrative.

This work is rooted in the experiences of the Irish and Jewish poor, as well as those of the religious and political figures who worked and made their homes in these communities. However, parallel to this 'history from below', the book will spend considerable time on the interactions and agendas of the Jewish and Catholic communal leaderships – anglicised, university-educated, upper middle class, and prosperous. 'History from below' is thus combined with 'history from above': the history of Chief Rabbis, Lords, Members of Parliament, Bishops, and Cardinals. This will be in part 'high' political history; a history of the elite as well as the underclass, the corridors of (relative) power as well as the backstreets of the slum. Locating the turn-of-the-century East End as an area of diaspora space in the terms defined by Avtar Brah, this work will illustrate interactions, commonalities, and contrasts between two diasporic communities, a socialist movement attempting to radicalise them, a trade union movement attempting to organise them, and communal leaderships attempting to maintain control over them. It will document how migrants or the children of migrants responded to these attempts to shape their lives and their identities. The broader narrative of entry into and settlement in the United Kingdom, both at the beginning of the last century and today, should not be viewed simply as a relationship between 'hosts' and 'guests', 'natives' and 'strangers'. One can reach a better understanding of the migrant experience in this country by framing it in terms of multiple relationships and negotiations, not between two binary opposites but a number of different groups creating, sharing, and contesting political, economic, and social space. In the case of the turn-of-the-century Irish and Jewish East End diasporas, we can learn more about each by comparing the two.

---

[46] Stefan Berger, 'Guest Editorial', *International and Comparative History, Socialist History* 17 (London: Rivers Oram Press, 2000), p. iv.

# 1

# Diaspora, Migration, and Irish–Jewish Interactions in London, 1800–1889

Before analysing left-wing attitudes to ethnicity and socialist interactions with minority communal institutions in the late-Victorian and Edwardian periods, the text will examine the processes by which Ashkenazi Jews and Irish Catholics came to settle in the East End from the early nineteenth century onwards. This chapter will identify both the similarities in the Jewish and Irish experiences of settlement in East London, the common factors involved in leaving a (predominantly rural) homeland for a distant urban metropolis, and also the crucial differences between the Irish and Jewish diasporic experience of migration, flight, and settlement in the nineteenth century. The varying political and economic circumstances in which Irish Catholics and Jews left their countries had important consequences for subsequent minority interactions with radical politics and with the wider host society. The post-Famine wave of migration from Ireland from the mid-1840s and the Jewish exodus from Eastern Europe post-1881 constituted the two great British immigration 'crises' of the nineteenth century. The ways in which the host society received those arrivals that had crossed the Irish Sea were substantially replicated in the reception awaiting those refugees who left the Pale of Settlement (the areas of Western Russia and Poland in which Jewish settlement was restricted under the Tsarist legal system) forty years later.

## The Roots of the Irish and Jewish Communities in East London

Jewish settlement in the metropolis dates back to the Norman Conquest. From the beginning, Jewish traders were a target for hostility and ethnic violence, particularly in times of economic distress or religious fervour. At the coronation of Richard I a widespread pogrom against London Jews formed a part of the events to mark the occasion. William of Newbury noted: '[A] pleasing rumour spread with incredible rapidity through all

London, namely that the King had ordered all the Jews to be exterminated.'[1] The attacks spread to the rest of the country. By the second half of the thirteenth century, monarch-sanctioned and Church-condoned anti-Jewish violence was a frequent occurrence.[2] In 1290, the entire Jewish population was expelled, the first example of a complete expulsion of Jews to take place in Western Europe. Jews would not be allowed openly to settle in England until 1655.[3] However, a complete absence of practising Jews in London did nothing to dampen antisemitism in popular and intellectual discourse. Julius refers to the pre-admission era as one of 'literary antisemitism', a period in which anti-Jewish prejudice continued to be articulated in a cultural sphere and still occupied a central part of the national psyche.[4]

From the readmission of the Jews in the second half of the seventeenth century, following the Whitehall Conference of 1655, East London became a focus of Jewish settlement and the hub of the new Anglo-Jewish community. Jewish neighbourhoods were formed in Spitalfields and then expanded into Whitechapel.[5] Houndsditch in the east of the metropolis was another early area of settlement.[6] As the eighteenth century progressed, Ashkenazi Jews, emigrating from Germany and Holland, began to outnumber their Sephardic co-religionists. By the middle of that century, with a total Anglo-Jewish population of 7,000 to 8,000, overwhelmingly located in London, Ashkenazi Jews made up some two-thirds of the community.[7] It was during this period that the 'problem' of the Jewish poor (a 'problem' felt most keenly by the Anglo-Jewish establishment, a situation that would repeat itself in the 1880s) and the awareness of the existence of a Jewish 'underclass' began to emerge. It was this eighteenth and early nineteenth-century Jewish residuum that had the first substantial social and economic interactions with London's Irish Catholic working-class population.

Irish Catholics had settled in East London in large numbers from the seventeenth century onwards, although there had been an Irish presence in the capital for centuries. There was no equivalent medieval persecution or

---

[1] Anthony Julius, *Trials of the Diaspora: A History of Anti-Semitism in England* (Oxford: Oxford University Press, 2010), p. 120.

[2] See Julius, *Trials of the Diaspora*, chapter 3, 'Medieval English Anti-Semitism'.

[3] Jews of mainly Spanish and Portuguese Sephardic origin, 'New Christians' following the Spanish Inquisition, had been practising their faith covertly and in secret in London during the Elizabethan period if not before.

[4] Julius, *Trials of the Diaspora*, p. 153.

[5] Todd. M. Endelman, *The Jews of Britain: 1656–2000* (Berkeley: University of California Press, 2002), p. 25.

[6] Beatrice Potter writing in Booth, *Life and Labour of the People in London*, First Series, *Poverty*, Vol. 3, p. 166.

[7] Endelman, *The Jews of Britain*, p. 43.

expulsion of the Irish, and until the Reformation the Irish shared a common faith with the host population. By the time of the readmission of the Jews, however, the Irish were viewed by the host society as not only the adherents of a hostile religion, but as members of an enemy nationality. In the Rookery of St. Giles, the oldest and densest of Irish settlements in London, Irish settlers first appear in Parish records in 1640.[8] By the eighteenth century, Irish men and women occupied roles across the economic spectrum in London, ranging from the criminal, semi-criminal, and begging underclass, to a large labouring proletariat, to skilled craftsmen, middle-class professional men, and a small Anglo-Irish gentry.[9] Even prior to the Famine, the Irish poor in London were viewed by the authorities and the wider population as a 'police problem, a sanitary problem, a Poor Law problem and an industrial problem'.[10] In the eyes of many contemporary observers, to be 'Irish' in London was to be part of the underclass, and the two terms were largely interchangeable. St. Giles in central London was known as 'Little Dublin', 'Little Ireland', and 'The Holy Land' (a reference to the Catholic faith of the settlers).[11] The issues raised by mass Irish immigration would be repeated to an extent in interactions with every subsequent substantial migrant group arriving in Britain.

Both the Irish and Jewish communities were therefore well established in the eastern environs of London by the time the first immigration 'crisis' of the nineteenth century occurred. Both migrant groups at this point were comparatively small numerically, yet, by virtue of their minority faith and ethnic difference, they already occupied the roles of the two predominant ethnic and religious 'others' in the national psyche. Both groups stood outside the dominant Protestant narrative.[12] Papist plots and Jewish conspiracies were conflated in this narrative and conflict with Britain's (Catholic) continental rivals often resulted in domestic acts of violence directed not solely against Catholics but against Jews as well.[13] From the early nineteenth century, Jews

---

[8] Jerry White, *London in the 19th Century* (London: Vintage, 2008), p. 132.

[9] See Lynn Hollen Lees, *Exiles of Erin: Irish Migrants in Victorian Britain* (Manchester: Manchester University Press, 1979), pp. 53–54; James Walvin, *Passage to Britain* (Harmondsworth: Penguin Books, 1984), pp. 24–25; White, *London*, p. 131.

[10] Dorothy George, quoted in Walvin, *Passage to Britain*, p. 25.

[11] White, *London*, p. 11. Whitechapel would in due course be referred to as 'Little Jerusalem' or 'Jew-Town', in antisemitic polemic.

[12] Keith Robbins, 'Ethnicity, Religion, Class and Gender and the 'Island Story/ies': Great Britain and Ireland', in Stefan Berger and Chris Lorenz (eds), *The Contested Nation: Ethnicity, Class, Religion and Gender in National Histories* (Basingstoke: Palgrave Macmillan, 2008), pp. 233–234.

[13] Frank Felsenstein, *Anti-Semitic Stereotypes: A Paradigm of Otherness in English Popular Culture, 1660–1830* (Baltimore, Md.: Johns Hopkins University Press, 1995), pp. 143–144, pp. 247–248. See John Marriott, *Beyond the Tower: A History of East London* (New Haven, Conn.: Yale University Press, 2012), pp. 80–81 for historical anti-Irish violence in East London.

and Irish Catholics were also perceived to be in connivance in the criminal underworld, the beginnings of a long association of migrant groups with a supposedly inherent criminality and delinquency.

## Interactions between the Irish and Jewish Communities, 1800–1889

Crowded into the same decaying and insanitary rookeries of the East End, Irish and Jewish communities overlapped socially and economically. In work typically involving heavy manual labour and later in the nineteenth century dock work, and in employment as stevedores and as porters, the Jewish poor did not compete with their Irish counterparts.[14] Economic contact, cooperation, and competition between poor Irish and Jewish immigrants in the first half of the nineteenth century took place on the streets and in the semi-criminal and criminal underworld of East London rather than on the docks or the building sites. Both groups engaged in the semi-legal occupation of hawking goods on the streets of London and the provinces, a mobile trade and one widely perceived as disreputable. The attraction of 'hawking' to newly arrived migrants was obvious. With a very small amount of capital, sometimes obtained on credit from a sympathetic compatriot, one could go into business.[15] The Irish poor in London had long engaged in itinerant trading and 'tinkering', and by 1800 both groups were heavily involved in hawking, selling everything from old clothes and cheap jewellery to oranges and gingerbread.[16] Another point of contact between the communities was bare-knuckle boxing, a sport in which both Irish and Jewish Londoners participated enthusiastically.[17]

Jews and Irish Catholics had been associated in public and judicial eyes with the criminal underworld in the East End since the Georgian period, with criminal violence in particular being seen as a peculiarly 'Irish' trait.[18]

[14] Geoffrey Alderman has questioned the existence of a separate Jewish working-class identity in London prior to the influx of the 1880s, outside certain small trades such as cigar- and cigarette-making industries. Geoffrey Alderman, *Modern British Jewry* (Oxford: Oxford University Press, 1992), p. 8. See Chapter 2 for analysis of where Jewish and Irish migrants fitted into socialist conceptions of the metropolitan class structure.

[15] Endelman, *The Jews of Britain*, p. 43.

[16] Endelman, *The Jews of Britain*, pp. 43–44.

[17] See Pierce Egan, *Boxiana; or Sketches of Ancient and Modern Pugilism: From the Days of the Renowned Broughton and Slack, to the Heroes of the Present Milling Era!* (London: G. Smeeton, 1812), 'Elisha Crabbe, the Jew', p. 243, 'Dan Mendoza', pp. 253–280 (the most detailed account of one boxer in the entire work), 'Bitton – the Jew', p. 470, 'Michael Ryan', p. 224, 'Jack O'Donnel', p. 315, 'Dogherty', p. 467 etc. for sketches of contemporary Jewish and Irish boxers.

[18] Roger Swift, 'Crime and the Irish in Nineteenth Century Britain', in Roger Swift and Sheridan Gilley (eds), *The Irish in Britain, 1815–1939* (London: Pinter Publishers Ltd, 1989), p. 164. See also Roger Swift, *Behaving Badly? Irish Migrants and Crime in the Victorian*

Whilst anti-Catholic or antisemitic prejudice no doubt played a part in many of these accusations of deviancy, a modicum of truth lay behind the perception. Jewish and Irish street gangs certainly existed and were active throughout the period. Patrick Colquhoun, Metropolitan Magistrate at the turn of the nineteenth century, writing in 1797 about the utterance of forged coins (something, according to Colquhoun, of a cottage industry among the Jewish underclass), suggested the existence of an 'unholy alliance' between Jewish and Irish immigrants:

> The lower ranks among the Irish, and the Jews, are the chief supporters of the trade of circulating base money in London ... there is said to be scarce an Irish labourer who does not exchange his week's wages for base money ... The Jews confine themselves principally to the coinage and circulation of copper; while the Irish women are the chief utterers and colourers of base silver. A vast number of these low females have acquired the mischievous art of colouring the bad shillings and sixpences which they purchase from the employers of Jew-boys who cry *bad shillings*.[19]

Colquhoun believed that criminality was a universal Jewish trait.[20] An assumption of widespread criminality as an inevitable result of the Irish or Jewish 'racial make-up' was common throughout the period. One result of this was a long-standing and mutually reciprocated hostility between Irish immigrants and the police. Second- or third-generation 'cockney Irish' were considered by contemporary commentators if anything as more criminally inclined than recent arrivals.[21]

Irish and Ashkenazi Jewish immigration continued to increase steadily throughout the 1830s. Streets and areas of East London had by this point definitely assumed 'Irish' or 'Jewish' characters in the descriptions of contemporary social commentators. Stereotypes which continued into the 1880s and beyond, of the violent and childish Irishman, or the criminal and avaricious Jew, were firmly in place by the 1830s. Both Jewish and Irish migrants were seen as spreaders of disease. An 1832 outbreak of cholera

---

*City: An Inaugural Lecture Delivered at Chester College of Higher Education* (Chester: Chester Academic Press, 2006), which discusses in detail the crimes Irish migrants were charged with in different parts of the country over the course of the nineteenth century, suggesting a preponderance of 'petty' rather than serious crime in Irish cases.

[19] Patrick Colquhoun, *A treatise on the police of the metropolis; containing a detail of the various crimes and misdemeanors by which public and private property and security are, at present, injured and endangered, and suggesting remedies for their prevention* (London: H. Fry, 1797), p. 119.

[20] Endelman, *The Jews of Britain*, p. 84.

[21] Booth, *Life and Labour of the People in London*, Third Series, *Religious Influences*, Vol. 7, *Summary* (London: Macmillan, 1903), p. 246.

in the city was blamed on the Jewish community.[22] The term 'Irish fever' became commonly used during this period as shorthand for a whole range of diseases thought to be suffered and spread by the Irish, and typhus in particular.[23]A report from the Select Committee on the Health of Towns, from 1840, described the inhabitants of Spitalfields thus, conflating ethnicity, poverty, dirt, and disease: '[They] are most intolerably filthy; they are the lowest description of Irish, many Germans, and many Jews, and they are, of all the people in the world, the most filthy.'[24] The visceral association with dirt and disease was a common trope employed against different migrant groups. This was partly the result of the condition in which immigrants arrived at British ports after lengthy and traumatic journeys, partly the inevitable result of life in urban slum conditions, and partly an articulation of racial prejudice. As with criminality, Jews and Irish Catholics were jointly equated by contemporary writers with disease and uncleanliness in the Victorian period. The Irish in the large urban areas were frequently compared in racist literature to pigs or dogs, their homes to 'pigsties', whilst 'dirty Jew' was a common antisemitic epithet of the period and beyond.[25] Both communities were portrayed in nineteenth-century racist literature as combining the worst elements of rural and urban existence, an agricultural proximity to livestock and waste coupled with the squalor of the inner-city. This supposed lack of hygiene and cleanliness within minority diasporic populations again formed a key indicator of 'otherness' and outsider status for Jewish and Irish migrant groups.

In the Famine years of 1845 to 1851 and in the decade following, Britain experienced its first immigration 'crisis' of the nineteenth century. In the space of a few years, hundreds of thousands of Irish men and women, fleeing starvation and destitution, left their homeland. They were often financially aided by landlords who desired to be rid of such a burden on the rates. In 1841, the census figures recorded 289,404 Irish-born immigrants resident in England and Wales; by 1851 this had leapt to 519,959 and by 1861 to 601,634.[26] These figures do not take account of those of Irish descent born

[22] Chaim Bermant, *Point of Arrival: A Study of London's East End* (London: Eyre Methuen, 1975), p. 126.

[23] MacRaild, *Irish Migrants in Modern Britain*, p. 58.

[24] White, *London*, pp. 32–33.

[25] Curtis, *Apes and Angels*, p. 12. W.H. Wilkins, *The Alien Invasion* (London: Methuen and Co., 1892), p. 95. See Joseph Banister, *England Under the Jews* (London: self-published, 1901), pp. 84–88 for the antisemitic equation between Jews and dirt and disease. See also Charles Chinn, *They Worked All Their Lives: Women of the Urban Poor in England, 1880–1939* (Manchester: Manchester University Press, 1988), pp. 129–130 for the demarcation in working-class neighbourhoods between 'clean' and 'dirty' as a benchmark of respectability.

[26] Holmes, *John Bull's Island*, p. 20.

on the mainland. Over a million Irish men and women crossed the Atlantic. Many migrants settled in Lancashire and in Scotland, but thousands headed for London, with its large established Irish community. This exodus had a profound effect on the social fabric of the city, creating 'Irish' areas in Shadwell, Wapping, Limehouse, and Poplar where there had been few migrants before, and reinforcing a perception of Irish dominance in areas already inhabited by compatriots. The Irish, in Chaim Bermant's words, 'made the north side of the Thames their own'.[27] This radical demographic change was documented in the work of Henry Mayhew, who published his *London Labour and the London Poor* in 1851 and 1861. Again and again, the poorest slums and rookeries he describes are inhabited by recent Irish immigrants. 'In almost all the poorer districts of London', Mayhew wrote, 'are to be found "nests of Irish" – as they are called – or courts solely inhabited by the Irish costermongers. These people form separate colonies, rarely visiting or mixing with the English costers.'[28]

> Of the other classes of persons admitted to the casual wards, the Irish generally form a large proportion … The Irish tramp generally makes his appearance with a large family and frequently with three or four generations together – grandfather, grandmother, father and mother, and children – all coming at the same time. In the year ending June 1848, the Irish vagrants increased to so great an extent that, of the entire number of casuals relieved, more than one-third in the first three quarters, and more than two-thirds in the last quarter, were from the sister isle.[29]

John Hollingshead, after a visit to one 'Irish' rookery in Shoreditch and again stressing this confluence of both urban and agricultural poverty that became such a feature of discourse of migrant groups in London, wrote:

> [These] courts are choked up with every variety of filth; their approaches wind round by the worst kind of slaughter houses … they are crowded with pigs, with fowls, and with dogs; they are strewn with oyster shells and fish refuse … their drainage lies in pools wherever it may be thrown.[30]

Overcrowding and subletting of slum housing in Irish neighbourhoods by Irish landlords was noted in strikingly similar language to that used about Jewish migrants by anti-immigrant campaigners and social investigators in the final decades of the nineteenth century:

[27] Bermant, *Point of Arrival*, p. 44.

[28] Henry Mayhew, *London Labour and the London Poor* (Harmondsworth: Penguin Books, 1985) (originally published 1861), pp. 56–57.

[29] Mayhew, *London Labour*, p. 373.

[30] John Hollingshead, *Ragged London in 1861* (London: J.M. Dent & Sons Ltd, 1986) (originally published 1861), p. 45.

An Irish landlord or landlady will rent a room at about two shillings a week, and then take in as many families, or individuals, at a small nightly rental, as the floor can possibly hold. This is openly done in defiance of the Lodging-house Act, or any other social reform law.[31]

It was during the Famine period that mass Irish employment on the London docksides began, although the Irish had been employed in the importation of sugar from the docks since the beginning of the century.[32] Both Mayhew's and Hollingshead's observations of the Irish poor in London are reminiscent of those made by Frederick Engels in his condemnation of industrial conditions in Manchester in the 1840s. *The Condition of the Working Class in England* (1844) also associates the Irish with the imagery of disease, poverty, and degraded living conditions, but adds a further element: the Irish man or woman as economic competitor and threat to the English working class.[33] For both Irish and Jewish migrants, this trope would come to dominate the political narrative of both left and right concerning their place in British society in the second half of the nineteenth century.

The influx of Irish immigrants into London between 1840 and 1860 coincided with significant political and social changes in the Jewish community. At the turn of the nineteenth century, Anglo-Jewry had consisted of a small number of well-to-do, mainly Sephardic, Jews and a larger, poorer, Ashkenazi community. Just as the faith-based and social prejudices expressed against Irish Catholic or Jewish immigrants were framed in a common language of religious preconception, with both groups sharing a common ecclesiastical outsider status, so the campaigns for political enfranchisement of the two minorities were linked. In the nineteenth century, the Jewish hierarchy took its lead from their Catholic counterparts. Following the granting of Catholic Emancipation in 1829, allowing Catholics MPs to take their seats in Parliament, the Jewish establishment intensified their efforts against prohibitive legislation in Parliament and in the City. These efforts were crowned with success in 1858, when the Jews Relief Act allowed Jews to take the oath of office.[34]

Parallel to the great wave of Irish migration into the capital during the Famine years was a demographic shift in Anglo-Jewry from a semi-criminal

[31] Hollingshead, *Ragged London in 1861*, p. 45.

[32] H. Llewellyn Smith, writing in Booth, *Life and Labour of the People in London, Poverty*, Vol. 3, pp. 90–92.

[33] Friedrich Engels, *The Condition of the Working Class in England* (Oxford: Oxford University Press, 1993) (originally published 1844), pp. 102–104.

[34] V.D. Lipman, *A History of the Jews in Britain since 1858* (Leicester: Leicester University Press, 1990), p. 9.

underclass towards a more prosperous working and lower middle class. In a pattern that would repeat itself throughout the nineteenth century and into the twentieth, new migrants arriving into the diaspora space of East London competed for trades and housing with older settled minority groups. Relationships between ethnic and religious 'others' underwent further changes as the demographics again shifted. In the fruit trade and similar occupations Jews were supplanted by Irish Catholics, whilst Irish residents as a percentage of the total metropolitan population increased from 4 per cent to 7 per cent and the Jewish figure fell from 1.7 per cent to 1 per cent.[35] The imagery of displacement that would become a feature of anti-Jewish rhetoric from the 1880s onwards was, during the mid-century, employed against the Irish competitor. Henry Mayhew wrote:

> The Irish boy could live *harder* than the Jew – often in his own country he subsisted on a stolen turnip a day. He could lodge harder ... he could dispense with the use of shoes and stockings ... he drank only water, or if he took tea or coffee, it was as a meal, and not merely as a beverage; to crown the whole, the city-bred Jew boy required some evening recreation ... but this the Irish boy, county bred, never thought of, for *his* sole luxury was a deep sleep, and being regardless or ignorant of all such recreations, he worked longer hours, and so sold more oranges, than his Hebrew competitor.[36]

As Irish migrants displaced Jews in traditional Jewish trades, and moved into traditional Jewish areas during the Famine period, poverty and street trading ceased to be the Jewish community's defining characteristic. The Jewish community was becoming more prosperous, more bourgeois, and more anglicised. Poorer Jews now definitely constituted a portion of the 'respectable' working class, whilst their more prosperous co-religionists adopted the values of the petit-bourgeoisie and middle classes, in recreational pursuits, education, and attitudes towards faith. The 1841 census revealed that 90 per cent of the Jewish population in the city were British-born.[37] By 1881, the Jewish community in London was relatively small and reasonably prosperous. Ashkenazi settlement had continued throughout the period, but at a slow and steady rate.[38] Jewish political emancipation had been achieved, Lord Rothschild having taken his seat in the House of Commons in 1858. The semi-criminal Jewish residuum of the eighteenth and early nineteenth centuries had largely been 'tamed', and the Jewish middle

---

[35] Alderman, *Modern British Jewry*, pp. 10–11.

[36] Mayhew, *London Labour*, pp. 195–196 (original emphasis).

[37] Lipman, *A History of the Jews in Britain Since 1858*, p. 14.

[38] Between the mid-1850s and the end of the 1870s the Jewish population of England grew from 35,000 to over 60,000 (Alderman, *Modern British Jewry*, p. 74).

class in London was blossoming.[39] London Jewry seemed set to take its place among other established non-Anglican denominations – Quakers, Baptists, and Methodists – tolerated and largely ignored by the wider population, with little of the sectarian baggage that invariably attached itself to Catholicism.

From 1881 onwards, the situation changed rapidly. Triggered by pogroms and oppressive legislature in the wake of the assassination of Tsar Alexander II, an unprecedented exodus of Jews from Poland, the Ukraine, the Baltic, and Romania occurred. The Jews of the Russian Empire had long laboured under second-class status and punitive discriminatory legislation, but in the last two decades of the nineteenth century this descended into state-sanctioned violence. The most brutal manifestations of this violence were the sporadic pogroms that took place across the Pale of Settlement and in other areas. Coupled with this was a worsening economic situation for Russian and Polish Jewry, which had demographic origins (during the nineteenth century the Jewish population in the Russian Empire grew from about 1 million to over 6 million) and was exacerbated by anti-Jewish economic legislation.[40] Between 1881 and 1914, around 2.5 million Eastern European Jews moved west, the majority settling in the USA, but some 150,000 moved to Britain and most found homes in London, and in particular in already overcrowded Whitechapel and Stepney.[41] This post-1881 wave of Jewish migration constituted Victorian Britain's second great immigration 'crisis'. The new influx of the Jewish diaspora would also radically alter the nature of Anglo-Jewry. The arrivals gravitated to those areas of East London already settled by Ashkenazi Jews over the last half century. The social trend towards the middle class in Anglo-Jewry in the 1840s and 1850s was transformed, as the immigrants, poor, sometimes illiterate, often with little English at their command, settled in East London. Jewish migrants made their homes in Glasgow, Liverpool, Leeds, Hull, and Manchester, but above all in the environs of the East End.

By the end of the 1880s, the economic and social relationship of Jewish and Irish immigrants had once again been transformed. The majority of Irish Catholics in London were now the children or grandchildren of the Famine influx. Parallel to the expansion of the Eastern European Jewish working class was a movement in the East End Irish population away

---

[39] A study published in 1883 by Joseph Jacobs, examining the incomes of London's 46,000 Jews, put 14.6 per cent in the upper or upper middle classes with family incomes over £1,000 a year; 42.3 per cent in the middle class with family incomes between £200 and £1,000 a year; and 19.6 per cent with family incomes around £100 a year, together with 23.6 per cent in receipt of at least occasional relief, with incomes of between £10 and £50 a year (Lipman, *A History of the Jews in Britain*, p. 19).

[40] Alderman, *Modern British Jewry*, pp. 111–112.

[41] Alderman, *Modern British Jewry*, pp. 110–111.

from the semi-criminal underclass and into the unskilled labour force, with a corresponding increase in living standards.[42] This is not to suggest a wholesale movement of Irish Catholic arrivals and Londoners of Irish descent out of poverty. The Irish community generally remained poor, and likely to live in sub-standard and crowded housing. There was no comparable demographic shift towards the middle and lower middle classes as took place in the Jewish community in the 1840s and would again take place in the twentieth century. The movement was from an extremely poor underclass to a still poor working class.

The territorial and economic trends that Mayhew had noted in *London Labour*, with Irish immigrants moving into Jewish areas and supplanting Jews in the street markets and trades, were again reversed. In areas such as Whitechapel, Stepney, and St. George's-in-the-East, 'Irish' and 'London Irish' areas were rapidly becoming 'Jewish', as the numbers of refugees from Eastern Europe entering the country continued to rise. 'Irish colonies' such as Inkhorn Court and Commercial Place in the East End were now being 'occupied' by Polish Jews.[43] The tailoring trade in East London, a partially Irish concern at the mid-point of the nineteenth century, was increasingly perceived to be a Jewish occupation. The Irish in East London were for the first time faced with another immigrant group of comparable size, a Jewish population competing economically and for housing, sharing geographical and cultural space, with communal and political interactions on a far greater scale than that of the Jewish and Irish residuum of the early nineteenth century. The complexity of East London diaspora space had increased with the new arrival of Eastern European refugees, providing fertile terrain for multiple interactions between the Irish and Jewish working classes, positive and negative.

## A Comparison of Factors Involved in Jewish and Irish Emigration

What distinguished those emigrants from Ireland or the Pale of Settlement who made the journey to Britain and settled in London from their compatriots who stayed at home? It became common for anti-migrant writers of the 1880s and 1890s to refer to the immigrants as 'rubbish', expelled from their homelands, 'the destitute and unfit of other lands'.[44] Moses Angel,

---

[42] M.A.G. O'Tuathaigh, 'The Irish in Nineteenth Century Britain: Problems of Integration', in Roger Swift and Sheridan Gilley (eds), *The Irish in the Victorian City* (Beckenham: Croom Helm, 1985), pp. 17–18.

[43] Jerry White, *Rothschild Buildings: Life in an East End Tenement Block, 1887–1920* (London: Routledge and Kegan Paul, 1980), p. 14.

[44] Wilkins, *The Alien Invasion*, p. 2.

headmaster of the Jews' Free School in Spitalfields for over half a century, described the foreign-born parents of his pupils (in 1871, before the great wave of Eastern European Jewish immigration) as 'the refuse population of the worst parts of Europe'.[45] Anti-immigrant rhetoric throughout the nineteenth century claimed that the migrant groups entering Britain were made up of the 'criminal classes', the diseased, the venereal, the politically suspect, no longer tolerated in the countries they were leaving and foisted upon British society.[46] The opposite was also argued, both by contemporary observers and by historians of immigration. Colin Holmes, discussing Italian immigration, attributed to those men and women who left Italy for Britain and the USA, a '"staunchness of soul", which not everyone possessed'.[47] To leave one's home, family network, and certainties for a strange destination, with no guarantee of work or shelter, required courage, ambition, and a certain awareness of the world beyond the village or town the migrant was leaving. Financial assistance, and kinsmen and women at the point of arrival, also facilitated matters. The men and women making the journey over land and sea were overwhelmingly young, willing to work long hours, to endure poor housing, and were ambitious for their children's futures. The stereotype of the immigrant being 'diseased' or 'filthy' sprang from the condition of migrants arriving at the East London docks, often after a long journey. On one point the contemporary critics of immigration like W.H. Wilkins were correct. Britain throughout the nineteenth century was a refuge for political radicals of all stripes exiled from their homelands across Europe, a haven where one could study, meet comrades, and agitate in relative freedom. London became a home from home for anarchists, socialists, and communists forced to leave their own countries – Marx, Engels, Mazzini, and Kropotkin being only the most prominent examples. This was particularly the case during periods of continental upheaval and strife such as 1848 and 1871. Liberal tolerance of foreign political refugees was seen as a distinguishing feature differentiating England from 'intolerant and unstable' European regimes.[48] English radical movements set up support networks and soup kitchens for foreign comrades. These initial impressions, both positive and negative, of migrants arriving on British shores clung not only to new arrivals, but would continue to inform discourse about settled diasporic communities into the twentieth century.

---

[45] Endelman, *The Jews of Britain*, p. 85.

[46] Garrard, *The English and Immigration*, p. 52.

[47] Holmes, *John Bull's Island*, p. 31. David Fitzpatrick conversely has argued that, with respect to the Irish diaspora, those who emigrated to Britain rather than the USA and the colonies formed a 'residue' amongst the migrants. David Fitzpatrick, 'The Irish in Britain, 1871–1921', in a W.E. Vaughan (ed.), *A New History of Ireland*, Vol. 6, *Ireland Under the Union, II: 1870–1921* (Oxford: Oxford University Press, 2010), p. 655.

[48] Panayi, *Immigration, Ethnicity and Racism*, p. 41.

What comparisons can be drawn between the Irish and Jewish diasporic experiences, the process by which Irish and Jewish settlers left their homelands and settled in new countries? For both Irish and Jewish migrants the destination most favoured was America.[49] In the shtetls and towns in the Pale of Settlement and Romania it was spoken of as 'the land of gold', *di goldene medine*. For the Irish, as well as its economic attractions, the USA had the undoubted advantage of being free from British rule. It is no surprise therefore that the majority of those leaving their homelands aspired to cross the Atlantic. Many Jewish immigrants, bound for the USA, settled in England inadvertently. Sometimes, an intended short sojourn on the way to America developed, for economic or personal reasons, into permanent settlement. This was sometimes through the dishonesty of those charged with transporting migrants out of the Pale of Settlement. The immigrants, many of whom had never travelled further than neighbouring settlements in Eastern Europe, were entirely in the hands of the 'operators'.

> The tour operators who arranged that escape … told each young client that he would be put on a train and travel on it for most of a day or night, and then he would be put on a ship (it was generally at Hamburg or Bremen or Rotterdam), and when he got off the ship he would be in *die goldene medina* [*sic*] … By implication *die goldene medina* was the United States, but it was only by implication: there wasn't any contract.[50]

Ian Mikardo, the future Labour politician, was the son of Jewish refugees from the Pale of Settlement. His father was one of many who were landed in the East India Docks believing themselves to be in New York. Morris Mikardo, illiterate and with limited English, did not realise that he had been deceived for several weeks.[51]

Irish immigrants, with only the Irish Sea to cross, and without the disorientating journey by foot, train, and boat across Europe that Jewish migrants were forced to make, would not be likely to confuse London with New York. However, many Irish settlers in East London did intend that their stay in England would be a short one, prior to crossing the Atlantic, and, as with many Ashkenazi Jews, this short stay would become a lifetime. In comparative terms, the age and gender profile of Irish and Jewish immigrants in the nineteenth century was similar, but their motives for leaving their homelands differed, as did the attitudes held towards the state that they were settling in. Both Irish and Jewish migrants were likely to be young, with a roughly equal proportion of men and women

---

[49] Holmes, *John Bull's Island*, p. 22.
[50] Ian Mikardo, *Ian Mikardo: Back-Bencher* (London: Weidenfeld & Nicolson, 1988), p. 17.
[51] Mikardo, *Ian Mikardo*, p. 17.

emigrating.[52] Both Irish and Jews were likely to emigrate as family units, though often in the case of Ashkenazi Jews with the husband or father arriving earlier and establishing himself before the family joined him.[53] The family were sometimes liable for a surprise when landing on English shores. Ivor Mairents, who left Poland with his mother at the age of five in 1913, recalled that his father, who had settled in the East End some months previously, did not even come to meet the family at the docks. When located he displayed perfect indifference to his wife and children as they arrived at the garret he inhabited in Grove Street in the heart of the East End. The mother and children had been led to expect a certain level of prosperity from the letters the father had sent; instead, he was living in poverty, dependent on the charity of already established family members.[54]

This equal gender distribution among immigrants distinguished the Jews and Irish from other migrant groups in the East End such as the Chinese and the Italians, the majority of whom were young unmarried men.[55] The rough parity in sex and age amongst Irish and Jewish migrants would have important ramifications for social life and gender relations on a number of levels. It determined the nature of these communities (the family as economic unit, the role of women (as mother, worker), and their place in church- or synagogue-centred life in the local neighbourhood) and how the Jewish and Irish populations were perceived by the host society. That families rather than individuals from minority communities were settling in urban areas such as East London pointed to a more permanent residence.[56] In the Irish and Jewish cases young unmarried men and women also made the journey alone to mainland Britain, often in danger of economic and/or sexual exploitation by those who preyed on the vulnerable disembarking from the quays.[57] Young single Irishwomen in particular found employment in positions related to domestic service.[58]

---

[52] Panayi, *Immigration, Ethnicity and Racism*, pp. 58–60.

[53] Alderman, *Modern British Jewry*, p. 74; Susan L. Tananbaum, *Jewish Immigrants in London, 1880–1939* (London: Pickering and Chatto, 2014), pp. 19–21.

[54] Tape J.M./381, Interview with Ivor Mairents, carried out by Cyril Silvertown on behalf of the Jewish Museum, London, 18 April 1994.

[55] Panayi, *Immigration, Ethnicity and Racism*, pp. 59–60; Holmes, *John Bull's Island*, p. 30.

[56] See Ultan Cowley, *The Men Who Built Britain: A History of the Irish Navvy* (Dublin: Wolfhound Press, 2001) (republished 2004), p. 91 for discussion of Irish family structures brought over from Ireland to mainland Britain.

[57] See Edward J. Bristow, *Prostitution and Prejudice: The Jewish Fight against White Slavery, 1870–1939* (Oxford: Clarendon Press, 1982).

[58] See Bronwen Walter, 'Strangers on the Inside: Irish Women Servants in England, 1881', in Roger Swift and Sheridan Gilley, *Irish Identities in Victorian Britain* (Abingdon: Routledge, 2011).

Irish and Jewish migrants had different motives at different times for leaving their homelands, and different expectations of what life would be like at the final destination. For the Irish, the threat of starvation during the Famine necessitated an immediate exodus, in particular from the rural south-west of the country (from where most Irish men and women settling in London had originated).[59] In Romania, Poland, and Russia, pogroms and massacres, or fear of such, forced many Jews to leave their villages and towns without any clear idea of where they were heading. However, the majority of Irish and Jewish immigrants took long-term considerations into account, rather than the basic need to keep the family and oneself from physical harm. Fears of future hunger or future persecution undoubtedly played a role, but the merits of the potential destination were carefully considered. On Jewish motives for migrating to England, Gartner writes:

> The composite picture which was formed by this knowledge regarded England as a free country where an immigrant would have to work extremely hard to earn very little, and a fortunate few might become prosperous. In this mental image, an immigrant might expect to live in freedom but almost sealed off from the rest of the population, and endure public dislike. All in all, the picture was essentially true.[60]

A crucial difference in the motivations of Irish and Eastern European Jewish migrants, and in how they interacted with the host society, lay in the situation they were leaving. For the Irish, whether in fact it ever took place, an eventual and ideally prosperous return to Ireland was always a factor in their migration. This return may have been conditional, dependent on an end to economic depression or the achievement of Home Rule, but it was there, and it influenced the behaviour of the Irish immigrants and their attitudes towards the host nation. The great numbers of second- and third-generation London Irish, Liverpool Irish, and Irish Americans testify to how many Irish migrants never did return, but the myth proved to be a strong and enduring one. The exceptions were those migrants who had left Ireland in the immediate wake of the starvation of the 1840s. The utter destitution wrought by the Famine, the depopulation of entire communities in the south-west, and the death or emigration of extended family networks, cut that generation off from the myth of the triumphant return.[61] The myth was re-established

---

[59] Roger Swift (ed.), *Irish Migrants in Britain, 1815–1914: A Documentary History* (Cork, Cork University Press), 2002, p. 27.

[60] Gartner, *The Jewish Immigrant in England*, p. 27. Colin Holmes describes this difference in motives for migration as being 'acute' or 'anticipatory' – the former a case of survival and escape from imminent attack or harm, the latter more carefully considered with a number of different factors being taken into account. Holmes, *John Bull's Island*, p. 28.

[61] White, *London*, pp. 133–134.

in the subsequent, smaller waves of Irish immigrants from the 1870s onwards, combined with a more widespread post-Famine political radicalism and antipathy towards the British state and its institutions. As important as the myth of return for the Irish who had settled in London was the geographical proximity of their homeland, its political union with the host country, and the common language shared by most Irish immigrants with that of the country in which they were settling.[62] For the Irish migrant in London, 'home' involved a railway journey of a few hours and a short sea crossing. Such a journey may have been beyond the financial means of many, but it was manifestly possible, and London Irish would socialise with and have relatives who had travelled back and forth between Ireland and England. The pre-Famine tradition of seasonal agricultural work, in which Irish labourers would travel to England for a time and then return, was also a factor.[63]

For the Jews leaving Eastern Europe the situation was more complex. As Anne Kershen writes:

> [The] location and definition of home is not straightforward. Was it to be found in the towns, villages and cities of the Pale of Settlement or in the biblical land from which the Jews were exiled almost two millennia before? Where ever they were in the diaspora, Jews prayed for a return to their spiritual homeland ... the majority of eastern European Jews migrating westwards carried two myths with them, one of return and one of home.[64]

There was no wish to return to a Russia or Poland under the Tsar under any economic conditions, with prospects only of discrimination, violence, and military conscription. The dreams of a return to Palestine for most of the period were just that, a religious dream, which was evoked in the Passover toast (the *Nirtzah*) at the end of Seder night, but never appeared likely to be fulfilled.[65] For most of the Jews landing in the East End, London was to be a permanent home, if they did not travel on to the USA.[66] For Jewish

---

[62] Most but not all. A substantial number of migrants leaving the southern counties of Ireland in the famine years for America and Britain spoke Irish only (see Chapter 4). The nomenclature for the native language of Ireland has evolved over the last century. 'Gaelic', 'Irish Gaelic' and 'Irish' have all been employed. In this book the language will be referred to as 'Irish' or 'Irish Gaelic' as the terms closest to those used by the people of the island of Ireland itself.

[63] Swift, *Irish Migrants in Britain*, pp. 8–9.

[64] Kershen, 'The Migrant at Home in Spitalfields: Memory, Myth and Reality', pp. 100–101.

[65] '*L'shanah haba'ah b'Yerushalayim*' ('Next year in Jerusalem').

[66] The exception were the several thousand Jewish immigrants persuaded by the Jewish Board of Guardians to return to Eastern Europe. See Mordechai Rozin, *The Rich and the Poor: Jewish Philanthropy and Social Control in Nineteenth Century London* (Brighton: Sussex Academic Press, 1999), pp. 143–144.

*Bundists* and social democrats an eventual return to a Russia freed from autocracy might be a long-term goal (and a number of Jewish socialists who had settled in the East End *did* return after the Russian Revolution), but for most Ashkenazi Jews, having left Eastern Europe, there was not the will, the desire, or the means to go back.[67] This irrevocable break from Eastern European shtetl life did not mean, however, any lessening on the part of the East End Jewish diaspora, English or foreign-born, of interest in and concern for the welfare of their co-religionists still living in the Pale of Settlement. The political affairs of the Russian Empire were followed closely. The way in which this concern over the treatment of Russian Jews was expressed proved a major division between socialists and radicals, both Jewish and Gentile, on one side, and the Anglo-Jewish hierarchy on the other.

Whilst the Irish certainly had less distance to travel than the Jews of Poland or Russia, the cultural dislocation and trauma experienced by Irish migrants, often from rural backgrounds, should not be underestimated. They may have shared a common language, the profession of a form of Christianity, and an interest in many of the pursuits of the host working-class culture, but life in London was still profoundly disorientating. It can be argued that many Irish immigrants lacked certain psychological defences possessed by the Ashkenazi Jewish community. Drawing individualising comparisons between the expectations of the two migrant groups, the Jews who had left behind the Pale of Settlement and the shtetl, unlike the Irish Catholic migrants, were accustomed to their role as a religious minority, the hostility of the wider population, and the prejudice of local authorities and institutions against them. Jewish immigrants expected passive religious and ethnic hostility, which was preferable to active religious and ethnic persecution. In addition, the Anglo-Jewish establishment, concerned about the ramifications of Eastern European immigration, took care to promote a negative (or perhaps realistic) picture of what life for the Jewish settler in East London would be like, hoping to discourage emigration. In a circular distributed among Eastern European rabbis by Chief Rabbi Nathan Adler at the close of 1888, the following bleak picture was painted:

> [M]any of [the migrants] are lost without livelihoods ... it is difficult for them to support themselves and their households, and at times they contravene the will of their Maker on account of poverty and overwork, and violate the Sabbath and Festivals. Some have been ensnared in the net of the missionaries and renounced their religion, may the Merciful save.

---

[67] See Sharman Kadish, *Bolsheviks and British Jews: The Anglo-Jewish Community, Britain and the Russian Revolution* (London: Frank Cass, 1992) for discussion of those Jewish socialists who returned to Russia following the events of 1917. The *Bund* was a Russian Jewish socialist organisation established in 1897.

Woe to the eyes which see and the ears which hear such things … There
are many who believe that all the cobblestones of London are precious
stones, and that it is a place of gold. Woe and alas, it is not so.[68]

For many rural Irish Catholics, particularly from the south of Ireland,
who would have had little contact with non-Catholics on any level, this new
status as a minority in a foreign land, and often a resented minority, was a
profound shock.[69] Equally disorientating was contact for the first time with
an English proletariat, with its own mores and customs. T.P. O'Connor,
arriving in London in 1870, expressed surprise at hearing English working-
class accents; his previous contact with the English in Ireland had been
limited to upper-class figures of authority.[70] Irish Catholics arriving in
London also had an ambivalent attitude towards the society they were joining
that was not present in the Jewish community. For Polish and Russian Jews,
Tsarist discrimination and persecution had forced the immigrants to leave
their homeland for a destination where they could live in relative peace and
freedom. Ashkenazi Jews were generally realistic about the privations and
problems they would encounter in England, but England, for all its faults,
was not under the rule of the Tsars. Ashkenazi Jews had left the source of
their persecution behind. But for Irish Catholics, there was a feeling that
migration to England was exchanging an oppressed homeland for the source
of that oppression.[71]

This bitterness felt against British colonial rule and the Empire that Irish
Catholic immigrants were reluctantly part of continued to play a significant
role in working-class Irish life. Into the Edwardian period, Irish communities
in the East End were judging grass-roots local political issues, even those
not obviously connected to Home Rule, by the impact or effect they would
have on the Irish Nationalist movement. Irish Nationalist MPs were never
elected in any East End constituency as T.P. O'Connor was in Liverpool (a
seat he retained for the Irish Nationalists into the 1920s), but throughout the
1889–1912 period there was a bedrock of Irish East London support for the
Nationalist movement.[72] For the majority of Jewish immigrants, conversely,

---

[68] Nathan Adler in the *Ha Meliz* XXVIII, 287 (30 December 1888–January 1889), in
Gartner, *The Jewish Immigrant*, p. 24.

[69] The majority of Irish migrants arriving in London, as opposed to Glasgow or Liverpool,
were from rural Munster in the south of the island. Giulia Ni Dhulchaointigh, 'The Irish
Population of London, 1900–14: Connections and Disconnections' (PhD thesis, Trinity
College Dublin, 2013), p. 4.

[70] Steven Fielding, *Class and Ethnicity: Irish Catholics in England, 1880–1939* (Buckingham:
Open University Press, 1993), p. 23.

[71] O'Tuathaigh, 'The Irish in Nineteenth Century Britain', p. 20.

[72] See L.W. Brady, *T.P. O'Connor and the Liverpool Irish* (London: Royal Historical
Society, 1983), p. 23.

there was no contradiction between a national loyalty and attachment to Britain, and a desire for change in the Russian Empire that they had left behind. Even for the Zionist movement in this period there was no apparent conflict of interest between the desire for a Jewish national home overseas and an enthusiastic loyalty towards the British Empire, the former being envisaged in some Zionist circles as a 'white' dominion under the protection of the crown on the lines of Canada, Australia, or New Zealand.[73] Irish communities had a far more ambiguous relationship with the country that they had settled in. Irish nationalism, unlike Zionism, was explicitly in opposition to the British Empire, and this would continue to colour the interactions of both a middle-class Irish intelligentsia and a working-class London Irish East End population with the wider host society into the inter-war period. Immigrant Jewry had a difficulty in conceptualising its true homeland, physical or spiritual, Eastern Europe or Palestine. This was not the case for the Irish diaspora. This enduring hostility to the British state as colonial power would be a key factor in the communal dynamic of the Irish East End.

Crucial to the establishment of immigrant communities in any town or city, and during any period, is the phenomenon of what is known in Yiddish as the *Landsman*, a relation or contact from the same town or village as the migrant who has already settled in the place of arrival, and can provide shelter, employment, or at least advice to the 'greener' or newly arrived migrant. The attractions of a shared language and culture were no less powerful in Victorian East London than anywhere else, and both Jewish and Irish immigrants tended to settle in areas already peopled by compatriots from the same town in Ireland or shtetl in Poland. Ian Mikardo, writing about the experiences of his parents in the East End, discusses the chain of support for new arrivals stretching from the land they had left behind to the new settlement in East London, the solidarity, protection, and support offered by these kinship networks.[74] The phenomenon of *landslayt*, the magnetic pull of new arrivals towards areas already settled by their kinsman from the 'old country', was strong for both Irish and Jewish settlers. This attraction, following the wave of mass Irish settlement in the 1840s and 1850s, and the Jewish arrivals of the 1880s and 1890s, led to areas very quickly assuming certain 'ethnic' characteristics, creating an impression

---

[73] David Feldman, 'Jews and the British Empire, c.1900', *History Workshop Journal*, No. 63 (Spring 2007), pp. 80–86 for discussion of the interaction between Zionism and British colonialism, and the project to establish an alternative Jewish national home in East Africa.

[74] Mikardo, *Back-Bencher*, p. 8. See also Lees, *Exiles of Erin*, on Irish kinship networks (p. 44).

of 'Jewish' or 'Irish' neighbourhoods. *Landslayt* acted to bind and solidify communities. It informed the immigrant's economic role, whether on the docks and building sites or in the smaller sweated trades, with prospects of employment for new arrivals often dependent on a shared local origin with their employer.[75] The *landslayt* networks were an important factor in the unionisation of immigrant groups and how receptive they were towards socialism, encouraging solidarity, but a solidarity that could traverse class or national loyalties; solidarity based on shared geographical background.

It is also possible to over-romanticise the comradeship and welcome offered to the new arrival of the *landsman*. 'Greeners' could be exploited by family and neighbour networks from the old country just as much as by strangers. However, these networks offered a modicum of protection for new arrivals. As discussed above, friendless strangers could become the victims of 'sharks' or 'bullies' who clustered around the docks where migrants arrived and targeted the naïve and single. Irish migrants were often met on disembarkation by a representative of the Catholic Church.[76] Kinship networks were a common factor in both Irish and Jewish settlement in the East End, playing an important role in determining not only where one lived and where one worked but where migrants worshipped and socialised in their leisure hours. These ties of localised identity and common diasporic experience acted as an informal grass-roots safety net for the very poor in a period before widespread welfare provision. *Landslayt* and the support networks provided was a force outside the control of the Catholic and Jewish communal hierarchies, a phenomenon made all the more potent when combined with radical left-wing political activity as it was during periods of industrial unrest in East End immigrant communities.

The diasporic umbilical cord between transnational Irish communities and Ireland itself was never wholly severed, even amongst the third generation of Irish East-Enders. Jewish migration from the Pale of Settlement in comparison represented a total and welcome break with Tsarist oppression and second-class status (if not with Eastern European culture, food, or language) – a new start, albeit with the accoutrements of old traditions and religious practice. By 1889, on the verge of widespread industrial action in the metropolis (and with the match-women having struck the year before), a number of leading figures in the nascent socialist movement were emerging from both diasporic communities. Socialists from outside the minority groups were also increasingly aware of the important role these communities

75  See Mary E. Daly, 'Irish Women and the Diaspora: Why They Matter', in MacPherson and Hickman, *Women and Irish Diaspora Identities*, p. 21 on chain migration in the Irish diaspora.

76  Panayi, *An Immigration History of Britain*, p. 148.

could potentially play in the approaching class struggle. The working-class migrant neighbourhoods of the East End – poorly housed, poorly paid, and largely un-unionised – seemed ready for radicalisation. The interactions between the socialist movement and these communities, and how the metropolitan left perceived the migrant experience, will now be examined.

# 2

# Socialist Ideology, Organisation, and Interaction with Diaspora and Ethnicity

It is now necessary to frame the ideological debates and conflicts taking place within late nineteenth- and early twentieth-century socialism in East London in the context of the ambiguous and sometimes quixotic relationships formed between the left and the Irish Catholic and Jewish populations. The socialist movement(s) of the period demarcated ideological space through a number of ethnically based oppositions. In particular, a contrast was stressed between a peaceful native socialist tradition on the one hand and a supposed propensity on the other for Irish or Jewish radical organisations to resort to violence to achieve political gains. The chapter locates the complex interplay present in socialist and trade union discourses on both the Jewish and Catholic communities within a wider radical narrative of national and international victims and villains; diasporic groups could find themselves simultaneously acting out both roles.

## Insular or International Socialism? Ideological Interactions between the Domestic Left and Foreign Émigrés

The fractious organisations that made up the radical left in the last decade of the nineteenth century were in a state of near-constant dispute with each other over ideological and tactical matters. These organisations ranged from anarchist groups through to the SDF, the Fabian Society, and the societies and trade union organisations that would coalesce into the Labour Party. These skirmishes took place at public meetings and in the columns of party organs, with groups forming, splitting, and re-forming, and with fluid memberships and loyalties. The socialist parties condemned the anarchists as 'individualists' and dangerous daydreamers, the SDF journal *Justice* belittled the Fabians both as 'almost entirely middle class', removed from their proletarian audience, and as 'men of the half-educated lower middle class [who] strive to make up by conceit and impertinence for their lack of capacity, knowledge and manners'.[1] H.M. Hyndman of the SDF was attacked for his 'upper-class' wardrobe, manner, and patrician attitude, and Bruce Glasier of the ILP wrote of the Social Democrats that 'the ways of the SDF are not our ways ... the SDF are more doctrinaire, more Calvinistic, more aggressively sectarian than the ILP'.[2] Robert Blatchford criticised Keir Hardie and the *Labour Leader* writers as 'Puritans, narrow, bigoted, puffed up with sour cant', who 'could never mix' with his own group based around the *Clarion* journal.[3] The anarchists themselves dismissed the 'permeation' tactics of the Fabians and the parliamentary road to socialism envisaged by the SDF and Labour Party as a distraction to the task of organising the working class.[4] Fratricidal in-fighting, ever the curse of the left, waxed and waned throughout the period under discussion. From the heady days of 1889, through the triumph of 'new unionism' in the early 1890s and its subsequent retreat, and up to the First World War, by which time syndicalist ideas from the continent were in the ascendency, groups formed, split, and reformed.[5] It was in this chaotic environment that the metropolitan left negotiated a relationship with ethnic difference and diasporic identity.

The various strands of the socialist movement were acutely aware that their ideological foundations were widely perceived and portrayed in the press and by their opponents as at best exotic, and at worst totally alien to the British political tradition. This was particularly the case for the anarchist groups and the Marxist SDF. Journals such as the *Pall Mall Gazette* stressed this foreign influence in their reports. On one socialist demonstration in East London the *Gazette* (which began as a Conservative-supporting organ then switched to the Liberals) commented: '[There was] the presence of a very large foreign element. Poles ... Italians who carried with them a fearful odour of garlic, and foreign Jews innumerable.'[6] A letter to the *Cork Examiner*, from a London correspondent, writing in 1896 during a flare up of popular anti-German feeling, claimed that 'a large proportion of the *English*

---

[1] *Justice* (20 April 1889) and (21 May 1892).

[2] Henry Pelling, *Origins of the Labour Party, 1880–1900* (Oxford: Oxford University Press, 1965) (republished 1979), p. 177.

[3] Deborah Mutch, 'The Merry England Triptych, Robert Blatchford, Edward Fay and the Didactic Use of Clarion Fiction', *Victorian Periodicals Review*, Vol. 38, No. 1 (Spring 2005), p. 97.

[4] Bevir, *The Making of British Socialism*, p. 134.

[5] See L.A. Pooler, 'The Socialist Movement', *Irish Church Quarterly*, Vol. 5, No. 2 (October 1912), pp. 297–298: 'What first strikes the student of Socialist literature is the fact that every Socialist writer is of the opinion that he is the only person who really understands what Socialism is.'

[6] *Pall Mall Gazette* (4 May 1891).

socialists are *foreigners*, most of them *Germans*'.[7] Reports such as these stressed the 'otherness' of socialism, something strange and unsavoury. The various socialist groups were aware of this popular perception, and struggled over the course of the 1890s to present a counter-narrative to this portrayal of socialism as a dangerous exogenous growth.[8]

Hyndman claimed a heritage for British socialism stretching back to the Peasants' Revolt and the Civil War, writing: 'It is well known that the idea of socialism is of no foreign importation into England'. On his list of radical heroes, Hyndman commented, 'not a foreigner in the whole batch'.[9] But, despite this emphasis on the SDF as forming the latest link in an unbroken radical English chain stretching back to the Levellers and beyond, the progress of socialism in London owed a great deal to the work of foreign exiles and refugees, and the descendants of migrants from Europe.[10] This was the case both practically and theoretically. Just as Irish radicals had been actively involved in the Chartist movement, so European émigrés, drawing on Britain's tradition of political asylum, provided experience and energy in invigorating the sluggish nascent movement in London.[11]

Nowhere in the world was the left more international than in London. The German anarcho-socialist Rudolf Rocker spoke of London as 'a hub, from which spokes went out in all directions, to a great number of people, in all countries'.[12] Walter Besant in his *East London* (1902) described a myriad of different exiled communities of political radicals settled in the area, from anarchists to Bonapartists.[13] This role as a place of refuge often engendered a form of patriotism in unlikely quarters. The anarchist leader Kropotkin, on seeing the Union Jack raised on the ship taking him to England, described the flag as 'under which so many refugees, Russian, Italian, French, Hungarian and of all nations, have found an asylum. I greeted that flag from the depth

---

[7] Quoted in *The Clarion* (8 February 1897) (original emphasis).

[8] Ward, *Red Flag and Union Jack*, p. 37.

[9] H.M. Hyndman, *The Historical Basis of Socialism in England* (London: Kegan Paul, Trench and Co.), 1883, p. 4. See Ward, *Red Flag and Union Jack*, p. 37.

[10] See Satnam Virdee, *Racism, Class and the Racialized Outsider* (Basingstoke: Palgrave Macmillan, 2014), chapter 3, 'The Contradictions of Socialist Nationalism', on the chauvinism of Hyndman and others in the SDF.

[11] See 'Introduction', Sabine Freitag (ed.), *Exiles from European Revolutions: Refugees in Mid-Victorian London* (London: Berghahn Books, 2003), p. 3. 'Between 1823 and the Aliens Act of 1905 no foreigner was ever refused entry into Britain, or expelled, whatever his or her status or political opinions.' See also Pelling, *Origins of the Labour Party*, p. 14 and Rachel O'Higgins, 'The Irish Influence in the Chartist Movement', *Past and Present*, No. 20 (November 1961).

[12] Rudolph Rocker, *The London Years* (Nottingham: Five Leaves Publications, 2005) (originally published 1956), p. 7.

[13] Walter Besant, *East London* (London: Chatto & Windus, 1902), pp. 206–207.

of my heart.'[14] However, the admiration and gratitude of these European political émigrés had its limits, and the character of socialism and the personal qualities of the leadership in London could provoke exasperation and contempt. For Kropotkin, the British anarchists were 'epicurean, a little Nietzschean, very *snobbish*, very proper, a little too Christian'.[15] Lenin, occupying a back room in SDF offices in Clerkenwell Green from where the Russian Social-Democratic Labour Party (RSDLP) journal *Iskra* was published, described his host Hyndman as 'a British bourgeois philistine who, being the pick of his class, finally makes his way to socialism, but never completely throws off bourgeois traditions, bourgeois views and prejudices.'[16] Hyndman's personal journey to revolutionary socialism was one that combined these international and parochial elements. Hyndman's socialist epiphany came after reading a French translation of *Capital*. He was vocal in his praise of Marx. Yet he never lost that element of 'Tory radicalism', rooted in an exclusive, somewhat paternalistic interpretation of a national form of socialism.[17] Whilst Hyndman paid tribute to Marx, and emphasised in positive language Marx's Jewish heritage, the SDF leader was uneasy about acknowledging the extent of the debt that British socialism owed to Marx, Engels, and other continental revolutionary thinkers.[18] For Hyndman and socialists such as Robert Blatchford, English socialism would be achieved by English workers expounding an English ideology. What role Irish and Jewish communities would play in a socialism that stressed English identity and a native English tradition remained unclear.

Parallel to the insular form of socialism propounded by men such as Hyndman and Blatchford was a strand of the left that explicitly viewed the movement and its membership in London as part of an international struggle. In this struggle both English socialists and foreign exiles and refugees situated in the capital had a crucial part to play. These elements perceived racial and religious discord as a capitalist chimera. For socialists such as Bruce Glasier and Keir Hardie, the crisis in the East End required, 'ultimately socialist solutions, rather than racist stereotyping, exclusion and restriction'.[19]

---

[14] A.J. Davies, *To Build A New Jerusalem: The British Labour Movement from the 1880s to the 1990s* (London: Michael Joseph, 1992), p. 52.

[15] Martin A. Miller, *Kropotkin* (Chicago: University of Chicago Press, 1976), p. 169 (original emphasis).

[16] Lindsey German and John Rees, *A People's History of London* (London: Verso, 2012), p. 161. V.I. Lenin, *On Britain* (Moscow: Progress Publishers, 1959) (republished 1979), p. 115.

[17] Bevir, *The Making of British Socialism*, pp. 17 and 45–46. See also Frederick J. Gould, *Hyndman as Prophet of Socialism* (London: Twentieth Century Press, 1924), p. 7.

[18] Gould, *Hyndman as Prophet of Socialism*, p. 7.

[19] Neville Kirk, *Comrades and Cousins: Globalisation, Workers and Labour Movements in Britain, the USA and Australia from the 1880s to 1914* (London: Merlin Press, 2003), p. 194.

William Morris in particular was vocal in his attacks on Hyndman's insularism and hostility towards émigrés and refugees. As early as 1885, in a letter to Robert Thompson, Morris commented on Hyndman's prejudices and tactics, condemning 'attacks on foreigners as foreigners ... [Hyndman] sneers at them: coquetting also with jingoism in various forms'.[20] In the same year, E. Belfort Bax wrote that 'Race-pride and class-pride are, from the standpoint of socialism, involved in the same condemnation ... Tall talk about the "Anglo-Saxon race" or "the great democracies of English speaking peoples" ... can [only] disgust the socialist who is at once logical and honest.'[21] This was a direct rebuke to Hyndman, who had written about 'the common interests and affinities of the great Celto-Teutonic peoples in America, in Australia, in these islands, and possibly in Germany'.[22]

None of the socialist organisations, including those that dabbled in chauvinism, rejected wholly the international dimension of radical left-wing politics. The Socialist League and the anarcho-socialist groups were probably the most internationally focused and sympathetic towards immigration in the East End, the right-wing of the SDF the most parochial, but all of the groups active in the capital combined elements of internationalism and insularism.[23] Indeed, *Justice*, the organ of the SDF, which indulged in anti-Jewish language, frequently made appeals for workers' solidarity to cross ethnic barriers: 'The position of the workers is the same, and their wants and interests are identical, all the world over. No matter what nationality a worker may be, no matter what race, creed or colour, if he is one of the proletariat.'[24]

John Burns, the Battersea-based 'Lib.-Lab.' socialist and trade unionist, combined the insular fears of socialists and trade unionists over foreign workers lowering wages and being used as 'blackleg' labour with an expressed concern for the international working class. Speaking at a meeting held at the Washington Music Hall in Battersea in 1890, Burns demanded the abolition of foreign contract labour, 'to prevent Hungarians, Germans, and Italians flooding our already overcrowded labour market, and it is in the interests, not only of Englishmen, but of the foreigners themselves'. Addressing the Irish radical Michael Davitt, Burns continued:

[T]he curse of your country [Ireland] and Germany has been that their best men and women have been driven from their own country into

---

20 'Introduction', Florence Boos (ed.), *William Morris's Socialist Diary* (London: Journeyman, 1985), p. 5.

21 *Commonweal* (February 1885).

22 Hyndman, *The Historical Basis of Socialism in England*, p. 433. See Chushichi Tsuzuki, *H.M. Hyndman and British Socialism* (Oxford: Oxford University Press, 1961), p. 51.

23 See Virdee, *Racism, Class and the Racialized Outsider*, chapter 3.

24 *Justice* (21 December 1901).

England, and elsewhere by landlordism and capitalistic oppression ... Instead of men flying from their countries it would be better for them to face and remove the cause that drives them abroad, and which often means out of the frying pan into the fire.[25]

Burns claimed the potential immigrants as comrades, but also as men and women who should stay and fight capitalism and 'landlordism' in their own lands, rather than move to Britain. Karl Kautsky, the Austrian socialist theoretician, wrote of capitalist 'blacklegging' as an international phenomenon that required an international response, capital subverting workers' organisation by the transnational movement of migrants. In Kautsky's words:

Slavs, Swedes, and Italians go as blacklegs to Germany; Germans, Belgians, Italians to France; Slavs, Germans, Italians, Irishmen, Swedes to England and the United States; Chinamen to America, South Africa and Australia, and perhaps before very long even to Europe ... These foreign workers are recruited partly from the ranks of expropriated peasants and small tradesmen, whom the capitalist system of production has ruined and driven from house and home, depriving them not only of these, but also of their native country.[26]

If 'blacklegging' was viewed as an international phenomenon rather than a purely national one, the British worker, the alleged victim of immigrant undercutting in the domestic trade union narrative, was also guilty. This was apparent in the Antwerp controversy of 1907, in which English dockers were shipped in to carry out work during a strike by Belgian comrades.[27] Both Burns and Kautsky draw together the insular fears of the various European socialist parties and trade unions over cheap immigrant labour with the demands of the international class struggle. This asserted the establishment of socialism on an international level as the only effective palliative against capitalist-inspired competition between 'native' workers and their foreign counterparts. Within British socialism ideological space was being defined in national and ethnic terms, between insiders and outsiders, between those included in the national narrative of progression towards the future socialist society and those standing outside. In East London this tension in the late nineteenth century in socialist discourse between inclusion and exclusion would centre on the Irish Catholic and Jewish communities.

[25] Warwick Modern Records Centre, MSS 240/W/3/29, Speech by John Burns at meeting held at the Washington Music Hall, Battersea, 21 September 1890.
[26] LSE ILP/13/1908/6, Karl Kautsky, *The Proletariat* (London: Twentieth Century Press, 1908), pp. 11–12.
[27] Warwick Modern Records Centre, MSS 292/PUB/4/1/7, Trade Union Congress Report, 1907.

## 'Merrie England', Darwinism, and Eugenics

One current of socialist thought in the last decades of the nineteenth century tended towards an idealisation of a rural mode of life stretching back to before the industrial revolution and perhaps before the Reformation, to a time before the 'dark satanic mills' of William Blake.[28] This fed into the wider trope that the countryside and rural existence represented a truer, purer form of English life, as opposed to the decaying and corrupting towns and cities.[29] For some socialist writers the dirt and overcrowding of London provoked a visceral disgust. The countryside was romanticised, just as earlier in the century William Cobbett had idealised the England of his youth, 'a land of peace and plenty, of hale and hearty yeomen, of home-baked bread and home-brewed ale, a country of villages and hamlets, a nation of pristine innocence and uncorrupted virtue'.[30] Going further back before industrialisation and Protestantism, life in the villages and small towns became idealised as a time of small-scale artisans, in control of their own labour and produce, of economic freedom and communality swept away by the 'individualism' of the Protestant ascendancy.[31]

Annie Besant framed the exploitation and dehumanisation that accompanied the industrial revolution as an indictment not solely of late nineteenth-century Britain, but of western civilisation as a whole, exposing the hypocrisy and failure of both capitalism and the imperial project. In *Why I Am a Socialist* (1886), Besant wrote:

> The savage has the forest and the open sea, the joy of physical strength, food easily won, leisure sweet after the excitement of the chase; the civilised toiler has the monotonous drudgery of the stuffy workshop, the hell of the gin-palace for his pleasure-ground, the pandemonium of reeking court and stifling alley for his lullaby; civilisation has robbed him of all natural beauty and physical joy, and has given him in exchange – the slum.[32]

This pre-industrial period and mode of life was compared favourably by William Morris's 'arts and crafts' circle in the late nineteenth century with the existing present lot of industrial workers, who did not control the means

---

[28]  William Blake, 'Jerusalem', in John Wain (ed.), *The Oxford Anthology of English Poetry*, Vol. 2 (Oxford: Oxford University Press, 1986) (republished 2003), p. 14.

[29]  Ward, *Britishness Since 1870*, pp. 55–62.

[30]  John W. Derry, *The Radical Tradition: Tom Paine to Lloyd George* (London: Macmillan, 1967), p. 46.

[31]  LSE ILP/13/1907/13, H.W. Lee, *The First of May: The International Labour Day* (London: First of May Celebration Committee, SDF Office, 1907), p. 6.

[32]  Annie Besant, *Why I Am a Socialist* (London: self-published, 1886), p. 4.

of production, who spent their days labouring to boost the profits of others, who paid extortionate rent for dismal housing, and who enjoyed no contact with nature. Crucially, for Morris, these lives also lacked beauty, either in work or in leisure. It was generally felt that a removal of the working classes from urban environments, if but temporarily, would alleviate the social and economic crisis.[33] But was there a role for urban diasporic minority communities in this rural socialist ideal?

Morris combined the utopian ideals of 'Merrie England' with his commitment to internationalism. For him the idealisation of rural simplicity and camaraderie was not backward looking, but a vision of the future.[34] In 'Merrie England', 'nationality' and therefore ethnic conflict would be subsumed and abolished. In *The Society of the Future* (1888), Morris writes:

> It is a society which does not know the meaning of the words rich or poor, or the rights of property, or law or legality, or nationality … It would be divided into small communities varying much within the limits allowed by due social ethics, but without rivalry between each other, looking with abhorrence at the idea of a holy race.[35]

Historians have identified the centrality of the idea of hospitality in Morris's vision – the welcoming of strangers and their treatment as guests.[36]

This evoking of the medieval traditions of hospitality, to be put into practice in a future socialist society, appeared to have opened the door for the participation of 'urban' immigrant groups such as Jews and Irish Catholics in building this future. But was this Utopia really available for ethnic and religious minorities? Waithe comments that 'Medievalism, with its concern for fellowship, for a fixed network of social bonds, is equally apt to inspire a suspicion of outsiders.'[37] 'Guests' might be well treated

---

[33] See William Booth, *In Darkest England and the Way Out* (London: McCorquodale & Co. Ltd, 1890), pp. 91–93 for discussion of a solution to the working-class 'problem' with the implementation of 'city colonies', 'farm colonies' and 'overseas colonies' and Robert Blatchford, *Merrie England: A Plain Exposition of Socialism (American Edition)* (New York: Commonwealth Company, 1895), p. 88.

[34] See Thomas Linehan, *Modernism and British Socialism* (Basingstoke: Palgrave Macmillan, 2012), chapter 3, 'Socialist Utopian Modernism: The Myths of the Kingdom and the Golden Age' for discussion of both forward- and backward-looking British socialist utopianism, with particular reference to Morris and Blatchford.

[35] William Morris, 'The Society of the Future' (1888), in Florence Boos and William Boos, 'The Utopian Communism of William Morris', *History of Political Thought*, Vol. 7, No. 3 (Winter 1986), pp. 495–496.

[36] Marcus Waithe, *William Morris's Utopia of Strangers: Victorian Medievalism and the Ideal of Hospitality* (Cambridge: D.S. Brewer, 2006), p. 197.

[37] Marcus Waithe, 'The Laws of Hospitality: Liberty, Generosity and the Limits of

and welcomed, but they remain 'guests', standing outside the society and looking in. The idealised pre-Reformation England was also a deeply antisemitic society. The medieval depiction of 'the Jew' as money-lender continued into the nineteenth century and informed late nineteenth-century medievalism.[38] Medievalism also drew on the ideas of William Cobbett, for whom disgust at industrialisation and anti-Jewish prejudice went hand in hand.[39] To what extent did the lauding of a medieval value system imply identification with these values? Morris, as discussed, successfully combined his commitment to international socialism and the working class with a localised rural utopianism. There is little evidence that Morris's medievalism was informed by antisemitic sentiment and he consistently made clear his support for refugees and political émigrés arriving in Britain in his writing and his campaigning.[40] In the first issue of *Commonweal*, Morris writes: 'The establishment of socialism … on any national or race basis is out of the question.'[41] Others, on both the left and the right, made more explicit links between the economic ideal of 'Merrie England' and idealisation of the ethnic and religious homogeneity of that period. Robert Blatchford, another exponent of the posited existence of a past golden age for the artisan, and author of the pamphlets *Merrie England* (1894) and *Britain for the British* (1902), made clear the patriotic and national nature of his interpretation of the future 'Merrie England':

> If you as a Briton are proud of your country and your race, if you as a man have any pride in your manhood, or as a worker have any pride in your class, men, come over to us and help in the just and wise policy of winning Britain for the British.[42]

Jewish immigrants were depicted by commentators across the political spectrum as 'irredeemably' urban, just as for the previous generation the term

Dissent in William Morris's "The Tables Turned" and "News from Nowhere"', *Yearbook of English Studies*, Vol. 36, No. 2 (2006), pp. 227–228.

[38] Waithe, 'The Laws of Hospitality', pp. 227–288. On the role of antisemitism in defining a medieval 'English' identity, see Colin Richmond, 'Englishness and Medieval Anglo-Jewry', in Tony Kushner (ed.), *The Jewish Heritage in British History: Englishness and Jewishness* (London: Frank Cass, 1992), p. 56.

[39] See William Cobbett, *Good Friday: The Murder of Jesus Christ by the Jews* (London: self-published, 1830); Felsenstein, *Anti-Semitic Stereotypes*, p. 233; and Derry, *The Radical Tradition*, pp. 76–77.

[40] See Philip Henderson (ed.), *The Letters of William Morris to his Family and Friends* (London: Longmans, Green and Co. Ltd, 1950).

[41] *Commonweal* (February 1885) in Fintan Lane, 'William Morris and Irish Politics', *History Ireland*, Vol. 8., No. 1 (Spring 2000), p. 23.

[42] Robert Blatchford, *Britain for the British* (London: Clarion Press, 1902), pp. 172–173.

'Irish' had been synonymous with inner-city squalor.[43] 'Merrie England' as a movement was not implicitly racist or sectarian. An artistic movement as much as a social and political one, it idealised a mythical past, but what particular aspects of this past should be celebrated and emulated was determined by individuals. For Morris and Annie Besant, 'Merrie England' was to be celebrated as a golden age for the artisan and small craftsman.[44] For Catholic intellectuals such as Hilaire Belloc, 'Merrie England' was a period of religious unity under an indivisible Catholic Church, before the iniquities of the Reformation. For other writers it was idealised precisely because it was a period before mass immigration, and Jewish settlement in particular.[45] This fed into a wider nostalgia that placed all social and economic problems at the door of the migrant.[46] The idealisation of 'Merrie England' formed part of a British radical narrative, with a focus on both the past and the future. This was a narrative which immigrant groups and religious minorities could be included in or excluded from, depending on the particular vision being expounded.[47] The undefined role of the East End diasporic communities in the future arcadia reveals the ambiguous and confused territory occupied by minority Jewish and Catholic communities in the socialist mindset during this period. The socialist and trade union movements wished to agitate within the diaspora space of East London and radicalise diasporic communities, but whether the minority groups they focused on would have a stake and a role to play in the eventual society created by the achievement of socialism was never made explicit in the 'Merrie England' discourses.

The complex interplay apparent here between insiders, outsiders, and 'guests' and the question of belonging brings to the surface another issue that was apparent both in contemporary socialist attitudes to Jewish and Irish immigrants and those of the wider society towards these groups. This was whether Irish or Jewish East-Enders could ever truly be considered 'British'. Whatever the level of integration or assimilation into the host society achieved by Irish Catholics or Jews, for some contemporary commentators, both groups, even men and women who were third- or fourth-generation London-born, retained the status of outsiders in the national narrative. In the case of East London Irish neighbourhoods this removal from the

---

[43] Paul B. Rich, *Race and Empire in British Politics* (Cambridge: University of Cambridge, 1986) (republished 1990), pp. 15–16.

[44] See Annie Besant, *The Evolution of Society* (London: Freethought Publishing Company, 1886), pp. 6–7, 11.

[45] Ward, *Red Flag and Union Jack*, p. 24.

[46] See Colin Holmes, *Anti-Semitism in British Society, 1876–1939* (London: Edward Arnold, 1979), p. 18.

[47] See Ward, *Red Flag and Union Jack*, chapter 2, 'Socialists and Oppositional Englishness' for further discussion of 'Merrie England'.

mainstream British body politic and a status as outsiders was at least in part voluntarily adopted by the community. Minority nationalism in Irish working-class communities maintained a vitality and dynamism clearly detached from purely local domestic concerns.[48]

Running parallel to the nostalgia and idealisation of the past that informed the 'Merrie England' movement was the adoption by some elements of the left of the eugenicist theories of Francis Galton and others, an intellectual current with its eyes fixed squarely on the future. Like the medievalists, the eugenicists stressed the dichotomy between rural and urban life, between a healthy and vigorous country life and a decadent or weakened city existence. As with the medievalists, London, the smog- and dirt-filled metropolis, was the villain, but its crimes were depicted not as an affront to beauty or fellowship between men and women but rather in terms of racial and social degeneration.[49] Again, tropes of decline, particularly when used in discussing the state of the poorest strata of the working class, turned easily towards ethnic categorisation and antipathy towards minority groups. Some parts of the socialist movement inclined towards a world view based around the pseudo-scientific racial pyramid so prevalent in the discourse of the second half of the nineteenth century.[50] An acceptance of Darwinism did not necessarily equate with a racially framed perspective. One could be attracted to the scientific rationalism of Darwinism, and apply its teachings to the class struggle, without endorsing an infallible Anglo-Saxon, Anglo-Celtic, or Teutonic superiority when viewing the world and its problems. David Stack writes of the prevalence of Darwinist views among the mainstream Victorian left, and the role of *The Origin of Species* in many individual conversions to socialist ideals:

> Darwinism was integral to socialism ... socialism, by necessity and choice, was developed within a Darwinian discursive space ... The socialism and socialist movements that arose in the [latter nineteenth century] were forged and matured in an era when Darwinism was an established part of the 'mental furniture'.[51]

[48] Panayi, *An Immigration History of Britain*, pp. 167–169 and 265. See Alan O'Day, *The English Face of Irish Nationalism: Parnellite Involvement in British Politics, 1880–86* (Dublin: Gill and Macmillan Ltd, 1977), chapter 7, 'The English Irish and Irish Nationalism' for discussion of this relationship in the context of the 1880s.

[49] Jack London, *The People of the Abyss* (Teddington: Echo Library, 2007) (originally published 1903), pp. 18–19: 'In short, the London Abyss is a vast shambles. Year by year, and decade after decade, rural England pours in a flood of vigorous strong life, that not only does not renew itself, but perishes by the third generation.'

[50] See West, *The Victorians and Race*, 'Introduction'.

[51] David Stack, *The First Darwinian Left: Socialism and Darwinism, 1859–1914* (Cheltenham: New Clarion Press, 2003), p. 2.

Galtonian theories were also attractive to socialists for their anti-aristo-cratic leanings, the suggestion that a decadent stratum at the top of society was as superfluous to progress, and in as much need of reforming, or purging, as that underclass at the bottom.[52] A strand also existed which combined socialism and a Darwinian-based perspective that focused on poverty and a racially-defined proletariat. Ethnic tensions in the East End were framed in physical terms, with men and women struggling physically for survival, locked in a conflict with new arrivals. The Jewish worker was depicted by both left and right as bodily able to work greater hours for less food, to survive on substandard food, and to prosper in conditions that the English worker could not bear.[53] The Irish worker was also portrayed as constitu-tionally stronger than his English rival.[54] Indeed, the new Irish arrivals were compared favourably to second- or third-generation Irish Londoners who had been sapped of strength by urban life. Diasporic economic transactions were framed in terms of ethnic conflict in a Hobbesian East End jungle: '[In] the battle of populations', commented the *ILP News* in an 1898 article on Chinese labour, 'it is the race which can eat least and work most that will survive.'[55] The 'fittest' were possibly not the 'best'. The capitalist system seemed to have perverted the Darwinian struggle. 'In the competitive struggle as we know it', wrote J. Connell in 1903, 'physical excellence counts for nothing, mental excellence counts for little, and moral excellence is simply ruinous.'[56]

For some, socialism was to be the preserve of the Anglo-Saxon, or the 'developed' white races. Sidney and Beatrice Webb concerned themselves with declining birth rates amongst the 'vigorous' Northern European races. Socialism could only be achieved through the efforts of certain European strata, and the demographic trends that threatened this predominance also threatened socialism.[57] Sidney Webb warned in *The Decline of the Birth Rate* (1907) that Anglo-Saxon predominance in the United Kingdom was under threat, that supremacy might be yielded to: '[The] Irish, the Jews or even the Chinese', and that the Anglo-Saxon people faced 'race suicide'.[58] In a 1913

---

[52] Arthur Herman, *The Idea of Decline in Western History* (New York: The Free Press, 1997), pp. 133–134; Greta Jones, *Social Darwinism and English Thought: The Interaction between Biological and Social Theory* (Chichester: Harvester Press, 1980), pp. 35–36.

[53] Wilkins, *The Alien Invasion*, pp. 15–16; Blatchford, *Merrie England*, p. 133.

[54] Fielding, *Class and Ethnicity*, p. 26.

[55] *ILP News* (February 1898).

[56] LSE ILP 5/1903/10, J. Connell, *Socialism and the Survival of the Fittest* (London: Twentieth Century Press, 1903), p. 18.

[57] See J.M. Winter, 'The Webbs and the Non-White World: A Case of Socialist Racialism', *Journal of Contemporary History*, Vol. 9, No. 1 (January 1974), pp. 182–183 and 190–191.

[58] Sidney Webb, *The Decline of the Birth Rate* (London: Fabian Society, 1907). See also

article, the Webbs predicted that 'the Western European races may go the way of half a dozen civilisations that have within historic times preceded it; to be succeeded by a new social order developed by one or other of the coloured races, the negro, the Kaffir or the Chinese.'[59] For the Webbs and their circle, without the demographic survival of that Anglo-Saxon civilisation, the achievement of socialism would be impossible. However, in a 1906 review of a tract, *The Anglo-Saxon*, by George E. Boxall, appearing in the *Labour Leader*, the reviewer, identified by his initials 'J.F.M.', attacked this particular world view in which society was framed solely in terms of race and racial conflict:

> It is equally absurd to attribute everything to race characteristics. It is as absurd to assert that despotism and superstition are inherent in the Latin as it would be to assert that money-grubbing is a racial characteristic of the Jew or Roman Catholicism of the Celt ... All these are the products of past and present conditions, and due as much to environment as to hereditary bent.[60]

Blatchford, four years earlier, in *Britain for the British*, attacked the callousness to which eugenicist ideas could lead:

> [N]o man is wise enough to select the 'fit' from the 'unfit' amongst the children. The thin, pale child killed by cold, by hunger, by smallpox, or by fever, maybe a seedling Stephenson, Hershel, or Wesley; and I take it that in the West End the parents would not be consoled for the sacrifice of their most delicate child by the brutal suggestion that it was one of the 'unfit'.[61]

Later in this tract Blatchford describes the British race as 'deteriorating'. The danger, for Blatchford, was not, however, from ethnic 'outsiders', but 'the worship of luxury, wealth and ease', a moral degeneration rather than a racial one.[62] The binary opposition in British society presented by Blatchford in *Britain for the British*, despite its title, was between the worthy and the unworthy. It was between those who made meaningful contributions to society and parasitical elements, rather than between the English host society and minorities.[63]

---

Geoffrey Bell, *Troublesome Business: The Labour Party and the Irish Question* (London: Pluto Press Ltd, 1982), pp. 5–6: Letter from the Webbs to a friend, 1892: 'The [Irish] people are charming but we detest them, as we should the Hottentots, for their very virtues. Home Rule is an absolute necessity in order to depopulate the country of this detestable race.'

[59] Beatrice Webb and Sidney Webb, 'What is Socialism? XXI The Great Alternative (1) The Answer of Pessimism', *New Statesman* (30 August 1913), p. 654.

[60] *Labour Leader* (15 June 1906). See George E. Boxall, *The Anglo-Saxon: A Study in Evolution* (London: T. Unwin, 1906).

[61] Blatchford, *Britain for the British*, p. 18.

[62] Blatchford, *Britain for the British*, p. 19.

[63] Tony Judge, *Tory Socialist: Robert Blatchford and Merrie England* (Dublin: Mentor

As with the differing conceptions of the relationship between 'Merrie England', ethnic difference, and outsider status, the role to be played by Irish and Jewish East End diasporic communities in the Darwinist narrative remained ambiguous and unclear. Webb's 1907 pamphlet illustrated the continuing role of the Irish, along with Jewish and non-white minority groups, as an explicitly racial and ethnic, as well as a class- or religion-based 'other', a continuing racial and demographic threat to Anglo-Saxon hegemony in Great Britain. The Irish and Jewish 'guests' of 'Merrie England' were, in a eugenicist analysis, potentially threatening outsiders: undermining the racial stock and health of the host society. For eugenicists of different political stripes, the very nature of the ethnic interactions taking place in East End diaspora space represented a threat to racial stability in the capital. A correspondent in *Blackwood's Magazine* issued dire warnings over the possible results of racial mixture between Jews and Chinese in East London, asking his readers to 'Imagine a struggle for existence in the tailoring trade between Polish Jew and Chinaman: the forty per cent of British who still keep their ground would go under, whichever of the other two might survive. Think if the slums were to bring to birth a slit-eyed mongrel.'[64] The multiple relationships taking place between different minorities within the neighbourhoods of East London and the perceived danger of 'miscegenation' between different minority communities appeared to constitute a potent demographic danger to British society for those on both right and left who viewed the world through the kaleidoscope of racial angst.

## Anarchism, Syndicalism, and 'Difference'

One of the major ideological differences that served to divide the late-Victorian and Edwardian left was the means through which power should be obtained, whether through the ballot box, unionisation of workers, or other methods, violent or otherwise. This could be framed as a choice between an English moderate social democracy on the one hand and an alien revolutionary socialism and nihilism on the other. This was a useful dichotomy for defining and occupying mainstream political space at the expense of ideological opponents. The majority of leading mainstream British socialists rejected violent revolutionary activity out of hand, and it

---

Books, 2013), pp. 82, 97–98, 108–109. As the first decade of the twentieth century progressed, however, Blatchford himself would increasingly be associated with the most chauvinistically inclined and insular sections of the British socialist movement and was eventually attacked by former comrades for being on a *Daily Mail* stipend.

[64] Anon., 'Foreign Undesirables', *Blackwood's Magazine*, No. 1024 (London: William Blackwood and Sons, February 1901), p. 289.

was on the fringes of the anarchist movement that direct and violent action was most seriously contemplated.[65] The SDF, the ILP, and Blatchford's *Clarion* all condemned violent action as contrary to the spirit and the beliefs of British socialism, and suggested that violence was the preserve of the foreigner. Robert Blatchford dismissed the notion of a violent revolutionary uprising in Britain:

> [T]here are very few socialists who believe in brute force, or think a revolution possible or desirable. The bulk of our socialists are for peaceful and lawful means ... I do not think a revolution is *possible* in Britain. Firstly because the people have too much sense; secondly, because the people are by nature patient and kindly; thirdly, because the people are too *free* to make force needful. I do not think a revolution is *advisable* ... after great bloodshed, trouble, labour and loss the people would almost surely slip down into worse evils than those against which they had fought, and would find that they had suffered and sinned in vain.[66]

William Morris rejected anarchism and broke with the journal *Commonweal* over this assumed propensity towards violent action, as well as for its individualism.[67] In correspondence with a young anarchist named James Tochatti, who had invited the veteran socialist to contribute articles to a putative journal, Morris concluded his final letter by stating: 'I could not in conscience allow anything with my name attached to it to appear in an anarchist paper ... I cannot for the life of me see how such principles, which propose the abolition of compulsion, can admit of promiscuous slaughter as a means of converting people.'[68]

In a 1901 lecture organised by the SDF, the speaker James Leatham claimed that:

> [The anarchist] demands 'absolute liberty' of action so far as the law is concerned – liberty limited only by the rules of sense, taste, and judgement – that is to say, *his* taste, *his* sense, and *his* judgement; but needless to say, public opinion is much more inquisitorial than any policeman, it interferes

---

[65] See George Woodcock, *Anarchism: A History of Libertarian Ideas and Movements* (Harmondsworth: Penguin Books, 1962); David Miller, *Anarchism* (London: J.M. Dent & Sons Ltd, 1984); and David Goodway, *Anarchist Seeds beneath The Snow: Left-Libertarian Thought and British Writers from William Morris to Colin Ward* (Liverpool: Liverpool University Press, 2006); as well as Alex Butterworth, *The World That Never Was: A True Story of Dreamers, Schemers, Anarchists and Secret Agents* (London: Vintage Books, 2011) for examination of the anarchist movement in a European context.

[66] Blatchford, *Britain for the British*, p. 75 (original emphasis).

[67] Goodway, *Anarchist Seeds beneath the Snow*, pp. 22–23.

[68] Letter from William Morris to James Tochatti, 12 December 1893, in Norman Kelvin (ed.), *The Collected Letters of William Morris*, Vol. 4 (Princeton, NJ: Princeton University Press, 1996), p. 113.

in many matters of which the law and officialdom take no cognisance, and is, on the whole, a greater tyrant than the law.[69]

Leatham concluded that 'The anarchists we have in this country are now almost entirely foreigners belonging to oppressed nationalities and themselves leading miserable lives.'[70] During the industrial unrest of 1911, with troops on the streets of Liverpool and attacks on blacklegs in London, *Justice* again attacked anarchism and denied its legitimacy: 'Although we understand how men can be driven by the tyrannies and injustices of capitalism into political madness so that they "run amok" … nevertheless, Social-Democrats can have no part with anything so insane as anarchism.'[71]

Key figures in Jewish metropolitan socialism also stressed the dangers of anarchist individualism, and the widely suspected infiltration of the anarchist groups by both the Metropolitan Police and the continental secret services. During a traumatic period for the Socialist League, Eleanor Marx had warned in an 1885 letter to her sister Laura that '[no one knows] what these Anarchists are: till they do find out it is a hard struggle to make head against them – the more that many of our English men taken in by Anarchists (half of whom I suspect to be police agents) are unquestionably the best men we have.'[72] Ten years later, Marx, in the introduction to a volume of Georgi Plekhanov's writings that she had translated, argued that the anarchist presence at the Congress of Revolutionary Socialists would make the wider movement 'a playground of reaction and international spydom [*sic*]'.[73]

Nevertheless, anarchism and political violence became entwined in the public perception with the Jewish community. For the wider public, this was a negative association which led to another popular antisemitic image, that of the wild-haired anarchist with a tract in one hand and a bomb in the other, alongside those of the Jewish financier, the moneylender, and the sweated worker keeping down wages. Jewish migrants were blamed for importing Russian nihilism into Britain. The model for the popular perception of the violent Jewish nihilist, carrying out assassinations and planting bombs causing indiscriminate carnage, which gained popular mileage in the Edwardian period, had already been in existence in an Irish context for several decades. Following quickly on the footsteps of Britain's

---

[69] LSE ILP/8/1901/28, James Leatham, *What is to be Done with the Anarchists? A Lecture by James Leatham* (London: Twentieth Century Press, 1901), pp. 8–9.

[70] Leathham, *What is to be Done with the Anarchists?*, p. 12.

[71] *Justice* (13 May 1911).

[72] Chushichi Tsuzuki, *The Life of Eleanor Marx, 1855–1898: A Socialist Tragedy* (Oxford: Clarendon Press, 1967), p. 129: letter from Eleanor Marx to Laura Lafargue, 12 April 1885.

[73] Tsuzuki, *The Life of Eleanor Marx*, p. 281.

first immigration 'crisis' in the aftermath of the Irish Famine of the 1840s came Britain's first terrorist panic. The periodic campaigns of the Fenian 'dynamiters' from the 1860s to the 1880s would set the pattern for both official and popular responses to terror campaigns over the course of the second half of the nineteenth century and up to the present day.[74] From the crisis of the mid-1860s onwards, political violence designated as terroristic on the British mainland would be associated with ethnic difference and blamed on ethnic 'outsiders'. As Britain's Irish communities would be blamed for harbouring Fenian 'dynamiters', so the Houndsditch murders and the Sidney Street siege would be laid (incorrectly as it turned out) at the door of Jewish radicals. Sir Howard Vincent, a leading campaigner against 'alien subversives' in the years before the First World War, had first come to notice directing operations in Scotland Yard against the Fenian campaign.[75] The preternaturally violent and quarrelsome Irishman was an old stereotype, and following bomb attacks by Irish Nationalists on the British mainland between the 1860s and 1880s the simian Irish caricature of *Punch* was increasingly depicted armed with dynamite as well as a thick wooden stick.[76] Between 1889 and 1912, Irish political violence had abated, at least on the English side of the Irish Sea. The Irish terrorist as political bogeyman would reappear in the British popular perception post-1916 and during the War of Independence of the early 1920s.[77]

The supposed militant qualities of Jewish anarchists were feted by some comrades. In a letter to William 'Woolf' Wess, a certain 'Mac' Duff wrote: 'Let them not be astonished when I say, I like the Jews best. They are the finest comrades and they don't play at being anarchists, they are in dead earnest.'[78] The militancy of the post-1905 intake of political refugees fleeing repressive measures in Russia was admired by many on the left, as men and

---

[74] Panayi, *An Immigration History of Britain*, pp. 216–217.

[75] Gainer, *The Alien Invasion*, pp. 105–106. S.H. Jeyes, *The Life of Sir Howard Vincent* (London: George Allen and Co., 1912), chapter 7, 'Fighting Fenians and Anarchists', p. 119: '[During the Fenian bomb scare of 1881] … any parcel left in a clubroom or forgotten in a railway carriage became an object of fear and suspicion, and in the facts known there was just enough to make the alarm not absolutely fantastic.'

[76] John Newsinger, *Fenianism in Mid-Victorian Britain* (London: Pluto Press, 1994), pp. 64–65.

[77] See Haia Shpayer-Makov, 'Anarchism in British Public Opinion, 1880–1914', *Victorian Studies*, Vol. 31, No. 4 (Summer 1988), p. 492 for the conflation in the public mind of 'anarchist' and 'Irish' terrorism, and for further discussion of the perception of 'anarchists'. 'When the anarchist movement appeared in the arena of British history, it was greeted with the stock rhetoric and imagery commonly applied to the Irish, the socialists, and other "deviant" groups.' See also Jones, *Immigration and Social Policy in Britain*, p. 8.

[78] Warwick Modern Records Centre, MSS 240/W/3/11, William Wess correspondence, letter dated 26 December 1897.

women who had *been* in a revolutionary situation, who had heard gunfire, experienced extreme political repression, perhaps some who knew how to handle dynamite. In some cases there were difficulties in restraining these radicals from violent action on British shores.[79]

However, prominent figureheads of the socialist movement such as Ben Tillett needed no schooling from 'foreign' anarchists, Jewish or otherwise, when it came to bloodcurdling language. During a 1908 visit to London by the American industrialist Andrew Carnegie, Tillett had publicly mused on the suitability of cutting Carnegie's throat. The trade union leader, in a letter to *Justice*, wrote: 'Would it be any more murder to rise up and cut the throats of the rich, than that the rich should be legalised to torture the poor with the vilest agonising death of all, that of starvation? ... There must come a day when the poor cut some throats.'[80] In May 1912, Tillett led the striking dockers in the prayer: 'May God strike Lord Devonport [the leader of the dock employers] dead!'[81] The designation by the mainstream socialist parties and trade unions of anarchism as intrinsically 'foreign' and 'Jewish' served its purpose – to bolster an ideological boundary and delegitimise anarchist claims to the loyalties of British workers. Following the Houndsditch murders and the siege of Sidney Street, the mere label of 'anarchist' was sufficient to draw public disapprobation and police attention.[82]

As anarchism in the capital drew widespread public and official hostility following the dramatic events of the winter of 1910–1911, another radical movement, syndicalism, began to gain increasing support in socialist circles and wider publicity in the mainstream press. Like anarchism, the ideological divide between syndicalist ideology and 'English' socialism was frequently framed in ethnic or national terms, both within the socialist movement and outside of it. Furthermore, the presumed violence of syndicalism was depicted by left-wing opponents as something foreign and alien to the British socialist tradition. The year 1889 had witnessed individual attacks on strike-breakers, but not the widespread disorder and battles with authority

---

[79] See Rocker, *The London Years*, pp. 108–109, in which Rocker discusses narrowly preventing 'a young Russian comrade', recently arrived, from planting a bomb at the Lord Mayor's Show.

[80] *Justice* (14 November 1908), in Jonathon Schneer, *Ben Tillett: Portrait of a Labour Leader* (Beckenham: Croom Helm, 1982), p. 134. See Barbara W. Tuchman, *The Proud Tower: A Portrait of the World Before the War, 1890–1914* (London: Hamish Hamilton, 1966), p. 72 for further examples of Tillett's bloodthirsty rhetoric during the coal strike of 1893, in this case the violence of which was challenged by Kropotkin.

[81] Rob Sewell, *In the Cause of Labour: A History of British Trade Unionism* (London: Wellred Books, 2003), p. 126.

[82] See Miller, *Anarchism*, pp. 112–113.

that characterised the strikes of the post-Edwardian period.[83] For some observers, this rise in violent militancy was a direct result of the proliferation of syndicalist ideas among the trade unions and the organised working class.

Employers stressed the un-English character of syndicalist trade unionism – that syndicalism was largely funded and organised by foreigners (and possibly Jews) – and left-wing rivals of the syndicalist movement bought into this designation. With Germanophobia sweeping Britain, it was alleged that syndicalist trade unionists were receiving strike funds from 'mysterious German waiters', that the industrial unrest was the result of an '"alien" continental ideology'.[84] Whilst anarchism was depicted as the preserve of Jews and political émigrés in the capital, syndicalism had a heritage combining the ideas of the French militants and the American 'De Leonists', followers of the radical labour leader Daniel De Leon. Syndicalism, working as it did through radical trade unionism, was more widespread and enjoyed more popular appeal than anarchism, which was confined largely to the East End and Clydeside. Nevertheless, the Industrial Union of Direct Actionists (IUDA) enjoyed particular support in East London.[85] An early and enthusiastic apostle of syndicalism was Tom Mann, who had travelled to France to find out more about the movement. Mann acknowledged the differences in the industrial situation in France compared with England, but wrote in the *Industrial Syndicalist*: '[Whilst] the temperament of the French is undoubtedly different from that of the British, their interests are exactly the same as ours, and their enemy is also ours – the Capitalist system.'[86] In the October edition of the *Industrial Syndicalist*, Mann compared British class organisation and radicalisation unfavourably with their French counterparts: 'The chief difference between British and French workmen is this: the French have instinctively and rationally a keener appreciation of class solidarity … they have developed a power to achieve altogether beyond what is possible with the compromising methods resorted to in Britain of late years.'[87]

Mann's former comrades in the wider socialist movement contested syndicalism's national character as much as the employers did, making use of the same tropes of alien ideology and a 'British' as opposed to a 'continental' way of conducting radical and industrial politics. Ramsay MacDonald, writing in 1912, questioned both syndicalism's character and its chances of success. He stressed syndicalism's alien way of conducting

[83] Bob Holton, *British Syndicalism 1900–1914* (London: Pluto Press, 1976), pp. 73–74.

[84] Holton, *British Syndicalism*, p. 76.

[85] Holton, *British Syndicalism*, p. 46.

[86] *Industrial Syndicalist*, Vol. 1, No. 1 (July 1910).

[87] *Industrial Syndicalist*, Vol. 1, No. 4 (October 1910). See Bantman, *The French Anarchists*, p. 173 for comparison of the British and French revolutionary movements.

politics, an import that would only lead the British working class down a costly blind alley. In the preface to the critique, MacDonald wrote: 'It is in vain that one searches English dictionaries for the word Syndicalism. It is a French stranger in our language, with no registered abode as yet.'[88] *Justice* compared syndicalist tactics to 'the Chinese method of starving themselves and their children on the door steps of their oppressors' – that is, harming the working class more than the employers.[89] For the SDP and its stepchild the BSP, syndicalist faith in the all-encompassing general strike as a means of obtaining political power (rather than the gradualist tactics adopted by the social democratic left) could only hinder the progression towards socialism. As with anarchism, ethnicity and national difference were both used to demarcate syndicalism from the native radical tradition and question its legitimacy compared with the mainstream socialist movement. This school of thought posited a division between a peaceful British route to socialism and an intemperate European one, and in an East End context between a native 'English' moderation and an 'alien', 'Irish', or 'Jewish' inclination towards political activity expressed in acts of violence.[90]

## Class Definitions, Economic Roles, and the East End Diasporic 'Other'

The East End Jewish and Irish communities both presented significant difficulties when outside observers, socialist, liberal, conservative, or otherwise, attempted to position diasporic groups in the late-Victorian and Edwardian class structure.[91] The poverty of large sections of the Jewish and Irish communities, the poor housing, the mortality rates, the long hours of labour in often extremely poor conditions, were not to be doubted. Yet contemporary observers struggled to place both communities on the class scale.

In the Jewish case, the fluidity between master and man in the tailoring sweatshops subverted the classic relationship between the boss and the hands, key to the socialist narrative of class conflict. Theodore Rothstein of the SDF traced this, and the barriers it formed against successful politicisation, to the class structure of the Pale of Settlement: 'Not being a proletarian at home [i.e., Russia] and seeing the potentialities of becoming

[88] J. Ramsay MacDonald, *Syndicalism: A Critical Examination* (London: Constable and Co. Ltd, 1912), p. v. See Ward, *Red Flag and Union Jack*, p. 91.

[89] *Justice* (1 June 1912).

[90] Ward, *Red Flag and Union Jack*, p. 90.

[91] See, for example, Charles Booth's designations in *Life and Labour of the People in London*, in Ben Gidley, *The Proletarian Other: Charles Booth and the Politics of Representation* (Goldsmiths College University of London, London, 2000), pp. 16–17.

a master ... the Jewish worker in England could never identify himself with the proletarian psychology.'[92] Elements of the left viewed Jewry as a whole as 'non-producers'. 'They [the Jews] do not toil neither do they spin', wrote one correspondent to *Justice* in November 1899, 'and under a Social-Democratic regime would either decline, like the Red Indians, or have to be absorbed amongst the democratic liberty-loving peoples of the world.'[93] This language drew on the classic trope that Jews were averse to physical toil.

Jewish labour was viewed, by both Jewish and Gentile trade unionists, as difficult to organise. Culturally, too, the East End Jewish community seemed to stand apart from the wider proletariat of the area. One Jewish woman from Bethnal Green reminisced years later that 'we were Jewish immigrants, and so we had no class really. It was different for us.'[94] Charles Booth observed that 'Broken windows are one of the surest signs of rough life, and it is curious to note that those of the Jews are intact, which would seem to show that where there is damage it comes from within, and not from without.'[95] It was this supposed cultural and social separation from the 'rough life' of the wider East End, rather than any comparative disparity in wealth, that seemed to differentiate the Jewish East-Enders from their Gentile neighbours, who were also likely to work in workshops and the 'sweated' industries.[96] Both economically and culturally, the socialist movement struggled to place the Jewish poor on the class gradient. It was clear that Jewish workers were being exploited. Where, however, the Jewish 'greener', the newly arrived immigrant, fitted in the struggle between labour and capital, painted in polemic in black and white terms, was uncertain, and troubled both Jewish and Gentile comrades. That sweated Jewish workers were sometimes related to their employer also complicated matters. The dislocation between the classic class definitions and oppositions so central to the socialist narrative and the complex class interactions actually at work in immigrant Jewry again fed into the general confusion and ambiguity that

92 Theodore Rothstein, quoted in William J. Fishman, *East End Jewish Radicals, 1875–1914* (London: Gerald Duckworth and Co. Ltd, 1975), p. 122.

93 *Justice* (4 November 1899). See Bryan Cheyette, *Constructions of 'the Jew' in English Literature and Society: Racial Representations, 1875–1945* (Cambridge: Cambridge University Press, 1993) (republished 1995), p. 95 on the discussion by H.G. Wells and George Bernard Shaw of the possible assimilation of Jewish 'difference' in the future socialist society.

94 Lee, 'Aspects of the Working-Class Response to the Jews in Britain, 1880–1914', p. 116.

95 Booth, *Life and Labour of the People in London*, Third Series, *Religious Influences*, Vol. 2, p. 9.

96 See the transition of streets that Booth described as inhabited by the 'vicious and semi-criminal' to 'Jewish and respectable' following Jewish settlement. David Feldman, *Englishmen and Jews: Social Relations and Political Culture* (New Haven, Conn.: Yale University Press, 1994), p. 182.

manifested itself in the relationship between the socialist movement and diasporic minorities.

The fluidity between master and workers in the Jewish clothes trades was certainly not present in the dockland industries in which large numbers of male Irish labourers worked. One might, as a docker, rise to the role of contractor, the middleman who hired causal labour, but a docker or stevedore was not likely to become an employer. The dock bosses were not small-scale masters running a business in their own back room, but men of property and influence, moving in a different world from the dockers, porters, and stevedores in their employment. But this fluidity was not entirely lacking in trades in which large numbers of Irish immigrants were involved. In the building trade, for example, it was possible for a bricklayer eventually to become an employer with his own business. At first glance the Irish Catholic community in the East End would appear to constitute a classic proletariat. Aside from a relatively small but politically and culturally influential middle class, and a significant number of Irish Catholics (and Irish Protestants) who had found employment in the Metropolitan Police and the army, the bulk of the Irish male population worked as manual labourers, on the docks, in the building industry, and as costers. A large number of Irish women worked in the tailoring trade and as domestic servants.[97] But the London Irish also remained difficult to place in the class structure. The perception formed in the mid-nineteenth century of Irish workers as temperamentally unwilling to work regular shifts for a regular wage, and thus resistant to political organisation, remained. Beatrice Potter, in a draft copy of an article for *Nineteenth Century* from 1887, stressed both the Irish aversion to regular employment and the physical decline among second- and third-generation Irish East-Enders:

Paddy enjoys more than his proportional share of dock work with its privileges and its miseries. He is to be found especially among the irregular hands, disliking as a rule the 'six to six business' for six days of the week. And the cockney-born Irishman, as distinguished from the immigrant, is not favourably looked upon by the majority of employers. In a literal and physical sense the sins of the forefather are visited tenfold upon the children, intensifying the evil of a growing Irish population.[98]

The perception that the Irish, like the Jewish 'greeners', were beyond political organisation was dealt a blow by the successful match-women's strike of 1888 and the dock strike of 1889. But the East End Irish community was throughout the period perceived to have one foot in the 'respectable'

[97] See Bronwen Walter, *Outsiders Inside: Whiteness, Place and Irish Women* (London: Routledge, 2001), chapters 3 and 4.
[98] LSE PASSFIELD 7/1/7, Beatrice Potter, 'London Dock Labour in 1887 (draft copy)', *Nineteenth Century*, No. 128 (October 1887).

working class in which the socialist movement placed much of its hope for the future, and one still in the residuum or underclass. Ben Tillett, of Irish descent himself, was sympathetic to the struggles of the East End Irish. He recalled the strength and comradeship of Irish workers on the docks and the days when 'the advertisement "No Irish need apply" was supposed to be the motto of loyalty and Christianity'.[99] In an exchange between Tillett and Professor Marshall during a meeting of the Royal Commission on Labour, the trade union leader dismissed Marshall's claims of an 'Irish temper' that preferred irregular work. 'I have seen a lot of Irishmen at regular work, and they have been most punctual and sober ... Under proper circumstances an Irishman as much as anybody else likes regular work.'[100] But for the residuum, and their ability to play a part in the coming struggle, Tillett placed little hope, describing that stratum of society as the 'hyenas of the revolution' and 'scum'.[101] This was the section of society that Annie Besant had warned the movement about in 1886. For Besant, only socialism could address the 'problem' of the East End underclass:

> [I]magine what would happen if those drunken men and women, singing, shouting, fighting in the streets, were to burst the barriers that hem them in, and were to surge westwards over London, wrecking the civilisation which has left them to putrefy in their misery, and had remained callous to their degradation. Is it not part of a good citizen to try to change a social system which bears such products as these in every great city?[102]

Thus both the Jewish and Irish Catholic communities in East London represented a challenge to conventional class categorisation. One individualising economic comparison that can be usefully employed is the identity of the employers in the casual trades Irish and Jewish migrants were working in. Jews in the East End were largely employed by (and paid rent to) other Jews.[103] Working-class Irish Catholics, on the other hand, whether on the docks or building sites or in domestic service, were not to any significant degree employed by other Irish Catholics. The East End Jewish workforce was predominantly employed in small-scale concerns and by small-scale bosses not substantially more prosperous than their employees; Irish Catholics in large-scale industries such as the docks and the gasworks, or as servants in

---

[99] Ben Tillett, *A Brief History of the Dockers Union* (London: Twentieth Century Press, 1910).

[100] Chushichi Tsuzuki, *Tom Mann, 1856–1941: The Challenges of Labour* (Oxford: Clarendon Press, 1991), p. 90.

[101] Ben Tillett, quoted in Rocker, *The London Years*, p. 25. See also Sarah Wise, *The Blackest Streets* (London: Vintage, 2009), p. 164.

[102] Besant, *Why I Am a Socialist*, pp. 4–5.

[103] Feldman, *Englishmen and Jews*, p. 174.

middle-class or lower middle-class households. Most Irish workers were employed by men and women they would never encounter socially outside the workplace or who shared a common diasporic or religious heritage with them. This removed one major factor involved in both inter-communal tensions within East End Jewry and the difficulties trade unionists found in organising Jewish workers in small-scale workshops – the shared ethnicity and the common economic status of boss and labourer, often involving ties to a particular region of Poland or Russia. It also fed into the potency of working-class Irish Nationalism in the East End; for the Nationalist, economically in London, just as politically in Ireland, the Irish Catholic worker was being exploited by the English Protestant master.

In 1891, the liberal economist H. Llewellyn Smith presented a paper explicitly comparing the presumed economic propensities of Irish Catholics and Jews in the metropolis, and the prospects for industrial organisation of both groups. 'Nowhere', Llewellyn Smith began, 'is the importance of attending to race characteristics in analysing economic problems better exemplified than in the case of the immigrant in East London. The two poorest classes in East London are the London Irish and the London Jews; but their poverty is of an entirely different description.'[104] The Irishman, he continued, is 'peculiarly attached to custom and tradition, and hence, as a labourer, peculiarly "immobile", using mobility in the wider economic sense. With these characteristics, however, he unites a clannishness which has always made the Irish strong in power of effective combination.' Describing Irish involvement in the strikes of 1889, he concluded that 'The social and class instinct is very powerful among the Irish, and this forms their economic strength, as their shiftlessness and want of power of persistent work form their economic weakness.'[105]

'The immigrant Jew', Llewellyn Smith continued, 'is an intense Individualist':

> Each for himself, unrestrained by the instinct of combination, pushes himself upward in the industrial scale. His standard of life readily adapts itself to his improved condition at every step. We have here all the conditions of the economist satisfied: mobility perfect; competition unremitting and unsparing; pursuit of gain an all-powerful motive.[106]

This analysis of the perceived economic virtues and vices of both communities, replete with stereotypes, depicted the Irish as willing to

---

[104] H. Llewellyn Smith, 'The Migration of Labour', in J.H. Levy (ed.), *The National Liberal Club Political Economy Circle, Transactions*, Vol. 1 (London: P.S. King and Son, 1891), pp. 122–123.

[105] Llewellyn Smith, 'The Migration of Labour', pp. 122–123.

[106] Llewellyn Smith, 'The Migration of Labour', pp. 122–123.

organise ('clannish') but reluctant to work regular shift patterns, the Jews as willing to work but impossible to organise due to their 'individualism' and love of profit. It illustrates the contemporary narrative, socialist as well as liberal, of the difficulties present in politically organising the diasporic East End of the 1890s. The difference was that for liberal economists such as Llewellyn Smith this supposed Jewish individualism was a virtue, whilst for the socialist it was an impediment to class solidarity and organisation, as well as an affront to proletarian identity. In the particular, the images of the Jew as reluctant trade unionist and the Irishman as hard-working but unable to keep to regular hours would prove to be persistent and tenacious ones. A correspondent in *Blackwood's Edinburgh Magazine*, writing in 1901 on the 'London Irish', claimed that

> If the [Irish] men [in the casual trades] would submit to the rigidity of the six-to-six hours, if they would condescend to work overtime, they might rise to permanent employment. But they prefer the short bustling job, followed by lordly ease, which they often spend, for days together, in bed. So as casuals they live, and as casuals they die.[107]

Gender relations, and in particular the role of women in the workplace, informed how migrant populations were perceived in economic and class terms. In the diaspora space of the East End two forms of chauvinism came up against each other. A masculine culture that had travelled with the migrants from rural Ireland and Eastern Europe, placing a high premium on submissive female roles (the domesticity and piety of the wife and mother, the chastity of unmarried girls), interacted with a native East End hyper-masculinity.[108] In both the minority communities and amongst the wider working-class East End population it was held that the role of the woman, especially the married woman, was in the home and taking care of children, not having an explicit contributory economic role in the family unit.[109] Contemporary observers pointed to the lack of employment

---

[107] Anon., 'The London Irish', *Blackwood's Edinburgh Magazine*, Vol. 170, No. 1029 (London: William Blackwood and Sons, July 1901), p. 131.

[108] See London, *People of the Abyss*, pp. 16–17 for illustrations of hyper-masculinity among the East End underclass and Bronwen Walter, *Outsiders Inside*, p. 275 for discussion of feminised roles within Irish culture.

[109] Deborah Thom, 'Free from Chains? The Image of Women's Labour in London, 1900–1920', in David Feldman and Gareth Stedman Jones (eds), *Metropolis London: Histories and Representations since 1800* (Oxford: Routledge, 1989), p. 92; Ellen Ross, 'Fierce Questions and Taunts: Married Life in Working-Class London, 1870–1914', in Feldman and Stedman Jones, *Metropolis London*, pp. 222–224; Elizabeth Roberts, *Women's Work, 1840–1940* (Basingstoke: Macmillan, 1988), pp. 12–13: 'Working wives and mothers especially were often regarded as unnatural, immoral and inadequate homeworkers and parents.'

amongst married women in the minority communities compared with the wider proletarian population of the host society. In *The Jew in London* (1900), C. Russell wrote that 'His [the Jewish immigrant's] wife, moreover, is probably a more costly encumbrance than the Gentile's, as she very rarely, indeed, brings in any wages.'[110] Later in the same book, H.S. Lewis commented on Jewish immigrant family life: 'They [the Jewish immigrants] seldom allow their wives to work for them.'[111] In the Irish neighbourhoods around the docklands a strict demarcation of gender roles was also apparent. Whilst religion and church-based social life was held as the preserve of the married woman, paid employment, 'putting bread on the table', was stressed to be a masculine prerogative.[112] Parallel to this, and conversely, anti-immigrant campaigners emphasised the employment in the small-scale sweated workshops of wives, sisters, and daughters by Jewish 'sweaters' as evidence of the unfair economic advantage held over the 'decent' Gentile worker who would not allow his womenfolk to work.[113]

In reality, employment of married women in the casual trades of the East End was common, even the norm, in the period, both in the minority communities and in the wider society, amongst the English, Irish, and Jewish working classes. In E.G. Howarth and M. Wilson's social study of working-class life in West Ham, conducted in 1907, it was found that the majority of women who earned wages by sewing clothes at home were the wives of men in the casual industries that employed large numbers of Irish- and London Irish-born men – the docks, the building sites, and general labouring jobs.[114] In the Jewish East End the degree to which married women were employed was hidden to an extent by the prevalence of small-scale workshops within the family home.[115] Moreover, much labour undertaken by women such as cleaning, taking in lodgers, and childcare did not appear on censuses, or indeed was not considered to be 'work' at

---

[110] C. Russell, 'The Jewish Question on the East End', in C. Russell and H.S. Lewis, *The Jew in London: A Study of Racial Character and Present-Day Conditions* (London: T. Fisher Unwin, 1900), p. 59.

[111] H. S. Lewis 'Another View of the Question', in Russell and Lewis, *The Jew in London*, p. 169.

[112] For discussion of multi-generational diasporic Irish masculinity, see Liviu Popoviciu, Chris Haywood and Máirtín Mac an Ghaill, 'Migrating Masculinities: The Irish Diaspora in Britain', *Irish Studies Review*, Vol. 14, No. 2 (May 2006), pp. 176–177.

[113] Feldman, *Englishmen and Jews*, pp. 284–285.

[114] E.G. Howarth and M. Wilson, *West Ham: A Struggle in Social and Industrial Problems* (London: J.M. Dent and Company, 1907), pp. 268–269. See Fitzpatrick, 'The Irish in Britain, 1871–1921', in Vaughan, *A New History of Ireland*, Vol. 6, p. 664 on contrasting Irish male and female economic roles.

[115] Marks, *Irish and Jewish Women's Experience of Childbirth and Infant Care in East London*, p. 28. See Kershen, *Strangers*, p. 89.

all. The attitudes towards the employment of married women in minority communities was another example of an artificial demarcation in cultural terms between diasporic groups and the host society, a demarcation that in this case had a basis in an abstract idealisation of family life and gender roles rather than in socio-economic realities.[116]

## Socialism, Oppression, and the Colonial Context

Attitudes towards the Jewish Community and Opposition to Tsarism

Many of the leading socialists active in London were naturally predisposed towards a sympathetic attitude regarding both Jewish refugees and Irish immigrants. This sympathy was in part occasioned by recognition of the traumatic circumstances that had led Jewish and Irish diasporas to settle in East London. The former were perceived as victims of continental autocratic oppression, the latter of a domestic colonialism that continued to sow the seeds of mistrust and discord in communities far removed from an Irish homeland. It is important to consider the comparisons that can be drawn concerning the lexicon of oppression and resistance that was used by the socialist movement and how this informed attitudes towards the diasporic communities. The 'Catholic' or the 'Jew' in radical discourse in a colonial context could serve as an archetype of an oppressed minority group, or, conversely, in the case of the Jewish 'capitalist' or the Catholic Jesuit, as a colonial oppressor and a pillar in a colonial structure.

Polish or Russian immigrants were fleeing the depredations of a regime that had been a *bête noire* for the left, and for a wider British public opinion, for many decades. The Russian autocracy seemed to embody all that was flawed in the old system, a system of government that defended its privileges by naked brute force. To quote David Feldman, '[The] notion of a backward and medieval [and antisemitic] Russia was, arguably, as significant as that of Darkest Africa in validating Britons' sense of their own modernity at the start of the twentieth century.'[117] It was natural that a socialist movement that generally evinced sympathy towards oppressed colonial subject groups in both the British and other empires should extend this sympathy to the Jewish migrant.

---

[116] Roberts, *Women's Work*, p. 49. In 1911, in the England and Wales census, some 13.7 per cent of married and widowed women were in full-time employment – the actual number was in all probability substantially higher. See Sonya O. Rose, *Limited Livelihoods: Gender and Class in Nineteenth Century England* (Berkeley: University of California Press, 1992), p. 78: 'In communities where it was generally a mark of shame for a married woman to have to earn wages, because it signified that her husband was unable to provide for her, the husband may have left blank the line reserved for his wife's occupation.'

[117] Feldman, 'Jews and the British Empire, c.1900', *History Workshop Journal*, p. 86.

Once settled in the capital, the victimisation of the Jewish worker seemed to be perpetuated by the long hours and backbreaking labour of the sweatshops, again drawing left-wing support. But this was but one side of the socialist attitude towards the Jewish community in London. Coupled with a widespread sympathy for the 'poor Jew', the émigré, the refugee, the 'greener', was a strong current that viewed the 'rich Jew', those members of the Jewish community, whether immigrants or part of Anglo-Jewry, who were successful in politics or finance, not as members of an oppressed group, but as oppressors themselves. This stressed the exploitation of other Jews, of Gentiles, of colonised peoples, or Boers in South Africa. Thus an uneasy dichotomy emerged, the 'good [oppressed] Jew', who must be defended, educated, organised, possibly assimilated, against the 'bad Jew', wielding sinister influence, who must be confronted, if possible with the aid of his poorer co-religionists. Parts of the socialist movement combined a forthright condemnation of antisemitism in principle with occasional polemic that was anti-Jewish in character. Jewish socialists working in the East End, it must be noted, did not passively accept these verbal and written attacks, but met them head on.

One matter that the whole of the turn-of-the-century left, from the anarchists to the ILP, were in concord on was the wickedness of Russian Tsarism, and sympathy for its enemies and victims. Indeed, the cry of 'Tsarism' or 'Tsarist tactics' was raised whenever the British government or employers acted with particular brutality, be it towards trade unionists, suffragettes, or Irish Nationalists. The British left condemned the persecution of Jews and other minorities in Russia, especially during periods of particular ferocity, such as the early 1880s and during the Kishinev pogroms of 1903 and the counter-reaction to the 1905 Revolution. The protection of minorities in Russia was linked with the achievement of socialism, both at home and abroad, and the shelter of refugees.[118] Opposition to Tsarism formed a common bond between Jewish and Gentile socialists of all political affiliations. Ben Tillett, whose attitude towards Jewish immigration from the Pale of Settlement was ambiguous at best, wrote in *Justice* on the occasion of a state visit by Nicholas II, 'of all the crowned heads (and tails) you are the most revolting brute and worst of the whole crew of evil despots ... Damn you Nick ... may your loathsome body sneak away from our shores as you cowardly creep to a crapulous welcome.'[119]

A London tailor, Mr Harris of Smithfield, expressed his opposition to the Tsar in an equally provocative but more practical means. The tailor produced a life-size wax model of the Russian monarch which he proposed

---

[118] *Labour Leader* (6 July 1906).
[119] *Justice* (19 June 1909), in Schneer, *Ben Tillett*, p. 138.

to try in effigy, for 'causing the slaughter of a large number of people', and then publicly to hang. Mr Harris's threatened action caused something of a headache for the Home Office and the Metropolitan police, anxious to prevent an insult to 'his Majesty the Tsar in so flagrant a manner'. The decision was reached not to prosecute the tailor, so as to avoid further publicity, and the Tsar was duly tried *in absentia*.[120] The year 1905 witnessed demonstrations across the country, jointly organised by the Labour Party, the SDF, Fabians, and the Trades Union Congress (TUC), in support of the revolution and against the oppressive tactics of the Russian government. Hatred of Tsarism brought together the different strands of the British left as few other issues could.[121] In a 1912 article, a writer in *Justice*, after a gloomy prognosis of the future of the British Empire, declared that, given the choice, they would prefer the rule of the 'Prussian Junker' to the 'Cossack'. 'Far better German rule than Russian.'[122]

## Depictions of the 'Good Jew' and the 'Bad Jew' in Socialist Discourse

Antisemitism as it manifested itself in Russia and Eastern Europe seemed something brutal, irrational, and uncontrollable, a prejudice that fed on the basest instincts. This most durable and vitriolic of prejudices seemed completely contrary to the rationality and ideal of continual progress so central to the socialist movement. The ways in which antisemitism manifested itself formed another demarcation line between a 'continental' and 'domestic' way of conducting politics, or, indeed, conducting prejudice. As early as 1885, Kautsky had described political antisemitism as an enemy of the international socialist movement, 'reactionary through and through'.[123] The metropolitan left was prepared to oppose avowed antisemites who spoke or were active in London, both home-grown and foreign.

One German socialist settled in London, under the pen-name 'Ahasverus', gave an early example of the left 'baiting the Jew-baiter'. This was occasioned by the arrival of Herr Stöcker, a notorious Prussian antisemite, who attempted a speaking-tour of London in 1883. Stöcker was barracked and challenged at every occasion, by a combination, in his words, of 'the worst class of foreigners, out-cast atheistic Socialists who had made close alliance with money-mongering Jews'. The speaking tour was abandoned. Ahasverus ended his article by exhorting Herr Stöcker to 'leave London and its Jews

---

120  National Archives, HO 45/10315/125890, Proposal to hang Czar of Russia in effigy, 1905.

121  Sewell, *In the Cause of Labour*, p. 116.

122  *Justice* (1 June 1912).

123  See Karl Kautsky, 'Der Antisemitismus', in *Österreichischer Arbeiter-Kalende für das Jahr, 1885*, p. 100, quoted in Jack Jacobs, *On Socialists and 'the Jewish Question' after Marx* (New York: New York University Pres, 1992), pp. 11–12.

alone'.[124] The disreputableness of anti-Jewish sentiment among progressive elements in the United Kingdom meant that articles in socialist journals attacking Jews as a group or as individuals were invariably qualified by the statement that the target was not being attacked for their religious or ethnic identity but for their actions or their class. *Justice*, the organ of the SDF, and Robert Blatchford's *Clarion*, argued that Jewish employers or communal leaders were singled out for attention by virtue of their capitalist rather than their Jewish identity, that the condemnation of the 'rich Jew' in no way implied an attack on his poor immigrant or English co-religionists. Together with this sentiment, an editorial in *Justice* from January 1898 implies that general persecution of Jews in Russia, or the individual persecution of Dreyfus in France, may be motivated in part by the actions of the 'rich Jews' themselves:

> While we condemn with all the force at our command the shameful manner in which Captain Dreyfus has been found guilty without a fair trial, and utterly despise the scurvy rabble in the press and in the streets of Paris, who howl for the blood of Jews merely because they are Jews … yet we cannot deny that the capitalist Jews of France, like the Jew moneylenders of Russia, have done something to aggravate the miserable cry against them. In all the recent financial troubles the Jews have been unpleasantly conspicuous … It is remarkable that no one has attacked capitalist Jews with more bitterness than Jews themselves. We hope however, that no sensitive Jew comrade will think we have any prejudice in the matter. We only state facts in order to account for symptoms.[125]

This paragraph in *Justice* is revealing, and summarises the issues that arise when discussing socialist attitudes towards Jews and the division of the Jewish community in left-wing eyes between 'good' and 'bad' elements. First, irrational racial or religious antisemitism, that of the press and the 'scurvy rabble', is condemned, calling for the 'blood of Jews merely because they are Jews'. Nevertheless, it is implied that this irrational hatred is partly the fault of elements of Jewry itself, 'the capitalist Jews of France', or the 'Jew moneylenders of Russia'. Again, antisemitic intent, a condemnation of *all* Jews, is disavowed, and the attack on 'capitalist Jews' is legitimised by the statement that Jewish comrades in the movement hold these sentiments themselves. No matter the strength of language used in these articles, the authors argued that these were not articulations of antisemitism, a prejudice motivated by ethnic, racial, or religious hatred against Jews as Jews, but a disinterested attack on a particular

---

[124] *To-Day* (1884). See also David Glover, *Literature, Immigration, and Diaspora in Fin-de-Siècle England: A Cultural History of the 1905 Aliens Act* (Cambridge: Cambridge University Press, 2012), p. 82.

[125] *Justice* (22 January 1898).

stratum of Jewry. However, in this matter, 'sensitive Jew comrades' did not let the matter rest. Theodore Rothstein, in correspondence printed in *Justice*, attacked what he saw as the creeping prevalence of antisemitic language and attitudes within the movement. The letters were occasioned not by the article quoted above, but by another published at the same time by a writer named Sandy MacFarlane. MacFarlane, discussing the situation in France, had expressed gratuitously racist sentiments over Jewish influence in the French republic. Rothstein identified what he perceived as the fundamental incompatibility of socialism and racial prejudice, and explicitly accused MacFarlane of antisemitism, 'in the ugliest sense of the word'.[126] Rothstein stressed that his opposition to MacFarlane's antisemitism and the language used by *Justice* generally stemmed not from his [Rothstein's] identity as a Jew, but as an affront to his politics as a socialist, writing that he acknowledged 'but two races – the bourgeoisie and the proletariat, but two nations – the exploiters and the exploited'.[127] Rothstein was not alone, the language used in *Justice* at the turn of the century was attacked by both Jewish socialists such as Joseph Finn and Gentile comrades such as E.B. Bax, who described the antisemitic tropes used, particularly in relation to the Boer War, as a 'disgrace to our movement'.[128]

This idea of acceptable and unacceptable forms of anti-Jewish prejudice is made explicit in the foreword to the publication *Within the Pale* (1903), an account of the Kishinev pogrom by the Irish radical writer and politician Michael Davitt. Davitt wrote:

> Where anti-Semitism stands, in fair political combat, in opposition to the foes of nationality, or against the engineers of a sordid war in South Africa, or as the assailant of the economic evils of unscrupulous capitalism anywhere, I am resolutely in line with its spirit and programme. Where, however, it only speaks and acts in a cowardly racial warfare, which descends to the use of an atrocious fabrication [the blood libel] responsible for odious and unspeakable crimes like those that are to its credit in the massacres of Kishineff [sic], it becomes a thing deserving of no more toleration from right-minded men than do the germs of some malady laden with the poison of a malignant disease.[129]

126  *Justice* (9 July 1898).

127  *Justice* (9 July 1898).

128  *Justice* (28 October 1899), in Claire Hirshfield, 'The Anglo-Boer War and the Issue of Jewish Culpability', *Journal of Contemporary History*, Vol. 15, No. 4 (October 1980), p. 622.

129  Michael Davitt, *Within the Pale: The True Story of Anti-Semitic Persecutions in Russia* (London: Hurst and Blackett Ltd, 1903), pp. viii–x. A year later, in response to the Limerick 'pogrom' of 1904, Davitt condemned the anti-Jewish violence as 'an Irishman and as a Catholic against the barbarous malignancy of anti-Semitism'. See K.H. Flynn, 'The Limerick Pogrom 1904', *History Ireland*, Vol. 12, No. 2 (Summer 2004), p. 31.

The mention by Davitt of the war in South Africa is significant. The outbreak and course of the Boer War brought with it a wave of anti-Jewish feeling within elements of the socialist movement. The blame for the war was laid at the door of South African Jewish financiers, the jingoistic feeling at home (which sometimes manifested itself in attacks on socialists campaigning against the war) was blamed on a press, 'owned and financed largely by stalwart patriots whose names have curiously foreign terminations and whose features seem to indicate they are part of the circumcision'.[130] The radical antisemitism that was expressed during the Boer War has been discussed at length by historians, but it formed only the most dramatic and most concentrated manifestation of what might be labelled 'anti-colonial antisemitism', which blamed the ills of British colonial oppression at least partly on a Jewish financial clique. As early as 1890, an article in *Commonweal* blamed Jewish financiers for the exploitation of 'negroes' in Jamaica, and over the next fifteen years this charge was often repeated, most often in connection with Africa, that Jews abroad were exploiting colonised peoples, and the 'Jewish' press at home was encouraging a colonial white supremacy.[131] On the subject of the delinquency of East End youth, *Alarm*, a short-lived anarchist weekly, described:

> how the press (run by Jewish usurers) laud the *officers* and *gentlemen* who takes trips to Africa, just for the lofty pleasure of potting *niggers*; and how the same press shout with joy when the potting of niggers is done on a larger scale than usual? ... when these boys have grown older and their desire to slaughter has been intensified by the incitements of the press – niggers or workmen on strike preferred – they may yet hope to be acclaimed as heroes.[132]

This idea of the parallel between racial exploitation abroad and class exploitation at home, and the culpability of shadowy financial elites for both, was echoed in the *Clarion*, which claimed that both 'Africa' and England belonged in part to 'Jew financiers'.[133]

Sympathy for the Boers on the left was often framed in that language stressing the rural as opposed to industrial dichotomy so dear to the proponents of 'Merrie England'. For Edward Carpenter, the healthy vigour and simple life of the Boer contrasted favourably with 'cosmopolitan' Johannesburg, a 'hell full of Jews, financiers, greedy speculators, adventurers,

---

130  *ILP News* (October 1899). Bruce Glaiser included the virulently anti-alien *Daily Mail* as one of the 'Capitalist and Jewish papers' whipping up nationalism. See Ward, *Red Flag and Union Jack*, p. 68.

131  *Commonweal* (9 August 1890).

132  *Alarm – Anarchist Weekly for the Workers* (13 September 1896) (original emphasis).

133  *Clarion* (29 January 1898).

prostitutes'.[134] Jewish mine magnates were blamed for the 'Chinese slavery' controversy in South Africa that became such a heated issue at the time of the 1906 General Election. John Burns, by this time an independent radical MP, made use of the themes of historical diasporic oppression and exploitation in a pamphlet entitled *Bondage for Black, Slavery for Yellow Labour*:

> The tragic irony of all this iniquity is that the financial Jew, whose race has been the slave of centuries, the persecuted of all countries, the hunted of all time, should be the central operating figure in reviving servitude, and voluntarily and gratuitously allow his vain and vulgar cupidity to enthral a race of men [the Chinese] who were a great and civilised race when the Chosen people of Israel were in Egyptian bondage.[135]

The British socialist movement condemned antisemitism in the form expressed by the Black Hundreds, and indeed that expressed by the British Brothers' League (BBL) and the right-wing of the Conservative Party. That said, elements of the SDF, the SL, the Labour Party, and the Fabians all made use of antisemitic language and imagery on occasion, often in an anti-colonial context. Hyndman, Quelch, MacFarlane, and others argued that their attacks extended to Gentile capitalists, financiers, and press barons as well as Jewish ones, and that prominent Jews formed only a fraction of their targets. This is true, but it does not diminish the cumulative effect of anti-Jewish stereotypes and phraseology that appeared with regularity in newspapers and pamphlets. *Justice* and other journals appealed to the class loyalty of East End Jewish workers over religious and ethnic loyalties to the Jewish middle and upper classes. However, the strength of this appeal, and the results of the work on the ground by Jewish and Gentile socialists against antisemitic prejudice and discrimination, was weakened by the use of antisemitic imagery in these publications. For Rothstein, left-wing anti-Jewish polemic served to push working-class Jews into the arms of the Zionist movement, seeming to prove the inevitability of antisemitism in any state, capitalist or otherwise, apart from a specifically Jewish homeland.[136]

At the SDF Annual Conference of 1900, whilst the Boer War was still being fought, a resolution was passed regretting that 'any impression should have gained ground that ... the SDF is in any way anti-Semitic' and

---

[134] Edward Carpenter, *Boer and Briton* (Labour Press: Manchester, 1900), quoted in Preben Kaarsholm, 'Pro-Boers', in Raphael Samuel (ed.), *Patriotism: The Making and Unmaking of British National Identity*, Vol. 1, *History and Politics* (London: Routledge, 1989), p. 113.

[135] LSE ILP/8/1904/7, John Burns, *Bondage for Black, Slavery for Yellow Labour* (London: Kent and Matthews Ltd, 1904), p. 2.

[136] See Julius, *Trials of the Diaspora*, pp. 272–273 and Hirshfield, 'The Anglo-Boer War and the Issue of Jewish Culpability', p. 622.

declaring 'determined opposition' to all 'anti-Semitic parties'. This resolution did not terminate antisemitic sentiment in the SDF, but it certainly reined it in.[137] After the conclusion of the Boer War the ferocity and frequency of anti-Jewish language in the socialist press declined noticeably. Racialised language in the SDF (which by the end of the period had transmuted into the SDP and then the BSP) did not wholly disappear, however. In the debates on rearmament between 1911 and 1913, Zelda Kahan, a Jewish socialist whose parents had emigrated from the Pale, drew a chauvinistic blast of vitriol from some senior members of the party. Kahan, a rising star in the movement, was referred to disparagingly as 'Fräulien Zelda Kahan', and it was claimed by fellow SDP members that she was 'alien in blood and race'.[138]

Contradictions are evident in the expression of these sentiments. Jews were associated with victimhood (itself a window into a particular vision of an emasculated Jewish proletariat without control of its own destiny) and simultaneously viewed as oppressors, both of the Jewish 'greener' within the minority community and the black colonial 'other' on the imperial periphery. This illuminates the wider confusion within the movement in the period in its attitudes towards diasporic identities that cut across class and national lines, an identity that encompassed both the refugee leaving Poland and the prospector arriving in the Transvaal.

## Socialism and Minority Nationalism in the Colonial Context

This confusion among the socialist movement and the simultaneous conferring of positive and negative narratives was also apparent in depictions of the Catholic diasporic experience and its interactions with colonialism. Irish Catholic immigrants were perceived by elements of the British left as victims of colonial ill-treatment and disenfranchisement in much the same way as refugees from Eastern Europe were viewed as victims of Tsarism. Parallel to this, the Catholic religious authorities, particularly the Jesuits, were seen as having a stake in imperial rule and mistreatment of colonised peoples. The Irish nationalist response to British rule, in Ireland and on what became known as the mainland, also complicated the narrative of oppression. For *Commonweal* and the anarchist groups in particular, Irish opposition to and suppression by the British Empire was reason enough to rally behind the Irish community settled in London.[139] For others, however,

---

[137] Social Democratic Federation annual conference report, 1900, in Graham Johnson, *Social Democratic Politics in Britain, 1881–1911* (New York: The Edwin Mellen Press, 2002), pp. 116–117.

[138] June Hannam and Karen Hunt, *Socialist Women: Britain, 1880s to 1920s* (London, Routledge, 2002), p. 182.

[139] Woodcock, *Anarchism*, pp. 415–416.

the resilience of Irish Nationalism formed a barrier to the spread of socialism in these neighbourhoods. For the mainstream socialist movement, minority nationalism, whether of the Irish or Zionist variety, without the backbone of socialism, could only replicate individualistic and capitalist tendencies.[140]

The parallels between Jewish and Irish diasporic identity, including a shared heritage of oppression, one the victim of autocracy, the other of imperialism, were used as political capital in the cut and thrust of East London electioneering. In political addresses to largely Jewish audiences in the East End the Home Rule debate was framed in the language of the diaspora, the common bonds of exile and flight, or discussion of how Jews might expect to be treated in a self-governing Ireland. At a debate held in Christchurch Hall in Spitalfields at the end of March 1889 between the Liberal MP for Whitechapel Samuel Montagu and the Conservative Colonel Trench, both men discussed the Home Rule issue in a Jewish context. As reported in the *East London Observer*:

> He [Mr Montagu] described the sufferings and persecutions through which the Jews had passed prior to their emancipation. He attempted to draw a parallel in the case of the Irish nation, which he described as struggling under the injustice and cruel persecution of the English Government.[141]

Trench responded by cautioning the audience against Montagu's appeal to them to approach Home Rule from a Jewish standpoint: '[According to Trench, the] members of his [Montagu's] community are not such fools as he thinks. They are as English in their feelings as their Anglo-Saxon fellow countrymen, with whom they did not wish to be set at variance.' Trench finished by warning that Home Rule could have dire consequences for Irish Jewry: 'All who knew Ireland knew how strong the anti-Semitism among the lower orders was.'[142] At a further meeting, attended by a mixture of Jews and Irish Catholics and held in Whitechapel in March 1890, Montagu reiterated his point in the strongest language:

> The members of his own faith belonged to a race which had been oppressed in olden times, even in this country, and were oppressed abroad at the present time, and therefore, they ought to have the greatest possible sympathy with their Irish fellow subjects, who had also an unconquerable national spirit, and who were being oppressed by 'special' and coercive laws.

---

[140] See Bornstein, *Colors of Zion*, for detailed discussion of the intersections between Zionism and Irish Republicanism, an account that traces the narrative into the post-First World War period and beyond.

[141] *East London Observer* (30 March 1889).

[142] *East London Observer* (30 March 1889).

That was the reason why he had always maintained that the Irish people should have the full measure of control over their own local affairs.[143]

In the heated debates of East End politics two visions of diasporic identity came into conflict with each other. One was a narrative of solidarity forged in adversity between different diasporic groups, the collective bonding of oppression. The other stressed an individualistic analysis emphasising the hostility of one minority group towards another, and the likely oppression to follow if one group was to achieve hegemony. These transnational narratives were made use of by both Liberal and Conservative politicians to advance purely local ambitions, as Westminster ventured into the complexities of East End diaspora space.[144]

It is worth briefly here examining the political status quo in East London that both Trench and Montagu, in their different ways, represented, and how Irish Catholics and Jews interacted with the Progressive and Moderate political machines in the East End. It was after all the Liberal/Radical working men's clubs, rather than any socialist grouping, that formed the political core of East End Irish Nationalism in the period. It was also these clubs, with their 'Lib.-Lab.' political complexion, that produced the first working-class elected officials in London.[145] These clubs had durable roots in working-class communities, cementing the belief that the Liberals were the 'natural' party of both the East End working class in general and minority groups in particular.[146] In the Irish case this was largely true, to the despair of James Connolly, amongst others. For that part of East End Jewry that enjoyed the vote the situation was rather more complex. In his study of grass-roots popular conservatism in the East End, *The Politics of the Poor* (2004), Marc Brodie has examined the skilful way in which the Conservatives/Moderates on the ground in East London wooed the Jewish vote, fielded Jewish candidates, and simultaneously appealed to the wider population on an anti-immigration ticket.[147]

---

[143] *East London Observer* (22 March 1890).

[144] In the 1886 General Election Leopold de Rothschild had backed Col. Trench against Montagu, standing for the Liberal Party, with an open letter urging the Jewish electorate of Whitechapel to vote for the Conservative and Unionist candidate. Despite this intervention, Montagu won the seat. This was an opening salvo in an ongoing rivalry within the Anglo-Jewish leadership between the two men. Both Montagu and Leopold and Nathan Rothschild would play a decisive role in the conclusion of the Jewish tailors' strike of 1889, discussed in the next chapter. Daniel Gutwein, *The Divided Elite: Economics, Politics and Anglo-Jewry, 1882–1917* (Leiden: E.J. Brill, 1992), p. 172.

[145] Pat Thorne, 'Labour and Local Politics: Radicalism, Democracy and Social Reform, 1880–1914', in Biagini and Reid, *Currents of Radicalism*.

[146] Pennybacker, *A Vision for London*, pp. 20–21.

[147] Marc Brodie, *The Politics of the Poor: The East End of London, 1885–1914* (Oxford: Oxford University Press, 2004), pp. 185–187, 191.

One of the policies of the London Municipal Society, formed in 1894 to provide a base for conservatism in the capital, was the limitation of 'alien' immigration.[148] The Moderates exploited racial hostility towards both Jews and Irish Catholics where the local ethnic and class dynamics were favourable to these tactics.[149] During the 1907 LCC elections, the Moderates made use of classic antisemitic imagery in their poster art when depicting a 'Progressive' 'capitalist' under the heading 'It's Your Money We Want!'[150] However, anti-Jewish sentiment was also present on the Liberal/ Progressive/Radical side. The Liberal and Radical Club in Bethnal Green in 1902 passed a resolution barring anybody of 'the Jewish race' from being a member. Two years later the Executive Committee of the St. George's and Wapping Liberal and Radical Association rejected a candidate put forward by the local Labour Party explicitly because he was a Jew.[151] Leaving overt prejudice to one side, what made local East London politics especially hard to break into for the various socialist groups was a tradition of paternalism in the East End. This drew on both English and Irish political customs and also on those of the Eastern European shtetl, where the interests of the people were guarded by a select group of respected communal leaders, who dealt with the outside world. Brodie has demonstrated the existence of this paternalism on both the Conservative/Moderate and Liberal/Radical/Progressive sides, pointing to Millwall (with its large Irish population) as an example. In the period under discussion this area was viewed as almost the private fiefdom of the charismatic local employer and Conservative politician F.A. Bullivant.[152] But the most significant example of this deep-seated paternalism in Jewish neighbourhoods of East London was Samuel Montagu himself. In Whitechapel voters were not electing Montagu solely, or even predominantly, on a Liberal ticket, but because of his close personal relationship with both Anglo and immigrant Jewry, and his adopted role as protector and defender of the community (amongst other things, from socialism).[153]

To return to the nationalist question, leading figures in the London labour movement, whilst acknowledging the Irish right to self-government, viewed

---

[148] Young, *Local Politics and the Rise of Party*, p. 59.

[149] Alan J. Lee, 'Conservatism, Traditionalism and the British Working Class', in David E. Martin and David Rubinstein (eds), *Ideology and the Labour Movement: Essays Presented to John Saville* (London: Croom Helm, 1979), p. 88.

[150] Young, *Local Politics and the Rise of Party*, p. 93.

[151] Holmes, *Anti-Semitism in British Society*, p. 110.

[152] Brodie, *Politics of the Poor*, p. 155. Conversely, the Irish dockers of Millwall were also viewed by the Catholic Church as particularly prone to both Irish Nationalism and militant trade unionism in the period.

[153] Brodie, *Politics of the Poor*, p. 187.

the continued predominance of the issue of Home Rule in long-established Irish communities as an impediment to socialism and a crutch for the Liberal Party. Keir Hardie, speaking in 1895 with some frustration at the electoral failure of socialism in East London, made the point:

> [If] the Irishmen or their leaders are foolish enough to rake up the dying embers of the old hatred, then on them and not us be the responsibility. Do you say that it is a question of Home Rule first? I can understand an Irishman in Connemara saying that, but here in South West Ham it is Labour first.[154]

For the Irish socialist and republican James Connolly, the mainstream Irish Nationalist movement in Britain, with its Liberal alliance, was a distraction for the Irish working class settled in British inner cities: 'One of the first and most bitter fruits of that alliance [between the Liberal Party and Irish capitalists] was the use of the Irish vote [in England] against the candidates of the Socialist and Labour Parties.'[155]

In London, in other words, domestic class-based issues must take precedence over the liberation of the old country. Moving from East to South London, at a meeting in Battersea in the summer of 1907, the Labour MP James O'Grady, born in Bristol of Irish parents, argued persuasively for Irish Catholic support for the Labour Party, but could not shake the support for Irish anti-colonialism above class politics: 'Ireland for them [concluded Cllr Brogan] was the first consideration, and any fight necessary for her cause would find the Battersea Irishmen in the thick of it. They had full confidence in the Irish leaders and would implicitly follow their advice.' The meeting was brought to a close by a rendition of 'God Save Ireland'.[156] In 1913, the Catholic radical John Richard Archer was elected mayor of Battersea. Archer, whose father was Barbadian and mother was Irish, had the distinction of being the first black mayor to attain the office in the British Isles. Identifying himself as both black and Irish, Archer was a fervent Home Ruler and Irish Nationalist, and a supporter of the early pan-African movement.[157] Archer's electoral success and his political agendas are key examples of the multiple interactions and adoption of identities possible in diaspora space, and illustrate the fluidity of identity and political loyalty over rigid and set ethnic demarcations.

[154] *Labour Leader* (20 July 1895).

[155] James Connolly, *Labour in Ireland: Labour in Irish History, the Re-Conquest of Ireland* (Dublin: Maunsel and Company Ltd, 1917), p. 212.

[156] *Catholic Herald* (21 June 1907).

[157] Westminster Diocesan Archives, AAW/BOX KV, Jean Olwen Maynard, *History of the Parish of Guardian Angels, Mile End*, Vol. 2, *1903–1918*.

The emergence of the radical Sinn Féin movement, which included a number of Irish socialists and rejected the Liberal alliance of the established Irish Nationalists, was greeted by *Justice* with some suspicion:

> It will not make the slightest difference to the workers of Ireland whether they are robbed by an English or an Irish capitalist. Ireland has been brutally treated by England we know ... and it would be a good thing for that little country if it could be rid of English oppression ... [However,] Nationalism, with race hatreds and strife between peoples, should be allowed to go down with the past. Internationalism, with its ideals of unsurpassed grandeur, of fraternity and peace, should be the creed of today.[158]

The *Socialist Standard*, writing in the same year, labelled the Sinn Féiners: 'Irish capitalist rebels'.[159] This is similar in sentiment to the comments in the *Labour Leader* on the growing Zionist movement in the East End. Having contrasted the poverty of East End Jewry, 'hoarded up in their workshops, foul from constantly burning gas fumes', with the wealth of the 'cosmopolitan financier', the article concludes: 'For the Jewish workman knows that a "Jewish State" means the building up of another capitalist State. Founded on individualism, it cannot be otherwise.'[160]

Zionism and Irish Nationalism were both subjects of socialist ambiguity. At best, such as in the case of the Zionist socialist *Poale Zion* movement or the left-wing socialist republican elements of Sinn Féin, minority nationalism could in fact actually advance the socialist cause. However, in its supplanting of class and labour concerns, nationalism, for metropolitan socialism, could be a distraction. At worst, minority nationalism would merely perpetuate and rebuild the structures of capitalist society, siphoning off political fervour and energy that would have been better applied to the class struggle. Hostility towards diasporic nationalism was occasionally made explicit. At a Jewish labour demonstration in Hyde Park to protest against the Kishinev pogroms of 1903, where socialists, social democrats, and anarchists were all in attendance, the SDF insisted that East End Zionist groups be barred from attending or speaking at the rally, and demanded a resolution be adopted condemning Zionism. When this resolution was refused the SDF representatives withdrew from the meeting.[161] On the fringes of the British socialist movement, 'socialist imperialists' such as J. Ernest Jones rejected any meeting of minds between socialism and Irish Nationalism:

---

158  *Justice* (6 April 1907).
159  *Socialist Standard* (1 September 1907).
160  *Labour Leader* (23 August 1907).
161  Rocker, *The London Years*, pp. 86–87.

[It] seems that the ILP and the SDF, the accredited representatives of British Socialism, have become the left wing of the Individualistic Irish Home Rule Party. The British democracy will have to keep in mind that they have little in common with Irish Nationalism – the programme of the Irish Nationalists is the most retrograde one ever inculcated.[162]

For Jones, Irish Nationalism, in Ireland and on the British mainland, was a smokescreen for the ambitions of the Catholic Church and the Irish clergy.

On one issue the late nineteenth-century Catholic Church in Britain was in agreement with the socialist movement, the Zionist organisations, and the East End Jewish community: the cruelty of the Russian Tsarist regime, the 'Cossack's knout'. *The Tablet* reported in March 1891 that 'Russia is undoubtedly the anti-Catholic power *par excellence*. Fresh details of her untiring persecution of the Church in matters petty and serious are daily filtering through the continental press.'[163] The British Catholic press carried horror stories of priests assaulted and churches desecrated in Poland and Lithuania. In January 1892, *The Tablet* compared the treatment of Catholic Poles in Russia with the plight of the Jews, and questioned the popular focus on Jewish suffering rather than that of Catholic minorities.[164] The Catholic press was not alone in stressing the suffering of non-Jewish groups in Russia. The *Jewish Chronicle*, in reporting the discrimination and persecution faced by Russian Jewry, consistently stressed the point that this was not solely a Jewish issue, but one that affected all the religious minorities of the Russian Empire, including Catholics, Old Believers, Protestants, Muslims, and Buddhists. The *Jewish Chronicle* and the Anglo-Jewish establishment, wary of 'Jewish exceptionalism', played down the specifically *Jewish* nature of the persecution. In fact, while minorities of all confessions, including Catholics, suffered discrimination and prejudice in the Russian Empire, it was the Jewish community that experienced the most extreme physical violence and the most far-reaching legal victimisation. It was Jewish migrants who left the Pale of Settlement in the greatest numbers. Radical Russian émigré newspapers, both Jewish and Gentile, could also play down the significance of Jewish identity in the Russian persecutions. While condemning the pogroms, these publications framed the attacks in class terms and demanded class solidarity with the non-Jewish proletariat and peasantry in the Pale (at the forefront of the anti-Jewish attacks themselves), against Tsarism, ignoring the ethnic and

---

162  LSE ILP 5/1903/19, J. Ernest Jones, *The Case for Progressive Imperialism (Demand for a Socialist Imperialist Party)* (Chester: Socialist Party, April 1903), p. 7.

163  *The Tablet* (14 March 1891).

164  *The Tablet* (16 January 1892).

religious context of the attacks. Russian socialists, both in their native land and in émigré communities in the west, were not free from antisemitic sentiment, with references to the *Bund* as 'yid socialists'.[165]

Sympathy for co-religionists in Poland aside, the Irish narrative of oppression and colonial misrule influenced a wider debate on imperial government, not only in Ireland but across the world. During the Boer War the sympathies of many left-wing Irish Nationalists, Michael Davitt and James Connolly among them, were firmly with the Afrikaners.[166] Prominent Irish socialists and Nationalists, expressing sympathy with the Boers, fell back on some of the language used in the domestic socialist movement, placing blame for the war on 'Jewish millionaires'.[167]

Roger Casement described the atrocities taking place in the Congo Free State as 'a tyranny beyond conception save only, perhaps, to an Irish mind alive to the horrors once daily enacted in this land [Ireland].'[168] For both Irish Nationalists and English critics of colonialism, England's treatment of Ireland, particularly in the Famine years, was the frame of reference for all other cases of imperial subjection. James Connolly in his history of the Irish labour struggle explicitly laid the blame for the Famine at the door not only of British misrule, but also the 'fetish' of 'capitalist political economy'.[169] The Irish labour leader Jim Connell, writing in 1898, demanded solidarity, not only between English and Irish workers, but between workers from both countries and colonised peoples as well:

> They [the British workers] are themselves victimised by landlords and capitalists, often to as great an extent as the Irish ... There are toilers on one side, and the exploiting class on the other. The latter traffic in the flesh and blood of their own countrymen just as freely as in that of the Irish, the Egyptians, the Afghans, or the Zulus ... We believe that self-government is the birth-right of every race, and that nobody

---

[165] See Fishman, *East End Jewish Radicals*, pp. 109–110.

[166] Kaarsholm, 'Pro-Boers', in *Patriotism*, Vol. 1, p. 117 and Hugh McLeod, *Class and Religion in the Late Victorian City* (London: Croom Helm, 1974), p. 76. It should be noted that Connolly was opposed to the scapegoating of Jews, whether from within the socialist movement or outside it. Virdee, *Racism, Class and the Racialized Outsider*, pp. 67–71.

[167] Hirshfield, 'The Anglo-Boer War and the Issue of Jewish Culpability', *Journal of Contemporary History*, pp. 624–625; Claire Hirshfield, 'The British Left and the "Jewish Conspiracy": A Case Study of Modern Antisemitism', *Jewish Social Studies*, Vol. 43, No. 2 (Spring 1981), pp. 102–103. See also LSE ILP/8/1901/19, Frederick Harrison, *The Boer War: Letters from Frederick Harrison*, reprinted from the *Daily News* (30 May–June 29 1901) for parallels between Ireland and South Africa.

[168] Bernard Porter, *Critics of Empire: British Radical Attitudes to Colonialism in Africa, 1895–1914* (London: Macmillan, 1968), p. 267.

[169] Connolly, *Labour in Ireland*, p. 170.

withholds that right from any people from any other motive than a desire to rob them.[170]

Catholics, like Jews, not only garnered socialist sympathy as an oppressed minority, but could also be the target of radical anti-colonialism. As the blame for the outbreak of the war in South Africa was laid by some at the door of the Jewish financier and press baron, so others made the same connection between African exploitation and the Catholic Church. The socialist pamphlet *In Memoriam, the British Empire* (1902) depicted the role of the Jesuits in strikingly similar terms to those used by Hyndman, Quelch, Hobson, et al. over Jewish influence:

> [Rhodes was] an enormously rich man because he could overreach any of the Petticoat-Lane Jews who were his companions in rascality ... acting upon the infamous Jesuit maxim, 'The end justifies the means,' he brought the Press, Parliament and the Priests by his ill-gotten millions, and by wholesale lying, by the aid of the infamous Order of Jesus, who helped him for their own ends, plunged the English people into war with the Transvaal and Orange Free State Republics ... The Church and the Stock Exchange have formed a Holy Alliance.[171]

*Justice* had suggested this connection between Jews and the Catholic clergy on the outbreak of the war in late 1899. The Jews were the 'principal promoters of the war'; the 'leading agents' would be the Jesuits.[172] As with the polemic attacking Jews, this apportioning of blame for colonial adventures focused on the supposed influence of the elite of a religious minority. Jesuits, like Jews, were blamed both for causing the war and stirring up jingoistic sentiment in support of it, and, in other quarters, for conspiring to damage the British war effort. J.A. Hobson voiced the sentiments of a significant part of the liberal left when he wrote:

> This conjunction of the forces of the press, the platform, and the pulpit, has succeeded in monopolising the mind of the British public, and imposing a policy calculated not to secure the interests of the British Empire, but to advance the private, political and business interests of a small body of men who have exploited the race feeling in South Africa.[173]

Catholic and Jewish minorities were similarly invested with victim status and at the same time perceived to contain transnational elements conspiring

---

[170] LSE ILP 5/1898/7, Jim Connell, *Brothers at Last – A Centenary Appeal to Celt and Saxon* (London: Labour Leader, 1898).

[171] LSE Coll Misc 1064, Anon., *In Memoriam, The British Empire, Died March 26th 1902* (1902).

[172] *Justice* (11 November 1899), in Julius, *Trials of the Diaspora*, pp. 274–275.

[173] J.A. Hobson, *The Psychology of Jingoism* (London: Grant Richards, 1901), p. 138.

and colluding in the exploitation of other oppressed and disenfranchised peoples. Both groups occupied an uncertain place in the turn-of-the-century British socialist pantheon of friends and enemies, comrades and opponents. Again, this confusion was grounded in the popular conceptions of Catholicism and the Jewish diaspora, a combination of posited 'power' that appeared to cross borders and a conferred status of victimhood that distinguished these two groups from other contemporary diasporic populations. No other minorities present in the metropolis embodied that confluence of supposed transnational wealth and influence and domestic poverty and vulnerability. This confused and complex interplay of perspectives on what constituted oppression is reflected in the presence of overtones of ethnic and religious hostility in socialist anti-colonial tracts of the period, and emphasises the lack of coherency or consistency in the socialist relationship with diasporic minority groups.

## Trade Unionism and Anti-Alienism

In the period 1889–1912, industrial action was a greater indicator of the success and tenacity of left-wing militancy among the East End working class than the electoral success of socialist parties or the size of their memberships, both of which were meagre. This situation only began to change with the breakthrough of the Labour Party in 1906. For migrant labour, socialism had to be practical and material to gain support.[174] At the same time, trade union leaders in their rhetoric, especially during industrial disputes, imputed economic and political characteristics wholesale to minority communities, largely on the basis of how members of the minority group in question behaved during times of industrial unrest.

Jewish trade unions, organised by workers in the garment trade, had begun to appear in East London from the mid-1870s onwards. These organisations were ambitious, idealistic, and short-lived.[175] Both Jewish and Irish workers remained largely untouched by the craft unions of the 1860s and 1870s.[176] The East End immigrant communities in the mid-1880s, a few years into the influx of Jewish refugees from Eastern Europe, contained a number

---

[174] Geoffrey Alderman, *The Jewish Community in British Politics* (Oxford: Clarendon Press, 1983), p. 58.

[175] In the spring of 1876 the *Agudah Hasozialstin Chaverim*, the Hebrew Socialist Union (HSU), the first metropolitan Jewish socialist organisation, was formed in Spitalfields, under the aegis of Aaron Lieberman. The HSU did not see out the New Year, disbanding in December 1876. See Nora Levin, *Jewish Socialist Movements, 1871–1917: While Messiah Tarried* (London: Routledge and Kegan Paul, 1978), p. 42.

[176] One exception to this was the Hebrew Cabinet Makers' Union, formed in 1887, whose rules, membership and fees were typical of a skilled 'craft union' of the period. Harold

of radical activists, but few organisations or structures, a surfeit of leaders who were without a substantial number of followers. Immigrant unionisation benefited enormously from the growth of militancy that followed the emergence of the 'new unions' from 1887 onwards, and which culminated in the great wave of industrial action of 1889. In the East End the key first step on the path to wider unionisation was undertaken by predominantly Irish women working in the match factories of Bryant and May in Bow, who, against all odds, successfully forced their employer to make terms in the summer of 1888.[177] Male Irish workers, particularly the stevedores, a minor labour aristocracy in the docks, were strongly involved in the Great Dock Strike, and the headquarters of the strike committee were, appropriately enough, located in an Irish pub, the Wade's Arms, in Poplar.[178] Public opinion, too, and the reports of even conservative broadsheets such as *The Times* and local journals such as the *East London Advertiser*, were favourable to the dockers. The discipline of the striking workers and the general good temper maintained through the strike (which was not, however, extended to strike-breakers) impressed observers favourably.[179] Those commentators, who during the Trafalgar Square unrest of 1887 had warned of bloody revolution and sedition emanating from the East End, evinced a mixture of surprise and relief at the generally calm progress of the dispute.[180]

The discipline of the dockers and the avoidance of large-scale violence should not obscure the bitterness of the dispute. The dock bosses had no intention of allowing the mass unionisation of their workforce, or the dismantlement of the casual system on the dock quays that placed unlimited power in the hands of the employer and the contractor. This latter was the figure described memorably by Beatrice Potter after the conclusion of the strike: 'This amphibious being, styled "the middleman", is the effect, and not the cause, of industrial disorder. Like the noxious fungus that breeds in dark places, he lives or dies on already decaying and disorganised matter.'[181]

After a fortnight, with strike-breakers imported from the British countryside breaking picket lines and the failure of other unions in the

---

Pollins, *Economic History of the Jews in England* (East Brunswick, NJ: Associated University Press, 1982), p. 155.

[177] See Raw, *Striking a Light*, pp. 173–176.

[178] Terry McCarthy (ed.), *The Great Dock Strike 1889* (London: Weidenfeld & Nicolson, 1988), p. 91.

[179] See *Commonweal* (31 August 1889): 'Even the roughest of strikers are very peaceful in their large processions; but woe to the scab upon whom an isolated party of them lay hands after working hours.'

[180] *East London Advertiser* (24 August 1889).

[181] Beatrice Potter, 'The Lords and the Sweating System', *Nineteenth Century*, No. 160, June 1890.

metropolis to join with the dockers, the strike committee faced bankruptcy and failure.[182] The strikers were saved by an extraordinary financial donation, when some £30,000, a substantial amount of money in 1889, was raised for the strike fund by sympathetic comrades in Australia.[183] The eventual success of the Great Dock Strike was due in part then to the continued interest and sympathy of the wider Irish Catholic diaspora with their co-religionists in the United Kingdom. The radical tradition of the English Chartists and Irish revolutionaries, imported into Australia through transportation, had come to the rescue of the nascent movement in London.[184] Transnational diasporic identity could cut across class lines and supplant the primacy of class, to the exasperation of the domestic socialist movement, but, as in the case of the Australian donation, it could also reaffirm class loyalties and solidarity between the working classes of different nations.

A general, London-wide strike in sympathy with the dockers, as demanded by *Commonweal*, did not materialise.[185] One section of the London proletariat, however, the tailors of the East End, contributed to the sense of a profound seismic shift with a list of demands of their own, which amounted to a dismantling of the worst excesses of the sweatshop system so prevalent in that trade. At a meeting held at the end of August 1889, the three Jewish tailoring unions active in the capital passed a resolution calling for a general strike across the tailoring trade.[186] By the beginning of September, over 6,000 tailors were out on strike, with the prospect of more workers joining the action and the dispute spreading to other trades with heavy Jewish involvement.[187] At a meeting with the tailoring employers on 12 September, the strike committee demanded an end to the abuses endemic in the trade.[188] Agreement between the masters and the strike committee proved elusive, and the tailors' strike

---

[182] See Tsuzuki, *Tom Mann*, pp. 78–79, in which these strike breakers were described as 'the finest workmen you could see anywhere, men from Rye, Romney, Lydd, men of splendid physique – nothing like it in London'. See Chapter 5 for detailed discussion of violence between strikers and 'blacklegs'.

[183] Henry Pelling, *A History of British Trade Unionism* (Basingstoke: Macmillan, 1963) (republished 1987), p. 96.

[184] See O'Higgins, 'The Irish Influence in the Chartist Movement', *Past and Present*, No. 20 (November 1961).

[185] *Commonweal* (7 September 1889).

[186] Fishman, *East End Jewish Radicals*, pp. 169–170.

[187] *The Times* (4 September 1889), in McCarthy, *The Great Dock Strike*, p. 146.

[188] Fishman, *East End Jewish Radicals*, pp. 172–173. These included demands for hours of work and overtime to be cut, the former to twelve hours a day, with an interval of an hour for dinner and a half-hour for tea. These meals were to be consumed away from the workshop. Overtime was to be cut to four hours in a week, and no more than two hours of overtime were to be worked on any one day.

continued. Outside commentators and the striking workers themselves explicitly linked the tailoring strike with the events taking place on the East End quays. The *Jewish World* described the strike as a 'contagion spread from the docks'.[189] The success of the dock strike became bound up in the public mind and in the perception of the strikers themselves with that of the tailors. In the *Balance Sheet of the Great Strike of East London Tailors*, published after the conclusion of the strike, it was revealed that the largest single donation to the tailors' strike fund (which had included contributions from dignitaries such as Lord Rothschild and socialist organisations including the Manchester International Working Men's Club), was issued by the Dock Labourers' Strike Committee, which had donated the sum of £100. In the preface to the account, the secretary of the strike committee wrote that the 'great lesson of solidarity' between the dock labourers and the tailors was a lesson 'for the workers of all countries'.[190] It was an example of inter-ethnic cooperation between Irish, English, and Jewish workers in the capital, a gesture that would be reciprocated in the support, moral and material, within the East End Jewish community for striking dockers in 1911–1912.

Both the dock strike and the industrial action in the Jewish East End concluded in victory for the strikers, and ushered in a new era for British trade unionism. The number of unionised workers, particularly those in unskilled trades, increased dramatically in the aftermath of the successful actions in the East End. On the docks, the Dock, Wharf and Riverside Labourers' Union was formed, with a membership of 24,000 in London and a national membership of 60,000 by the end of 1890.[191] Total national trade union membership had risen to upwards of 1.5 million by 1890.[192] The wave of strikes that took place in 1889 enjoyed a high success rate, with Eric Hobsbawm estimating that some 40 per cent ended in outright victory for the striking workers, and 35 per cent settled by compromise.[193] The socialist press was fulsome in its praise for the determination and cohesive action displayed by the Jewish strikers. *Justice* held up the striking East End tailor as an example to the wider English and international proletariat: 'When the struggle does come, it will be well for the Gentile worker if he fights

[189] *Jewish World* (6 September 1889), in Feldman, *Englishmen and Jews*, p. 218.

[190] Warwick Modern Records Centre, MSS/240/W/3/2, Balance Sheet of the Great Strike of East London Tailors.

[191] Thompson, *Socialists, Liberals and Labour*, p. 51.

[192] Keith Laybourn, *A History of British Trade Unionism* (Stroud: Alan Sutton Publishing, 1992) (republished 1997), p. 76.

[193] Eric J. Hobsbawm, 'The "New Unionism" Reconsidered', in Wolfgang J. Mommsen and Hans-Gerhard Husung, *The Development of Trade Unionism in Great Britain and Germany, 1880–1914* (London: George Allen & Unwin, 1985), p. 17.

as bravely and suffers as nobly as the Jewish workmen have done in their struggle.'[194]

Meanwhile, the dockers, both English and Irish, were lionised by the wider movement, their struggle passing almost immediately in to socialist folklore. This state of affairs, however, was not to last long. If the period from 1888 to 1891 was defined by growth in union expansion and confidence, the next five years witnessed a sustained campaign by employers in the causal trades to roll back the concessions forced by the unions during 1889 and 1890. The cooperation between English, Irish, and Jewish workers as displayed during the strikes, and the successful unionisation of immigrant labourers, suffered a severe reversal as conditions worsened. The unions in the casual trades lost members, funds, and bargaining power. The dockers' union survived, but was severely weakened over the course of the 1890s, while the Jewish clothing trade unions, after the unparalleled cooperation and unity of purpose of 1889, proved mostly transient, divided, and unable to hold on to members for any length of time.[195] This was at least partly a result of the general lack of stability in employment in the East End clothes workshops, with substantial numbers of workers being laid off during quiet periods in the trade, which greatly increased the difficulty in unionisation.[196] Comparing Jewish and Irish unionisation, the industries employing large numbers of male Irish workers in East and South London, such as the docks and the gasworks, tended to experience unionisation on a large scale, with hundreds or thousands of labourers in a particular union. By contrast, the Jewish unions in the sweated workshops, at least at the commencement of the 1890s, were predominantly on a small scale, disparate and short-lived. This reflected the different economic circumstances in which Irish and Jewish workers in the East End laboured. For the large number of Irish women employed in domestic service in the late nineteenth century there was little prospect of any unionisation or labour organisation at all.[197]

---

[194] *Justice* (12 October 1889).

[195] Anne J. Kershen, *Uniting the Tailors: Trade Unionism among the Tailors of London and Leeds, 1870–1939* (Ilford: Frank Cass, 1995), p. 127.

[196] White, *Rothschild Buildings*, p. 197.

[197] See Mark Ebery and Brian Preston, *Domestic Service in Late Victorian and Edwardian England* (Reading: University of Reading, 1976), p. 99 for discussion of the extreme difficulties placed in the way of servants attempting to organise trade unions, not least the need for a reference of 'good character' from previous employers to take up a new position, a recommendation certain to be withheld if a servant went on strike. At the end of the period under discussion in East London this situation was being challenged by working-class female domestics in the Domestic Workers' Union. See Laura Schwartz, '"What We Feel is Needed is a Union for Domestics Such as the Miners Have": The Domestic Workers' Union of Great

Resentment and conflict in the East End between unionised and non-unionised labour, and between labourers and contractors, grew increasingly bitter in the last decade of the nineteenth century. The familiar charge that Jewish immigrants lowered wages, increased rents, and lengthened hours to a degree intolerable for 'native' workmen was repeated; that, in the words of a couple of itinerants overheard by Jack London amongst the unemployed of Mile End, in *People of the Abyss*, 'The Jews of Whitechapel [are], say, a-cutting our throats right along.'[198]

At the conferences of the TUC from the mid-1890s onwards until the end of the century, the attention of the trade union leadership was increasingly focused on restricting 'alien' entry into the United Kingdom, that policy should be directed towards *preventing* immigration, parallel to attempting to organise those migrants who had already settled. The possible adoption by the TUC of a restrictive policy on immigration proved divisive. The TUC debates highlighted a fracture in British trade unionism. This was the difficulty in reconciling the need to represent trade union memberships, concerned with wages, hours, overtime, and blacklegging with an idealistic international world view and cooperative ideology. Discussion on the prevention of entry of immigrants into the United Kingdom in the 1890s and the Edwardian period was focused primarily on Jewish refugees; the Irish migrant before the First World War was after all merely moving from one part of the Kingdom to another. Irish immigrants were certainly regarded as 'foreign' on an intrinsic level; they were also seen as a source of economic competition. But before Home Rule debate on controls on immigration and repatriation fixed on Jews rather than their Irish neighbours.

This divergence in the trade union movement over the treatment of 'aliens' became explicit in the TUC annual meeting of 1894. One delegate moved an amendment calling for the Government to:

[Close] the ports of this country against the entrance of any workers belonging to any trade or industry which the *Labour Gazette* shows to have 8 per cent of its workers unemployed ... since there was not enough work for English people, they [immigrants] should not be allowed to enter the country.[199]

Opposition to the amendment was led by the delegate Mr Pye. Pye 'opposed the amendment on international grounds ... Trade was not local or national; it was international. Though they might suffer, it was impossible to draw

---

Britain and Ireland, 1908–1914', *Twentieth-Century British History*, Vol. 25, No. 2 (2014), pp. 173–192.

[198] London, *People of the Abyss*, p. 81.

[199] Warwick Modern Records Centre, MSS 292/PUB/4/1/1, Trade Union Congress Report, 1894.

a line anywhere. The only way was that they must teach each other the power of organising which they themselves possessed.'[200] Pye's appeal for the organisation and unionisation of 'alien' workers was rejected by Charles Freak, who consistently argued for restrictions and against Jewish immigration throughout the 1890s and 1900s. Freak responded to Pye with the claim that 'Though there were not many paupers among the Jews, they made others paupers by working all hours and at any price … These people [immigrants] were incorrigible; they were either sweaters or sweated.'[201] Freak represented the Shoemaker Society, a trade that had its roots in the Bethnal Green/Whitechapel area, which Freak perceived to be suffering from migrant competition. For Freak, 'these Jew foreigners … make a lot of cheap and nasty stuff that destroys the market and injures us'.[202]

The following year the debate was resumed. At the beginning of the conference William Inskip moved that the Congress adopt the following resolution: 'In view of the injury done to a large number of trades and trade unions by the wholesale importation of foreign destitute paupers, this congress calls upon the Government to take the necessary steps to prohibit the landing of all pauper aliens who have no visible means of subsistence.'[203] T. Walker, supporting an amendment to the resolution, called instead for the organisation of foreigners resident in the United Kingdom and particularly London, and for the establishment of 'a world-wide brotherhood to prevent the workmen from being robbed of their rights'.[204] Freak again supported an anti-alien resolution, in stronger terms than the year before. The alien was a 'blighting blister', East London 'had been made the dumping ground for the common refuse of the world'. 'There was no manhood in the alien workman, and it was impossible to appeal to him through his heart. Therefore the British must take compulsory means of getting rid of him.'[205] The response of Jewish comrades present was not recorded, but Jas MacDonald of the London Tailors Union answered Freak that he was aware of Jews who were starving in the East End while 'English workmen were

---

[200] Warwick Modern Records Centre, MSS 292/PUB/4/1/1, Trade Union Congress Report, 1894.

[201] Warwick Modern Records Centre, MSS 292/PUB/4/1/1, Trade Union Congress Report, 1894.

[202] William J. Fishman, *East End 1888* (Nottingham: Five Leaves Publications, 2005) (originally published 1988), p. 185.

[203] Warwick Modern Records Centre, MSS 292/PUB/4/1/2, Trade Union Congress Report, 1895.

[204] Warwick Modern Records Centre, MSS 292/PUB/4/1/2, Trade Union Congress Report, 1895. See Burns and Kautsky, above.

[205] Warwick Modern Records Centre, MSS 292/PUB/4/1/2, Trade Union Congress Report, 1895.

blacklegs'. The resolution calling for restrictions on entry into the United Kingdom was carried by a majority of 20,000, with 266,000 votes cast in favour opposed to 246,000 against.[206] The trade union movement was thus neatly split in two by the debate on entry restriction.

The reaction in the socialist press to the passing of the resolution was mixed. In the *Clarion*, Leonard Hall argued in favour of the move, responding to Sam Hobson, who in the *Labour Leader* had characterised the resolution to restrict immigration as 'stupid'. For Hall, 'A large percentage of the class of continental immigrants settling here from the moment of landing are compelled to wage mercilessly fratricidal war against British labour ... It is not a race question but an economic one.'[207] *Justice*, on the other hand, in an article headed 'Aliens', strongly condemned the resolution. 'Nothing', the article started,

> can be more unsocialistic than the resolution of the Cardiff Congress on the alien question ... What we deny is that the introduction of legislation prohibiting the landing of foreigners, or hanging over them the threat of expulsion when landed, can serve any useful purpose whatsoever. It may, however, very easily prove a descent which will lead to the virtual abrogation of the rights of asylum for political offenders.[208]

The final condemnatory sentence of the article formed the crux of socialist opposition to the TUC moves to restrict immigration. Any legislation, especially that likely to be passed by a Conservative government, would certainly restrict the movements of political refugees, socialists, and other progressives from Central and Eastern Europe. An anti-alien bill could also possibly be employed to expel foreign socialists already settled in Britain. In his article in favour of restriction, Leonard Hall had included a caveat supporting the free movement of political refugees. In a letter in response to the article, published a few weeks later, J. Fyvie-Mayo wondered how 'politicals' could be distinguished from the mass of immigrants fleeing general persecution: 'is Leonard Hall's sympathy limited to those whose *spoken* or *organising* action has made them what he calls "political refugees in the definite sense"? Has he no sympathy to spare for the many, whose wrongs have goaded these few into utterance or organisation?'[209]

A meeting of Jewish trade unionists at the Great Assembly Hall at Mile End, meanwhile, condemned the 1895 proposition as a 'futile, un-English measure', the result of 'groundless accusations, gross misrepresentations,

[206] Warwick Modern Records Centre, MSS 292/PUB/4/1/2, Trade Union Congress Report, 1895.

[207] *Clarion* (12 October 1895).

[208] *Justice* (7 December 1895).

[209] *Clarion* (9 November 1895) (original emphasis).

and perversion of facts on the part of some Labour misleaders [*sic*] ...
we, the assembled Jewish working men, against whom the poison arrows
are chiefly pointed, condemn this crusade against us and its instigators'.[210]
The tension between trade unionists opposed to immigration for economic
reasons, and those in the socialist movement who wished to maintain open
borders for political and ideological reasons, continued up to the passing
of the Aliens Act by the Conservatives in 1905. By the time anti-alien
legislation had become law the bulk of the socialist and labour movement
had moved to a position opposed to the legal restriction of migrants. The
ten years between the motion proposing the anti-immigration resolution
by the TUC in 1895 and the implementation of the Aliens Act saw a
significant shift in the attitudes of the socialist-inclined trade unions
towards the 'alien problem'. At the 1903 Congress, Mr Policoff, speaking
as a representative of the Jewish tailoring organisations, proposed a motion
to reduce the naturalisation fees paid by foreign workmen and women who
lived and worked for a number of years in the country, 'so that it may be
within the reach of every workman to become a loyal subject as well as a
useful citizen of this country'. The resolution was carried unanimously.[211] In
1905, as anti-alien legislation passed through parliament, the TUC, which
ten years before had moved to restrict the entry of migrants into British
ports, condemned the putative bill. It was described as a device to end the
tradition of asylum offered to political refugees, whilst not addressing the
issue of foreign economic competition:

> [The Alien Act] will be made use of to exclude the genuine political
> refugee, such as Father Gapon and Prince Kropotkin, men who have
> sacrificed everything worth sacrificing in their own country in the protests
> against inhumanity and injustice ... It is, therefore, to be hoped that the
> British workman will not be led into the bog of prejudice by this political
> will-o-the-wisp.[212]

---

210  *Daily Chronicle* (10 December 1895).

211  Warwick Modern Records Centre, MSS 292/PUB/4/1/3, Annual Trade Union Congress
Report, 1903.

212  Gapon, who had been at the forefront of the initial protests that acted as a catalyst
for the 1905 Russian Revolution, was briefly a darling for the European political left. It
soon transpired that Gapon had in fact been an agent of the Okhrana, the Tsarist secret
police, and he died in mysterious circumstances in April 1906. Warwick Modern Records
Centre, MSS 292/PUB/4/1/5, Annual Trade Union Congress Report, 1905. H. Snell in his
1904 pamphlet, *The Foreigner in England*, listed 'Mazzini, Lewis Blanc, Karl Marx, Engels
... Kropotkin, Bernstein, Emile Zola and thousands of less known but heroic personalities'
who had benefited from the tradition of political asylum. LSE ILP 5/1904/64, H. Snell,
*The Foreigner in England: An Examination of the Problem of Alien Immigration* (London:
Independent Labour Party, 1904).

That the Aliens Act was essentially a distraction for the working class which would not solve the problems bound up in economic exploitation was echoed in the *Socialist Standard*, the journal of the Socialist Party of Great Britain (SPGB), a splinter group from the SDF, which described the anti-immigrant campaign as 'glaringly fraudulent'.[213] As well as fears that the Act was a smokescreen to allow the government to exclude and to expel foreigners with disagreeable political views, the class element – that the Act was confined to 'steerage class' passengers – was also condemned by the left.[214] In 1911, the *Socialist Standard*, which steadily aimed throughout the period to challenge popular assumptions surrounding the negative results of migration, condemned Robert Blatchford as an 'anti-socialist of the worst type' for comments he had made in the *Weekly Dispatch* about 'foreign thugs' and 'undesirable aliens'. The *Socialist Standard* concluded:

> between worker and worker there can be no alienism, because there can be no alienation. They are bound together by the common ties of their class position – a common class interest. On the other hand, they have nothing in common with the master class, whose interests are everywhere opposed to theirs. Therefore it is the master class who are the aliens.[215]

To summarise interactions taking place with trade unionism, Jewish strike action in the small-scale workshops had a different quality from the industrial disputes that London Irish workers on the docks were involved in, and the resultant class tensions arising from these conflicts were of a different nature. Strikes in the Jewish community were inter-communal, between predominantly Jewish employers and Jewish workers; in the Irish case, the 'boss' was generally an English Protestant, and thus class and ethnic tensions were projected outwards. The difficulty in both communities was maintaining union membership and subscriptions between the periods of explicit and open class conflict. Another significant factor in working-class Jewish attitudes towards unionisation was the popularity amongst left-inclined and politically aware Jewish immigrants of the anarchist and anarcho-socialist groups, semi-clandestine organisations that enjoyed greater influence in the Jewish East End than in the wider working class of the area.[216] Elements of the *Arbeter Fraynt* and their circle dismissed unionisation as a distraction from revolutionary activity. The Jewish anarchist Isaac Stone, writing in the first edition of that journal, claimed that the effect of the unions 'is even actually harmful, because they divert the workers

---

[213] *The Socialist Standard* (23 June 1905).

[214] T.W.E. Roche, *The Key in the Lock: A History of Immigration Control in England from 1066 to the Present Day* (London: John Murray, 1969), p. 69.

[215] *The Socialist Standard* (March 1911).

[216] Goodway, *Anarchist Seeds Beneath the Snow*, p. 9.

from the right path, which is socialism'.[217] The issue of unionisation led to conflict and division among the East End Jewish left, and a bitter dispute between the social democrat trade unionist Lewis Lyons and the anarchist leader S. Yanovsky. Lyons advocated the combination of Jewish trade unions and the small master tailors, whilst Yanovsky rejected the plan as an 'unnatural alliance', objectively harmful to the movement.[218] For Lyons, combination between workers and employers who were barely any better off than their employees, made practical sense. Indeed, it was not unknown for the poorer class of Jewish master to join their workers during industrial action.[219] For Yanovsky and others, however, this proposal was akin to supping with the enemy. The disagreement between the two and their followers was heated; at the end of one meeting Yanovsky was assaulted with an iron bar whilst walking home down a quiet side-street, and was treated in hospital for some time.[220] At a meeting held at the Jewish Working Men's Club in Whitechapel to discuss industrial action, Lyons was attacked as the platform was stormed, with the speaker injured by blows from a heavy stick.[221]

The unions representing the significant Irish trades in East and South London, the dockers, the stevedores, and the gas workers, suffered a decline in numbers and influence during the fallow period of the late 1890s, as did the movement generally. Ben Tillett's attempt to achieve a 'closed shop' in the London docks, with only unionised labour being employed, was a failure. By the end of the decade practices such as subcontracting and casual employment had reappeared.[222] Nevertheless, these unions, less fragmented than those in the East End tailoring trade, survived, and, as with the wider movement, benefited from the upsurge in membership and militancy at the end of the Edwardian period. There was little ambiguity in Irish communities about the relationship between employer and worker. The Irish worker settled in the East End had not shaken off the role of ethnic and religious 'other' in turn-of-the-century London; but the term 'alien' in anti-immigrant discourse from the 1890s onwards was applied overwhelmingly to Jews, the two terms becoming almost synonymous.[223] The range of responses to proposals for restriction of entry into the United Kingdom highlighted the

---

217 *Arbeter Fraynt*, quoted in Rocker, *The London Years*, pp. 58–59.

218 Rocker, *The London Years*, p. 62.

219 Gartner, *The Jewish Immigrant in England*, p. 79.

220 Rocker, *The London Years*, pp. 62–63.

221 *Jewish Chronicle* (4 September 1896).

222 W. Hamish Fraser, *A History of British Trade Unionism, 1700–1998* (Basingstoke: Macmillan, 1999), p. 79.

223 The terminology of 'alien' and 'Jew' is discussed in Glover, *Literature, Immigration, and Diaspora in Fin-de-Siècle England*. See also Gainer, *The Alien Invasion*, pp. 4–5.

contested and continuing question of whether it was the primary duty of the movement to maintain solidarity with persecuted or exploited minorities or to protect domestic wages and conditions. In the early twentieth century, groups emerged from outside the socialist organisations and trade unions which attempted to exploit this ambiguity for political ends.

## The Challenge of the Radical Right in East London

The stance adopted by the leading trade unions between 1895 and 1905 thus shifted from an essentially anti-immigration and pro-restriction position to one that condemned anti-alien legislation as an ideologically motivated policy directed at keeping out the very poor and the politically unsuitable. This was at least partly occasioned by the composition of those political elements that by the turn of the twentieth century were most bellicose in their support for such an act. The majority of British trade union leaders, socialist or otherwise, instinctively recoiled from the jingoistic, anti-immigrant, anti-union right-wing of the Conservative Party. The vocal support of such elements for a restriction on entry in to the United Kingdom effectively decided the position for the bulk of the left-leaning labour movement.[224] However, the demand for closing British borders to refugees was just one manifestation of a current of radical right-wing popularism that emerged in Britain between the conclusion of the Boer War and the outbreak of the First World War. Ranging from the radical Tory right-wing 'die-hards', the Primrose League, and the various navy leagues, to the campaign group the British Brothers' League, and at its most extreme individuals such as Joseph Banister, wielding little influence but much invective, these disparate groups campaigned on a number of issues. These included the prevention of Home Rule for Ireland, an increase in military spending, and opposition to female suffrage. In East London these organisations converged on the issue of anti-alienism, the evils of current and potential future immigration.[225] The Jewish community in East London was the main target of this political agitation, which in some respects constituted a foreshadowing of the activities of the various fascist groups of the 1920s and 1930s.[226] The other predominant diasporic 'other' present in East London, the Irish Catholics, largely escaped the attentions of the BBL. In any case

[224] See Jill Pellew, 'The Home Office and the Aliens Act, 1905', *Historical Journal*, Vol. 32, Issue 2 (1989) for discussion of attitudes within the mainstream British right towards restriction of migration and the explicit class connotations of the Act.

[225] See Glover, *Literature, Immigration and Diaspora*, chapter 3 for discussion of the different strands of the Edwardian radical right.

[226] Gainer, *The Alien Invasion*, p. 70.

the opposition of the radical right to Home Rule in Ireland, the support for Ulster-based loyalist groups, and the jingoism and flag-waving of the BBL and other groups alienated working-class Irish Catholics still concerned with the political situation back in Ireland.[227] This new current of populist anti-immigrant sentiment, explicitly canvassed among the more prosperous elements of the East End English working class, with opposition to Jewish immigration framed in speeches and pamphlets around a series of 'bread and butter' issues: housing, employment, and education. This agitation brought into question what the 'correct' position of a socialist party drawing on working-class support should be as regarded immigration.

During the Edwardian period, the radical right consistently portrayed progressive forces in the metropolis as 'soft' on immigration, which was taken also to mean 'soft' on sweatshops, and on the perceived economic exploitation or marginalisation of the English working class. This theme was taken up by the press office of the Conservative Party, particularly at election times, when both Liberal and socialist opponents were attacked for being 'pro-alien'.[228] A 1906 pamphlet read: 'The whole scum of Europe may come to this country by merely concocting stories about being political or religious "refugees", however obviously improbable their stories may be.'[229] In a lecture delivered to a Conservative and Unionist Club by Joseph Hurst in 1907 the socialist movement was portrayed as opposing restrictions for its own sinister reasons. 'Shall we not have cheap importation of foreign Socialists to assist their "comrades" here, and to instruct them in their foreign methods from which up to now we have been greatly shielded?' Hurst also warned of the effects of immigration on 'the British political scale' and the possibility of 'a great increase in foreign crime'.[230] The concerns raised in this lecture directly mirror one of the primary objections raised by the socialist movement to the Alien Bill, that it would be used to prevent political refugees from settling in Britain. But while socialists saw the issue as a matter of both international solidarity and the British tradition of hospitality, for Hurst, the prospect of

---

[227] David Feldman, 'The Importance of Being English: Jewish Immigration and the Decay of Liberal England', in Feldman and Stedman Jones, *Metropolis London*, p. 72. See Martin Pugh, *'Hurrah for the Blackshirts!': Fascists and Fascism in Britain between the Wars* (London: Pimlico, 2006), pp. 18–20; Richard Thurlow, *Fascism in Britain: A History, 1918–1985* (Oxford: Basil Blackwell, 1987), pp. 4–5; and Glover, *Literature, Immigration and Diaspora*, pp. 103–104 for the relationship between the pre-First World War radical right and Ulster loyalism.

[228] LSE JF2 (42C)/266, Anon., *Chinese and Aliens* (London, Conservative Publication Department) (*c*.1904–1906).

[229] LSE JF2 (42C)/267, Anon., *The Aliens Act Made Useless – Following Liberal Amendments to the 1905 Aliens Act* (London: Conservative Publication Department, 1906).

[230] Anon., *Socialism: What it is, and How to Meet it, Lecture delivered by Joseph Hurst to the Hitchen Junior Conservative and Unionist Club* (London: Paternoster and Hales, 1907).

'foreign socialists' landing on British shores seemed to presage a possible violent uprising on the continental model. These fears on the far-right intensified during the strikes of 1911–1912, where the success of syndicalism was frequently cited as evidence of 'alien' influence.[231] Conservative rhetoric, like that of their socialist counterparts, drew heavily on the opposition of 'British' (peaceful) and 'continental' (violent) ways of conducting politics, with immigrants portrayed as importing an alien, aggressive strain of political radicalism.

At the Royal Commission on Alien Immigration held in 1903, one BBL member, questioned by the leading light of the League, Major William Evans-Gordon, framed his objections to immigration in terms that played on fears of displacement, physical and political: 'I want to live, as I consider myself a decent working man, and I want to live in a respectable neighbourhood … they [immigrants] are turning the street into one of the worst streets I know of in the neighbourhood.'[232] The BBL exploited traditional East End working-class concerns over territory and neighbourhood. This fed into what Kirk describes as the 'defensive appeal' of working-class Conservatism: 'us' and 'them', with self-identity defined against 'hostile communities'.[233] At the first meeting of the BBL in the summer of 1901, Arnold White made the class focus of the movement explicit, blaming the 'alien' for slum landlording and high rents: 'The people who invented key money in east London belong to the race of whom the majority are poor, but of whom some are very, very rich.'[234] This rhetoric fed on the ambiguity of diasporic identities that cut across class lines, a transnational community encompassing both the Rothschild family and the sweated worker. David Hope Kyd, a Conservative parliamentary candidate, warned of 'the extermination of the British workingman in the East End of London'.[235]

The movement of the trade unions and the Labour Party towards opposition to restriction before the 1906 election had caused concern amongst those unions that felt themselves most under threat from foreign competition. If the Labour Party refused to protect these workers from the 'alien' and all the evils supposed to flow from that source, who would? This

---

[231] Holton, *British Syndicalism*, p. 76.

[232] Minutes of Evidence taken before the Royal Commission on Alien Immigration, 1903, interview with a member of the BBL (questioned by Major Evans Gordon) in David Englander (ed.), *A Documentary History of Jewish Immigrants in Britain, 1840–1920* (London: Leicester University Press, 1994), p. 91.

[233] Neville Kirk, *Change, Continuity and Class: Labour in British Society, 1850–1920* (Manchester: Manchester University Press, 1998), p. 204. Irish Catholics formed one of these 'hostile communities' along with Jews and other 'outsider' groups.

[234] Bermant, *Point of Arrival*, pp. 141–142.

[235] Holmes, *John Bull's Island*, p. 69; Gainer, *Alien Invasion*, p. 113.

sentiment was strongest in the docks and in the sailors' unions, occupations that by their nature attracted a large number of foreign casual workers. In a letter to Ramsay MacDonald in his position as secretary of the Labour Representation Committee (LRC), dated 19 January 1906, a representative of the Sailors' and Firemen's Union expressed these concerns and fears of abandonment by the wider movement:

> we have little to hope for from the Liberal Party, containing as it does, many shipowners who employ these foreigners in preference to our own people. Our only hope is in a Labour Party, who, one would think, would favour restrictive legislation in their own interest, for it seems quite clear to me that if the workers on British ships can with impunity be displaced by cheap, imported labour, so also can the worker in any or every form of employment, in the country. But we are not quite sure that [we] will receive the support of even the Labour Party, as we have seen the present 'free and easy' entry of the Alien into this country advocated and defended by men with whom previously we had no cause to quarrel.[236]

Jewish settlement in East London ('the present "free and easy" entry of the Alien') was conflated with the employment of non-white minorities on dock quays and aboard ships, with both posing a threat to the 'native' working class. Such organisations considered themselves out of step with the prevalent mood of internationalism and opposition to restriction. This would seem to be fertile ground for recruitment by the radical right. At the end of the Edwardian period a right-wing, anti-socialist, anti-immigrant workers organisation did emerge from the 'die-hard' wing of the Conservative Party, the Workers' Defence Union (WDU). Originating in the Battersea branch of the Tariff Reform League, the WDU defined itself in opposition to a labour movement perceived as siding with the immigrant and the 'alien' against the 'Conservative workingmen' of London.[237] The left-wing trade unions were accused by the WDU of betraying British workers. An article in the *Worker*, the WDU journal, declared: 'Such of us as are Trade Unionists have seen our efforts at cooperation defeated by the unrestricted competition of the foreign "blackleg". Others have had their livings filched from them by the unchecked advance of a horde of aliens who will accept conditions under which we cannot live.'[238] In *WDU Notes*, an editorial declared the socialist and left-wing trade unionist to be 'hairy, foreign and

---

[236] Manchester People's History Museum, LRC/19/397, Letter to J.R. MacDonald of the LRC from Joseph Foley of the British Sailors' and Firemen's Union, 19 January 1906.

[237] Alan Sykes, 'Radical Conservatism and the Working Classes in Edwardian England: The Case of the Workers Defence Union', *English Historical Review*, Vol. 113, No. 545 (November 1988), p. 1186.

[238] *The Worker* (November 1910), in Sykes, 'Radical Conservatism', p. 1191.

unwashed, speaking English as he learnt it in the State schools of Posen or Moscow, before he fled to avoid the service of his country, or the attentions of the police'.[239]

The radical right agitating in the East End in the early twentieth century made some overtures to the Irish community. Fears of 'Jewish invasion' in East London were certainly present in Catholic as well as Protestant East End neighbourhoods, as the content of the *Catholic Herald* in the first decade of the twentieth century will attest.[240] In April 1904, the BBL had passed a resolution thanking the antisemitic agitator Father Creagh, the driving force behind the Limerick boycott of Jewish businesses earlier in the year, a campaign that resulted in some violence against property and persons. The resolution spoke of the 'misery' caused by 'undesirable aliens' to 'our Irish Brothers and Sisters [*sic*]'.[241] As early as 1893, Michael Davitt, in a letter to the *Jewish Chronicle*, cautioned Irish workers against the 'delusion' that 'low wages and trade depression in the East End of London … are traceable for cause to the influx of foreign workmen, mainly Jews'.[242] The Union flag-waving 'jingo' element involved in these organisations, and above all the opposition to Home Rule, largely alienated the Irish communities around the docklands who might have otherwise been sympathetic to the anti-alien campaign. Concurrently to the BBL campaign against Jewish immigration, the Irish Catholic neighbourhoods of the East End had their own antithetical pressure group to contend with, the Protestant Alliance, an organisation that endeavoured to import the sectarian tensions of Belfast, Liverpool, and Glasgow to East London through provocative demonstrations and acts. The Irish Catholic reaction to these efforts will be examined in more detail in Chapter 5.

In London, the BBL made a great deal of noise, and had an impressive roster of speakers, but the actual political threat to the support bases of progressive forces in the capital was not great. At its peak, in 1902, the BBL claimed a membership of 12,000 East End residents.[243] By 1912, however, the movement had largely dissipated, its main campaigning point, an act to restrict immigration, having been achieved, and the League was made more or less redundant. The BBL was a pressure group rather than a political party. The WDU failed to supplant the mainstream trade unions, and even

[239] *WDU Notes* (June 1910).

[240] See Chapter 5 for discussion of the *Catholic Herald* and the relationship between ethnicity and territory in the East End.

[241] Dermot Keogh and Andrew McCarthy, *Limerick Boycott of 1904: Anti-Semitism in Ireland* (Cork: Mercier Press, 2005), p. 65.

[242] Quoted in *Jewish Chronicle* (21 November 1902).

[243] David Feldman, 'The Importance of Being English: Jewish Immigration and the Decay of Liberal England', in Feldman and Stedman Jones, *Metropolis London*, p. 70.

the unions that indulged particularly in anti-immigrant rhetoric, such as those representing sailors and associated trades, remained affiliated to the TUC. Although claiming to be a cross-party pressure group, the WDU grew out of the right-wing of the Conservative Party, again limiting its appeal to East End Irish communities and trade unionists generally.

Prior to the growth and dominance of the Labour Party which began to take shape at the end of the period, the various socialist organisations displayed an extraordinary variety of attitudes towards diasporic minorities in East London. None of the socialist groups had a firm 'line' towards minority groups, as examination of the leading left-wing publications of the time illustrates. Attitudes were shaped by international events such as the Boer War or the Kishinev pogroms, and socialists such as Michael Davitt condemned Jews for the former and expressed sympathy and outrage on their behalf for the latter. How the Irish Catholic diaspora was viewed by the socialist movement was also ambiguous, particularly over the key question of whether Irish or English politics took primacy in those communities, in other words whether class or nationality was the cornerstone of loyalty and solidarity. But minority nationalism was not the only force competing with socialism and trade unionism for purchase in migrant communies. Competition also came from the Jewish and Catholic religious bodies that claimed responsibility not only for the immigrant's spiritual well-being, but their political affiliations as well. How the minority hierarchies and the beliefs they espoused interacted with metropolitan socialism will now be addressed.

# 3

# Socialism and the Religious 'Other'

The religious beliefs of the Jewish and Irish communities in East London played a key role in demarcating their differences from wider mainstream British society. It was religious faith that helped cement a diasporic identity that crossed class and national boundaries. Religious institutions also provided a ready-made structure of communal leadership for migrant communities. The durability of minority religious observance was noted by contemporary observers, as compared with a largely non-religious wider working-class culture.[1] However, there were negative as well as positive ramifications for the strength of faith amongst the Irish Catholic and Jewish communities, as far as the diasporic groups were perceived in the wider society. The way in which religion cut across class and national lines, as well as its seemingly alien elements, with unfamiliar rituals and prayers recited in a foreign language, could lead to accusations of conspiracy and suggestions of hidden transnational ecclesiastical networks by both the political right and the left. For H.M. Hyndman, the supranational element of ecclesiastical commitment smacked of reactionary conspiracy, whilst for Beatrice Webb and Robert Blatchford, the strength of Jewish and Catholic religious loyalty caused ideological difficulties. Other socialists, such as the now obscure one-time Catholic Fabian Robert Dell, spent a part of their political careers attempting to reconcile socialist politics and minority religion.

For both the Irish Catholic and Jewish diasporas transnational belonging and identity were a complex composite mixture of both religious and ethnic loyalties and roles. These roles, and identification with a wider minority community, were not set in stone, but were conditional and often changing. For the BoD, the United Synagogue, and the *Beth Din* in the 1890s, involvement by a Jewish socialist or trade unionist in 'extreme' left-wing political activity could effectively negate the Jewish identity of the offender.

---

[1] McLeod, *Class and Religion in the Late Victorian City*, p. 72.

Similarly, a failure, particularly by certain radical members of the clergy, to follow the strictures of the Church, or to fall into such 'deviations' as Modernism, could potentially forfeit Catholic belonging not only in this world but in the next. The Church had the ultimate sanction of excommunication and the withholding of religious rites at the individual's funeral and burial were the potential consequences of political or spiritual 'deviation'.[2]

Sheridan Gilley, examining the interaction of Catholicism and socialism in Scotland between 1900 and 1930, divides British socialism into three main 'schools' regarding attitudes towards religion. The first argued that socialism and faith were more than compatible, in the case of Christian socialists that 'Christianity was the religion of which socialism was the practice'.[3] The second school rejected organised religion absolutely, and argued that socialism was an antidote to religious belief, or 'superstition' as the secularists would term it. The third position, which would come to constitute the policy of the Labour Party in respect to individual party members' beliefs, declared itself neutral as regarded religion, positing that faith was an essentially private matter to be separated from political activity, and that the socialist movement should embrace those of any faith or denomination, or of none.[4]

This discussion will concentrate on the first two 'schools' that Gilley mentions, that is synthesis and rejection, rather than the compromise and moderation of the third. It will place in context attempts by Christian and Jewish socialists to reconcile religious and political beliefs, and ideological socialist hostility towards minority religion. The first part of this chapter, however, will concentrate on religious communal institutions, examining and comparing the structures of the Catholic and Jewish hierarchies and their attitudes towards Irish and Jewish unionisation following the strikes of 1889.

## Socialism and Minority Communal Institutions

The ways in which the Jewish and Catholic communal leaderships responded to the series of strikes that broke across London in the second half of 1889 were influenced by a number of inter-connected factors. First, the structures of the communal, particularly religious institutions, and their supposed legitimacy in the eyes of the migrant proletariat, were decisive in

---

[2] Dennis Sewell, *Catholics: Britain's Largest Minority* (London: Viking, 2001).

[3] Sheridan Gilley, 'Catholics and Socialists in Scotland, 1900–1930', in Roger Swift and Sheridan Gilley (eds), *The Irish in Britain, 1815–1939* (London: Pinter Publishers Ltd, 1989), p. 213.

[4] Gilley, 'Catholics and Socialists', p. 213.

influencing attitudes towards labour unrest and the subsequent increase in unionisation and exposure to left-wing politics. These structures affected the confidence with which communal bodies faced an increasingly militant migrant working class, and the internal cohesiveness of these structures determined to what extent political organisation of an immigrant proletariat was a threat to communal hegemony.

The personalities of the individual communal leaders, their backgrounds, and the political and cultural baggage that they brought with them, was another factor. The personal element conditioned the sympathy or lack of the same that was felt by the communal representatives towards the strikes and the beginnings of mass unionisation of migrant communities post-1889. The force of personality was relevant in the response of the Catholic hierarchy towards Irish unionisation in the late 1880s, and that of the BoD and the office of Chief Rabbi towards Jewish socialism.

On an international level socialism had been viewed by the Catholic Church as a potential threat since the 1840s. The centralised and hierar-chical nature of Catholic religious structures as compared with their Jewish counterparts gave the pronouncements of the Roman hierarchy an influence beyond that of a domestic Chief Rabbi. Pius IX, writing in 1849, condemned in the strongest language 'Communism or Socialism'.[5] His successor, Leo XIII, writing some thirty years later, articulated the antipathy the Church felt towards the socialist movement with a strong defence of private property. This was a stance that would be stressed in the doctrine of both the Catholic and Jewish establishments, an assertion that economic inequality was part of the natural and ordained order of things.[6]

The international Roman Catholic Church regarded liberalism with distaste, and modernistic tendencies within the Catholic clergy were strongly discouraged. But it was the various strands of the socialist movement that drew the most opprobrium. Through the nineteenth century and into the twentieth, socialism on the European continent was a bugbear for the Church.[7] In Britain, both Catholicism and the socialist movement were relatively small and marginal minority groups, neither one powerful or influential enough to provoke a head on confrontation between the Papacy and the Socialist International.[8] Nevertheless, the hostility that the Vatican

---

[5] Kenelm Digby Best, *Why No Good Catholic Can be a Socialist* (London: Burns and Oates Ltd, 1890), pp. 6–7.

[6] Best, *Why No Good Catholic Can be a Socialist*, pp. 8–9. See Claudia Carlen, *The Papal Encyclicals, 1740–1878* (Wilmington, NC: McGrath Publishing Company, 1981) for an accurate English translation of the encyclicals.

[7] See Hilaire Belloc, *The Church and Socialism* (London: Catholic Truth Society, 1909), p. 1. and Fielding, *Class and Ethnicity*, p. 111.

[8] In *Life and Labour*, Charles Booth suggests the figure of slightly under 200,000

felt towards the international left was replicated to a degree in the attitudes of the domestic Catholic hierarchy. It was of great significance, then, that in 1889, the head of the Catholic Church in Britain, Cardinal Manning, should play such a decisive part in bringing the dockers' strike to an end, to evince such broad sympathy for their aims, and in the process become a folk-hero among sections of the London Irish working class.[9]

### Catholic and Jewish Communal Leaderships: Contrasts and Comparisons

Manning was a convert to Catholicism, beginning his career as an Anglican clergyman. That Manning was a convert rather than an 'Old Catholic' would take on political significance, especially regarding his attitudes towards the Irish. Manning carried none of the 'Old Catholic' prejudice against Irish immigrants that had manifested itself from the time of the Famine.[10] Becoming Cardinal in 1865, Manning was possibly the most influential and certainly the most socially aware religious leader active in late nineteenth-century Britain. As priest, Archbishop, and finally Cardinal, Manning was present during that great demographic shift in British Catholicism that followed the post-Famine exodus from Ireland, with all the possibilities and problems that that influx had raised. Manning's active championing of the Irish and the reciprocation of good feeling by the London Irish diaspora would be a crucial factor during the 1889 dock strike.

Manning had had previous contact with dire poverty and want. He came from a wealthy background, but a tenure as Archdeacon of Chichester had exposed Manning to the level of hardship felt in the countryside.[11] A possibly apocryphal tale concerning the Cardinal and two priests points to Manning's politics and a dry sense of humour. When asked what they would be if not a priest, Manning responded that he would be 'Radical member for Marylebone'.[12] Manning was certainly not a socialist, though some in the Catholic establishment suspected otherwise.[13] What Manning did believe in was the beneficial role that the Catholic working class could play in the future of the Church, both in Britain and internationally, an

---

Catholics residing in turn of the century London. Booth, *Life and Labour of the People in London*, Third Series, *Religious Influences*, Vol. 7, p. 250.

9  H. Llewellyn Smith and Vaughan Nash, *The Story of the Dockers Strike* (London: T. Fisher Unwin, 1890), pp. 149–150.

10  Mary J. Hickman, *Religion, Class and Identity: The State, the Catholic Church and the Education of the Irish in Britain* (Aldershot: Avebury, 1995), p. 116.

11  Vincent Alan McCelland, *Cardinal Manning: His Public Life and Influence, 1865–1892* (London: Oxford University Press, 1962), p. 11.

12  Georgiana Putnam McEntee, *The Social Catholic Movement in Great Britain* (New York: The Macmillan Company, 1927), p. 20.

13  McCelland, *Cardinal Manning*, p. 23.

'alliance between the papacy and the poor'.[14] In Manning, therefore, we have a communal leader comfortable with the migrant working class, aware of social conditions, and commanding respect amongst both employers and workers.[15] This placed him in a uniquely favourable position to mediate in the 1889 dockers' strike. Manning also enjoyed the friendship of Ben Tillett, for whom the Cardinal was something of a spiritual mentor. Tillett described an early correspondence thus:

> One of the master forces of my life at that period was Cardinal Manning ... I was sick to death of life and of the movement, and said so to the Cardinal, giving fair reasons for my attitude of mind. I received a letter back, which condoled with me, but which contained so subtle a castigation that it stung me to effort and faith again, a faith I have never lost since. In effect it thanked me for the courage and sacrifice of the past; it then stated what type of man was wanted for the work of the true agitator.[16]

For Tillett, there was no contradiction between religious faith and union militancy.

Manning held a high card during negotiations to end the strike that he could use either against Tillett and the strikers or the employers as he chose. This was his 'sacred battalion', the Irish Catholic dockers themselves, whom Manning could appeal to above either the heads of the trade union or the employers. It is questioned whether Manning ever made this threat explicit but both sides of the dispute were aware that Manning had this power.[17] As Colin Davis writes, the (Catholic section of the) dockers accepted leaders such as Tillett, 'not because of their socialism but in spite of it'.[18] Manning prevailed on the dockers to accept terms offering less than was demanded, but which was still considered a great victory for the labour movement.

---

[14] McEntee, *Social Catholic Movement*, p. 33.

[15] Manning's father had been the director of one dock company and his brother director of another. See Llewellyn Smith and Nash, *The Story of the Dockers Strike*, p. 125.

[16] Warwick Modern Records Centre, MSS 74/4/1/5, pamphlet, Ben Tillett, *A Brief History of the Dockers Union*, p. 15.

[17] McCelland rejects what he argues is a historical fallacy that Manning at the meeting in the Kirby Street schools explicitly threatened to break up the strike by appealing to the Irish Catholics at the docks. 'No such appeal is to be found recorded in any contemporary accounts of the meeting.' McCelland, *Cardinal Manning*, p. 144.

[18] Colin Davis, 'The Elusive Irishman: Ethnicity and the Post-War World of New York City and London Dockers', in Peter Alexander and Rick Halpern (eds), *Racializing Class, Classifying Race: Labour and Difference in Britain, the USA and Africa* (Basingstoke: Macmillan, 2000), p. 91. See also Gareth Stedman Jones, *Outcast London: A Study in the Relationship Between Classes in Victorian Society* (Harmondsworth: Penguin, 1971), p. 348. 'Casual workers [on the docks] ... remained readier to listen to a few well-chosen homilies from Cardinal Manning than to a torrent of speeches from the SDF.'

The 'Cardinal's Peace' was subsequently mythologised, and his intervention depicted in frankly religious terms. An 1890 account of the previous year's events came close to suggesting a miracle had taken place at the Kirby Street Catholic School where negotiations were being held:

> He [the Cardinal] urged, with the air of gentle authority, which won the hearts of all who had dealings with him throughout the strike, that from a business point of view they would do well to accept an offer which gave them practically all they asked in six weeks time. They must consider not only themselves, but the suffering the strike was bringing on their families … It was late before Cardinal Manning summed up. In an address which deeply moved his hearers, he reviewed the arguments on both sides. He himself was accountable to no human authority for standing there: he was responsible only to one above. Unaccustomed tears glistened in the eyes of his rough and work-stained hearers as he raised his hand … Just above his lifted hand was a carved figure of the Madonna and Child, and some among the men tell how a sudden light seemed to swim around it as the speaker pleaded for the women and children.[19]

This emphasis on religious faith that surrounded the conclusion of the dockers' strike was perhaps unique in the industrial disputes of the period. This was a subtext that could only have emerged from the heady mixture of religious belief and union militancy that characterised the docks and the significant number of Catholic dockers and stevedores at work there. Tillett later wrote: 'I have the greatest reverence and gratitude for the memory of dear Cardinal Manning, as for others who served, and I give thanks to all who helped us and to Almighty God, Who gave us strength.'[20]

The Jewish religious establishment at the end of the 1880s had no equivalent figure, no leader who combined the authority and the respect of the establishment with such empathy for the industrial immigrant working class and their concerns. This was made clear in the response to the tailors' strike that began on 29 August 1889. Chief Rabbi Nathan Adler and his son Hermann, who would take up the post on his father's death, were sympathetic to the plight of the Ashkenazi Jews of the East End.[21] Nathan Adler himself was an immigrant from Germany. But both Adlers were strongly conservative in regard to the social and political situation in East London, and regarded the strike of the Jewish tailors as a harbinger of anarchy and violence that would reflect badly on the community as a whole.

---

[19] Llewellyn Smith and Nash, *Story of the Dockers Strike*, pp. 148–149.

[20] Warwick Modern Records Centre, MSS 74/4/1/5, pamphlet, Ben Tillett, *Ben Tillett: Fighter and Pioneer* (London: Blanford Press, 1943), p. 7.

[21] In Nathan Adler's final years, when he was beset by ill health, his son Hermann took on the greater part of his duties as 'Delegate Chief Rabbi'.

Contrasting the tenures of Manning and the Adlers, and the differing political sympathies of these men, would suggest the efficacy of an individualising comparison to be drawn between the Catholic and Jewish leaderships, stressing the differences both of personality and of organisation.[22] On a purely personal level this has merit. Manning had a radically different attitude towards working-class co-religionists than either Adler. Structurally, there were intrinsic differences between the set-up of the Roman Catholic Church on the one hand and the Jewish authorities on the other. However, focusing on *wider* attitudes towards both the poor and radical politics held within the hierarchies, there are more similarities than differences. Manning was very much the exception. The rest of the Catholic leadership in the capital, and the Cardinals who would take up the role after Manning, were much closer in attitude towards that of Adler *père* and his son. Certainly no other senior member of the Catholic authorities commanded the affection Manning enjoyed among the London Irish working class. When Herbert Vaughan became Cardinal following Manning's death in 1892, his conservatism was far more in keeping with the direction which the Catholic establishment was moving towards, rather than the democratic and socially aware instincts of Manning.[23] Compared with his predecessor, Vaughan was unsympathetic to the labour movement. Although concerned with the spiritual well-being of the Irish faithful, he lacked the emotional bond Manning had enjoyed, particularly with East End parishioners. After Manning's death, Vaughan suggested that Manning's support for the trade unions had been a product of the onset of senility.[24]

The Jewish religious authorities, as represented by Hermann Adler, were also seemingly out of step and out of sympathy with the striking tailoring workers.[25] The men who interceded and attempted to broker an agreement between masters and striking workers in 1889 were from the *secular* Jewish establishment, most notably Samuel Montagu and Lord Rothschild.[26] Montagu, as well as being the MP for many of the workers concerned, was the founder of the Federation of Synagogues. This organisation had been formed in October 1887, established to bring a degree of unity to the numerous *chevrot* (small-scale Jewish places of worship) that had sprung up across the East End. Montagu had also founded the London Tailors' Machiners' Society

[22] See Daniel Renshaw, 'Control, Cohesion and Faith', *Socialist History* 45 (2014), pp. 28–32.

[23] Sewell, *Catholics*, p. 42.

[24] McCelland, *Cardinal Manning*, p. 146.

[25] *Jewish Chronicle* (22 February 1889).

[26] See Eugene C. Black, *The Social Politics of Anglo-Jewry, 1880–1920* (Oxford: Basil Blackwell, 1988), chapter 1, 'A Dramatis Personae', for portraits of the leading secular and religious figures in late nineteenth-century Anglo-Jewry.

in March 1886.[27] Montagu was closer to being a 'Manning' in the Jewish community than any of the Jewish religious leadership.[28] For Rothschild and other members of the Jewish aristocracy who concerned themselves in the matter, the strikes were very much a 'family affair', the outcome of which would reflect on Jewry as a whole, to be decided within the Jewish community and not by perceived outsiders. The *Arbeter Fraynt* on the other hand warned its readers against the palliatives to striking Jewish workers offered by Rothschild, Montagu, and the Anglo-Jewish establishment.[29]

The failure of the Jewish ecclesiastical authorities to intervene in the strike and effectively to delegate this role to the secular leadership of Anglo-Jewry can be attributed to a mixture of lack of influence and lack of will. There was a reluctance to take decisive action in response to industrial disputes within the East End community, as their Catholic counterparts had done. The differences in the responses were also informed by the radically different structures in the two hierarchies, and the relative intellectual prestige that they enjoyed. Hermann Adler was greatly respected as a pillar of the community, but not as a biblical scholar. The intellectual status enjoyed by Jewish religious leaders in Eastern Europe had been largely jettisoned by an English hierarchy attempting to create something approximating a Jewish version of Anglicanism.[30] This lack of authority was partly caused by the confused and self-appointed nature of the Jewish leadership, which contrasted sharply with the disciplined and clearly demarcated gradations of leadership to be found in Catholicism.[31]

The Catholic Church had a clearly defined hierarchy, which had existed for centuries and was international in structure. Below the Pope were the archbishops, below them various orders of clergy, at street level the priests and the congregations. On Catholicism, Charles Booth wrote that 'the leading characteristic is strength of authority ... the human conscience is placed in the hands of a priest, and each priest is a member of a highly organised and powerful hierarchy'.[32] The Jewish establishment on the other hand was self-appointed and relatively recent in formation: the BoD formed in 1760 and the United Synagogue in 1870. There was no Jewish equivalent

---

[27] Kershen, *Uniting the Tailors*, p. 132.

[28] Alderman, *Modern British Jewry*, p. 158.

[29] *Arbeter Fraynt* (4 October 1889) in Fishman, *East End Jewish Radicals 1875–1914*, p. 178.

[30] Rubinstein, *A History of the Jews in the English-Speaking World*, p. 63. See Alderman, *Modern British Jewry*, p. 38 on the responsibilities for dealing with the outside world assumed by the local Jewish religious leadership (*Landesrabbinat*) in the Pale of Settlement, and the failure of the English leadership to take on this role.

[31] Renshaw, 'Control, Cohesion and Faith', p. 29.

[32] Booth, *Life and Labour of the People in London*, Third Series, *Religious Influences*, Vol. 7, pp. 252–253.

papal figure whose pronouncements could not be challenged, either in Britain or on the continent. A rabbi might command a good degree of authority, and be admired as a biblical scholar, but this did not make his assertions or interpretations of religious obligations or practices beyond challenge or contention. Indeed, the ability successfully to contend and argue with one's instructors was praised in the Talmudic religious schools of the Pale of Settlement.[33] There was no infallible figure in Jewry, domestic or international, no comparable 'chain of command' that in London's Catholic community linked and connected Cardinal Manning and Cardinal Vaughan both with the Vatican and with the priest and his congregation in Bethnal Green. There was also the sentiment in the wider Jewish community that it was simply not the role of the religious authorities to become involved in trade union disputes, and that it was right to devolve responsibility to the secular leadership. Attempts by Dr Gaster, the religious leader of the Sephardic community, to involve himself in the tailors' strike were met with scorn in the letters page of the *Jewish Chronicle*.[34] A report to the United Synagogue in April 1897 reiterated this stance. 'It is not intended that the Board shall interfere in labour disputes, but simply endeavour to arrange [*sic*] petty quarrels between master and servant.'[35]

This belief that religious leaders had no place interfering in industrial disputes was shared by Jewish socialists. Woolf Wess, speaking at a meeting at Berner Street in the East End, condemned the 'interference' in the strikes by 'Chief Rabbis, Lord Mayors, Cardinals, Boards of Conciliation, and MPs', and demanded 'direct action by workmen themselves and through their organisations'.[36] In October 1890, *Commonweal* published a 'blacklist' of pro-sweating journals, including the *Banner of Israel*, the *Jewish Chronicle*, *Jewish World*, and the *Catholic Times*, with the comment: 'It is surely strange that the salvation of men's souls should be so closely bound up with the starvation of their bodies. Sweating and piety seem to go together nowadays.'[37]

---

[33] See Shaul Stampfer, *Families, Rabbis and Education: Traditional Jewish Society in Nineteenth-Century Eastern Europe* (Portland, Oreg.: Litman Library of Jewish Civilization, 2014), p. 157 on the autonomy and independence enjoyed by rabbinical scholars in the yeshivas of Eastern Europe, and the emphasis placed on independent thought, independent research and the ability to argue with one's teacher and peers, certainly emphasised to a greater extent than in the theological instruction imparted to young seminarians in Catholic institutions of the time.

[34] *Jewish Chronicle* (15 November 1889).

[35] Special Collections, Hartley Library, University of Southampton, MS 147, Papers of D. Mellows, Report of the Sub-Committee of the Special Committee of the United Synagogue, 14 April 1897.

[36] *Commonweal* (4 January 1890).

[37] *Commonweal* (11 October 1890).

Thus, preparing to face the challenges both of trade union organisation and socialism within working-class immigrant communities at the end of the 1880s, the Catholic Church entered the fray both stronger and more confident than its Jewish counterparts. The structure of the Church made it resilient to challenges and allowed it to be proactive in dealing with left-wing and Modernist threats to its authority. The sermons of the priest on the ground and the policies of the Catholic leadership were backed up by the support of a complex political and religious machine invested with the ultimate authority of the Vatican. This was support and sanction that no rabbi, English or migrant, in the East End enjoyed. Jewish religious authority and instruction in the capital was fragmented to an extent not apparent in Catholicism. The Jewish hierarchy in Britain had neither the political nor spiritual authority of the Catholic Church. It had forfeited the intellectual and biblical gravitas of the Eastern European religious leadership without being fully comfortable either in the secular position adopted by the BoD or the 'anglicised' religious authority of Hermann Adler.[38] These factors made the Jewish metropolitan leadership more vulnerable to left-wing activities in East London, and more aware of its vulnerabilities. It also lacked the sanctions that could ultimately be employed by the Catholic Church. This would become evident in the parallel emergence of Catholic Modernism and Liberal Judaism in the Edwardian period and the hierarchies' responses to these challenges.

Neither the Jewish nor Catholic communal authorities were against trade unions per se.[39] Both the BoD and the Church recognised the need for the collective organisation of workers, that bad pay and worse conditions for immigrants in the sweatshops and the docks fostered social problems that could injure the community as a whole. In the Catholic case this had been recognised by the Vatican in the *Rerum Novarum* of 1891. Samuel Montagu claimed that unionisation of the unskilled immigrant labour force would act as a catalyst for anglicisation.[40] Some form of trade union was clearly necessary. But these unions should be malleable, deferring to the communal leaderships, and, crucially, shorn of socialist ideology and perhaps the right to strike.[41]

The utmost sympathy must be felt for the East End tailors who have attempted to strike against the oppressive conditions of their labour …

---

[38] Stampfer, *Families, Rabbis and Education*, p. 164.

[39] See the *Jewish Chronicle* (22 February 1889), which urged working-class Jews to 'join a good trades union. There were already two Jewish trade unions established, but it was not by any means necessary that they should join only Jewish unions.'

[40] Kershen, *Uniting the Tailors*, p. 132.

[41] See the *Jewish Chronicle* (22 February 1889), 'those true friends of the working classes who had devoted their lives to a consideration of this question'.

An amelioration of the conditions under which the 'sweated' Jewish tailors slave is greatly to be desired. They must not, however, estrange the sympathy of the public with their unhappy lots by acts of violence. If these poor people are to be rescued from being the innocent dupes of designing men, some active steps must be taken to organise the workers into a Trades Union of an innocuous character – with the ominous word 'International' carefully omitted.[42]

This editorial in the *Jewish Chronicle* is instructive. It presents the Jewish workers of the East End as essentially passive, not involved in determining their own fate or in improving their own conditions. These are the 'innocent dupes' of 'designing men', agitators from outside the community, socialist wolves circling around the immigrant flock. The word 'International' was to be avoided, with its connotations of both transnational workers' solidarity and, crucially, *diasporic Jewish* solidarity, that English Jews, Polish Jews, or American Jews could share a class or economic bond rather than solely a religious or ethnic one.[43]

In the Catholic case Manning envisaged the trade unions, whose foundation and success he encouraged, as being on the model of the medieval guilds, 'societies for mutual protection and benefit, not political institutions', again shorn of political power and socialist ideology.[44] Young Irish men and women were also depicted as being 'preyed on' by a vampiric socialist movement, again seen as a malevolent foreign body threatening the spiritual health of the community, and taking advantage of the naivety of youth through dissimulation.[45] Far more preferable in the view of the Church were the church-based and priest-led 'friendly societies', firmly under the control of the hierarchy, the most significant of which was the Catholic Social Union (CSU) formed in December 1893.[46] Both the Jewish and Catholic leaderships desired what were for them the positive results of trade unionism. This was the union as the facilitator of integration and as a means of reducing class tensions in immigrant communities, without the potential political radicalism that could result from unionisation, in sum an emasculated ideal.[47]

---

[42] *Jewish Chronicle* (5 June 1891).

[43] See Ben Gidley's PhD thesis, 'Citizenship and Belonging: East London Jewish Radicals 1903–1918' (Goldsmiths, University of London, 2003), for discussion of the BoD's attitude towards Jewish transnational identity.

[44] McCelland, *Cardinal Manning*, p. 135.

[45] Joseph Rickaby, *The Creed of Socialism* (London: Anti-Socialist Union Publication Department, 1910), p. 7.

[46] See MacRaild, *Irish Migrants in Modern Britain*, p. 91 and Donald M. MacRaild and David E. Martin, *Labour in British Society, 1830–1914* (Basingstoke: Macmillan, 2000), pp. 129–130.

[47] Fishman, *East End Jewish Radicals*, pp. 137–138.

## Challenges to Communal Control

Irish involvement in radical politics was discouraged by the Catholic Church, in its most extreme form by excommunication, a weapon not available to the Anglo-Jewish leadership.[48] Irish involvement in the trade unions was accepted, albeit grudgingly. However, on a purely domestic level the adoption of socialism by a minority of Irish Catholics did not threaten cohesion or the influence of the Church leadership. In the Jewish community, on the other hand, socialists and anarchists appeared to present a very real and immediate challenge to the communal authorities. The BoD and the United Synagogue were being attacked on two sides in East London. On the one hand there were the independent *chevrot*, a challenge to religious authority, an alternative claim for the heart and soul of Jewish religious orthodoxy.[49] On the other were Jewish radical groups, who staked a claim for East-Enders' political loyalty. In the 1890s and 1900s, the question of who exercised control in Jewish East London, who truly represented the community, was an issue of paramount importance. Irish socialists and Nationalists might reject the Catholic Church and everything that went with it, but the possibility that socialism might supplant the Catholic Church as the primary loyalty for the Irish working class was a remote one. The Anglo-Jewish leadership, by contrast, were acutely aware of the precariousness of their position in East London.

This anxiety manifested by the BoD and the religious authorities over any attempts by the Jewish left to claim the right to speak for the wider community is illustrated in the Great Assembly Hall controversy of November 1890, a year after the conclusion of the tailors' strike. At the end of October 1890, a group of Gentile and Jewish socialists belonging to the International Working Men's Club, situated in Berner Street in the East End, had booked the Assembly Hall in Mile End for a meeting to protest against the Russian persecutions. The meeting had been given wide publicity, preceded by an extensive poster campaign and the distribution of

---

[48] The Jewish equivalent to Catholic excommunication is *Herem*. *Herem* has different levels of severity, from limited censure to complete condemnation. However, as authority was devolved to national and local Jewish leaderships in the early modern period, this movement of religious censure largely fell out of common use. Although, as discussed below, Hermann Adler certainly questioned the Jewish identity of socialists and anarchists, the Jewish religious authorities did not employ this against leading Jewish radicals in this country, even those socialists and anarchists who explicitly challenged and flouted religious laws. See Stampfer, *Families, Rabbis and Education* for discussion of *Herem* and its falling out of usage in most Jewish communities.

[49] C. Russell, in Russell and Lewis, *The Jew in London*, pp. 97–99.

thousands of handbills, as well as newspaper advertisements.[50] The event had been organised by the prominent Jewish socialist Woolf Wess, and was to be addressed by, amongst others, William Morris and Dr Edward Aveling, the partner of Eleanor Marx. On the Thursday afternoon before the meeting, however, Wess received a telegram from F.N. Charrington of the Assembly Hall, with the brief message: 'Use of Great Assembly Hall cancelled, Dr Adler repudiates on behalf of the Jewish people.'[51] Charrington had in fact received a delegation led by Chief Rabbi Adler and Samuel Montagu the day before, the Jewish leaders declaring that the meeting would do 'more harm than good', and further that the convenors of the meeting had 'no right whatever to speak on behalf of the Jewish community'.[52] Charrington deferred to the Chief Rabbi, stating that 'we, at the Great Assembly Hall, have always been very friendly with the very large Jewish community existing in the East End of London ... it is advisable to keep up that friendship and to make them our friends, instead of doing anything that would make enemies of them.'[53] What had brought about this last-minute intervention by Adler and Montagu? It was certainly not the essential sentiment of the meeting, to condemn the Russian pogroms. What raised the ire of the Anglo-Jewish establishment, secular and religious, was Wess's reputed claim to Charrington to represent East End Jewry; that the Hall was being booked by the socialists in the name of the wider Jewish community.

Charrington subsequently claimed that Wess had 'misled him' into believing that the socialist leader had communal authority. 'I do contend that I was right, when the avowed representatives of the Jewish people called upon me to disavow any connection with this meeting, and to suggest that the convenors had no right whatever to speak on behalf of the Jewish community, to refuse permission for the meeting be held in the Hall.'[54] The acrimony and recriminations continued. Dr Adler refused to receive a deputation led by Wess to discuss the matter, claiming that 'Jews did not want the intervention of Socialists, Nihilists, Revolutionists, and Anarchists.'[55] The *Jewish Standard* claimed that the cancelled meeting would have been counterproductive, that 'the presence of avowed nihilists and revolutionists in their ranks could only tend to embitter the Russian Government against the Jews, instead of doing any good ... And in any case,

---

[50] *Daily Chronicle* (1 November 1890).
[51] *Daily Chronicle* (1 November 1890).
[52] *East London Observer* (15 November 1890).
[53] *East London Observer* (15 November 1890).
[54] *East London Observer* (15 November 1890).
[55] *Weekly Times and Echo* (2 November 1890).

even with the revolutionaries removed, such a meeting would not carry the necessary prestige.'[56]

The International Working Men's Club responded in kind. Wess alleged that Adler had suggested that if he (Wess) would sign a paper pledging them not to hold the advertised meeting the Jewish authorities would reimburse the Club.[57] This alleged offer was refused, and the meeting went ahead on waste ground outside the Hall. During the meeting there was loud and frequent condemnation of Adler and Montagu for their 'unmanly and cowardly action'.[58] A resolution was passed, with barbs aimed directly against the leadership: 'Besides protesting against persecution by the Russian Government, we also have to protest now against those richer members of the Jewish community who always remain on good terms with the Russian Government ... They know how to remain on friendly terms with all governments, however execrable.'[59] As a footnote to the affair, Hermann Adler arranged an alternative meeting with 'respectable' speakers at the London Guildhall to protest against the Russian persecutions a month later, with a statement issued on behalf of his office signed by various Dukes, Bishops, and the Archbishop of Canterbury.[60] The whole affair illustrates the insecurity felt by both the office of the Chief Rabbi and the secular Jewish establishment over their right to speak for the wider Jewish community and the potential threat of socialism from within this community. The role that the Catholic Church assumed as communal representatives of working-class diasporic co-religionists, the hegemonic right to speak for the Irish proletariat, was never in this period challenged or contested in such an explicit manner as took place on the Mile End Waste.

A section of the Jewish left, the most radical socialist/anarchist contingent, based around the *Arbeter Fraynt*, went beyond contesting the communal control of the Jewish religious and political authorities and attacked the tenets and the traditions of the Jewish religion itself.[61] In March 1889,

---

[56] *Jewish Standard* (6 November 1890).

[57] *Daily Chronicle* (1 November 1890).

[58] *Daily Graphic* (3 November 1890).

[59] *Daily Graphic* (3 November 1890).

[60] *Jewish Chronicle* (14 November 1890). *Illustrated London News* (20 December 1890), in Anne Cowen and Roger Cowen (eds), *Victorian Jews through British Eyes* (Oxford: Oxford University Press, 1986), p. 127.

[61] See Thomas G. Eyges, *Beyond the Horizon: The Story of a Radical Emigrant* (Boston: Group Free Society, 1944), p. 75: 'To become a radical in those days, one had invariably first to abandon religious belief, to deny the existence of God. Then, as a matter of course, one became convinced of the uselessness of religious ceremonies, and then followed the abandonment of church or synagogue attendance.'

following a refusal by the Chief Rabbi to preach a sermon on sweating and unemployment, the *Arbeter Fraynt* organised a march on the Great Synagogue, an unprecedented action.[62] These radicals rejected any meeting between socialism and the Orthodox Jewish religion, or any compromise between the two. Those who maintained a religious faith were dismissed as 'Synagogue Socialists'. A correspondent in the *Arbeter Fraynt* attacked the conflation of political radicalism and religious observance: 'They talk of socialism and revolution, but marriage must be celebrated in a synagogue. For this one day they reveal themselves as false hypocrites.'[63] The actions of these groups went beyond editorials, or even parades, but manifested themselves in deliberately provocative acts. These included the 'Yom Kippur' picnics and balls, taking place on one of the holiest days in the Jewish religious calendar, a day of fast and contemplation. These displays alienated the majority of working-class East End Jews, who might be contemptuous of the religious and social failings of their West End leadership, but could not very well put up with such desecrations of Jewish religious law on their doorsteps. The Yom Kippur Ball, first held in 1889 in East London and then made an annual event, eventually led to violent confrontation between radical Jewish anarchists and socialists and Orthodox Jews:

> Thousands of Jews were walking along the streets, when they were met by a body of socialist Jews, who had driven a van containing food along the streets. All the Orthodox Jews were fasting and they at once resented this unseemly display. The socialists being driven into their club responded by throwing glass bottles out of the windows. Several cases of minor injury occurred and the disorder thus started to spread quickly ... Excited groups of Orthodox Jews were parading the streets threatening the socialists with dire consequences for their insults and stones were thrown at the homes of prominent socialists.[64]

For conservative journals such as the *Jewish Chronicle*, the actions of certain socialists effectively forfeited the protagonists' status as Jews, or their membership of the community. This denial of 'Jewishness' could be extended to *all* Jewish socialists, the majority of whom did not reject, at least so publicly, the laws of the Jewish holy texts:

> It is an odd sort of Judaism that publicly and deliberately desecrates the Jewish Sabbath by parading the streets with a band of music, by making inflammatory speeches, principally directed against the Delegate Chief Rabbi, and by assaulting inoffensive citizens and the police as an

---

[62] Fishman, *East End Jewish Radicals*, p. 165.
[63] *Arbeter Fraynt* (27 June 1890) in Fishman, *East End Jewish Radicals*, p. 195.
[64] *East London Observer* (24 September 1904), quoted in Bermant, *Point of Arrival*, p. 212.

appropriate method of winding up the day ... It is a fact that among the demonstrators on Saturday were men of *Jewish birth* ... But it is clearly idle to talk of these persons as Jews ... It is a notorious fact that they have from time to time gone out of their way to repudiate any connection with Judaism. They are men who determined to hold a banquet on the Day of Atonement as the most striking means of expressing their hatred and contempt for Jewish Law.[65]

Hermann Adler, in a speech given in Manchester, complained about press reports describing 'noisy blatant atheists' as 'Jews'. '[A]lthough by birth they might be Jews, they could not be identified with Jewish congregations.' He asked whether Gentile 'agitators' would be referred to in the press as 'Christians'.[66] Conservative elements in Anglo-Jewry, in denying that anarchists and Marxists from within the community who flouted and rejected Jewish religious law and Jewish festivals were in fact Jewish, were advancing a particular view of what constituted 'Jewishness' in late nineteenth-century Britain. This narrative simplified that complex and almost intangible confluence of religion, ethnicity, history, and diasporic belonging that defined Jewish identity through a particular political and social categorisation that stressed religious observance, respect for the hierarchy, and conservative politics.[67] In effect, Adler was conferring the status of social, cultural, religious, and political 'other' to those elements of Jewry that embraced socialism, at the same time as the Anglo-Jewish leadership sought to remove that status from the broader Jewish community.

There is little evidence for any equivalent public rejection of Roman Catholicism by Irish socialists and trade unionists, or at least not in such a dramatic manner as exhibited by the followers of the *Arbeter Fraynt*. A loss of faith in the majority of Irish Catholic cases was an essentially private affair, as indeed it was for most Jewish socialists. There were no demonstrations outside churches, no flouting of Catholic religious festivals and parades. The priest might be seen as a bastion of reaction by the Irish socialist, or an agent of anglicisation by the Irish Nationalist, but an open challenge was rare. Irish workers on the docks were not generally employed by co-religionists, and this limited to an extent the communal resentment and cynicism felt in contrast by both Jewish and English Protestant sweated workers. These men and women were often employed by a church- or synagogue-going boss, who, in the perception of the exploited, prayed and

---

[65] *Jewish Chronicle* (22 March 1889) (my emphasis).

[66] *Pall Mall Gazette* (25 March 1889). See Renshaw, 'Control, Cohesion and Faith', p. 27.

[67] See Douglas A. Lorimer, 'Race, Science and Culture', in West, *The Victorians and Race*, p. 15 on Disraeli's conception of 'true' Jewish identity – the 'Semitic Principle', which was 'spiritual, aristocratic and conservative, and opposed to pernicious egalitarian ideas'.

listened to uplifting sermons on a Sunday (or Saturday) and sweated their employees during the week.[68] Charles Booth commented that 'Amongst the Irish, rebellious blood turns not against both Church and State as in Italy, but against State alone.'[69]

Gender issues also informed these public or private confirmations or rejections of religious faith, with publicly expressed religious devotion demarcated by sex in diasporic communities to a large degree. In Irish neighbourhoods the maintenance of religious observance and church attendance, particularly of children on a Sunday and on religious holidays, was seen as predominantly the responsibility of the women in the family unit, demarcated in the allocation of roles as a female task.[70] Mothers were also expected, by both husbands and the wider society, to ensure the maintenance of correct religious belief by children, and religious instruction at church-based Sunday school. The public religious face of an Irish Catholic working-class family in the East End was that of the wife and mother, the woman in control of interactions with the local clergy, with the husband and father attending certain key events such as first communion, weddings, and funerals.[71] Orthodox Jewish religious observance, on the other hand, was publicly a male affair. The important roles in religious life in the community, both within and outside the family and in the rituals of the synagogue, were undertaken by men, with the husband and father assuming the public face of Orthodox piety.[72] Many women from Poland and the Baltic States did not attend shul, and within the Orthodox synagogue seating was demarcated by gender. However, this did not prevent Jewish women from enjoying a public as well as private spiritual life, as the transcripts available for the interviews carried out by Jerry White for *Rothschild Buildings* (1980) in the 1970s testify. The men and women being interviewed here recall Jewish mothers steeped in the knowledge of the scriptures and prepared to impart that knowledge to illiterate but devout neighbours, literacy being of a premium in the community.[73] In some cases,

[68] Brodie, *The Politics of the Poor*, pp. 83–84.

[69] Charles Booth, quoted in Raphael Samuel, 'The Roman Catholic Church and the Irish Poor', in Swift and Gilley, *The Irish in the Victorian City*, p. 278.

[70] Marks, *Working Wives and Working Mothers*, p. 19.

[71] Marks, *Working Wives and Working Mothers*, p. 10.

[72] See Amy Levy, *Reuben Sachs: A Sketch* (London: Macmillan and Co., 1889), pp. 48–49 for a description of gender roles in Orthodox Judaism in a late nineteenth-century fictional context, and Lewis in Lewis and Russell, *The Jew in London*, p. 205: 'whilst in most Church congregations there is a large preponderance of women and children, they are in a minority in the East End synagogue'.

[73] See Rothschild Buildings Transcripts – interviews carried out by Jerry White, held in Tower Hamlets Local History Library and Archives.

the premature death of a husband and father meant that the mother took on that public responsibility for maintaining religious observances and sensibilities, as recounted by Hymie Fagan, who would become a prominent East End communist in the inter-war period:

> After father died mother saw to it that I said my prayers daily and kept all the religious customs, for she was very religious herself ... What kept her going was her faith in God. He was her protector. She read Yiddish very fluently, and every Saturday afternoon she would read from the Old Testament aloud, and weep over the sufferings of her people, in which her own sufferings mingled ... Her faith was a solid rock.[74]

Oral history of the period immediately before the First World War also emphasises the importance of Jewish women in ensuring the upholding of religious observance and dietary laws within the domestic sphere. Nate Zamet, born in 1906, recalled:

> [It] was owing to the *frumkeit* [observance of kosher laws] of the women that things were going, because I know it was my mother who kept a kosher home ... had it been left to [the father] he would probably have smoked on Shabbos and that sort of thing, but with mum there was nothing like that about.[75]

Jean Austin, growing up in the Edwardian period, again stressed the importance of the Jewish woman in maintaining a kosher household. Discussing her parents' attendance of synagogue, she reminisced: 'My father didn't [go to synagogue]. No ... because he used to keep his shop open on Saturday, so he couldn't go to shul. My mother was on the *frum* [kosher] side.'[76] One of the key tenets of Orthodox Anglo-Judaism challenged by the Jewish Liberal movement in the Edwardian period was the dominance of men in the religious service and the separation of men and women in the physical space of the synagogue. There was no such spatial division between men and women in the physical confines of a Catholic church.

[74] Manchester People's History Museum, CP/IND/FAG/1/5, Childhood memories of Hymie Fagan (unpublished autobiography).

[75] Tape J.M./320, Interview with Nate Zamet, carried out by Debbie Seedburgh on behalf of the Jewish Museum, London, (unknown date).

[76] Tape J.M./378, Interview with Jean Austin, carried out by Debbie Seedburgh on behalf of the Jewish Museum, London, 17 May 1994.

## Socialism and Minority Religion: Ideological Interactions

### Socialism and Catholicism

Socialist thought and socialist activists interacted with minority religious observance on both ideological and grass-roots levels. Catholic and Jewish religious hierarchies also both attempted to halt efforts at religious modernisation, which embodied explicit or implicit challenges to the hegemony of the communal leadership, in their infancy. Catholic strictures against Modernism were far more effective than their Jewish counterparts' attempts to undermine and expurgate Liberal Judaism.

The dockers' strike of 1889, like the match-women's strike of the previous year, proved that trade unions formed by unskilled workers, with determined leadership and communal intercession and mediation, could achieve substantial and practical gains. Holding onto these gains was a different matter. In the docks especially, the 1890s witnessed a 'rolling back' by the docking companies of the increases in pay and hours won in the strike. The much-hated 'casual' system of taking on labour on a daily or even hourly basis through the 'gang-masters' also survived the strike.[77] As with the clothing sweatshop employers in the East End, the dock bosses rightly assumed that the dockers and stevedores, English and Irish, would not be able to maintain the vigilance and militancy needed to protect the advances achieved. But if gains were lost the unions remained and survived, and by the turn of the twentieth century trades employing large numbers of Irish Catholics in the East End were some of the most unionised in the capital.[78] The London Irish community produced some of the most notable labour leaders of the next few decades, the docks acting as a 'finishing school' for effective trade union leadership in the 1890s and 1900s.[79] Catholicism and trade unionism, then, if not sitting comfortably together, were clearly compatible. However, reconciling Catholicism and socialist ideology was a different matter. Throughout the period the Papacy had periodically issued edicts condemning forms of socialism. In spite of this, much time and ink were spent attempting to resolve this opposition, to prove not only that socialism and religious Catholicism could coexist, but in fact could not exist without each other – that Catholicism was intrinsic to socialism; that socialism was the ultimate expression of Catholicism.

---

[77] Fraser, *A History of British Trade Unionism*, p. 79.

[78] Connolly, *Labour in Ireland*, pp. 195–196.

[79] Connolly, *Labour in Ireland*, pp. 195–196. See Gearoid O'Tuathaigh, 'A Tangled Legacy: The Irish "Inheritance" of British Labour', in Lawrence Marley (ed.), *The British Labour Party and Twentieth Century Ireland* (Manchester: Manchester University Press, 2016), p. 26 and Virdee, *Racism, Class and the Racialized Outsider*, pp. 43–44.

This attempt to reconcile the two drew on both a particular interpretation of how various popes expressed Catholic policy on social issues and a Catholic-socialist historical narrative stressing the collectivism of the policy of the pre-Reformation Catholic Church. Attempts to create an explicitly Catholic socialism also coincided and overlapped with the Modernist movement within the Catholic clergy in Britain and in Europe, and the point at which the Modernist current transmuted into socialism is sometimes hard to determine.

Although throughout the nineteenth century popes had consistently issued condemnations of the left, individualism (and especially the perceived callousness towards the poor and vulnerable within capitalist society) had drawn censure as well. Leo XIII's encyclical, 'The Rights and Duties of Capital and Labour', of 1891, explicitly attacked modern capitalism.[80] The Papal attacks on the excesses of capitalism produced the movement known as 'Social Catholicism' or 'Catholic [or Christian] Democracy'. Catholic Democracy claimed that the tenets of 'Liberty, Equality, Fraternity, and Natural Right' were the natural inheritance of Catholicism rather than the post-1789 radical movements. 'Taken away from their [Catholic] pre-suppositions they are entirely void of truth or authority, and constantly tend to degenerate into the wildest licence.'[81] Social Catholicism accepted that the industrial revolution and the machinery of modern capitalism had created social injustice and that capitalism could be viewed as on some level 'ungodly', even 'Deistic'.[82]

Catholic intellectuals of the early twentieth century, such as Hilaire Belloc (better known today for his extremely grisly cautionary tales for children), resolutely opposed to socialism in any manifestation, viewed the effects of industrialisation and capitalism as 'an abomination which should vanish as soon as possible from the face of the earth'.[83] Belloc suggested that one disagreeable result of capitalism and the Reformation was an increase in 'Jewish influence', writing of 'non-Catholic societies of Northern and Industrial Europe, with their subservience to Jewish finance'.[84] The pastoral Catholic English past, with its homogenous ethnic population, was held by Belloc to be the ideal.

These intellectuals, whether socialist or social Catholic, drew on this strain of anti-individualism in the Church and used it to construct a particular

---

[80]  See *The Tablet* (23 May 1891).

[81]  Revd J.J. Welch, *Socialism, Individualism and Catholicism* (London: Sands and Co., 1910), p. 9.

[82]  Welch, *Socialism, Individualism and Catholicism*, p. 14.

[83]  McEntee, *Social Catholic Movement*, pp. 111–112.

[84]  Belloc, *The Church and Socialism*, p. 16.

narrative of the history of medieval society and the Reformation. This placed the pre-sixteenth-century Church as the bestower and arbitrator of social justice and social coherence, the centre of a pre-capitalist golden age, a period of small landowners and self-sufficient artisans. This was essentially the 'Merrie England' of the mainstream socialist movement as conceptualised by William Morris but with the Protestant Reformation placed in the role of villain. Protestant 'Individualism' had overthrown Catholic 'Collectivism' and so brought on the horrors of industrialisation and ruthless commerce. The Protestant 'work ethic', so vaunted in mainstream Victorian society, was depicted in this narrative as the oppressor of the 'small man', the farmer or the craftsman. It stressed the parochial care practised by the Church in the medieval period and the relatively high standard of life enjoyed by the artisan and the labourer. This tied in with the Catholic belief in 'Holy Poverty' and charity, that pauperism was a blessing that brought one closer to God.[85] Socialists diverged from mainstream Catholic thinking in their emphasis on the organised, politicised quality of such relief. For T.D. Benson, in his *Socialist's View of the Reformation* (1902), the actions of the Roman Church pre-Reformation verged 'upon Communism'.[86] The Revd Stewart Headlam, although (very) High Anglican rather than Catholic, similarly condemned the spiritual and economic selfishness of political and religious 'individualism' as compared with synthesised religious socialism in an 1895 pamphlet: 'Individualism in religion (Protestantism, Atheism, etc.) destroys the bond between man and man, making the believer otherworldly and inhuman, and the unbeliever self-centred and unsocial.'[87] Headlam concluded the pamphlet with the challenge to his readers: 'Is the reader of this paper a Catholic? Then let him ask himself why he is not a socialist. Is he a socialist? Then what hinders him from declaring himself a Catholic? The issues are clear.'[88]

The Fabian socialist and convert Robert Dell, writing in 1899, set English history in the context of a struggle between a Collectivist Catholic Church, for which the socialist movement had taken up the mantle, and an extreme Individualistic Protestantism/capitalism.[89] Dell stressed the 'rights of the

---

[85] In Chapter 5 of this book differing Jewish and Catholic attitudes towards poverty and the Poor Law are discussed.

[86] LSE ILP 5/1902/5, T.D. Benson, *A Socialist's View of the Reformation* (Manchester: National Labour Press, 1902), p. 6.

[87] LSE ILP 8/1906/25, Revd Stewart D. Headlam, *The Guild of St. Matthew – What it is and Who Should Join it* (London: Guild of St. Matthew, 1895) (reprinted 1906). See F.G. Bettany, *Stewart Headlam: A Biography* (London: John Murray, 1926), pp. 75–76 and 210–211 for discussion of Headlam's prolonged but never consummated relationship with Catholicism.

[88] Headlam, *The Guild of St. Matthew.*

[89] Dell was born in 1865, the son of a Church of England clergyman. He converted to

community' under Catholicism, the cooperative as opposed to competitive nature of agriculture and industry under the Church, and that society in this period was 'working for the common good'.[90] The Reformation, in this view of historical progress, was a 'great and terrible change for the workers'.[91] It was a 'tragedy' that had led to 'The commercial spirit [overthrowing] authority in matters of opinion and faith ... in which true religion perished and atheism rose amidst the clash of creeds ... above all, licence to a few to exploit, enslave and degrade the many.'[92] Luther, Calvin, and their followers were depicted as proto-capitalist exploiters, 'on the side of privilege and Mammon'.[93] Protestantism resurrected 'the brutal and lawless ideas of paganism ... once more applied to industry and commerce'.[94]

The simultaneous rise of Protestantism and the beginnings of capitalism were noted both by non-Catholic socialists and by non-socialist Catholics, the former of which proposed a cure based around socialist ideology, the latter around religious faith and piety. The militantly atheistic E.B. Bax declared that, 'as the religion of serfage [*sic*] was Catholic Christianity; as the religion of Capitalism is Protestant Christianity ... so the religion of collective and co-operative industry is Humanism, which is only another name for Socialism'.[95] For both Catholic and socialist intellectuals a surfeit of 'Individualism' was the problem, but while mainstream socialism looked to the future alone for the remedy, Catholic socialism looked at both the future and the past.

A critical question for Robert Dell and others was whether the Papal condemnation of radical politics extended to all forms of socialism, or only its most extreme manifestations. For Dell, in the early stages of his decade-long attempt to reconcile his Fabianism and his Catholicism, it quite clearly was the case that these edicts applied only to certain forms of socialism. He felt that Leo XIII's attack on the 'deadly plant of socialism' extended only to that form of socialism that held private property to be immoral.[96] This was not socialism 'as we understand it in England', but rather that violent, anarchist/communist strain to be found on the continent (a form believed by most

---

Catholicism in the early 1890s. He described himself as a Catholic 'not by inheritance or early training or habit but by deliberate choice'. LSE DELL 6/2.

[90] LSE DELL 6/1, Robert Dell, *The Catholic Church and the Social Question* (London: Catholic Press Company, 1899), pp. 21–23.

[91] LSE ILP 13/1907/13, H.W. Lee, *The First of May: The International Labour Day* (London: First of May Celebration Committee, SDF Office, 1907), p. 7.

[92] Benson, *A Socialist's View of the Reformation*, p. 10.

[93] Dell, *The Catholic Church*, p. 54.

[94] Welch, *Socialism*, p. 51.

[95] E.B. Bax, quoted in Day, *Catholic Democracy*, p. 166.

[96] Dell, *The Catholic Church*, p. 37.

moderate socialists in England to be on the decline in the early twentieth century).[97] He continued: 'Communism and Anarchism are in England almost entirely confined to foreigners ... "Catastrophic socialism" ... is now rapidly dying out, and in England is almost extinct.'[98]

> To apply the Holy Father's words to the entirely constitutional collectivism of the Fabian Society or the Independent Labour Party ... would be a distortion of language as monstrous as it would be to interpret the equally severe condemnation of 'Liberalism' to the Encyclical on Human Liberty as if it applied to Liberalism as it is understood in English politics.[99]

This statement stresses the dichotomy drawn by both socialists and their opponents between domestic and continental forms of radicalism – a safe, moderate social democracy qualitatively different from violent forms of communism, anarchism, and syndicalism, the preserve in Britain of 'foreigners'. For Dell, England was, historically and contemporaneously, the exception. Those from within the Catholic Church and Catholic intellectuals opposed to the confluence of socialism and Catholicism, however, argued that this was fundamentally a false distinction, that socialism of any kind, whether of the violent continental model or of the defanged British variety, was both immoral and impracticable.[100]

At the same time as Dell sought to effect a meeting of minds between socialism and Catholicism, a domestic non-socialist challenge to Papal authority from within the Church in Britain emerged, which was decisively suppressed by the hierarchy. This challenge took the form of 'Catholic Modernism', not a call for socialism as such but for a re-evaluation of what were seen as outmoded aspects of Catholic theology.[101] The movement had been building for some time, but first manifested itself in Britain in reaction to the perceived complicity of the Church in France in the legal persecution of Alfred Dreyfus and the subsequent fallout from that affair. Calls for change were led by the Catholic biologist St. George Mivart, who also argued for a greater amount of scientific rationality within the Church and an abandonment of what he saw as superstitious practices.[102] Cardinal Vaughan responded with a demand that Mivart sign a 'profession of faith' admitting his errors. Mivart refused, and was promptly excommunicated. He died soon after, and was denied Catholic burial. Eventually, a

---

[97] Dell, *The Catholic Church*, p. 37.

[98] Dell, *The Catholic Church*, pp. 29–30.

[99] Dell, *The Catholic Church*, pp. 37–38.

[100] See Best, *Why No Good Catholic can be a Socialist*, p. 10.

[101] Sewell, *Catholics*, pp. 43–44; Clyde F. Crews, *English Catholic Modernism: Maude Petre's Way of Faith* (Tunbridge Wells: University of Notre Dame Press, 1984), pp. 24–25.

[102] Sewell, *Catholics*, p. 42.

compromise was reached with Mivart's family, declaring that Mivart had been of 'unsound mind' when he had made these statements, and the burial took place.[103] The prominent Catholic priest and reformer Father George Tyrrell was also excommunicated after the publication in 1903 of his book *The Church and the Future*, an attack on the conservatism of the Catholic establishment.[104] Tyrrell had concluded his treatise with the provocative statement: 'That the Church of Christ should be governed by the methods of Russian autocracy and terrorism is an abuse that must revolt the conscience of every Christian who is even moderately imbued with the spirit of Gospel-liberty.'[105] The swift and decisive actions of the Catholic establishment to isolate and condemn these liberal Catholic reformers occasioned Robert Dell's final break with the Church and his attempts to reconcile Catholicism and socialism. Dell moved to France after the fallout from the Tyrrell affair, occasionally launching broadsides against the Catholic establishment, and in the inter-war period towards the end of his life devoted himself to warning of the dangers posed by Nazi Germany.[106]

The Modernist movement in English Catholicism could be viewed as roughly analogous to the emergence of Liberal Judaism during the Edwardian period. Both movements wished to reform their religious structures from within, to banish what was seen as outmoded superstition, to reconcile faith and science, to remove the barriers of language and ritual that were seen as preventing working-class followers from a true appreciation of religious practice.[107] The leading lights of Liberal Judaism were Lily Montagu and Claude Montefiore, both of whom had been raised in the heart of the Anglo-Jewish communal leadership. Unlike East End Jewish socialism, the founders of the Jewish Religious Union (JRU) came from the same social demographic as the West End Orthodox hierarchy they challenged.[108]

---

[103] Sewell, *Catholics*, p. 43. See correspondence between Vaughan and Mivart held at the Westminster Diocesan Archives (AAW/V.1/2/3–4) for some idea of the bitterness of the break between the two men.

[104] Hilaire Bourdon (George Tyrrell), *The Church and the Future* (Edinburgh: Turnbull and Spears, 1903). See Michael Hurley, 'George Tyrrell: Some post-Vatican II Impressions', and Gabriel Daly 'Some Reflections on the Character of George Tyrrell', *Heythrop Journal: A Quarterly Review of Philosophy and Theology*, Vol. 10, No. 3 (July 1969) for discussion of Tyrrell's faith and politics.

[105] Bourdon, *The Church and the Future*, p. 162.

[106] *The Times* (22 July 1940).

[107] For example, both Hebrew and Latin being learnt by rote rather than being truly understood, and the practice of religious ceremonies being held in these languages. See V.D. Lipman in *A History of the Jews in Britain*, pp. 90–91: 'Very few are capable of reading their prayers and less are able to understand what they read.'

[108] Lawrence Rigal and Rosita Rosenberg, *Liberal Judaism: The First Hundred Years* (London: Union of Liberal and Progressive Synagogues, 2004), pp. 11–13.

Under Montagu and Montefiore, Liberal Judaism went significantly further than Reform Judaism had in the nineteenth century, itself viewed for a long period of time by the Orthodox religious leaders as dangerously radical. To quote Endelman, 'Unlike Reform, Liberal Judaism broke root and branch with traditional Judaism, even its polite English form.'[109] Montefiore rejected the divine nature of the Bible, and the ritual laws, and the belief that the Jews were a divinely elected 'chosen people'. 'They were not a nation, not even a people, but rather a "religious brotherhood".'[110]

Within Liberal Jewish worship, class and gender distinctions were also moderated, and lacked the strict segregation of the sexes to be found in Orthodox synagogues. Lily Montagu, in her role as founder of the Jewish Girls' Club and later as a leader of the JRU, worked to transform religious faith into something relevant to the lives of young working-class Jewish women. These were women who had been excluded from the Orthodox religious mainstream by virtue of both social position and gender. As early as 1895, Lily Montagu had published a booklet entitled *Prayers for Jewish Working Girls*.[111] Liberal Judaism explicitly courted sections of Jewish society for whom synagogue worship had lost relevance, or who felt they had no role in Orthodox services, or were not welcome at them. It also displayed a realistic appreciation of the difficulties that religiously observant Jews of both sexes working in the tailoring and boot-making sweatshops faced in obeying the demands of faith.[112] Liberal Judaism drew as much opprobrium from the Orthodox Jewish authorities as Modernism had done from the Catholic leadership, but proved harder to suppress. At the first service of the JRU, with its abandonment of gender segregation, the *Jewish World* reported that men and women had sat together 'promiscuously'.[113] The Orthodox leadership, religious and secular, did not have the powers so effectively exercised by their Catholic counterparts to halt the Liberal challenge at an embryonic stage. Instead they applied social pressures, 'cutting' the leading figures of the JRU when encountered in society. Lily Montagu's father Samuel did not speak to his daughter for the last two years of his life.[114] Despite these attempts at ostracisation, Liberal Judaism survived. Into the 1940s, the debate carried on about whether marriages

---

[109] Endelman, *The Jews of Britain*, p. 169.

[110] Endelman, *The Jews of Britain*, p. 169.

[111] Rigal and Rosenberg, *Liberal Judaism*, p. 57.

[112] Ellen M. Umansky, *Lily Montagu and the Advancement of Liberal Judaism: From Vision to Vocation* (New York: The Edwin Mellen Press, 1983), pp. 122–123. One prayer published by Lily Montagu was entitled 'a prayer for those who are unavoidably prevented from keeping the Sabbath'.

[113] *Jewish World* (24 October 1902).

[114] Umansky, *Lily Montagu*, p. 111.

performed in Liberal synagogues could be viewed as legally binding in the Jewish community. Only in the post-war period was a reconciliation of sorts between Orthodox and Liberal Judaism effected, but the relationship continued to be an uneasy and uncomfortable one.[115]

By contrast, the Edwardian Catholic Modernist movement was so effectively halted in its infancy in Britain that it cannot be known if an English form of 'Liberal Catholicism' would have mirrored the evolution of 'Liberal Judaism'. If Cardinal Vaughan had been more temperamentally like his predecessor, an accommodation between conservative elements and the Modernists could perhaps have been effected, although the condemnations of the Vatican were so intense they could not easily be ignored. The rise of an inclusive Labour Party meant that the majority of left-wing Catholics could reconcile their religion and their progressive politics without an explicit adoption of proscribed Modernism. It was from *within* the Labour Party and the trade unions that working-class Catholics could use their influence both to amend and to discourage policies considered harmful to their faith and at the same time press for a more liberal and socially aware form of Catholicism. In its brief existence, Catholic Modernism had been very much a middle-class affair, with little influence in working-class Catholic neighbourhoods.

The structure of the Catholic religious hierarchy and the power, temporal and spiritual, enjoyed by the leadership allowed them to deal decisively with ecclesiastical challenges to Church hegemony in their infancy. Jewish religious worship, on the other hand, was significantly decentralised, with East End immigrant rabbis already in reality outside the writ of the BoD and the United Synagogue. Religious Jewry had already experienced the nineteenth-century schism between Orthodoxy and Reform, so that, beyond condemnations and a long-lasting refusal to recognise marriages solemnised in a Liberal synagogue, there was little the authorities could do. The Anglo-Jewish religious leadership found itself in an uncomfortable position by the end of the Edwardian period. It was situated between a Liberal movement that desired to update religious practice and accelerate the anglicisation and modernisation of religious Judaism, and a conservative immigrant Orthodoxy brought over from the Pale of Settlement, that believed that the Anglo-Jewish authorities had already gone too far down the road of religious compromise. Migrant rabbis also questioned the Chief Rabbi's position as a Talmudic scholar.[116] Catholic priests in the East End were by no means automatons, and they varied greatly in political stance and attitude, as well as in social and ethnic background. Nevertheless, the various Catholic churches located in East London and the parish priests were not competing with each other for the fidelity of their congregations. When Modernism did appear as a challenge, it was silenced by the Church leadership, whilst Liberal Judaism became a permanent feature of the Jewish religious landscape.

## Socialism and Scripture: Ideological Interactions with Judaism

In Israel Zangwill's *Children of the Ghetto* (1892), Pinchas, the archetypal schemer, chancer, and poet, a figure of fun speaking a peculiar phonetic form of English that Zangwill employs exclusively for him, persuades an up-and-coming Jewish socialist, Simon Wolf, of the *Arbeter Fraynt* school, to jettison his blasphemous language and attitudes. Pinchas instead suggests that they use the Jewish scriptures to win East End Jewry over to the cause. Pinchas himself addresses the crowd, and makes the following speech: 'Our great teacher Moses was the first Socialist. The legislation of the Old Testament, the land laws, the jubilee regulations, the tender care of the poor, the subordination of the rights of property to the interests of the working man, all this is pure socialism!'[117] He continues:

> Socialism is Judaism and Judaism is Socialism, and Karl Marx and Lassalle, the founders of Socialism, were Jews. Judaism does not bother with the next world; it says 'Eat, drink and be satisfied, and thank the Lord thy God, who brought thee out of Egypt from the land of bondage' ... My brothers, how can we keep Judaism in a land where there is no Socialism? We must become better Jews, we must bring on Judaism ... yes brothers, the only true Jews of England are the Socialists. Phylacteries, praying-shawls – all nonsense! Work for Socialism – that pleases the Almighty.[118]

The meeting ends in chaos and a brawl between Wolf and Pinchas over the smoking of a cigar on the Sabbath. The cynical nature of Pinchas and Wolf's agreement, and the fact that Pinchas, essentially a joke character (prior to his brief stint as a socialist he proclaims his intention to become Chief Rabbi), is employed by Zangwill to give the speech perhaps reflect the author's views on reconciling socialism and the tenets of Judaism. Just as a minority of Jewish socialists openly rejected the Jewish faith and flouted its laws, others went in the opposite direction and, no doubt with greater sincerity than Pinchas, attempted to prove either that the *Tanakh* condoned socialism or presented a template for the construction of socialism. This

---

[117] Israel Zangwill, *Children of the Ghetto* (London: J.M. Dent and Sons Ltd, 1892) (republished 1909), pp. 249–250.
[118] Zangwill, *Children of the Ghetto*, pp. 249–250.

was not the view of radicals alone. An article in the *Jewish Chronicle* of 2 May 1890 stated, in very similar terms to Pinchas:

> [Referring to Marx and Lassalle,] is it not more than a coincidence that they, the strenuous advocates of the rights of labour, should have sprung from the loins of men whose religious doctrines were saturated with a quick sympathy for the workman ... The Bible is at once the labourer's charter and his text-book .... There is no sacred book that evinces so lively a concern for the well-being of the labourer enjoined with so deep an appreciation of the nobility of labour.[119]

Politically, invoking the scriptures rather than trampling over their laws made sense in a Jewish community defined by the orthodoxy and religious faith of the new arrivals. This group regarded the Anglo-Jewish establishment as religiously lax, and had brought over from Eastern Europe a strict and rigorous attitude towards Jewish religious laws and the observance of the Sabbath. Socialists such as Morris Winchevsky quickly realised that Yom Kippur Balls and other provocations were counter-productive.[120] Yet within the atheistic Jewish socialist fringe there is little evidence of a change in direction, or any moderation in the name of political expediency. For the *Arbeter Fraynt* strand of Jewish socialism, victory was to be obtained through organisation of labour and revolution, not by winning elections. The fact that in the Jewish East End the bulk of the labouring class who needed to be organised were strong religious believers was not addressed. Socialists, whether atheistic or otherwise, were acquiring a bad reputation across the Jewish community for the provocative actions of a minority. The majority of Jewish socialists did not flout religious laws so publicly. Prayer in the synagogue and activism in the workplace sat comfortably for many working-class Jews, but this did not necessarily indicate an explicit synthesis of radical socialist politics and religious Judaism.[121]

For all of the debates taking place within the Jewish community over the confluence of Judaism and socialism, the bulk of the literature produced in Britain in the period attempting to bring together the teachings of the biblical scriptures and modern socialism was in fact produced by Christian socialists for Christians, rather than being directed at Jewish workers. The primary aim was not to reconcile Jewish socialists with their own religious

---

[119] *Jewish Chronicle* (2 May 1890).

[120] Fishman, *East End Jewish Radicals*, p. 140. See Vivi Lachs, 'The Yiddish *Veker* in London: Morris Winchevsky, Building a Broad Left Through Poetry, 1884–1894', *Socialist History* 45 (2014) for Winchevsky's attempts to reconcile socialist criticism of both the Anglo and immigrant Jewish religious leaderships and the religious sensibilities of working-class Jews.

[121] See Alderman, *Modern British Jewry*, p. 176.

teachings, but to prove to left-wing Christians that radical politics and biblical scripture were not mutually exclusive. This interest in the Jewish roots of socialism was partly a product of traditional Nonconformist sympathy with and regard for Judaism, a Protestant-Jewish nexus stretching back to the readmittance of the Jews in the seventeenth century.[122] The interests of the Jewish community and the smaller Protestant groups were often seen as converging; both were relatively small religious minorities, both were perceived by outsiders as embodying a particular work ethic, and were seen on the ground in East London as detached in class and social terms from the wider East End proletariat. Both Nonconformists and Jews were associated with temperance and moderation in respect to alcohol. Socialists from Nonconformist backgrounds inherited a positive predisposition towards the Jewish faith, just as they inherited a suspicion of Catholicism and 'Romanism' generally, particularly its manifestations within the Church of England.[123]

The pamphlets distributed by organisations such as the 'The Church Socialist League Library' and the 'Social Crusade Book Depot' in the Edwardian period drew on Jewish scripture and used it to critique capitalism and, as with Catholic socialists, the 'individualistic' spirit of the age:

> The ancient Jewish conception of the Kingdom of Heaven or theocracy involved a sense of democracy, of fellowship, of justice between man and man, of the value of the whole of life, material as well as spiritual ... It was this idea that dominated their revolutionary leaders, from Moses onwards, and wielded scattered tribes into a compact nation ... they [the Israelites] were divinely guided to realise that no nation can prosper unless it is based in justice (righteousness) and they early came to the modern socialist conclusion that justice is not compatible with private ground rents or private interest.[124]

J. Stitt Wilson of the Social Crusade Book Depot produced a number of pamphlets on similar themes. He begins the tract *The Hebrew Prophets and the Social Revolution* with an attack on contemporary religious hierarchies, Jewish, Catholic, and Protestant:

> The Bible is a dangerous book. I do not wonder that for centuries the ruling classes sought to keep it out of the hands of the masses. It is one of the

[122] Endelman, *The Jews of Britain*, p. 19.

[123] See LSE ILP 8/1903/60, C.B. Stanton, *Why We Should Agitate* (Aberdare: Haylings and Co., 1903), p. 11: 'the Church of England, with its Romish formulas, its priestly pomp and vanities, to me appears the very incarnation of hypocrisy; the bishops, vicars, with their fine fat livings, compare badly with the Man of Nazareth'.

[124] LSE ILP 8/1904/47, Conrad Noel, *Socialism and the Kingdom of God (Jewish Scriptures and Gospels)* (London: Church Socialist League, 1904), p. 3.

tragedies of history that this charter of human liberty has been perverted by the priesthoods of succeeding centuries, and made the bulwark of Social Injustice. These Hebrew Prophets were the Social Revolutionaries of their time. They defied kings, rulers, and priests.[125]

The Jewish prophet as proto-revolutionary is also stressed in this literature. 'These Hebrew prophets were social reformers of the most radical type ... They were the voices of Social Revolution in their day, according to its need.'[126]

Ultimately, the contemporary socialist movement was presented as the rightful heir of the Jewish biblical prophets. In *Moses, The Greatest of Labour Leaders*, Wilson declares:

> The work of Moses belongs to us. Eliminating those elements that are purely local and racial, and seeking for those essentially human and universal elements in the work of Moses, it is the Social Movement that to-day inherits the spirit that led the great Israelite from Horeb to the Court of Pharaoh. It is the Socialist Movement that utters to-day the modern cry 'Let my People Go'.[127]

In *The Hebrew Prophets and the Social Revolution*, he writes:

> [I]f you wish to see this passion for social justice, of which the Hebrew prophets are our great exemplars, sweeping over people irrespective of their creed, colour or nationality, inspiring men and women with the spirit of devotion to a great social ideal, leaping forward to capture political power in order to establish economic freedom and justice in social institutions – if you wish to see this as never before exhibited in power or sanity of programme, you must behold the Socialist Movement of the world.[128]

The attempts in this literature to bring together the scriptures of the *Tanakh* and socialism are not always comfortable, with occasional awkward analogies. Wilson describes Moses organising the Hebrews in Egypt into a 'vast labour union'.[129] The internal strife of ancient Israel is presented as a 'Class Struggle'.[130] The Ten Commandments are described as 'Social Legislation' and a 'Social Programme', that 'correspond with the movement

[125] LSE ILP 8/1909/85, J. Stitt Wilson, *The Hebrew Prophets and the Social Revolution* (Huddersfield: Social Crusade Book Depot, 1909), p. 1.

[126] Wilson, *The Hebrew Prophets*, p. 11.

[127] LSE ILP 8/1909/89, J. Stitt Wilson, *Moses, The Greatest of Labour Leaders* (Huddersfield: Social Crusade Book Depot, 1909), p. 12.

[128] Wilson, *The Hebrew Prophets*, p. 12.

[129] Wilson, *The Hebrew Prophets*, p. 11.

[130] Wilson, *The Hebrew Prophets*, p. 13.

of Labour to-day to Socialise Land, Capital and Machinery', and it is claimed that Moses organised 'the first General Strike'.[131] But these tracts were not produced for theological debate, but rather to stress continuity between Judaism, the early Christian Church and contemporary socialism, and to condemn conservative religious leaders for flouting or diluting the religious teachings contained in the Bible.

The pamphleteers stressed the combination of spirituality and materialism in ancient Judaism, of morality and practicality, a combination upon which the socialist movement should base its beliefs and message. Just as Catholic socialists like Dell chose to interpret the pronouncements of the Vatican as to some extent endorsing progressive left-wing politics, so these socialists quoted the biblical texts to create a basis of socialism acceptable to the religious believer, Jewish or Gentile. This adoption of the language of the scriptures to articulate the social issues of the day was not the sole preserve of elements of the socialist movement. William Booth, founder of the Salvation Army, employed scripture to powerful effect in his writings on the state of the poor in East London, and cultivated an appearance and manner appropriate to a biblical prophet.[132]

Antisemitism and xenophobia could also be framed in the imagery of Jewish scripture. William Evans Gordon of the BBL discussed Jewish immigration into the area in a volume entitled *The Alien Immigrant* (1903), which evoked ancient biblical battles in language calculated to inflame feeling in the area: 'The Christian fares as the Canaanite fared. He is expropriated. Chapel after Chapel has closed, many mission halls have been abandoned, and the congregation of the few that remain are dwindling every day.'[133] In a speech given on 24 November 1902, the Bishop of Stepney used the imagery of the plagues of Egypt to voice similar sentiments: 'In some districts every vestige of comfort had been absolutely wiped out, the foreigners coming in like an army of locusts, eating up the English inhabitants or driving them out.'[134] In both cases, the language used in describing this Jewish threat to the 'old', 'Christian' East End was deliberate. Evans Gordon drew parallels with the seizure of land and displacement of other tribes by the Israelites,

[131] Wilson, *Moses*, p. 16.

[132] Bermant, *Point of Arrival*, pp. 102–103.

[133] William Evans Gordon, *The Alien Immigrant* (London: William Heinemann, 1903), p. 12.

[134] Cosmo Gordon Lang, Bishop of Stepney, quoted in Evans Gordon, *The Alien Immigrant*, p. 12. See also Lara Trubowitz, 'Acting like an Alien: "Civil" Antisemitism, the Rhetoricized Jew, and Early Twentieth-Century British Immigration Law', in Eitan Bar-Yosef and Nadia Valman (eds), *The 'Jew' in Late-Victorian and Edwardian Culture: Between the East End and East Africa* (Basingstoke: Palgrave Macmillan, 2009), p. 73.

whilst the Bishop of Stepney used the imagery of plague and pestilence befalling a host society that had mistreated its Hebrew minority, as well as references to cannibalism.

The text and imagery of the biblical scriptures and the Jewish religious tradition could therefore be drawn on by a number of different groups. First, it was employed by different elements of the Jewish community itself. This was obvious in the *chevrot* and in the synagogues, but was also apparent also among Jewish radicals, those that the *Arbeter Fraynt* labelled 'Synagogue Socialists'. It was argued that the adoption of socialism did not mean the end of one's identity as a religiously observant Jew. Conversely, the Torah was employed by those within Anglo-Jewry, and the East End immigrant population opposed to socialist politics, to prove that socialism had no place within religious Jewry.

Secondly, the scriptures were cited by Christian socialists, portraying Moses as a revolutionary leader, Isaiah as a prophet of social change, and the jubilees a form of wealth-redistribution. Quoted in conjunction with the New Testament, this had a similar aim to that of the Jewish socialists, to prove to Christians that socialism would not mean the end of religion and Christian ethics, that in fact the triumph of socialism would be the triumph of Judaeo-Christian morality. The subtext to this was that the current Christian church hierarchy, of whatever denomination, were no longer worthy shepherds of the faith, a role which had passed to socialism.[135] The Christian clergy themselves used this language in their sermons on the dire state of class conflict and religious apathy of East London.[136]

Finally, the imagery of the Bible was employed by those opposed to Jewish immigration or the Jewish community generally. Resentment and hostility could easily be whipped up by selective references from the biblical scriptural texts to the 'chosen', 'exclusive' nature of the Jews and the displacement of other nations when the Israelites settled in the Holy Land.[137] For some antisemites, Jewish religious writing, again with selective and misleading quotation, was portrayed as a mandate to cheat and abuse Gentiles. Coupled with this was a denial in some antisemitic quarters of the existence of any true Jewish spirituality or religion at

[135] See Wilson, *The Hebrew Prophets*, p. 2: 'The shepherds have not only abandoned the sheep to the industrial wolves, which fleece and devour the people, but these shepherds openly defend the wolf in his depredations by appeal to the Word of God, which they are ordained to preach.'

[136] Seth Koven, *Slumming: Sexual and Social Politics in Victorian London* (Princeton, NJ: Princeton University Press, 2004), pp. 228–229.

[137] In their 'Introduction' to *The 'Jew' in Late-Victorian and Edwardian Culture*, Bar-Yosef and Valman discuss the British imperial view of themselves as a 'chosen people' and 'modern day Israelites' (p. 16).

all.[138] The racist writer and theorist Houston Stewart Chamberlain, the son-in-law of Richard Wagner, not only denied Jewish spirituality, but the Jewish origins of Christianity as well.[139]

Both Catholic and Jewish socialists attempted to prove the common ground, or even the inter-dependence of the strictures of faith and belief in socialist principles with varying degrees of success. The extent to which these efforts succeeded was influenced by a number of factors, most importantly the structures of the religious leaderships, their ability to silence internal dissent, and the class dynamic existing within diasporic communities. Attempts to prove that the tenets of minority religious belief and left-wing politics were in fact one and the same, as proposed by Robert Dell, foundered. In the Catholic case this was largely because of the intractable hostility of the Church hierarchy, domestic and European, towards any such confluence of faith and radical ideology. In the writings of Catholic socialists the aesthetic spirituality of Roman Catholicism and the rough and ready rural equality of the Middle Ages were contrasted with the materialism, rigid class structure and economic exploitation of the Protestant ascendancy. In comparison, those socialists, both Jewish and Christian, arguing for the ideological rooting of socialism in the books of the Bible, stressed spirituality deriving from scripture *and* a bread and butter materialism – the 'practical socialism' and wealth redistribution of the jubilee, for example.[140]

However, the religious hierarchies of both communities consistently rejected these analogies. More successful were attempts to suggest *compatibility* between minority faith and socialism, that the two were not mutually exclusive, but not one and the same. Yet even the possibility of compatibility between religious belief and socialism was questioned by the hierarchies, as Chief Rabbi Adler's Manchester speech illustrates, with the designation by communal leaders of socialism as an 'other', outside the communal narrative. For both Adler and Catholic anti-socialist writers, 'socialism' was a blanket term – the nuances stressed by Blatchford, Dell, and others between peaceful domestic manifestations and violent European counterparts were ignored. The responses to this question of the synthesis of religion and politics varied. The career of one man, Robert Dell, who in the course of

---

[138] See Herman, *The Idea of Decline*, p. 72 and Leon Poliakov, *The Aryan Myth: A History of Racist and Nationalist Ideas in Europe* (London: Sussex University Press, 1974), pp. 314–320 for discussion of antisemitic denial of Jewish spirituality.

[139] Julius, *Trials of the Diaspora*, p. 395.

[140] See Noel, *Socialism and the Kingdom of God*, p. 3 for calls for social justice in the Psalms and the pamphlet written by Daniel De Leon, *Socialism Versus Anarchism – An Address by Daniel De Leon* (Edinburgh: Socialist Labour Press, 1908), pp. 20–21 on the jubilee of the Old Testament: 'there was to be every fifty years a grand jubilee, there was to be a complete readjustment of property'.

two decades journeyed from Anglicanism to Fabian socialism to Catholic socialism to a form of disillusioned agnosticism, illustrates the diffuse and confused nature of the multiple interactions and negotiations taking place between religion and radical politics.

## Ideological Opposition to Minority Religion

Alongside a section of the left that wished to meld left-wing politics and faith together there existed a substantial current in turn-of-the-century socialism that viewed the deeply rooted Orthodox Judaism of the Ashkenazi community and the Catholicism of the Irish as an ideological impediment to class consciousness. In this diagnosis religious beliefs objectively supported and defended the status quo and retarded the immigrant proletariats' political awareness. Churches and the *chevrot* were perceived as a powerful magnetic force attracting and keeping hold of Catholic and Jewish workers to the detriment of socialism, their priests and rabbis exercising, in socialist eyes, an unhealthy influence, often directed against the socialist movement. Just as the minority communal leaderships viewed socialist propaganda as predatory, preying on the weakest and most naive members of the communities, so elements of the socialist movement viewed religion in the same light:

> A child or person intellectually incapable, either naturally or through ignorance or both, comes under the influence of the Salvation Army or the worst kind of Catholic Priest, it matters not which, is terrified by threats of the wrath of God into 'conversion', becomes the slave of General Booth or the 'Church', is warped mentally or morally for life, and in the worst case possibly driven to religious mania.[141]

It is the radical suspicion of the international nature of Catholicism and Judaism, the transnational structure of the former and the diasporic character of the latter, that the final part of this chapter is primarily concerned with. Socialist hostility towards minority faith was as uncertain and variable from group to group and individual to individual as those attempts to fuse faith and left-wing politics described above. Moreover, the socialist concern with the supranational loyalties of the religious 'others', and the supposed power concentrated in the hands of religious minorities sometimes closely resembled prejudices held by elements of the Victorian political establishment during the same period, and the nascent radical right that began to emerge in the twentieth century.

---

[141] *Commonweal* (April 1886).

The Four Internationals

H.M. Hyndman, writing in *Justice* in March 1900, headlined a lecture he had given previously and was now committing to print with the title: 'The Four Internationals: The Jews, the Catholics, the Monarchs, the Socialists'. Out of the four, only the socialists, for Hyndman, emerged with any credit.[142] The implication was that these four transnational affiliations were locked in a battle for British, or indeed worldwide supremacy. Hyndman had gained a degree of notoriety for his antisemitic pronouncements. These were combined with a strong streak of anti-Catholicism and antipathy towards the Irish diaspora in Britain both historically and in a contemporary context.[143] In this article Hyndman drew on a tradition of hostility and suspicion towards 'Rome' and 'Jewry' that was present in both the Victorian radical and conservative traditions. The nineteenth-century depiction of the Catholic Church as an international 'octopus' spreading tentacles of influence, or as a 'vampire', is strikingly similar to the portrayal of international Judaism in antisemitic circles from the late nineteenth century onwards.[144]

In certain quarters, Catholicism, 'with its Irish base and Italian [Vatican] allegiance', was viewed as an insidious foreign body, one that could never owe its loyalty entirely to England.[145] These doubts were accentuated by the nature of the Irish diaspora. Transnational Irish connections to the lands in which migrants had settled, 'a spiritual empire both in Ireland and across the seas', meant that the Irish were perceived as holding multiple national identities but a single religious one, defined by faith rather than citizenship.[146] The Jewish community in England, as well being part of a religious diaspora, was perceived as holding economic allegiances that stretched across national boundaries. The name 'Rothschild' was used both by the left and by right-wing antisemites in this period as a shorthand for 'international Jewish finance', and by Hyndman and some on the left for capitalism generally.[147] Just as domestic Jewry constituted both a small elite

---

[142] *Justice* (10 March 1900). See Hirshfield, 'The British Left and the "Jewish Conspiracy"', *Jewish Social Studies*, p. 97; Ward, *Red Flag and Union Jack*, p. 67.

[143] Hyndman, *The Historical Basis of Socialism in England*, pp. 174–175.

[144] Rubinstein, *A History of the Jews*, p. 8.

[145] Walvin, *Passage to Britian*, p. 56.

[146] Swift and Gilley, 'Introduction', *The Irish in the Victorian City*, p. 12.

[147] See LSE ILP/1898/50, Alex M. Thompson, *Towards Conscription* (London: Clarion Press, 1898), p. 11: 'the Rothschild makes his alliances with Rothschilds of other lands to keep John Smith in proper subjection' and LSE ILP/5/1912/1, Norman Angel, *War and the Workers* (London: National Labour Press, 1912), p. 37: 'the type of capitalists represented by the Rothschilds, Cassels, Sterns, Oppenheims ... and Bleichroeders – men whose activities disregard completely national and political divisions'.

and a large immigrant working class, so Catholicism seemed to exercise influence over rich and poor through a prosperous 'old Catholic' upper-class community and a clergy ministering to an Irish and continental European proletariat. For socialists concerned with minority religious loyalties, these not only challenged patriotism, but workers' solidarity. The parallel between international Catholicism and Judaism, and their supposed influence, was drawn in the (at the time) Liberal Party-supporting *Pall Mall Gazette*:

> Is there to be a Jerusalem question as well as a Roman question? ... For the simple fact is that there is a kingdom of the Jews already, just as there is a kingdom of the Papacy. But the one, like the other, is not national, but international; not local, but universal. The kingdom of the Jews, and the power thereof, is in every capital of the civilised world, just as the rule of the Papacy is in every country and among every people.[148]

As well as suspected conflicting loyalties, there was the belief that international connections were allowing Catholics and Jews to gain disproportionate influence over domestic politics, as evident in a *Justice* article headlined 'Catholic Supremacy':

> We do not believe the Catholic Church in Great Britain is gaining adherents ... but we do believe it is daily gaining in political influence. To begin with, was ever a Church so advertised gratuitously in Protestant countries? ... Catholics have political influence out of all proportion to their numbers. For some inscrutable reason, English statesmen are nowadays singularly deferential to the dexterous men of God who are so careful to pervade the best or worst of English society.[149]

This fear of Catholic influence was fuelled by the number of prominent converts to Catholicism in positions of power throughout the nineteenth century. In his frequently republished 'Who's Who' of Victorian and Edwardian Catholic converts, W. Gordon Gorman, writing in 1910, estimated that '29 peers, 432 members of the nobility, 470 writers and poets, 306 army officers, 64 naval officers, 192 lawyers, and 92 doctors' as well as 'almost 600 Anglican clergymen' had converted over the course of the last sixty years.[150] The figures can be taken as accurate, Gorman providing details of employment and status for each convert. Such a text could easily inflame anti-Catholic sentiment and feed suspicions of 'Roman' influence

---

[148] *Pall Mall Gazette* (3 January 1889).

[149] *Justice* (29 August 1903).

[150] W. Gordon Gorman, *Converts to Rome: A Biographical List of the More Notable Converts to the Catholic Church in the United Kingdom During the Last Sixty Years* (London: Sands & Co., 1910).

in high places.[151] After all, it was Catholics in Whitehall and in the high ranks of the military, rather than their co-religionists in Wapping and Bethnal Green, who presented a threat to those concerned with the power of the Roman Church. 'Their [the Catholic Church's] exercise extends from high statecraft, through the whole range of appeal to intellect and emotion … down to every form of guidance and control that can be exercised in the interest of religion upon men and women of all conditions', wrote Charles Booth.[152] But this was not the spirit in which Gorman presented his encyclopaedia of converted Catholics. In the preface to *Converts to Rome* he wrote:

> The publication of such a list speaks eloquently for the vitality of the Church. It may be regarded as a challenge by some, but nothing is further from the wish of the author. To all fair-minded men the movement towards the Church cannot fail to be of great interest. With the bigot the author has no concern except to remind him that in yielding allegiance to the Old Faith the convert becomes no less loyal to his native country. His Gracious Majesty King George V has not in the thousands enumerated in these pages lost a single subject; rather has he gained, for loyalty like all the virtues only grows stronger in the fuller life.[153]

But such assertions of loyalty to crown and country did not wholly alleviate the suspicion with which the Catholic Church was viewed, on both left and right. Under particular scrutiny were the Jesuits, whose membership crossed national boundaries, and who were widely perceived to be a shadowy but influential force in Catholic countries, and working for the restoration of the faith in non-Catholic countries. Their religious and political conservatism also made them a target for the left, as well as Catholic Modernists such as Father Tyrrell. A series of articles in *Commonweal* claimed that the Jesuits were infiltrating both the establishment and the revolutionary movement: '[They] send men into revolutionary parties, and into States that have thrown off the yoke of Rome, to urge rulers and rebels alike into deeds that may bring about their destruction.'[154] *Commonweal* and the Socialist League also accused the Jesuits of bolstering domestic antisemitism and opposing the entry of 'political refugees' who had 'been responsible for the diffusion of advanced ideas among the English workers'.[155] The depictions of Jesuits in

---

[151] Gorman, *Converts to Rome*.

[152] Booth, Charles, *Life and Labour of the People in London*, Third Series, *Religious Influences*, Vol. 7, p. 241.

[153] Gorman, *Converts to Rome*, pp. ix–x.

[154] *Commonweal* (19 April 1900). Compare with the twentieth-century antisemitic trope of the Jew as both capitalist and revolutionary.

[155] *Commonweal* (5 October 1900).

this polemic were strikingly similar to contemporary antisemitic portrayals of 'Jewish finance'.

Coupled with fears of undue influence was acute anxiety about what would follow if the religious minorities outside the Protestant national narrative ever gained political power in Britain. Dell, in his disillusionment, had warned of the consequences to British liberty if the Catholic Church ever re-established itself as the dominant force in British society.[156] However, dire prophecies of a future Catholic or Jewish dominion over 'native-born' Protestant Gentiles were generally a preserve of the anti-immigrant far-right that began to emerge in Britain during the Edwardian period, rather than of the left. This irrational fear was not dampened by the small number of Catholics and the even smaller number of Jews settled in the country. The idea of Jewish or Catholic 'supremacy' had such a firm hold on a particular anti-alien or sectarian mentality that numbers and statistics did little to shake it. The idea of minority groups, with very little actual power, gaining ascension over the host population allowed the imaginations of antisemites and anti-Catholics free rein, describing a situation that would never conceivably arise, but on to which every racist fiction and fantasy was projected.[157]

Beatrice and Sidney Webb at times made use of the imagery of Jewish 'control', and framed these ideas in religious terms: 'The Polish and Russian Jews have centred their thoughts and feelings in the literature of their race – in the Old Testament, with its magnificent promises of universal domination; in the Talmud, with its minute instructions as to the means of gaining it.'[158] *Problems of Modern Industry* (1898), co-authored by the Webbs, included a chapter on East End Jewry in which the language of conspiracy is again employed: 'He [the Jewish immigrant] suffers oppression and bears ridicule with imperturbable good humour; in the face of insult and abuse he remains silent. For why resent when your object is to overcome? Why bluster and fight when you may manipulate or control in secret?'[159] The portrayal

---

[156] Robert Dell, 'The Papal Attack on France', *Nineteenth Century and After* (April 1906), p. 642: 'Would there even be any toleration or religious equality if the Catholic Church had retained her hold on England?'

[157] Such anti-Jewish fantasies proliferated in the tense period in the run-up to the First World War. The popular writer William Le Queux, given to fantasising about London pogroms and foreign invasions, claimed that European Jewry owed its loyalty to Germany.

[158] Beatrice Webb in Booth, *Life and Labour of the People in London*, First Series, *Poverty*, Vol. 3, p. 181. See David Englander, 'Booth's Jews: The Presentation of Jews and Judaism in *Life and Labour of the People in London*', in Englander and O'Day, *Retrieved Riches* for an extended discussion of Charles Booth's magnum opus and the East End Jewish community.

[159] Beatrice Webb and Sidney Webb, *Problems of Modern Industry* (London: Longman, Green and Co., 1898), p. 43.

of religious Judaism by the Webbs was not wholly negative. On the same page of *Problems of Modern Industry*, the writers refer to '[the] perfection of family life, in obedience towards parents, in self-devotion for children, in the chastity of the girl, in support and protection of the wife', all as positive results of the Jewish scriptures.[160] But the use of the language of conspiracy and tropes of clandestine activity were unmistakable.

In the same way that religious prejudice, whether of the anti-Catholic, anti-Protestant, or anti-Jewish type, actually subverted racist sentiment through holding out the possibility of the group in question converting to the faith held by the other party, the basic socialist tenet of workers' solidarity and international brotherhood undermined antisemitism or anti-Catholic feeling. Any Jew or any Catholic could potentially become a socialist. What could be described as ethnic or religious prejudice on the left was generally not directed at the minority groups as a whole, but at what were perceived as 'bad' or 'undesirable' (from a socialist stance) elements of the ethnic group or faith. The difficult question was where hostility towards the institution or the occupation stopped, and where racial or religious stereotyping of the minority group as a whole began. In the Catholic case, the foremost of these 'undesirable' groups was the priesthood. The Catholic clergy was seen as a bulwark of conservatism amongst the Irish working class, and a parasitical stratum of 'non-producers'. 'The claims and prescriptions of the Roman priesthood (there are of course individual exceptions) are hostile to almost every movement for the political and social emancipation of the people.'[161] They had also been a target throughout the nineteenth century for sectarian attacks based around sexuality. The celibacy of the Catholic priesthood had been depicted by anti-Catholic 'penny dreadful' publications throughout the Victorian period as a cover for seduction of female confessors or pederasty. The Old Catholic upper class meanwhile was depicted as 'unmanly' and 'effeminate'. This literature frequently recounted the supposed exploits of priests, monks, and nuns within their religious orders.[162] The historian Denis G. Paz located this anti-Catholicism as a social safety-valve in wider Victorian society for repressed sexuality: 'There can be no doubt that some male anti-Catholics found in this [sexualised literature] a godly, uplifting and acceptable way of consuming pornography.'[163] Both Paz and the historians of the Irish diaspora, Swift and Gilley, have identified priests and nuns as pre-eminent social and sexual 'others' and outsiders in mid-Victorian

---

[160] Webb and Webb, *Problems of Modern Industry*, p. 43.

[161] *Labour Leader* (15 May 1908).

[162] D.G. Paz, *Popular Anti-Catholicism in Mid-Victorian England* (Stanford, Calif.: Stanford University Press, 1992), p. 62.

[163] Paz, *Popular Anti-Catholicism in Mid-Victorian England*, pp. 275–276.

Britain, with the clergy depicted as either sexually emasculated or a sexual threat, in either case a challenge to robust and 'normal' Victorian Anglican heterosexuality.[164]

The Jesuits, the targets for much anti-Catholic opprobrium, sexual or otherwise, were explicitly a transnational organisation, as discussed above. Conspiracy theories would prove durable and long-lasting; the death of Edward VII in 1910 was blamed in some sectarian quarters on Catholic poisoners acting upon the orders of the international Roman Catholic Church. This drew on another popular narrative of the time that referred back to the activities of the Borgias and other Italian ruling families with links to the Renaissance Vatican that had an inclination towards despatching enemies with poison.[165]

In their attacks on the Catholic hierarchy, and in particular the Jesuits, socialist groups could call on the imagery of priestly perversion and corruption of the young. An 1890 attack on organised religion in *Commonweal* concluded with the following paragraph: 'The writer remembers, with disgust, that he was taught in a Catholic school never to rebel against any laws, or anyone in authority, however palpably unjust they might be, because there was such merit in obeying bad laws and bad governors.'[166] But one article, the last in a series of attacks on the Jesuits by the *Commonweal* between April 1900 and October 1902, went beyond attacking Catholic education for its collusion with the status quo and discussed in detail allegations of the sexual abuse of the young by priests in England and France. It concluded:

> Why do Clericals and Jesuits defend these vices? Because they know that men addicted to them are emotional, unstable and fall an easy prey to their wiles ... Celibate priests are also very prone to them. There is hardly a month passes, in England, without some priest getting 'time' through these cases, and for one that appears before the courts, hundreds are 'hushed up' ... These men are worse than ordinary murderers who slay the body. They corrupt and ruin utterly God-like reason and imagination in the young ... *And it is to men like these a reactionary Government, placed in power by their infernal intrigues would hand over your sons and daughters to be 'educated!'*[167]

---

[164] See Paz, *Popular Anti-Catholicism in Mid-Victorian England*; E.H. Norman, *Anti-Catholicism in Victorian England* (London: George Allen & Unwin, 1968), p. 14; Swift and Gilley, 'Introduction', *The Irish in the Victorian City*, p. 8.

[165] J.E.B. Munson, 'A Study of Nonconformity in Edwardian England as Revealed by the Passive Resistance Movement against the 1902 Education Act' (DPhil thesis, University of Oxford, 1973), p. 370.

[166] *Commonweal* (15 November 1890).

[167] *Commonweal* (October 1902) (my emphasis).

This article was published in the midst of the ongoing debate on elementary secular education, a movement that the socialist parties and trade unions were generally supportive of and the Catholic Church resolutely opposed. *Commonweal* was largely sympathetic to religious and ethnic minorities labouring under the oppression of capitalism, Tsarism, or colonialism, but viewed the official institutions of minority faith, in particular the Jesuits, as both reactionary and conspiratorial. Whilst the prejudices against both Jews and Catholics examined above could not be described as symbiotic, when one was prevalent, in a period of national crisis or extreme xenophobic sentiment such as the Napoleonic Wars or the late-Edwardian period, the other was likely to come to the surface as well. Although the British socialist movement(s) almost across the board rejected the most lurid aspects of these racial and religious conspiracy theories, they too could make use in rhetoric and discussion of the tropes of an international and influential Jewish or Catholic religious and political cabal. In *Socialism: A Reply to the Pope's Encyclical* (1895), Robert Blatchford drew a distinction between the domestic clergy and the international structure and leaderships of the Church:

> I have often met the Catholic priests and sisters, and I believe them to be sincere and charitable people. I have often met them in the slums engaged in works of mercy; I have met them in Ireland fighting for the people. I am satisfied that they are the most devoted and the most unselfish of all clergymen; but we must have justice, and we must have truth, and the Pope's message is neither true nor just.[168]

Nevertheless, as the representative of the power structure on the ground in East London, the parish priest attracted a share of the criticism from the socialist movement aimed at his international and domestic superiors.[169]

Aside from the most militantly anti-religious groups, the mainstream socialist movement declared itself indifferent to the theological and moral advantages of one religious faith over another, or of religion over atheism or agnosticism. *Commonweal* and the Socialist League attacked elements of the clergy, but not the faithful congregations being 'duped'. *Justice* and the SDF hinted darkly at 'Catholic supremacy' and 'political influence', but this influence was manifestly not wielded by the Irish or Italian working class in East London. Nevertheless, the line between principled ideological opposition to Catholic religious tenets and hostility towards Catholics themselves was often blurred.[170] This was also true in relation to separating

---

[168] LSE ILP 8/1895/9, Robert Blatchford, *Socialism: A Reply to the Pope's Encyclical* (London: Clarion Press, 1895), p. 16.

[169] *Justice* (22 July 1911).

[170] Paz, *Popular Anti-Catholicsm*, p. 26.

socialist hostility (from outside the Jewish community rather than that
of Jewish atheistic socialists themselves) towards Judaism as a faith from
hostility towards the Jewish community generally. Secular antagonism
towards the tenets of a minority faith could easily become ethnic antipathy
against a minority community, and it was not clear at what point the one
transmogrified into the other. This was particularly the case for Jewish and
Irish diasporic communities, in which ethnic and religious belonging were
bound tightly together in a complex web of multiple identities.

Left-wing hostility towards religion also tended to view immigrants
themselves as passive receptacles unquestioningly absorbing the teachings of
their communal and religious leaders. The migrant workers were portrayed
as politically unaware and spiritually naive, and in need of being weaned
off religious influences. In fact, working-class migrant religious faith in
East London, and the relationship between leaderships and worshippers,
formed a reciprocal process, with immigrant religious belief often eclipsing
in fervency that of the communal leaderships, and their structures and forms
of religious worship arising from the grass roots. This relationship between
hierarchies and migrant groups in the East End will now be considered. We
will examine the common ground held by the Catholic and Jewish communal
authorities as they struggled to weather challenges to their authority not
only from socialists but also minority nationalists, Protestant missionaries,
Liberal educational reformers, Tory anti-immigrant campaigners, and the
wider secular culture of working-class London.

# 4

# Concerns of the Communal Leaderships

The Catholic religious hierarchy and the Ashkenazi Jewish secular and denominational leaderships shared common concerns and apprehensions over the direction that communal politics in the East End was taking. These fears were accentuated by the strikes of 1889 and the corresponding growth in working-class militancy. However, distrust of socialism was not the only concern that the two leaderships had in common. With respect to education, to dealing with wayward youth, to language, and to the preservation of a minority culture, the issues confronting the upper echelons of the Catholic Church and the Jewish authorities were strikingly similar. Both were aware of their vulnerable positions in wider English society, and the dual imperative simultaneously to maintain a minority religious faith whilst encouraging social integration in other fields. The hierarchies were conscious that socialism was not the only distraction. As well as the lure of the political left, evangelical Protestantism was seen as a threat, as was, conversely, the overt religious orthodoxy and decentralised forms of worship that Jewish and Irish immigrants had brought from the countries they had left.

Perhaps the greatest challenge for the hierarchies, more so than either Protestantism or left-wing political involvement, was religious apathy and assimilation of the young into a wider working-class culture with the pleasures and the temptations that that society presented. As Andrew Godley wrote, referring to Jewish youth in an East End context: 'The younger immigrants ... rather looked at the world around them and, not surprisingly ... they liked what they saw.'[1] This book will now examine the efforts of the Catholic and Jewish leaderships to maintain control, facilitate cohesion, and promote a particular form of anglicisation and approved acculturation within East End communities. There were multiple confluences between two hierarchies that were separated by religious profession and practice.

[1] Godley, *Jewish Immigrant Entrepreneurship in New York and London*, p. 109.

These communal bodies differed radically in organisational structure, but their attitudes towards working-class migrant co-religionists were similar. Indeed, the ways in which the Jewish metropolitan leadership attempted to maintain influence over the new East End Jewish populations from 1881 onwards followed closely the strategies adopted by the Catholic Church regarding the presence of the Irish diaspora of the generation before. But before comparing the agendas and actions of the hierarchies it is worth first analysing the interactions taking place between the minority communal leaderships in the period and the issues that united and divided the Catholic Church and its Jewish religious and secular counterparts.

## Catholic–Jewish Relations: The Hierarchies

A distinction should first be drawn when discussing the relationship between the Catholic Church and Anglo-Jewry between the attitudes of domestic English Catholicism towards Judaism and the Jewish community, and that held by the Vatican. The upper echelons of the English hierarchy were largely cordial towards or at least tolerant of assimilated Anglo-Jewry, recognising both the common concerns held and a common social demographic origin among the leaderships. These hierarchies were upper middle-class, generally English-born, and university educated.[2] The class backgrounds and formative experiences of the men who staked a claim to represent the Catholic and Jewish communities would be a key factor in determining the similar concerns held by both hierarchies over the moral and political direction that the Jewish and Irish Catholic proletariats were taking. The position of the Papacy on Catholic–Jewish relations in the nineteenth and early twentieth centuries was rather more ambiguous.

Catholic–Jewish hierarchical interactions were perhaps at their warmest during the latter years of the tenure of Cardinal Manning as leader of the English Catholic Church. Manning had frequently expressed public admiration for Jewish philanthropy among the very poor, moral examples that should be noted, he suggested, by wealthier Catholic families. For the Cardinal, piety was not sufficient – it must be coupled with practical assistance, with measurable results. In a sarcastic aside, Manning commented: 'The Jews are taking better care of their working girls in the East End than we are. What are our people doing? Oh, I forget, they have no time. They are examining their consciences or praying ... for success in finding a really satisfactory maid.'[3]

---

[2] See Benjamin J. Elton, *Britain's Chief Rabbis and the Religious Character of Anglo-Jewry, 1880–1970* (Manchester: Manchester University Press, 2009), p. 13.

[3] McEntee, *The Social Catholic Movement*, p. 38.

In the early 1880s, Manning had condemned the Russian and Romanian pogroms, and denounced and fully refuted the blood libel accusations that surfaced sporadically in Catholic countries such as Austria and Poland. Manning's forthright and explicit condemnation of continental antisemitism was recognised by Chief Rabbi Adler and the Jewish leadership. In an address to the Cardinal by a delegation of leading British Jews in October 1890 the Chief Rabbi lauded Manning thus:

> When a persecution, great and terrible, came upon our unhappy brethren in Russia, you were pre-eminent among those who lifted up their voices against outrage and oppression, and you gave utterance to your sympathy in words aglow with brotherly love and pity ... By your enthusiastic pleading for justice and humanity, by your noble denunciation of religious intolerance ... you have proved yourself a Minister of Religion in the highest and holiest sense of the term.[4]

In his reply, Manning made explicit what he considered the spiritual bonds between Catholicism and Judaism, stating: 'I should not be true to my own faith if I did not venerate yours.' 'There are', he continued, 'only three indestructible elements in the history of man: the People and Faith of Israel; the Catholic Church, sprung from it; and the world which has persecuted both.'[5] Manning drew a comparison between antisemitism on an international level and the historical domestic campaigns against the Roman Catholic Church – between privations suffered by Jews in the Pale of Settlement and Catholics in both Ireland and Poland.[6] Other contemporary Catholic writers echoed Manning's belief in a fundamental spiritual debt owed to the Jewish faith by Christianity. In an article discussing the appointment of the first Jewish Chief Magistrate of London that appeared in the *Catholic Household*, the correspondent wrote approvingly: 'We Catholics have indeed many things which should make us gentle and tolerant of our Jewish brethren, one is that through them we trace our way step by step back to all the glorious prophets and patriarchs whom we and they equally reverence.'[7] In a letter to Sir John Simon, Manning described the Jews as 'a race with a sacred history of nearly four thousand years ... visibly reserved for a future of signal mercy.'[8]

---

[4] London Metropolitan Archives, ACC/3121/G/01/001/003, Board of Deputies of British Jews, Annual Report, April 1891.

[5] London Metropolitan Archives, ACC/3121/G/01/001/003, Board of Deputies of British Jews, Annual Report, April 1891.

[6] Bornstein, *Colors of Zion*, p. 124.

[7] *Catholic Household*, quoted in the *Jewish World* (22 November 1889).

[8] McEntee, *The Social Catholic Movement*, p. 88.

The Socialist League journal, *Commonweal*, had its own view of the close relationship between Manning and the BoD, and the agendas behind it. In an editorial headed 'Cardinal Manning and the Jews', and with an ironic opening biblical reference, *Commonweal* framed the October 1890 meeting in the language of reactionary conspiracy:

> Surely the Millennium has come at last, with its lion lying down with its lamb. The affecting spectacle of Cardinal Manning being presented with an address by the arch enemies of his creed and Lord would lead one to think so. This remarkable incident has no parallel in history. On the contrary, the Catholics of the Middle Ages would have thought it an indelible disgrace to allow a Jew to eat at the same table ... What is the cause of this great change? A common danger, a common enemy to resist ... This, we are told, is the age of religious toleration; in other words, the age of shame and hypocrisy.[9]

The writer continued, with more than a hint of antisemitism: 'Does this not prove that intrinsically there is only one religion, i.e. that of money-getting, and that Commercialism had Judaised the so-called Christians of today?'[10] For *Commonweal*, friendly relations between the Cardinal and the Chief Rabbi were a cynical tactical manoeuvre to retard the political progress of the immigrant working class. This dismissal of all local communal religious bodies, Jewish, Catholic, or Protestant, and the motives behind inter-communal religious solidarity as stressed by bourgeois leaderships, was also the position held by militantly atheistic Jewish radical organisations such as the *Arbeter Fraynt* group.

Manning's close relationship with the Jewish establishment in London was not wholly sustained by his successors, Cardinals Vaughan and Bourne. Nevertheless, respect and regard between the leaderships was maintained. Vaughan, in his tenure as Bishop of Salford, had enjoyed amicable relations with Manchester's Jewish community and their Chief Rabbi, the Revd Dr Salomon.[11] He continued to do so with the leaders of London Anglo-Jewry on becoming Cardinal of Westminster. Vaughan was, as Manning had been, a contributor to the Mansion House fund established in support of the victims of the Russian pogroms.[12] But this relationship was complicated

---

[9] *Commonweal* (15 November 1890).

[10] *Commonweal* (15 November 1890).

[11] *Manchester Courier* (26 June 1903).

[12] William D. Rubinstein and Hilary L. Rubinstein, *Philosemitism: Admiration and Support in the English-speaking World for Jews, 1840–1939* (Basingstoke: Macmillan, 1999), p. 43. See William Kenefick, 'Jewish and Catholic Irish Relations: The Glasgow Waterfront', in David Cesarani and Gemma Romain (eds), *Jews and Port Cities, 1590–1990: Commerce, Community and Cosmopolitanism* (London: Vallentine Mitchell, 2006) for discussion of the reaction of the Scottish Catholic Church to the Russian pogroms.

by the changing position towards Jewry held by the Vatican, which veered between tolerance, ambiguity, and at times guarded hostility. The complicated and factional nature of Papal politics caused further confusion, with various cardinals and clerics making contradictory statements on the official Catholic 'position' with regard to European Jewry.

In the period under discussion, three issues caused particular concern for both the Jewish leadership and elements of the domestic Catholic Church, as well as a degree of embarrassment for the latter. First, the Church's position on the Dreyfus affair, which over the course of the 1890s grew from a localised miscarriage of justice in the French military to a Europe-wide scandal. A significant number (but by no means the entirety) of the French Catholic clergy had sided with the anti-*Dreyfusards*.[13] Secondly, the veracity of the recurring blood libel made against Jewish communities across Central and Eastern Europe. Finally, there was the conflation by some in the Catholic hierarchy of 'Jews' with anarchists, socialists, and revolutionaries of all kinds. There was no consistent Vatican 'line' on these three points, but the fact that the Papacy did not explicitly disavow these various claims caused concern not only for Jewish bodies but for Catholic liberals and Modernists. It was the Dreyfus affair, after all, that had acted as the catalyst for the excommunication of both St. George Mivart and George Tyrrell, and the disillusionment of Robert Dell. In a letter to *The Times* of 17 October 1899, Mivart publicly condemned the Vatican's silence on the guilt or innocence of Dreyfus, and the detrimental effects it was having on Catholicism, concluding: 'No trial of any other Jew has had such world-wide consequences since that of Christ.'[14] This letter precipitated the exchange of correspondence between Mivart and Cardinal Vaughan that ended with Mivart's excommunication. Vaughan's lack of a firm position on the Dreyfus affair was noted in his obituary in *The Times*: 'in his utterances ... he gave the impression of being driven into a compromise in which he mingled semi-apology for his brethren and his personal belief in the innocence of the unhappy victim of anti-Semitism.'[15]

Senior members of the European Catholic clergy occasionally expressed anti-Jewish opinions, spoken or in print. Sometimes there was confusion whether the sentiments were intended or not, or endorsed by the hierarchy. In a foreword to an 1889 French antisemitic diatribe repeating the blood

---

[13] Vicki Caron, 'Catholic Political Mobilization and Anti-Semitic Violence in Fin-de-Siècle France: The Case of the Union Nationale', *Journal of Modern History*, Vol. 81, No. 2 (June 2009), pp. 338–341.

[14] Westminster Diocesan Archives, AAW/V.1/2/1a, Extract from Dr Mivart's letter to *The Times* (17 October 1899).

[15] *The Times* (22 June 1903).

libel, the notorious author Edouard Drumont claimed that: 'Cardinal Rampolla [had] publicly written to the author, telling him of the joy of his Holiness [Leo XIII] at having received the book in question' on the 'horrible customs of the "Rabbinical Jews"'.[16] This controversy led to an exchange of correspondence between Adler and Manning, resulting in a letter by the latter to the *Jewish Chronicle*. Manning accused Drumont of lying in claiming the approval of Cardinal Rampolla and the Pope for the work, suggesting that the response received by Drumont was the standard one sent to all authors before the monograph had actually been read.[17] The *Jewish Chronicle*, in an editorial, voiced the need for the Pope to issue 'as clear a denunciation of the Blood Accusation as was given by some of his predecessors', that 'his Holiness ... declare to the world in unequivocal terms that there exists not the slightest foundation for the "blood" calumny.'[18] The English Catholic clergy could reassure their Jewish counterparts that no insult or slander was intended, but fears and suspicions of the position that the Vatican took on such issues remained. In 1901, it was reported that in an address by the Pope to a group of bishops in Southern Italy, the Pontiff had said that 'it is the duty of all to combat Socialism in the form in which it is at present developing, which attacks society and threatens it with ruin. In the presence of the perils of Socialism, Freemasonry, *Judaism* and Anarchism, we must multiply our endeavours.'[19] This belief that Judaism was inherently subversive was in strong contrast to Manning's recognition of the essential conservatism of religious Anglo-Jewry and the social and political concerns it shared in common with the English Catholic Church.

The relationship between the Catholic and Jewish leaderships in the 1890s and 1900s was not wholly free of suspicion and hostility. However, Catholic–Jewish antipathy was largely manifested either at a European level, in the words and writing of antisemitic clerics on the continent and the ambiguous position of some of the Vatican leadership, or at a grass-roots level, as evident in the English Catholic communal press. The English Catholic leadership maintained good relations with Anglo-Jewish bodies. The sentiment of cooperation was reciprocated, coupled with recognition of their shared roles as religious minorities in a Protestant country. In a letter to the Lord Cardinal Archbishop of Armagh, protesting against the anti-Jewish disturbances that broke out across Limerick in 1904, David L. Alexander of the BoD wrote:

---

[16] *Pall Mall Gazette* (3 November 1889).
[17] *Jewish Chronicle* (7 February 1890).
[18] *Jewish Chronicle* (28 February 1890).
[19] *The Jewish World* (27 September 1901) (my emphasis).

The fact that we Jews have always received active sympathy from the Church to which your eminence belongs adds poignancy to the grief with which we regard this outbreak ... In fact, whenever we have had occasion to seek for aid or cooperation on behalf of our brethren we have never failed to obtain ... sympathy and help from the Roman Catholics of the United Kingdom.[20]

The verbal excesses of certain Catholic intellectuals and clerics on the continent were a source of embarrassment to the English hierarchy. In an article published in the Catholic journal *The Tablet* in the winter of 1899 and subsequently reprinted in part in the *Jewish Chronicle*, disapproval of antisemitic sentiment as expressed by authors in France and Austria-Hungary was juxtaposed with recognition of the common outsider status still accorded to both Catholicism and Judaism in Britain:

We can only declare, in regard to all such writers, that anti-Semitism, as a religion, is a very poor substitute for the practical Catholicism which teaches us to love God above all things and our neighbours as ourselves. We Catholics who, especially in this country, have had to suffer so much from fierce and unreasoning prejudice ought to be the last to withhold our sympathy from those who labour unjustly under a similar weight of odium.[21]

In the late nineteenth-century metropolitan context both the Catholic and Jewish hierarchies were 'respectable', English, or thoroughly anglicised, and determined to defend the interests of a wider establishment that they supported yet from which they were still partially excluded by virtue of faith. The continued ambiguity of Catholicism's relationship (or lack of the same) with the mainstream British establishment was made clear by the so-called 'Jubilee controversy' of June 1897, when a proposed Catholic delegation to the Queen, chosen by Vaughan, was denied audience by the royal authorities. Subsequent to this a letter of congratulation sent by Vaughan to the Queen was returned by the Home Office, on the semantic issue that Vaughan should sign himself 'Roman Catholic Archbishop' rather than 'Cardinal'. Vaughan in turn rejected this request, writing that 'The term Roman, Romish, Popish, Papist as designating an Englishman's religion was brought from abroad in the 16th century ... Roman Catholic is a term taken out of context ... to create an unfavourable impression in the public's mind, as signifying something foreign.'[22] Despite the Prince of Wales's much

---

[20] London Metropolitan Archives, ACC/3121/A/015, Board of Deputies of British Jews, Minutes, Vol. 14.

[21] Extract from *The Tablet*, reprinted in the *Jewish Chronicle* (1 December 1899).

[22] Westminster Diocesan Archives, AAW/V.1/1/74, correspondence of Cardinal Vaughan. June 1897.

discussed partiality for Jewish society, the metropolitan Jewish leadership too were aware of the continued precariousness of their position with regard to acceptance by the wider elite, which was still conditional and at times reluctant.[23]

## The Communal Hierarchies and Anglicisation

### Language: Irish, Yiddish, and English

In a letter to the editor of the *Jewish Chronicle*, dated 10 July 1891, a concerned correspondent lamented a linguistic trend he had observed in the East End, spoken by 'our humbler brethren and … those not so humble', a 'vile jargon' being employed in the back streets and the *chevrot*. 'Let us do nothing to perpetuate the existence of that linguistic monstrosity now flourishing on English soil', the correspondent concluded, 'the offspring of deformed parents, a cross between Yiddish and Cockney'.[24] Although the language was outspoken, this writer's desire for 'the English language for the Jews of England' only reflected a wider disapproval and disavowal by elements of Anglo-Jewry for the 'dialect' that refugees had brought over from Poland and Russia. To make matters worse, Yiddish had experienced cross-pollination with the existing argot of the East End. The prevalent use of Yiddish by working-class Jews in the inner cities presented an obstacle to the efforts being made to anglicise and integrate the immigrant population. It also served as a symbol of the cultural and social gap between the middle classes and their poorer co-religionists.[25] In November 1901, at a meeting of the Council of the Jewish Colonization Association, Yiddish was described by one member as a 'cancer' that provoked antisemitism, an indicator of difference with the host society.[26] An internal report of the Special Committee of the United Synagogue, discussing ways and means of approaching the perceived social 'problem' in the East End, lamented the fact that proposed 'magic lantern' lectures, intended both for moral

---

[23] Julius, *Trials of the Diaspora*, p. 375 and Lipman, *A History of the Jews in Britain*, pp. 80–81. See Mervyn Busteed, 'Resistance and Respectability: Dilemmas of Irish Migrant Politics in Victorian Britain', in *Immigrants and Minorities*, Vol. 27, Nos. 2–3 (2009) for the relationship between the Catholic Church, Irish migrants and Victorian concepts of decorum and respectability.

[24] *Jewish Chronicle* (10 June 1891). See Kershen, *Strangers*, pp. 138–145.

[25] See Lulla Adler Rosenfeld, *The Yiddish Theatre and Jacob P. Adler* (New York: Shapolsky Publishers Inc., 1977) (republished 1988), pp. 164–165 for the class connotations of Yiddish, and the specific disapproval of both Nathan and Hermann Adler over the use of Yiddish.

[26] Rozin, *The Rich and the Poor*, p. 139. The Jewish ecclesiastical body, the Federation of Synagogues, also led a campaign amongst the East End poor for English to supplant Yiddish as the *lingua franca* of the Jewish working class. Black, *The Social Politics of Anglo-Jewry*, p. 62.

uplift and the teaching of practical life skills, would have to be carried out in 'Yiddish-Deutsch'. The communication regretted that this was 'the only language understood by the people'.[27] Subjects for these uplifting (if not perhaps terribly exciting) lectures included 'Hygiene (including sanitation, temperance, first aid and nursing); ambulance work, the science of common things; and, for women, Domestic Economy (including housekeeping), needlework, cookery, cutting out etc., etc.'[28]

This movement against Yiddish by the Jewish hierarchy in the last quarter of the nineteenth century closely mirrored the highly effective campaign instituted by the English Catholic Church against the Irish language in the 1850s and 1860s during the tail-end of the great Famine-induced influx of Irish migrants. For the Church, as for the United Synagogue, the use of the language of the old country was a signifier of difference and an implicit challenge to the control of the anglicised leaderships. One-third of Irish arrivals into the Commercial Road in East London in the years immediately following the Famine of the 1840s only spoke Irish.[29] In a considered response to these linguistic limitations in Church-run Catholic schools, English was taught exclusively.[30] Priests, even that minority with Irish Gaelic at their command, were strongly discouraged from conversing in it with their Irish congregations, or to give sermons in the language, although there were important metropolitan exceptions, such as Dockhead Catholic Church in Bermondsey.[31] Irish Gaelic, at the mid-century point, was a language synonymous with poverty, hunger, and a form of Catholicism and associated practices not wholly approved of by the hierarchy.[32] By the turn of the twentieth century, Irish had undergone a revival of sorts through the efforts of the Gaelic League and Irish sport associations. But these were largely the preserve of the middle classes.[33] These metropolitan

---

[27] Special Collections, Hartley Library, University of Southampton, M147, Papers of D. Mellows, Report of the Sub-Committee of the Special Committee of the United Synagogue, 14 April 1897, pp. 9–10.

[28] Special Collections, Hartley Library, University of Southampton, M147, Papers of D. Mellows, Report of the Sub-Committee of the Special Committee of the United Synagogue, 14 April 1897, pp. 9–10.

[29] Hickman, *Religion, Class and Identity*, p. 109.

[30] Hickman, *Religion, Class and Identity*, pp. 108–109 and Lees, *Exiles of Erin*, p. 190.

[31] Ni Dhulchaointigh, 'The Irish Population of London', p. 175.

[32] Booth, *Life and Labour of the People in London*, Third Series, *Religious Influences*, Vol. 7, p. 247; Hickman, *Religion, Class and Identity*, pp. 98–99; Sheridan Gilley, 'Roman Catholicism and the Irish in England', p. 154.

[33] John Hutchinson, 'Diaspora Dilemmas and Shifting Allegiances: The Irish in London between Nationalism, Catholicism and Labourism, 1900 to 1922', *Studies in Ethnicity and Nationalism*, Vol. 10, No. 1 (2010), pp. 109–110; Ni Dhulchaointigh, 'The Irish Population of London', p. 17. For an excellent, concise and well-illustrated text on the middle-class

Irish-speaking organisations attempted to reintroduce the language into Catholic social and religious life in the capital, most notably in the annual St Patrick's Day service held in Westminster Cathedral. The prohibition by the metropolitan Catholic leadership on an Irish-language service in the run-up to the 1908 celebration, after a number of years of services in Irish and Latin (but not English), caused 'considerable indignation in Irish circles', and the ban was blamed by Irish Nationalists on 'Tory Catholics' at work in the hierarchy.[34] A statement issued by the Gaelic League of London in response to the ban read:

> The Committee of the Gaelic League of London, and its members, non-Catholic as well as Catholic, all recognised the importance to the Gaelic movement of the restoration to its rightful position, in the Churches, of the national language of Ireland; and that the most fitting way to celebrate the memory of the apostle of Ireland was in the language that he spoke.[35]

Just as during the Mile End controversy of 1890, discussed in the last chapter, Jewish socialists switched venue from the Great Assembly Hall to Mile End Waste, so Irish Nationalists, as represented by the Irish Religious Celebration Committee, surmounted this prohibition by relocating. A service in Irish was instead held at Holy Trinity Church, Dockhead.[36] For a large number of working-class London Irish, however, in the first decade of the twentieth century and after fifty years of Church education, English was the only tongue spoken. The exceptions were those children whose parents or grandparents had made the deliberate choice to pass the language down to the next generation or, at the end of our period, through priests and school teachers who wished to facilitate a renewed interest in Irish cultural identity and taught poetry and song in Irish Gaelic.[37] There were also those who had learnt the language through classes organised by branches of the London Gaelic League (amongst this grouping was a young Irish civil servant working in London named Michael Collins).[38] But the majority of the latter were part of the London Irish middle class or petit-bourgeoisie. In speech the Irish proletariat were observed to be 'more cockney than the cockneys'.[39]

---

London-based Irish intelligentsia, see Fintan Cullen and R.F. Foster, *'Conquering England': Ireland in Victorian London* (London: National Portrait Gallery Publications, 2005).

[34]  *Daily News* (25 February 1908).

[35]  Westminster Diocesan Archives, AAW/Bo.5/83g, The Gaelic League of London, 'Irish Celebration 1908'.

[36]  *Freeman's Journal* (20 February 1908).

[37]  Ni Dhulchaointigh, 'The Irish Population of London', p. 195.

[38]  Ni Dhulchaointigh, 'The Irish Population of London', p. 186.

[39]  White, *London*, p. 139.

These linguistic trends did not reflect any lessening of nationalist and pro-Home Rule sentiments among the Irish working class of East London, but it did condition the language in which these sentiments were expressed. The highly effective way in which the Church had marginalised Irish, the better for hierarchically approved integration and anglicisation, served as a ready model for the BoD and those institutions of Anglo-Jewry which wished to eliminate Yiddish. But once again the highly fragmented nature of Jewish religious authority, as compared with their Catholic counterparts, undermined these efforts. English might well be the only language spoken in class at Jewish voluntary schools, but Yiddish was still the language in which lessons in the *chedarim* outside the school system were conducted in. Unlike Irish (with some exceptions), the children and grandchildren of refugees from the Pale of Settlement retained everyday Yiddish, certainly as the language spoken in the home.[40] Language could serve as an indicator of hegemonic control, and lack of fluency in English in its received pronunciation form was a marker of class and social inferiority. This extended beyond Yiddish and took in 'Cockney English' and other regional accents.[41] The existence or non-existence of a common language shared by communal leadership and a migrant working class was on one level an indication of communal and social control. The fact that the BoD failed to eliminate Yiddish (as compared with the success of the Church's campaign against Irish the generation before) was an indicator of the limited writ of the Anglo-Jewish authorities in East London as compared with their Catholic counterparts.

But a desire for English to replace Yiddish as the *lingua franca* of the Jewish East End was not simply a matter of an anglicised elite dictating to an immigrant working class. David Feldman has illustrated how the socialist movement in the East End championed the rapid mastering of the English language and integration, the better to accelerate unionisation and to increase solidarity with English workers. Yiddish-language radical journals urged their readers to become proficient in the language of the land in which they had settled.[42] There was a profusion of various radical Yiddish-language newssheets in East London from the 1880s onwards, beginning with the short-lived *Dos Poilishe Yidl*, established by Morris

---

[40] White, *Rothschild Buildings*, pp. 81–83.

[41] Gidley, 'Citizenship and Belonging', p. 117. See also Stedman Jones, 'The Cockney and the Nation', *Metropolis London*, p. 279: 'the "cockney" was one who could not wield political authority, above all because he or she could not speak with authority'.

[42] David Feldman, 'Jews in London, 1880–1914', in Raphael Samuel (ed.), *Patriotism: The Making and Unmaking of British National Identity*, Vol. 2, *Minorities and Outsiders* (London: Routledge, 1989), p. 216. See the radical journal *Die Freie Welt* (November 1892), on the necessity of assimilation for Jewish workers prior to taking part in the wider class struggle. Fishman, *East End Jewish Radicals*, p. 206.

Winchevsky in 1884, of which the *Arbeter Fraynt* was the most resilient and durable.[43] The very existence of these revolutionary journals, using the Yiddish language and the Hebrew script, served as an indicator of Jewish 'difference' for contemporary observers. In *The Alien Invasion* (1892), W.H. Wilkins wrote that 'There is [in East London] even a foreign newspaper half printed in "Yiddish", and the sentiments expressed therein are often of the most dangerous order.'[44] Wilkins was reluctant even to afford Yiddish the status of a language. More benignly, S. Gelberg described the Jewish migrant taking his leisure during a quiet period at the Spitalfields market: 'behind his stall absorbed in the political columns of one or other of the new-born Yiddish Press'.[45] Yiddish, like Irish, was a language associated with revolution, as well as an indicator of continued transnational diasporic identity.[46] Nevertheless, the International Working Men's Educational Club in Berner Street provided English lessons for Yiddish-speaking Jewish socialist arrivals to the East End, and the socialist journal *Der Vekker* urged its readers to 'Cast away your wild tongue and learn the language of the land in which you live.'[47] Woolf Wess's bilingualism was crucial in cementing his role as a 'permanent liaison officer' between Jewish and Gentile socialists.[48] Conversely, the Gentile socialist Rudolf Rocker learned Yiddish (similar phonetically but with a different alphabet from his native German) the better to work with Jewish comrades.[49] Illiteracy, whether in Yiddish or English, was also a concern, both for the BoD and the socialist movement, especially in a community that had historically prized scholarship (in a religious context).[50]

Proficiency in English was also an indicator of generational difference, between old and young, between new arrivals and those who had found their

[43] See Fishman, *East End Jewish Radicals*, pp. 140–151 for a description of the brief but busy life of *Dos Poilishe Yidl* and p. 327 for a breakdown in Yiddish-language London and Leeds-based socialist journals and their durations. See Leonard Prager, 'A Bibliography of Yiddish Periodicals in Great Britain (1867–1967)', *Studies in Bibliography and Booklore*, Vol. 9, No. 1 (Spring 1969).

[44] Wilkins, *The Alien Invasion*, p. 20.

[45] S. Gelberg, 'Jewish London', in George R. Sims (ed.), *Living London* (London: Cassell & Company Ltd, 1906), p. 31.

[46] See Nathan Cohen, 'The Yiddish Press and Yiddish Literature: A Fertile but Complex Relationship', *Modern Judaism*, Vol. 28, No. 2 (May 2008) for discussion of the wider Yiddish literary diaspora, and the relationship between Yiddish writing in Eastern Europe and North America.

[47] Rachael Holmes, *Eleanor Marx: A Life* (London: Bloomsbury, 2014), p. 352. *Der Vekker*, quoted in Fishman, *East End Jewish Radicals*, p. 206.

[48] Fishman, *East End Jewish Radicals*, pp. 171–172.

[49] Rocker, *The London Years*, pp. 46–48.

[50] Stampfer, *Families, Rabbis and Education*, p. 147.

feet in the new environment of East London. In Zangwill's *Children of the Ghetto*, Esther Ansell 'led a double life, just as she spoke two tongues'.[51] This 'double life', the common experience of the children of recent arrivals, was divided between home and school (or work), between an inner religious life and an outer social one. For many Jewish children, Yiddish was the language one talked with one's parents, just as Hebrew was learned at synagogue, and English talked in the streets and the playground. The linguistic anglicisation that the BoD, the United Synagogue and the Federation of Synagogues struggled so to encourage amongst the first generation of arrivals from the Pale seemed to occur naturally among the children and grandchildren of these arrivals. But it was an *organic* process, that grew out of social interaction, in the school, at work, at the concert hall, rather than some pre-conceived plan by the hierarchy put into operation.[52]

It was that 'linguistic monstrosity', the confluence of Yiddish and cockney, that proved so enduring, its day-to-day interactions taking place within the diaspora space of East London.[53] Among the Jewish middle classes of the late Edwardian period, as the language of the shtetl that had travelled with the migrants to the East End began to give way to English, Yiddish, 'possessing a rich literature ... attracting more and more the attention of students', was increasingly to be celebrated rather than dismissed, just as Irish Gaelic was revived in Irish Nationalist circles at the same time.[54] Increasingly, for the Jewish leadership, just as for their Catholic counterparts, the difficulty was not solely the integration of minority youth, but also the prevention of complete assimilation and abandonment of culture and religion.

## Youth Organisations

Various youth organisations were formed in the late Victorian period to cater for the young working-class men and women of the inner cities. Those groups established for second- and third-generation Jewish and Irish

---

[51] Zangwill, *Children of the Ghetto*, p. 117.

[52] See Leonard Prager, *Yiddish Culture in Britain: A Guide* (Frankfurt am Main: Peter Lang, 1990), p. 9 on *yidishkeyt* ('Jewishness' through language) among second- and third-generation Jewish youth.

[53] The ever-evolving East End underworld slang quickly assimilated Yiddish words and phrases, as it had done with Romany and other languages.

[54] *Jewish World* (1 June 1906). See Paul Kriwaczek, *Yiddish Civilisation: The Rise and Fall of a Forgotten Nation* (London: Phoenix, 2005) (republished 2006), p. 9 and pp. 304–305 for discussion of the role of Yiddish in British Jewry. For the Gaelic revival, see John Hutchinson, *The Dynamics of Cultural Nationalism: The Gaelic Revival and the Creation of the Irish Nation State* (London: Allen & Unwin, 1987), chapter 5, 'The Gaelic Revival (*c.*1890–1921): Its Socio-Political Articulation' and chapter 7, 'The Origins and Character of the Gaelic Revival' for discussion of the forces behind the Gaelic revival on both sides of the Irish Sea.

youth were created to serve a number of purposes. They were intended as a vehicle of what supporters would describe as social elevation and opponents (including those in the socialist movement) as communal control. Organisations such as the Catholic Working Lads' Club and the Jewish Lads' and Girls' Brigades took great trouble to arrange excursions to the seaside and the countryside, away from the supposed stultifying effects of urban life in the slums and backstreets, and, though not explicitly stated, removed from the influence of parents as well. This, the organisers of such groups argued, expanded the horizons of minority youth, offering a picture of English life and custom outside the East End, furthering a sense of common citizenship and encouraging ambitions beyond an existence in the slums. Opponents argued the converse, that such groups encouraged class control, that they were a means of preparing working-class youth for a life at the lowest strata of society.[55] These organisations also promoted anglicisation, an English-based patriotism, a sense of shared national identity, and identification with the mores and ideology of the wider Victorian and Edwardian society.[56] Lastly, in the case of Catholic and Jewish youth organisations, the groups strived to maintain religious adhesion and belonging, a continuing loyalty to the traditional faith brought over from Ireland or Eastern Europe. It was a bugbear of both the Jewish and Catholic religious bodies that having left school and religious instruction at thirteen (also the age of bar mitzvah for young Jewish men), all but nominal religious practice ceased for many young men and women. 'There are ... special dangers for our youth', Cardinal Vaughan wrote in an 1895 pamphlet:

> [During] the critical period between the ages of 14 and 21, when the mind and the passions become restless and venturesome – a danger lest they should prepare, by a life of indifference and neglect of religion, to drift eventually into the ranks of those societies which are the active organisation of unbelief and disorder.[57]

If socialism did not tempt wayward youth, the amoral pleasures of a sinful city might do so. In 1900, Vaughan, continuing along the same lines, wrote:

> [They] are carried away, at least for a time, on the stream of materialism, indifference and vice that surges around them ... It is no reproach to

---

55  Sharman Kadish, 'A Good Jew and a Good Englishman': The Jewish Lads' & Girls' Brigade, 1895–1995 (London: Valentine Mitchell, 1995), p. 38.

56  See Nigel Scotland, Squires in the Slums: Settlements and Missions in Late-Victorian Britain (London: I.B. Tauris, 2006), pp. 170–171 for discussion of the involvement of upper-class English Catholics in organisations such as the Catholic Social Union, which catered for Irish Catholic working-class youth.

57  Herbert Vaughan, A Key to the Social Problem: An Appeal to the Laity (London: Burns and Oates, 1895), p. 1.

religion that Catholic boys and girls, flung at a tender age into the vortex of such a life as London life, cannot, unaided, resist the strength of the current.[58]

The nature of both Catholic and Jewish religious teaching, whether in Sunday school or the *chedarim*, a schooling often characterised by heavy discipline, also encouraged rebellion and rejection of faith.[59] Beyond radicalism and hedonistic pleasure was sometimes complete ignorance in the second or third generation of a past religious and cultural heritage.[60] The Catholic and Jewish brigades therefore served a dual purpose: to integrate and anglicise young working-class co-religionists, and at the same time preserve religious observance and loyalty. In the words of the founder of the Jewish Lads' Brigade, Colonel Albert E.W. Goldsmid, these organisations inculcated 'a true God fearing manliness'.[61] What the hierarchies aimed for could be described as integration (anglicisation) without assimilation (loss of faith). The Jewish Lads' Brigade and the Catholic Boys' Brigade were founded within a year of each other, the former in Whitechapel in 1895, the latter in Bermondsey in 1896.[62] Both were enormously popular. The excursions organised, the patriotic tales of colonial victories related round the campfire, the militaristic drilling, allowed marginalised groups of working-class youth a share, however tenuous, in the public school ethos of 'fair play', patriotism, and hard physical exercise so prevalent and popular at the turn of the century. This constituted part of what John M. MacKenzie has described as an 'ideological cluster' that had formed during the Victorian period.[63] Tales of Empire and public school exploits, recounted in various journals, were eagerly devoured by second- and third-generation Jewish and Irish East-Enders, just as they were by working-class and lower middle-class youth more generally.[64] The literate children of often illiterate migrants were part of a generation consuming the second wave of the genre of leisure literature that had emerged in the mid-nineteenth

---

[58] Herbert Vaughan, *A Call on the Laity for Christian Work* (London: Burns and Oates, 1900), p. 6.

[59] Stephen Humphries, *Hooligans or Rebels? An Oral History of Working-Class Childhood and Youth, 1889–1939* (Oxford: Blackwell, 1995), p. 38.

[60] F.A. McKenzie, *Famishing London – A Study of the Unemployed and Unemployable* (London: Hodder and Stoughton, 1903), p. 14.

[61] Kadish, '*A Good Jew and a Good Englishman*', p. 2.

[62] John M. MacKenzie, *Propaganda and Empire: The Manipulation of British Public Opinion* (Manchester: Manchester University Press, 1984) (republished 1988), pp. 242–243.

[63] MacKenzie, *Propaganda and Empire*, p. 2.

[64] In 1912 the ever popular *Greyfriars* series by Frank Richards gained its first Jewish character, Monty Newland, 'wise and generous in his ways, and [he] has lots of pluck'. J.S. Butcher, *Greyfriars School: A Prospectus* (London: Cassell, 1965), p. 50.

century. Tales of plucky public school boys and girls were seen as suitable and uplifting as compared with 'subversive' and sensationalist alternatives.[65] The first metropolitan organisations that catered for working-class and lower middle-class adolescents had emerged out of the Church of England and the Protestant nonconformist groups in the 1880s, stressing a particular form of 'muscular Christianity', most notably the Boys' Brigade.[66] The subsequent Jewish and Catholic groups that were created in the 1890s followed this successful template of religious affirmation and semi-military organisation.

Again, the attitude of the leaderships was ambiguous. Patriotism and identification with the ethos of the wider society by the coming generation was to be encouraged. But at what point did integration become assimilation? In *Children of the Ghetto*, for Esther Ansell, 'far keener than her pride in Judas Maccabaeus was her pride in Nelson and Wellington; she rejoiced to find that her ancestors had always beaten the French'.[67] Her brother Solomon does not care for the 'literature and history' of the Jews, but rather 'the history of Daredevil Dick and his congeners'.[68] The BoD and the *Jewish Chronicle* both strove to create a Jewish identity that combined British patriotism and fidelity with observance of traditional customs and religion. In the pages of the *Jewish Chronicle*, potted biographies of English Jewish heroes were prominent, as were the obituaries of young Jewish men who had died on active service during the Boer War.

Concern for the moral condition and progress of young Irish and Jewish women was even more pronounced than the fears expressed for the young men of the community. In the Jewish community, 'Young women were deemed to be more "at risk" than their male counterparts who were presumed to be at school, *yeshiva* or work'.[69] The unspoken concern was prostitution or sexual exploitation, or assimilation of the perceived immoral sexual attitudes of the wider East End.[70] The belief in bourgeois propriety held by the hierarchies, combined with the conservative sexual and religious politics carried from rural Ireland and the Pale of Settlement by migrants, placed a premium on respectability and protection from temptation for young women. The opinion of Charles Booth, that 'on the whole ... immoral relations before

---

[65] Jenny Holt, *Public School Literature, Civic Education and the Politics of Male Adolescence* (Farnham: Ashgate Publishing, 2008), p. 146.

[66] John Springhall, Brian Fraser and Michael Hoare, *Sure & Steadfast: A History of the Boys' Brigade, 1883 to 1983* (London: Collins, 1983), pp. 18–21.

[67] Zangwill, *Children of the Ghetto*, p. 117.

[68] Zangwill, *Children of the Ghetto*, p. 88.

[69] Kadish, 'A Good Jew and a Good Englishman', p. 2.

[70] Peter Ackroyd, *London: The Biography* (London: Vintage, 2001), p. 376: 'Even in areas where the more respectable working class lived, it was customary for couples as young as thirteen and fourteen to live and procreate without the need for marriage vows.'

marriage among the lower classes are not unusual, and are indulgently regarded' did not hold true with respect to the minority communities.[71] A more usual reaction would be disgrace and disavowal.[72] In an article dated 10 March 1887, Chief Rabbi Adler lamented the growing number of 'unchaste Hebrew maiden[s]' in the East End, blaming the labour market and the social strains occasioned by mass immigration from Eastern Europe.[73] In migrant culture, there was little middle ground for unmarried young women between 'innocence' and 'corruption'.[74]

To avoid the temptations that music halls and dances in the East End threw in the paths of young women, societies such as the Jewish Girls' Club were formed, again encouraging patriotism, identification with wider society, as well as the necessities required to lead a respectable anglicised home life. The hierarchies also took an interest in the economic occupations of girls who had left school at thirteen. Both the Catholic Church and the Jewish authorities strongly encouraged domestic service as a 'respectable' occupation for young working-class women. For the Church, domestic service was compared favourably in moral terms with factory work. It was also seen as a means of preparing young Catholic girls for domesticity and family life.[75] The numerous cases of (often unreported) seduction and sexual abuse that took place within domestic service were not apparently taken into account.[76] The Jewish leadership also encouraged working-class Jewish girls to become servants. This could even serve as a form of integration, '[completing] the work of their social emancipation', as the *Jewish Chronicle* phrased it. The want of Jewish servants in the capital had been noted, and the *Chronicle* suggested that this lack of Jewish domestic staff 'would but perpetuate a spirit of separateness'.[77]

[71] Charles Booth, *Life and Labour of the People in London, Notes on Social Influences and Conclusion* (London: Macmillan, 1903), p. 44.

[72] In *The London Years*, Rocker discusses the 'Free Love' movement in Jewish radicalism. See the slogan 'Love without marriage rather than marriage without love.'

[73] Chief Rabbi Adler, quoted in Arnold White, *The Modern Jew* (London: William Heinemann, 1899), p. 142.

[74] Bermant, *Point of Arrival*, p. 157. Lara Marks, '"The Luckless Waifs and Strays of Humanity": Irish and Jewish Immigrant Unwed Mothers in London, 1870–1939', *Twentieth Century British History*, Vol. 3, No. 2 (1992), p. 118.

[75] Walter, *Outsiders Inside*, p. 146; Daly, 'Irish Women and the Diaspora', p. 25.

[76] Pamela Horn, *The Rise and Fall of the Victorian Servant* (Dublin: Gill and Macmillan, 1975) (republished by Sutton Publishing Ltd, 2004), pp. 148–151.

[77] *Jewish Chronicle* (23 November 1888) in Fishman, *East End 1888*, p. 176. See also Susan L. Tananbaum, 'Jewish Feminist Organisations in Britain and Germany at the Turn of the Century', in Michael Brenner, Rainer Liedtke and David Rechter (eds), *Two Nations: British and German Jews in Comparative Perspective* (London: Leo Baeck Institute, 1999), p. 385 for discussion of the activities of the Union of Jewish Women in encouraging working-class Jewish girls to enter nursing or domestic service.

In other words, for a middle-class hierarchy, the Jewish working class should strive to adopt the economic roles of a conventional proletariat, the better for acceptance in the host society. The large majority of young Jewish women in employment, however, continued to work in small-scale workshops, often employed by their families.[78]

These youth organisations were generally popular, both among the leaderships and the East End communities. However, a degree of hostility and antagonism was directed at the groups, both politically and on a grass-roots level. As discussed above, strands of the socialist movement could not help but regard organisations such as the Boys' Brigade and its minority cousins as a device employed to facilitate communal control and cohesion. These groups, in this narrative, were formed to head off a supposed burgeoning class identity and offer instead a share in the wider conservative Victorian hegemonic ideology of patriotism, empire, thrift, and hard work. For the Jewish and Catholic youth organisations adhesion to these values was combined with a desire to maintain and protect a minority religious faith, again promoting an identity based around religion rather than class. But socialists were not alone in holding reservations about the overtly militaristic element that was a feature of both the Catholic Boys' Brigade and the Jewish Lads' Brigade. Sections of the East End Irish community in particular feared that the Catholic Boys' Brigade and Catholic Working Lads' Club were smokescreens for recruitment by the British Army.[79] In a letter to the *Catholic Herald*, a correspondent signing himself 'Padraic', articulated these fears:

> [T]he Catholic Boys' Brigades, whatever may have been the intention of their founder, are little better than mere recruiting depots ... 'But what must the fathers who permit such a thing be like – don't they know it is all planned to entice the boys into the army?' Such was the sensible comment of a robust old Irishman ... The parents and the parents only can kill this stupid Jingo spirit, and it is to them that I earnestly appeal to take heed for the sake of the boys before it is too late.[80]

Whilst the Catholic youth organisations stressed adhesion to English Victorian values, they also appeared to subvert the Irish identity held on to tenaciously by the previous generation. The militarism, rifle practice, and drilling of the brigades fed into an *English* rather than an *Irish* patriotism. It was English tales of pluck and derring-do narrated round the camp fire, the heroes of Empire lauded, not of Erin.[81] Irish Nationalists feared that

---

78  Marks, *Working Wives and Working Mothers*, p. 16.

79  Renshaw, 'Control, Cohesion and Faith', p. 40.

80  *Catholic Herald* (18 April 1902).

81  The Gaelic League and the United Irish League attempted to counter this with their

the brigades were effectively divorcing Catholic religious piety from Irish national and cultural identity among second- and third-generation London Irish. The antagonism between a residual Irish nationalism and distrust of British imperialism on the one hand and the creation by the youth organisations of an English patriotism and militarism on the other, created problems and raised issues not apparent in the relationship between East End Jewry and the Jewish Lads' and Girls' Brigades. In this period nascent Jewish nationalism, in its Zionist form, was both a recent phenomenon and in its early years apparently able to coexist with a British imperial identity. The contradictions and strained loyalties of the Catholic youth organisations were a by-product of the mutual legacy of distrust and suspicion between England and Ireland, still able to work its influence over communities who had left Ireland decades before.

Catholic Boys' Brigaders also came under attack from their own peers. Young men in the Bermondsey Catholic Boys' Brigade went to the lengths of carrying their uniforms in brown paper bags to change into once inside the sanctuary of the premises of the club.[82] This caution had been occasioned by the verbal insults and occasional physical attacks by what were termed 'local hooligans'. This tension and violence, between young men sharing an ethnic and religious background (Irish Catholic) and a similar socio-economic background, was a symptom of a larger cultural battle taking place within metropolitan working-class youth culture. One strand embraced and emulated the public school ethos whilst the other formed a subculture that celebrated 'an alternative cultural ethos of working class masculinity which placed a heavy emphasis on drinking and fighting'.[83] Whilst both groups embraced 'manliness' and admired physical strength and activity, the former viewed this in the context of a national patriotism, to be employed in the service of country or Church and displayed on track and field, whilst for the latter it fed into the strong territorialism of the East End, semi-criminality, gang life, and distrust of outsiders generally and the police in particular. The former looked beyond the confines of the East End, the latter celebrated the parochialism of the local neighbourhood as territory to be defended against interlopers. These tensions were not limited to second-generation minority youth, but reflected a cultural conflict taking place amongst the

---

own classes for Irish Catholic children – with limited success. Ni Dhulchaointigh, 'The Irish Population of London', p. 238.

[82] John Springhall, 'Building Character in the British Boy: The Attempt to Extend Christian Manliness to Working Class Adolescents, 1880–1914', in J.A. Mangan and James Walvin (eds), *Manliness and Morality: Middle-Class Masculinity in Britain and America, 1800–1940* (Manchester: Manchester University Press, 1987), p. 60.

[83] See Springhall, 'Building Character in the British Boy', p. 69 and Humphries, *Hooligans or Rebels?*

young in working-class communities across London and Britain.[84] However, they illuminate the complexity of issues of identity and the forces shaping self-definition for male and female youth in diasporic communities separated physically and culturally from the homeland of their parents or grandparents, but with their attachment to the culture of the host country their forebears had settled in still a fraught and confused matter. The hierarchy-approved organisations and the street gangs with ethnically based memberships both represented attempts by Jewish and Irish young men and women to negotiate and settle these questions of belonging.[85]

## Temperance and Gambling

The most obvious outward manifestations of an undesired and uncontrolled assimilation of the children of immigrants into the culture of the wider East End were the adoption of its vices: sexual promiscuity, excessive consumption of alcohol, and gambling. In fact, none of these illicit pleasures was new to the communities or the homelands which the previous generation had left. But it was useful to blame an amoral city and its native inhabitants for the feared moral 'corruption' of second- or third-generation minority youth. Alcohol, the socialist movement, the Catholic Church, Protestant evangelists, and social investigators were agreed, was the curse of the poorest sections of society, and in particular of the Irish Catholic working class. In social investigation and local newspaper reports of the time alcohol-induced horror stories involving Irish East-Enders were a common feature:

> Mary O'Shaugnessey, aged 25, the wife of a ship's fireman, living at 46 Well Street, East India Road, Poplar, burned to death on the night of Saturday 12 January. William O'Shaugnessey had that evening landed back in England, and he and his wife had spent their wages on rum, with the result that the husband was too drunk to realise his wife, who had upset a lamp, was burning to death downstairs. 'The coroner, in summing up, said the case as the most disgraceful one it had ever been his lot to inquire into. That human beings could get into such a state of intoxication is dreadful to think of, but he hoped the husband would take warning by it.[86]

Of the father of one Irish family, Charles Booth wrote: 'He had been a great drunkard, signing the pledge from time to time and after a while

---

[84]   See Geoffrey Pearson, *Hooligan: A History of Respectable Fears* (Basingstoke: Macmillan, 1983) on the late-Victorian 'moral panic' over the deviant behaviour of certain subcultures of British urban youth.

[85]   A testament to the influence of the Jewish Lads' Brigade was the statistic that one-third of British Jews who died on the Western Front had been members of the Brigade. Joanna Bourke, *Working Class Cultures in Britain, 1890–1960* (London: Routledge, 1994), p. 196.

[86]   *East London Observer* (26 January 1889).

breaking out again. He would earn a little in the morning but would spend nearly all of it on drink before he came home, would then swear and knock his wife about.'[87] Excessive consumption of alcohol was certainly a problem in the Irish community in the late nineteenth century, but it is debateable whether alcoholic abuse was any less prevalent among the wider East End poor.[88] Nevertheless, drunken debauchery fitted in with the popular image, cultivated in the cartoons of *Punch* and on the music hall stage, of the 'Paddy' and 'Bridget' stereotypes, the feckless, lazy, violent, and drunken Irishman or Irishwoman.[89] To combat both the very real evils of alcoholism and the domestic violence that accompanied it, and the popular association of the Irish in London en masse with drinking and drunkenness, the League of the Cross was formed. This was a temperance organisation that recruited mainly in Catholic schools. The League focused on the next generation of Catholic youth rather than their parents: 'Love of drink in the adult is a terribly tough bough to lop; but one may hope that these tens of thousands of little temperance twigs will tell on the sobriety of the generation that is to follow our own.'[90] John Denvir, in his contemporary *The Irish in Britain* (1894), linked alcoholism in Irish communities with the traumatic circumstances in which the diaspora had arrived in Britain: 'nine-tenths of the misery and faults of the Irish arose from the way in which they had been driven from their country, where, with all their poverty, those who are now but too often a scandal to creed and country here, would, if still at home, be living virtuous and happy lives.'[91] With respect to alcohol, as with other issues, domestic East End Irish Catholic social, cultural, and economic tensions were externalised, pushed outwards, and framed in the language of anti-colonialism, drawing a connection between colonial subjection in Ireland and poverty and destitution in East London.

Gambling, rather than alcoholism, was considered by the Anglo-Jewish leadership to be a particular problem for the Jewish community. Both Jewish and non-Jewish contemporary observers made much of the absence

[87] Charles Booth, *On the City: Physical Patterns and Social Structure* (Chicago: University of Chicago Press, 1967), pp. 197–198.

[88] See Donald M. MacRaild, *The Irish Diaspora in Britain, 1750–1939* (Basingstoke: Palgrave Macmillan, 2011), p. 169 for discussion of the depiction of Irish alcoholism in anti-Irish discourse.

[89] See G.C. Duggan, *The Stage Irishman: A History of the Irish Play and Stage Character from the Earliest Times* (London: Longmans, Green and Co., 1937), pp. 288–289 and Annelise Truninger, *Paddy and the Paycock: A Study of the Stage Irishman from Shakespeare to O'Casey* (Berne: Francke Verlag, 1976), p. 51.

[90] Mary C. Tabor, in Booth, *Life and Labour of the People in London*, First Series, *Poverty*, Vol. 3, p. 225.

[91] John Denvir, *The Irish in Britain* (London: Trench, Trubner and Co., Ltd, 1894), p. 255.

of alcoholic abuse in East End Jewry, as contrasted with their English and Irish neighbours.[92] This was partly because for many Jewish immigrants the East End public house was a zone of cultural and ethnic exclusion. Games of chance, however, were a different matter. In a March 1891 report by the *Beth Din*, 'A Scheme for Alleviating the Social Condition of the Jewish Working Classes', the 'temptations of gambling houses' are mentioned alongside 'anarchist and anti-religious clubs' and '[Christian] mission halls' as the greatest threats to working-class Jewry.[93] Betting and bookmaking thus ranked as high as the lures of socialism or Christianity in the concerns of those elements of the Jewish establishment worried about the moral and social welfare of the East End Jews. Card-playing went on illicitly in dens behind shops and restaurants.[94] Just as alcoholism in East End Irish communities, although a real problem, was also exploited to bolster a popular ethnic stereotype, so the popularity of gambling among East End Jewry, whilst not a fabrication, was frequently presented by those outside the community in terms of the familiar antisemitic trope of a Jewish love for money and profit. 'The Jews especially, of all classes, are great gamblers. I have in my mind a picture of a little Jew boy in a very poor street, playing pitch and toss all by himself, studying the laws of chance in this humble fashion.'[95] As with the Church and alcohol, the campaigns of the BoD and *Beth Din* were two-pronged, attacking a concrete problem manifesting itself on the streets, and the issue of the popular perception of immigrant communities by the wider population.

Youth organisations played an important role in the Jewish and Catholic campaigns against alcohol and gambling. The Stepney Lads Club, catering for young Jewish men, explicitly condemned gambling amongst its members.[96] The Catholic League of the Cross meanwhile encouraged female members not to court young Irishmen who drank.[97] The League of the Cross attempted to challenge the culture of drinking in the Catholic immigrant communities, to use peer pressure to make alcoholism unacceptable. 'Try and get your neighbours to look upon the drunkard as a pariah … hoot the drunkard in the street … You would stop the pickpocket from robbing, why not stop the drunkard and protect his wife and children from his cruelty.'[98]

---

[92] Russell and Lewis, *The Jew in London*, p. 64.

[93] London Metropolitan Archives, ACC/2712/GTS/366, Notices and circulars from various Jewish organisations.

[94] Fishman, *East End 1888*, p. 186.

[95] Booth, *Life and Labour of the People in London, Notes on Social Influences and Conclusion*, p. 57.

[96] *Jewish World* (31 March 1905).

[97] *Catholic Herald* (February 1902).

[98] *Catholic Herald* (5 December 1902).

To what extent the organisations established to promote temperance and challenge gambling were successful is debateable. Certainly, Charles Booth, in his final volume of *Life and Labour*, had noted a change in drinking patterns, a certain moderation, in the poorest areas:

> Among men who drink more shame is felt than used to be the case at having been drunk. 'Much more is drunk than formerly', says one witness, speaking of some of the rough Irish, 'but there is less drunkenness, partly because the beer is lighter, but more because of a change in manners; nowadays you drink, and the more you drink the better man you are, but you must not be visibly drunk. Outward drunkenness is an offence against the manners of all classes.' The ideal is to 'carry your drink like a gentleman'.[99]

The success of Jewish campaigns against gambling are harder to quantify, these semi-legal activities going on by necessity behind closed doors, without the violence, noise, and discord that accompanied alcoholic excess. Both the efforts of the Catholic Church against drunkenness and the campaign of the BoD against gambling constituted part of a wider process of encouraging integration and anglicisation, and, as with the youth organisations, hope was placed on and efforts aimed at the rising generation, the children or grandchildren of immigrants. The campaigns against drunkenness carried on by the Catholic Church are also noticeable for the stress laid on the influence of young women over their male peers in a hyper-masculine culture. It was integration and acceptance of a particular set of values and mores, those of the 'respectable' working and middle classes (strata that the Catholic and the Jewish leaderships encouraged their parishioners to emulate), rather than the culture of the wider East End and of the poorest sections of the English proletariat. In many ways these concerns of the hierarchies, over integration of co-religionists and the adoption of 'respectability', paralleled those of the socialist movement. Proficiency in English, as discussed, was seen as a means of furthering unionisation and inter-ethnic cooperation. Alcoholism, particularly in the docks, was an impediment to solidarity and organisation. Teetotalism was largely encouraged by the socialist organisations and the trade unions, with the view that it was easier to organise men and women who were sober.[100] The practice in the docks of weekly wages being collected in the nearest public

---

[99] Booth, *Life and Labour of the People in London, Notes on Social Influences and Conclusion*, p. 60.

[100] See *The Clarion* (25 March 1889): 'I have no wish to rob a poor man of his beer ... but I am convinced that the poor man would be immensely richer in health, mind and pocket, if there wasn't a public house at every corner'.

house, and those wages being spent largely on liquor, was also condemned by socialists and trade unionists.[101] Similarly, gambling was seen as a means of tricking workers out of their wages, money that could have been spent on self-improvement, family, or union subscription fees. J. Ernest Jones, the self-styled 'socialist imperialist', in a 1903 pamphlet, set out a list of temptations besetting working-class youth in terms very similar to those of the Church or the United Synagogue: 'vice, drinking, smoking, gambling and attending exciting professional sports'.[102] His remedy would have met with the approval of Goldsmid and Vaughan: 'They must, without conscription and barrack life, simply by living at home, be compulsorily made to drill, shoot, and go through gymnastic exercises and healthy sports.'[103] Jones was on the 'progressive imperialist' wing of the socialist movement, far removed from the Socialist Leaguers who condemned the militarism of the various brigades. Nevertheless, these sentiments reveal an overlap of concerns between communal leaderships and elements of British socialism, on the desirability of integration, and in particular fluency in English, and the dangers of alcohol and other East End vices. The ultimate goals of the socialist movement may have been radically different from those of the communal hierarchies, but the means of getting there, through the creation of a sober, anglicised, and educated proletariat, were desired by Church, Jewish communal bodies, and socialists alike.

## Religious Education

So far in this chapter the common concerns of the Jewish and Catholic hierarchies in East London have run parallel to each other, but have not overlapped. In the secular education controversies of the Edwardian period, however, and in particular the reaction to the various proposed Liberal Education bills that were debated in the Commons and the Lords from 1906 onwards, the Church authorities and Jewish communal leaders in the capital formed an alliance to resist attempts to undo the Education Act of 1902. This culminated in the election in 1904 of Henry Herman Gordon, son of the Revd A.E. Gordon of the United Synagogue, standing as an independent candidate in Whitechapel to the LCC. Gordon was elected on an anti-secular education ticket, receiving the great majority of both

---

[101] Brodie, *Politics of the Poor*, p. 145. See also H.A. Mess, *Casual Labour at the Docks* (London: G. Bell and Sons Ltd, 1916) for discussion of the role of alcohol in the docklands culture, the practice of alcoholic inducements to be 'taken on' by a foreman and the role of the pub as an unofficial labour exchange.

[102] LSE ILP/5/1903/19, Jones, *The Case for Progressive Imperialism*, p. 19.

[103] LSE ILP/5/1903/19, Jones, *The Case for Progressive Imperialism*, p. 19.

the Jewish and Irish votes.[104] Gordon was lauded by both rabbi and priest in the pulpits of the East End, by Cardinal Bourne and Lord Rothschild alike. This convergence of synagogue and church was not the only unlikely temporary alliance formed over the issue of how religion was to be taught in elementary schools, with Irish Nationalists voting in parliament with Tory Unionists, and the leaders of immigrant Jewry sharing common ground with the anti-alien Primrose League.

In the matter of Edwardian elementary education, the usual political allegiances did not hold. The socialist and trade unionist movements too were split by the debate, the majority in favour of completely secular education, but with a small and vocal minority resolutely determined to defend religious provision, even at the expense of continued allegiance to the Labour Party and the TUC. The alliances formed by the Catholic and Jewish hierarchies and working-class Irish and Jewish electorates to defend what were perceived as interests vital to communal well-being illustrate the complex and adaptable negotiations of identity and loyalty taking place within East London diaspora space. They also proved that acting upon the shared agendas of both religious leaderships, when acknowledged, could result in concrete political gains on the ground in the East End, if the hierarchies chose to advance these agendas in confluence.

Two political issues arose from Irish and Jewish involvement in the education debate. First, it brought into sharp focus the long-term question of whether ethnic and religious minorities should use their votes to further the interests of their particular religious denomination or ethnic loyalty, to form a 'bloc' based around ethnic or sectarian belonging. As part of the movement towards integration, both the Catholic and Jewish hierarchies had previously cautioned against forming such cross-political religious alignments. The education battles of the Edwardian period for a time led communal leaders to question this prohibition. Secondly, it forced minority, particularly Irish Catholic, trade unionists and socialists to acknowledge the difficulty in reconciling two competing allegiances, one to the religious authorities, the other to the TUC and its resolutions. Throughout the period under discussion, and the twenty years preceding it, education of working-class children was perhaps *the* major issue for the leaderships of London's religious groupings. All of the other concerns discussed in this chapter, from language to the lure of socialism or Protestantism, were felt to have their roots in the quality of the instruction received in the classroom.

The 1870 Education Act had split the provision of elementary education between locally funded board schools, in which a broad, non-denominational religious instruction was given, and voluntary schools, independent of state

---

[104] Alderman, *London Jewry and London Politics*, p. 49.

control, self-financed and under the control of particular religious denominations. The largest Jewish voluntary school was the Jewish Free School, founded in Spitalfields in 1817. It had capacity for some 3,000 pupils, making it the largest institution of its kind in London.[105] Under the long tenure of its formidable headmaster Moses Angel, for half a century generations of East End Jewish youth passed through the Free School, with its dual emphasis on English cultural integration and the preservation of Jewish religious faith. Angel, arguably more than any other individual in nineteenth-century Anglo-Jewry, successfully drove forward the hierarchy's aim of achieving migrant integration while not jettisoning the Jewish religion.[106]

The divide between board and voluntary schools was blurred, however, in that in areas of East London with large minority faith populations, some provision was made for minority religious observance within the secular board schools. Jewish children in these schools were usually excused from studying the New Testament and explicitly Christian instruction. 'The Jewish children, as a rule, take some secular subject while the Bible is being taught. At some schools in the East End, however, where the Jews equal or outnumber the Christians, the children all take Scripture, but the little Hebrews, of course, are given only Old Testament lessons.'[107] There was also an unofficial policy in East End board schools in heavily Jewish areas of appointing Jewish headmasters, who would be sympathetic to the religious requirements of their pupils.[108] In addition to the board and voluntary schools were the institutions that provided religious education outside of the schools: in the Catholic case, church Sunday Schools, and in the Jewish East End the traditional *chedarim* (small-scale religious classes, presided over by a rabbi), the larger scale Talmud Torah schools, and the synagogue classes, in which the Torah was studied and Hebrew taught. A premium was placed on learning Hebrew, at least up until bar mitzvah. Nevertheless, a significant number of East End Jewish children received no formal religious instruction not imparted from their parents.[109]

The board school versus voluntary school divide again brought to the surface the question of balancing integration on the one hand and preservation of

[105] Irving Osborne, *Jewish Junior County Awards in East London Schools, 1893–1914, An Interim Report and Guide to Sources*, East London Research Papers, Centre for East London Studies, Queen Mary College, University of London, 1988, pp. 1–2.

[106] Lipman, *A History of the Jews in Britain since 1858*, pp. 29–30.

[107] H.A. Kennedy, 'Council School London', pp. 91–92. See also Jones, *Immigration and Social Policy*, pp. 104–109 on the essential 'Jewishness' of many East End Board Schools.

[108] Alderman, *Modern British Jewry*, pp. 189–190 and David Feldman, '"Jews in the East End, Jews in the Polity": The Jew in the Text', *Interdisciplinary Studies in the Long Nineteenth Century*, No. 13 (2011).

[109] Tananbaum, *Jewish Immigrants in London*, p. 98.

religious faith on the other. Certainly, the migrant communities and their leaderships did not desire the religious instruction of their children to be left in the hands of a non-believer. Jewish oral history from the period reveals the problems Jewish children could experience in largely Gentile board and later state schools, from teachers as much as fellow pupils. One Jewish girl recalled the antisemitism of certain teachers at her board school, and the particular victimisation by the staff of one pupil accused of mocking the Christian religion.[110] Stories occasionally surfaced in the Jewish press of Jewish children in board schools being expected to take part in Christian prayers. But the Jewish leadership recognised the efficacy of the board schools as a means of integrating and anglicising children.[111] The Gentile headmaster of one predominantly Jewish East End board school reported to the Royal Commission on Immigration: 'Jewish boys soon become anglicised and cease to be foreigners ... practically the whole of these children are of foreign parentage. Notwithstanding this fact, the lads have become thoroughly English ... Jewish lads who pass through our schools will grow up to be intelligent, industrious, temperate and law-abiding citizens.'[112]

The Jewish Free School and similar smaller voluntary institutions occupied a middle ground between the secular board schools with their non-denominational religious provision (albeit a provision that Jewish children could usually opt out of) and the out-of-school hours *chedarim*, often conducted by rabbis from Eastern Europe. The more affluent sections of the Jewish community sent their sons to 'synagogue classes', modelled on the church Sunday school, rather than the working-class, immigrant-led *chedarim*. For more conservative religious East End Jews, however, the Anglo-Jewish 'synagogue classes', rather like the dog collars adopted by some West End Jewish ministers, seemed to imitate Gentile religious instruction and methods. There were suggestions that the working-class children of immigrants were receiving a more thorough religious education in the *chedarim* than their more prosperous peers were imbibing in the synagogue classes that took their inspiration from equivalent Catholic and Protestant organisations.[113]

The Catholic Church strongly encouraged its parishioners to send their children to church schools, with board schools viewed with some suspicion as possible agents of Protestant evangelism or atheism. Given the choice between modern, well-equipped, and secular board schools and resource-starved Catholic voluntary schools, many parents, under the influence of the

---

[110] White, *Rothschild Buildings*, p. 169.
[111] *Jewish Chronicle* (17 September 1898) in Feldman, 'Jews in London', p. 215.
[112] Lipman, *A History of the Jews in Britain since 1858*, p. 107.
[113] *The Jewish World* (10 January 1890).

Church, still chose the 'tumbledown and badly equipped schools of their own faith'.[114] Working-class Catholic parents supported their local church schools financially and involved themselves in school activities, giving them a stake in both their children's education and the administration of the church as a whole.[115] But this, of course, was dependent on a suitable voluntary school being in the vicinity, and having the requisite capacity for students. For working-class Jews and Irish Catholics, the board school was sometimes the only choice.

By the last decade of the nineteenth century, the voluntary schools were suffering financially, being largely dependent on the charity of wealthy co-religionists and the contributions of poor local communities. Father Amigo, of a Catholic voluntary school on the Commercial Road, in appealing for funds to maintain his school, put the matter thus:

> We have 1200 children, nearly all poor Irish children, on the registers of our schools, but accommodation for 1000 only. We know the addresses of 500 Catholic children in the parish going to non-Catholic schools and losing their faith – both boys and girls with fine Irish names without Mass and without their first confession.[116]

A Catholic priest, writing in 1896, asked: 'Why ... should the state starve the voluntary schools and pamper the board schools? Why put a conscience tax upon the religious supporters of the voluntary schools?'[117]

The voluntary schools were rescued by the Education Acts of 1902 and 1903, the first of which overhauled the national elementary school system and the latter dealing with provision for education in London in particular. The Conservative Act, passed with the support of the Irish Nationalists, incorporated the voluntary schools into a national system, one that allowed the schools to preserve their denominational character whilst receiving financial support from the state.[118] The board school system was abolished, the new 'provided' schools falling under the control of county councils and county boroughs. For supporters of the Act, it was a measure that protected religious freedom and the right of religious minorities to educate their children in their chosen faith. For opponents, the Act was a rearguard piece of legislation designed to protect the primacy of the Anglican Church.

[114] T.P. O'Connor, quoted in Englander, *A Documentary History of Jewish Immigrants*, p. 235.

[115] Hickman, *Religion, Class and Identity*, pp. 171 and 203. The complex interactions between working-class parishioners and the local churches largely kept running by their financial assistance will be discussed in the next chapter.

[116] *Catholic Herald* (18 May 1900).

[117] J.E.B. Munson, 'A Study of Nonconformity in Edwardian England', p. 64.

[118] J.E.B. Munson, 'A Study of Nonconformity in Edwardian England', p. 111.

More sinister interpretations were also advanced, referring back to the traditional suspicion towards Catholicism, that this was 'Rome on the rates', the public purse supporting creeds alien to the great majority of taxpayers, to the detriment or even destruction of the Protestant Nonconformist groups.[119] Politically, the 1902 Act meant that the religiously observant members of migrant communities, Jewish and Catholic, who on other issues could be counted upon to support progressive organisations, here stood behind the Conservatives and the resistance towards subsequent Liberal attempts to alter the Act. In 1890, Father Edmund Buckley of the Southwark school board, the parish priest of one East London diocese, and thus closely concerned with the issue, had framed the dilemma posed by the education controversy in the following terms: 'While our sympathies are Liberal in everything else, in this we are conservatives of conservatives.'[120] Even Home Rule, for the religious East End Irish Catholic, had, according to the Church, to cede precedence to religious education.[121]

The support by voters from minorities for the Conservative policy on education, and for the Moderates in the LCC elections, is incongruous when one considers the anti-alien agitation being carried out by the right wing of the Conservative Party parallel to the education legislation. This campaign, anticipating Government moves towards enshrining formal restrictions on immigration into the country, was not above using the changing ethnic make-up of East End schools as a political tool. An undated pamphlet issued by Conservative Central Office at the time reads:

> Even from the schools the English children are being driven by the alien. In January 1892, at the Rutland Street Board School, there were 862 Christian and 207 Jewish pupils. In the same month of 1902 there were 268 Christian and 878 Jewish pupils. It is only right that these children should be educated, but it is not right that the native children should be supplanted by the Jewish alien.[122]

The changing demographic in the board schools of East London was fixed upon by the right wing of the Conservative Party, the Primrose League,

[119] J.E.B. Munson, *A Study of Nonconformity in Edwardian England*, p. 74.

[120] *Pall Mall Gazette* (14 January 1890).

[121] See Joan Allen, 'Uneasy Transitions: Irish Nationalism, the Rise of Labour and the *Catholic Herald*, 1888–1918', in Marley, *The British Labour Party and Twentieth Century Ireland*, p. 46 for the stance of the editor of the *Catholic Herald*, Charles Diamond, as regards the Education versus Home Rule controversy in British Catholicism.

[122] LSE JF2(42C)265 Anon., *Alien Immigration, Issued by the Conservative Central Office, Report of the Royal Commission on Alien Immigration, Extracts from the Evidence Given before Royal Commission and from the Commissionaires Report* (London: Conservative Central Office, undated).

and the BBL as evidence of 'alien' encroachment into the territory of the native working class. The Jewish authorities would have concurred with the attack on Liberal policy set out by the Primrose League in a 1905 pamphlet that: 'By supporting mere secular education in our elementary schools, they aim a fatal blow at the cause of religious teaching and promote a policy which is ruinous to the best interests of all religion.'[123] Yet at the same time the Primrose League was busy campaigning against immigration in Whitechapel and Stepney, a campaign that on occasions descended into antisemitism. The Revd Parry stated at a Primrose League meeting in Whitechapel that 'He did not like to be represented in Parliament by a Jew', drawing loud applause for his remarks.[124] There were also concerns among elements of the Conservative Party over Christian children receiving religious instruction from a Jewish teacher, reversing the concerns of the Jewish communal leadership. Viscount Cranborne warned of Christian children being 'governed for six days [i.e., at school] by the morality of a Jewess [a Jewish schoolteacher]', incidentally revealing a casual antisemitism still present in the upper echelons of the Tory front bench.[125]

The Liberal Party, having been returned to power in the electoral landslide of 1906, partly on the strength of public feeling over the Education Act, and with the support of Nonconformist allies and the Labour Party, set about legislating to reverse Conservative policies. This included financial support for denominational schools, implemented by the Conservatives in 1902–1903. Sectarian religious instruction in the erstwhile voluntary schools would be replaced by a blanket non-denominational religious teaching that had been a feature of the board schools before their abolition. Any denominational religious instruction would have to be paid for by the religious communities themselves. For the Jewish and Catholic religious and secular leaderships, the importance of retaining the 1902 Act against Liberal and Nonconformist incursions crossed party political lines, and required a united response from political representatives, of whatever ideological persuasion. That voters belonging to religious minorities should vote *as* Jews or *as* Catholics, and that politicians should vote in parliament according to their faith rather than according to their secular political loyalties, represented a significant departure.

---

[123] LSE ILP/08/1905/95, Anon., *'What is the Primrose League?'* (London: Primrose League, 1905).

[124] David Feldman, 'The Importance of Being English: Jewish Immigration and the Decay of Liberal England', in Feldman and Stedman Jones, *Metropolis London*, p. 69.

[125] Tony Taylor, *The Politics of Reaction: The Ideology of the Cecils and the Challenge of Secular Education, 1889–1902* (Leeds: University of Leeds Educational Administration and History Monographs, 1997), p. 28.

Both hierarchies had consistently stressed the separation of religious faith and political allegiance. Discussing the question of a Jewish 'bloc' in 1885, the *Jewish Chronicle* had poured scorn on the notion: 'Surprise, or no surprise, Jews actually do support Radicals, wonder or no wonder, Jews are often Tory. The fact is that Jews have become so thoroughly English that they regard their responsibility as voters entirely as Englishmen.'[126] 'Your vote should not be decided simply by the religion which a candidate may profess, even though that religion be Catholic', Cardinal Vaughan had written in 1894, 'You must consider the work to be done and the fitness of the candidate to do it.'[127] St. George Mivart wrote in 1883 that: 'Their duty [as Catholics] is to vote according to their conviction as individual citizens, and not at all as *Catholics*, for in England there is not and cannot be a Catholic party.'[128] The historical reluctance of both leaderships to promote political activity on sectarian lines was partly rooted in their acute awareness of antisemitic and anti-Catholic conspiracy theories. These accusations, expressed on both the political left and the right, of shadowy, underground alliances held by Jews or Catholics that crossed the political divides visible on the surface, would only be bolstered by political organisation on religious lines.[129] The Liberal proposals, however, were deemed so serious, that cross-party consultation and cooperation between co-religionists to resist the legislation was openly called for by the Jewish and Catholic press, and encouraged by communal leaders.

In a debate at the Maccabaean Club in May 1906, H.S.Q. Henriques spoke in favour of a pooling of resources by Liberal and Conservative Jewish politicians, and suggested that they should consult each other on matters pertaining to education.[130] At the same meeting Henriques had declared, 'it would be a monstrous thing for any form of Christianity to be taught in a Jewish school. It was all very well for Christian schools, but nobody desired [non-denominational] Christian teaching for Jewish children.'[131] The 'four-fifths rule', a Liberal compromise proposal that would allow for denominational religious education in an area where a religious group formed such a majority, would, he suggested, lead to the ghettoisation of Jewish and Irish communities, 'the establishment of an Irish quarter in every city in this country'. 'It might be possible', Henriques concluded, 'to appoint

---

[126] *Jewish Chronicle* (26 November 1885), in Brodie, *The Politics of the Poor*, p. 185.

[127] Herbert Vaughan, *Catholics and their Civic Duties* (London: Burns and Oakes, 1894), p. 12.

[128] McEntee, *Social Catholic Movement in Great Britain*, pp. 139–140 (original emphasis).

[129] The education controversy did lead to a minor resurgence of anti-Catholic sentiment and conspiracy theories in certain areas of the country.

[130] *Jewish Chronicle* (18 May 1906).

[131] *Jewish Chronicle* (18 May 1906).

a Council to look after the interests of the Catholics and the Jews, though a more satisfactory means would be the exemption of Jewish and Catholic schools from the Act.'[132]

The Catholic Church urged an anti-Education Bill alliance amongst the faithful, with the clergy, Liberal and Conservative believers, Irish Nationalists, and Catholic trade unionists making common cause.[133] On the ground in East London, the spirit of cooperation against attacks on the voluntary schools resulted in the election of Gordon as an independent candidate to the LCC. Gordon enjoyed the support of the Anglo-Jewish leadership, local Jewish immigrant communal leaders, and the local Catholic population, an unprecedented joint action and pooling of resources by the two diasporic communities.[134]

The *Jewish World* editorial of 6 March 1908, headlined 'A Menace to Judaism', articulated Anglo-Jewish fears on the issue: 'from the point of view of the Jewish voluntary schools, the Government's new Education Bill stands condemned as a particularly gross piece of injustice'. Secular education would threaten the survival of a religiously observant Jewish community:

> The process by which the modern English Jew is gradually becoming more and more estranged from the practice of his religious observations must be arrested if English Judaism is to preserve its existence ... If the Education Bill now before parliament becomes law ... English Judaism will have been dealt the severest blow it has experienced in modern times.[135]

The move towards minority religious communities forming political 'blocs' on the continental model, however, never evolved further than polemic and informal consultations. The domestic British model, of a political framework that cut across ethnic and religious stratifications, proved extremely durable. The proposed alliances between the different strands of political and religious Catholicism were intended to address a particular issue, if an important and emotive one, and did not hold fast when education began to take a back seat to other concerns. Similarly, the support by both Jewish and Catholic religious leaderships for H.H. Gordon, the convergence of Jewish and Catholic interests in East End politics that culminated in his election, was not repeated, at least in the Edwardian period. The education controversies made for exceptional political alliances and allegiances, but when the issue

---

132 *Jewish Chronicle* (18 May 1906).

133 Eric G. Tenbus in *English Catholics and the Education of the Poor 1847–1902* (London: Pickering and Chatto, 2010) discusses in detail the relationship between Catholic conservatives and the Irish Nationalists and their responses to the education controversy.

134 Alderman, *London Jewry and London Politics*, p. 49.

135 *Jewish World* (6 March 1908).

had died down traditional loyalties were again resumed. In some respects, the cross-political and cross-faith alliances were ultimately unnecessary. The Liberal Education Bills were effectively checked by the House of Lords, and abandoned before the outbreak of the First World War.[136] Denominational schools, and explicitly Jewish and Catholic religious education, survived. So did the problem of balancing the integration of minority youth into the wider society with the maintenance of religious loyalty. The events of 1904 proved, however, the power, at least on a purely local level, that minorities, their interests often overlooked by the mainstream political parties, could wield electorally if prepared to unite over an issue judged vital to the interests of the community. No other issue in the Edwardian period acted as a catalyst for the repetition of this confluence.

## Socialism, the Trade Unions, and Religious Education

The bulk of the socialist movement supported a policy of wholly secular education in elementary schools. Ideologically, religious education as practised in the voluntary schools was seen as at best a distraction and at worst an anti-progressive form of indoctrination. Clerical control of education, in socialist eyes, promoted irrationality and worked against the scientific rationalism that needed to be developed in the coming generation if socialism was to be achieved.[137] The school boards abolished in the 1902 Act were 'invariably seen [by the socialist movement] as democratically elected bodies enabling the working class to have some control over their own children'.[138] This sentiment, though approached from the opposite angle, was shared by the Catholic Church, which argued that faith-based voluntary schools were a desirable barrier against political radicalism and subversion.[139] Many on the left would have agreed with this statement, that sectarian religious instruction, now strengthened and enshrined by the 1902 Act, worked against socialism. For Philip Snowden, the Bill was 'anti-social, reactionary, and anti-educational ... and so should be fought by all socialists'.[140] The final stage of the Education controversy was reached whilst Labour was still involved in a 'progressive alliance' with the Liberal Party that was pushing forward the campaign for repeal. This was an informal agreement that would reap dividends for the new Labour Party

---

[136] N.R. Gullifer, 'Opposition to the 1902 Education Act', *Oxford Review of Education*, Vol. 8, No. 1 (1982), p. 93.

[137] Brian Simon, *Education and the Labour Movement, 1870–1920* (London: Lawrence and Wishart, 1965), pp. 142–143 and Kevin Manton, *Socialism and Education in Britain, 1893–1902* (London: Woburn Press, 2001), pp. 147–148.

[138] Simon, *Education and the Labour Movement*, pp. 225–226.

[139] Tenbus, *English Catholics and the Education of the Poor*, p. 94.

[140] *Labour Leader* (26 April 1902), in Simon, *Education and the Labour Movement*, p. 227.

in the 1906 General Election, and had manifested itself prior to this point in frequent joint Liberal–Labour organisation and campaigning in East London.[141] Labour was inclined to support Liberal policy on this issue in any case, whilst many in the movement wished to push the repeal of the Act further, and establish a uniform secularity in the education system.

As well as opposition to religious instruction on a theoretical level, Labour Party leaders such as Keir Hardie argued that, as the elementary school problem affected working-class families especially, it was the right and responsibility of the Labour Party to formulate policy and campaign on the matter.[142] Rather than the non-denominational but Christian-based religious provision envisaged by the Nonconformists, the Labour Party and the SDF pressed for an entirely secular education, with religious instruction of whatever kind to be private and carried on out of school hours. But the labour movement was not unanimous in this position. From 1902 onwards a rear-guard action was mounted by socialists and trade unionists, mainly from the Catholic faith or representing Catholic members. The matter came to a head in the successive TUC congresses held between 1907 and 1910.

In 1907, the TUC had passed a resolution calling for 'a national education system under popular control, free and secular'.[143] The resolution, and the policy of the Labour Party and the TUC towards education generally, was opposed and resisted by a minority of union leaders, in particular those men representing trades with significant Irish involvement such as the docking and building industries. In December 1907, the Executive Committee of the Labour Party received a communication from the 'Trade Union Section of the Catholic Federation' expressing deep concern at the direction of the trade union movement:

> We, the members of the Trade Union Section of the Catholic Federation, and trades affiliated to the Labour Party, desire to place on record, our strong protest, against the Secular System of Education, for our Elementary Schools, which has been placed on the Programme of the Labour Party ... It is opposed to the conscientious belief of many ardent and sympathetic members of the labour cause, on whose behalf we speak ... There are enough reforms to engage our attention for many years to come, & upon which we are united. *Why allow then this discontent to grow in our ranks?*[144]

[141] See Paul Adelman, *The Decline of the Liberal Party, 1910–1931* (Harlow: Longman Group Ltd, 1981), p. 7; Biagini, *British Democracy and Irish Nationalism*, pp. 314 and 364; Dutton, *A History of the Liberal Party since 1900*, p. 37.

[142] Munson, *A Study of Nonconformity*, p. 368.

[143] Warwick Modern Records Centre, MSS/292/PUB/4/1/7, Trade Union Congress Report, 1907.

[144] Manchester People's History Museum, LPGC/22/68, Letter from the Trade Union

At the subsequent TUC Congress, resistance by Catholic trade unionists was led by James Sexton, the Liverpool dockers' representative, whose members were '75 per cent Catholic'.[145] Sexton argued against the prevalent sentiment of the Congress:

[It] is a distinct breach of faith with those who have deep religious convictions to introduce anything of a secular character like this … They joined the Labour movement for labour purposes. Had they been asked to join it with the idea of introducing secularism into schools they would have kept out of the movement altogether.[146]

G.H. Roberts, on the other hand, arguing in favour of the wholly secular resolution, posited that a completely secular curriculum was more equitable to religious minorities such as Jews and Irish Catholics than the alternative, a form of non-denominational Christian teaching unacceptable to either group. He followed with a plea for unity:

The governing classes are glad to see any apple of discord thrown into our midst in the hopes that we may be set at each other's throats. It is utterly impossible to reconcile the conflicting interests of the various sects of the community … The only way out of the difficulty is to be found in the resolution.[147]

Despite the dockers' opposition, the resolution was overwhelmingly carried, with a majority in favour of 1,302,000.[148]

The 1910 and 1911 Congresses were if anything more fraught. Neither the majority in favour of completely secular education nor the minority against it had shifted its position; the same arguments were put forward with increasingly bad temper. At the 1910 Sheffield TUC Congress, Roberts, again appealing for unity, concluded that he:

absolutely declined to admit the right of the parent to say what theological views the child should attach to itself. He wanted the children to be so educated that when they reached the age that they were able to form their own opinions they should not do it as a matter of instinct because

---

Section of the Catholic Federation to the Executive Committee of the Labour Party (original emphasis).

[145] Warwick Modern Records Centre, MSS/292/PUB/4/1/8, Annual Trade Union Congress Report, 1908.

[146] Warwick Modern Records Centre, MSS/292/PUB/4/1/8, Annual Trade Union Congress Report, 1908.

[147] Warwick Modern Records Centre, MSS/292/PUB/4/1/8, Annual Trade Union Congress Report, 1908.

[148] Warwick Modern Records Centre, MSS/292/PUB/4/1/8, Annual Trade Union Congress Report, 1908.

of what their fathers have impressed upon them, but as a result of reason and conviction.[149]

James O'Grady, representing the Furnishing Trades unions and picking up the baton of the anti-secularist members, warned that the policy would harm the party politically in key areas of East London. Will Thorne, hero of the 1889 Gasworkers' strike, countered:

> [The] 700 Roman Catholic voters in my constituency [West Ham] agree with me [in support of secular education] because I play the straight game. As soon as you start pandering to any of them, you are bound to have division in your ranks. That is why Catholics have always worked unanimously with me.[150]

The 1911 debate almost ended in violence when James Sexton took the stand again to argue against secularism. 'Taunts were flung at Mr Sexton from the gallery and other parts of the hall, and at one time an ugly rush was made up the central pathway towards the would-be speaker, who shook his fist and shouted in protest at the refusal of Congress to hear him speak.'[151] O'Grady concluded his speech with the following warning:

> You may pass your laws and your resolutions on this question, but the Catholics of this country will still resist your attitude. If that be so, are you going to say that we as Catholics shall not work shoulder to shoulder with our fellow Trade Unionists until we have swallowed this bitter pill?[152]

O'Grady and Sexton threatened an unprecedented break with the mainstream British labour movement, a movement they had both been involved with from their youth. It is evidence of how bitter the dispute was, and how determined the representatives of Catholic trade union members were to resist either secularism in schools or a version of Christian instruction that they did not agree with, that the threat was even made. O'Grady and Sexton contemplated a split from the mainstream trade union movement on religious grounds; the idea of a Catholic union on the continental model, to go further than the Catholic Federation, essentially a pressure group working within the TUC, had gone. It is doubtful whether such a movement could have succeeded. Irish Catholics were numerically strong in a small number

---

[149] Warwick Modern Records Centre, MSS/292/PUB/4/1/10, Annual Trade Union Congress Report, 1910.

[150] Warwick Modern Records Centre, MSS/292/PUB/4/1/10, Annual Trade Union Congress Report, 1910.

[151] Warwick Modern Records Centre, MSS/292/PUB/4/1/11, Annual Trade Union Congress Report, 1911.

[152] Warwick Modern Records Centre, MSS/292/PUB/4/1/11, Annual Trade Union Congress Report, 1911.

of industries, but a small minority in the labour movement as a whole, as the majorities carried by the pro-secular elements of the TUC show.[153] It is also questionable whether Catholic workers themselves, as opposed to their leaders, would have accepted such a move, which could only have weakened union strength and bargaining power.

From the TUC reports, there is no evidence of comparable protest from Jewish socialists and trade unionists over the secular education resolutions. Whilst the heated debates conducted at TUC congresses suggest Catholic trade unionists, or those union leaders representing Irish Catholic members, broadly sharing the aims and reflecting the fears of the Catholic hierarchy on education, Jewish trade unionists, in contrast, articulated no such common ground with the BoD and the United Synagogue. This was symptomatic of a greater prevalence of atheistic sentiment, or at least secularism, within the Jewish left, as compared with their Irish Catholic counterparts. It points to a greater divide within the Jewish community between trade unionists and the communal hierarchy, the radicalism of Jewish trade unionists and possibly greater acceptance that religious instruction could and should take place outside of school hours, in the synagogue school or *chedarim* rather than the school classroom. For the labour movement, the issue of religious education, like immigration restrictions and attitudes towards anarchist and syndicalist activity, had become defined through the prism of ethnic and religious difference and outsider status, through Irish Catholic opposition to the position adopted by the majority of the TUC.

## Outsider Proselytisation

Together with the insidious threat of cultural submergence of migrant communities, and in particular youth, by an irreligious wider East End working-class culture, and the overt challenge to communal loyalty presented by the socialist movement, was a third factor perceived as contesting the authority of the Jewish and Catholic hierarchies. This was the presence of Protestant organisations in East London, and in particular those groups that attempted actively to proselytise among Jewish and Irish Catholic communities. These bodies, ranging from William Booth's Salvation Army, which worked amongst the homeless and destitute, to the East London Mission for the Jews, founded in 1877 by Revd M. Rosenthal, a Jewish convert to Christianity, were viewed with suspicion and hostility by the

---

[153]  In 1910 a Conference of Catholic Trade Unionists was indeed organised in Salford, 'for the purposes of safeguarding the Catholic interests of the Catholic members of the Trade Union and Labour movements'; however, this movement operated *within* the broader TUC organisation. McEntee, *The Social Catholic Movement in Great Britain*, pp. 205–206.

minority religious leaderships.[154] On occasion they met with violence from Irish Catholic and Jewish East-Enders themselves.[155]

The fears of Protestant evangelism were tied in with the concerns discussed already, whether over apathy and cultural assimilation or sympathy and involvement with radical politics. The cultural and religious alienation of young Irish men and women so feared by Cardinal Vaughan was perceived as leaving the youth vulnerable to the appeals of Protestant evangelism, a first step on the road not only towards the abandonment of the old faith but the adoption of a new one. Socialism, for all the anti-religious polemic of men such as Robert Blatchford and Ernest Bax, was also viewed as a first step towards Protestantism.[156] Of particular concern, and much discussed in communal newspapers such as the *Jewish Chronicle* and *The Tablet*, was the fate of young Jewish or Catholic children orphaned or separated from their parents, and subsequently raised in families or institutions belonging to another faith.[157] There was also reluctance by the leaderships to accept that those who did convert were acting through genuine religious sentiment and belief, but rather held that adoption of the new faith was motivated by greed, ambition, or some deep-seated moral failing. The issues raised by proselytisation, like provision of religious education, bring to the surface the complex interplay of affirmation and negation of identity. Public conversion to another faith, in minority communities, involved an exchange of identities, desired or forced, that socialist political beliefs or trade union membership did not.

The challenge presented by Christian evangelism in the East End concerned the BoD sufficiently for a body to be set up whose specific role was to counter attempts at conversion. The 1906 report of the Mission Committee reflects the deep suspicion held of the motives of Jewish converts to the Christian faith, and contains dire warnings for the fate of 'Hebrew Christians', their ultimate fate as 'social outcast[s] and ... business failure[s].[158] The attitude of the Jewish hierarchy towards Christian evangelism was summed up by the *Jewish Chronicle*, which described successful proselytising as the 'conversion of bad Jews into worse Christians'.[159] The East End Christian clergy itself

---

[154] Renshaw, 'Control, Cohesion and Faith', pp. 37–38.

[155] W.T. Gidney, *The Jews and their Evangelisation* (London: Student Volunteer Missionary Union, 1899), p. 97.

[156] Fishman, *East End Jewish Radicals*, pp. 118–119.

[157] Renshaw, 'Control, Cohesion and Faith', p. 38.

[158] London Metropolitan Archives, ACC/3121/E/03/028, Missionary Activities: Counter Action to Attempted Conversions, Report of the Mission Committee.

[159] *Jewish Chronicle* (10 March 1899). The sensationalist writer Edgar Wallace, in *The Council of Justice*, a late-Edwardian work permeated with suspicion of radical politics in general and Jewish East End socialism in particular, makes a similar claim on the failure of Christian

was split on the issue of Jewish conversion, with attitudes ranging from enthusiasm for the 'gathering of the lost sheep of the House of Israel' to attitudes very similar to those expressed by the BoD, questioning the moral stamina and wholeheartedness of 'genuine converts'.[160] There were other Christian clergymen in the East End, such as the Revd G. Martyold of the German Lutheran Church in Whitechapel, who frankly viewed efforts to convert Jews as a waste of time and money.[161] There was a sub-genre of popular Yiddish-language fiction on the dangers of Christian evangelism, such as 'The Girl from Kovno and the London Missionary: A True Story of Jewish Life', a serial published in 1899.[162]

Both the Jewish and Catholic leaderships were particularly sensitive to cases in which young children, through the death of parents or some other separation, came to be in the care of organisations outside the religion. Cardinal Vaughan especially involved himself with the issue. In his appeal for 'A Crusade of Rescue for the Orphans', the Cardinal wrote:

> Thousands and thousands of Catholic children have been robbed of their faith in past years ... they have been spirited from one place to another; they have been cut off from all Catholic influence; their very names have been changed; and they have been sent out into the world aliens to the religion of their baptism.[163]

For Vaughan, the destitution of the elder generation resulted in the apostasy of the younger one:

> The condition of the children of drunken, loafing, vicious, criminal parents – who have lost all sense of self-respect, and all trace of Catholic conscience – is painful in the extreme, not only for the obvious reasons, but also because ... many of them [the children] are liable at any time to be placed in Institutions, in which they must lose their faith.[164]

One institution that repeatedly clashed with the Catholic hierarchy was Dr Barnardo's orphanage and adoption agencies. Although the charity

---

proselytization among a community he describes as 'curious low-down Jews who stand in the same relation to their brethren as White Kaffirs [sic] to a European community'. Edgar Wallace, *The Council of Justice* (London: Ward Lock and Co. Ltd, 1908), p. 20.

[160] Booth, *Life and Labour of the People in London*, Third Series, *Religious Influences*, Vol. 2, pp. 8–9.

[161] LSE/BOOTH/ B/224 pp. 150–157, Interview with Revd G. Martyold, minister of the German Lutheran Church, Little Alie Street, 21 February 1898.

[162] Prager, *Yiddish Culture*, p. 27.

[163] Booth, *Life and Labour of the People in London*, Third Series, *Religious Influences*, Vol. 7, *Summary*, p. 268.

[164] Herbert Vaughan, *A Crusade of Rescue for the Orphans* (London: Burns and Oates, 1899), p. 7.

was generally esteemed for its good work, the Catholic Church perceived Barnardo's as having a Protestant bias and a reluctance to place children born into the Catholic faith in Catholic homes. These disputes occasionally ended in litigation. Coupled with this, the Irish Nationalist movement defined the threat not only in religious but also in demographic terms, as an instrument of an explicit policy of detaching Irish Catholic children from a second- or third-generation London Gaelic culture and politics, through adoption or the workhouse. John Denvir wrote:

> There cannot be a doubt but that the Catholic population of Great Britain … would be much greater now had it not been that, up to a comparatively recent date, Catholic children in workhouses could not be educated in the religion of their parents. This proselytism … accounts for the large number of characteristically Irish names borne by many who are lost to both creed and country.[165]

The policy of placing Catholic boys and girls with non-Catholic families, and the refusal of institutions such as the workhouse to provide Catholic religious education was thus condemned both by the Church as an attack on religion, and by Irish Nationalists, who saw it as an attempt to instil an English Protestant affiliation at the expense of Irish patriotic sentiment. This fed the *externalisation* of Catholic social tensions in the East End. The BoD also interested themselves in Jewish children who had ended up in charitable institutions, intervening in certain cases, 'to prevent the [child] from being brought up in another faith', and ensuring that 'the child was placed under the care of a respectable Jewish woman'.[166]

Whilst the communal hierarchies involved themselves in countering outside attempts at proselytisation, working-class Jews and Irish Catholics on the ground in East London also responded to missionary efforts in various ways. These responses ranged from hostility and even violence, through good-natured contempt or chaff, to acceptance and conversion. A hostile physical response, especially during a missionary's first foray into the East End, was not uncommon. This tied in with a wider East End working-class suspicion of outsiders of any kind, and in particular so-called 'do-gooders'.[167] Class tensions exacerbated such disconnection, pious observance being viewed in some quarters as the preserve of the bosses, 'as belonging to a

[165] Denvir, *The Irish in Britain*, p. 255.

[166] London Metropolitan Archives, ACC/3121/G/01/001/004, Reports 1901–1905, April 1901: Jewish Lad in Dr Barnardo's Home.

[167] McLeod, *Class and Religion in the late Victorian City*, pp. 44–45. See Arthur Morrison, *A Child of the Jago* (Chicago: Academy Chicago Publishers, 1995) (originally published 1896), chapter 2 for a fictionalised (and cynical) description of mission work in the poorest areas of the East End.

wholly different class from themselves'.[168] Early Salvation Army excursions into Tower Hamlets were met with orange peel, stones, and jeering.[169]

Missionaries, or those mistaken for missionaries, found themselves under attack from both diasporic communities. As Bermant writes: 'Any "toff", which is to say, anyone respectably dressed, might be taken for a missionary, and many an innocent passer-by, who had nothing more sinister to him than a stiff collar and shiny boots, suffered indignity and assault.'[170] In certain respects this victimisation of 'respectable' interlopers into the East End recalls the tensions that surrounded the Ripper murders of 1888. Just as any well-to-do stranger during those traumatic few months might be mistaken for 'Jack', so in Jewish or Irish Catholic areas middle-class outsiders were labelled as evangelists, with all the unwanted attention that entailed.[171] Israel Zangwill, in the introduction to *Children of the Ghetto*, recalled Jewish ministers from more prosperous or suburban congregations dressed in the costume of their Anglican contemporaries being mistaken for missionaries in Whitechapel and pelted with debris.[172]

Violence was one response to outsider evangelism. Perhaps a more common reaction was indifference, annoyance, or enjoyment of the spectacle of preaching and the back-and-forth arguments of preacher and crowd. However, proselytisation in the East End by Protestant missionaries was not wholly a failure. There were converts. Their numbers are difficult to ascertain: the missionary groups overestimated the number of those who had been converted, and the minority communal organisations underestimated them. By the 1890s, much missionary work amongst the Jewish community in East London was being undertaken by Jews who had themselves converted to Christianity. The Hebrew–Christian Prayer Union, established in 1882 by the Revd Henry Aaron Stern, stressed (much as had Cardinal Manning, in a different context) the Jewish roots of Christianity and the essential compatibility of Jewish culture and the Christian religion.[173] Booth describes

---

[168] Bishop Walsham How, quoted in Thompson, *Socialists, Liberals and Labour*, p. 17.

[169] See Pamela J. Walker, *Putting the Devil's Kingdom Down: The Salvation Army in Victorian Britain* (Berkeley: University of California Press, 2001), pp. 26 and 30–31 for descriptions of violence against the Salvation Army.

[170] Bermant, *Point of Arrival*, p. 57.

[171] For the supposed 'respectable' (or indeed Jewish or Irish or socialist) identity of 'Jack', see Christopher Frayling, 'The House that Jack Built', in Alexandra Warwick and Martin Willis, *Jack the Ripper: Media, Culture, History* (Manchester: Manchester University Press, 2007) and Judith Walkowitz, *City of Dreadful Delight* (London: Virago Press, 1992), chapter 7, 'Jack the Ripper'.

[172] Zangwill, *Children of the Ghetto*, p. 10.

[173] Todd M. Endelman, *Radical Assimilation in English Jewish History, 1656–1945* (Indianapolis: Indiana University Press, 1990), p. 161.

a Christian meeting in an East End basement with prayers in Yiddish, overseen by a missionary and his wife, both of whom were Jews who had converted.[174] Despite the claim of a speaker at the meeting that 'they are coming over in thousands!', the actual number of Jews who converted was probably small, as was the number of working-class Irish or Italian Catholics who embraced Protestantism.[175]

A major contributing factor to the rarity of successful conversions in the diasporic communities, apart from the strong disapproval of religious and secular leaderships, was the isolation and hostility faced by converts from within the working-class neighbourhoods. Converts who openly took up another faith faced permanent outsider status for themselves and their families. One had the choice of leaving the area or accepting ostracism by neighbours and kinsfolk. Conversion to another religious creed brought a pariah status that political activity or religious indifference did not.[176] Irish Catholic and Jewish socialists and anarchists certainly faced disapproval and suspicion from within the community, as did their counterparts back in the homelands of their parents.[177] The Chief Rabbi denounced Jewish anarchists and questioned their Jewish status, and the threat of potential excommunication by the Catholic Church hung over Irish radicals. But from *within* their neighbourhoods, from within the working-class migrant populations of the East End, socialists were generally recognised as still belonging in some sense to the wider community. A Jewish anarchist was still a Jew. Similarly, religious indifference or disinterest, attendance at church or synagogue on holy days if at all, the attitude among some male Irish Catholics that religion was 'woman's business', did not lead to social isolation and rejection. Lack of any strong religious faith did not impede Irish East-Enders defining themselves on a fundamental level as Catholic. For Jewish self-identity, faith was only one aspect of a self-definition that embraced not only religion but also culture, language, nationality, and politics. One did not have to be religiously observant to be Irish Catholic, as defined by self and as defined by the community; one did not have to attend synagogue to view oneself, and be viewed by one's neighbours, as a Jew. 'Once a Jew, always a Jew, whether he follows the Mosaic laws or disregards them', Benjamin Farjeon wrote in *Aaron the Jew*, published

---

174    Booth, *Life and Labour of the People in London, Religious Influences*, Vol. 2, pp. 231–232.

175    Booth, *Life and Labour of the People in London, Religious Influences*, Vol. 2, pp. 231–232.

176    Booth, *Life and Labour of the People in London, Religious Influences*, Vol. 2, pp. 231–232.

177    To the extent that in the Pale of Settlement *Shiva* (ceremonial mourning) was sometimes held by families for Jewish young men or women who had joined the revolutionary movement. Leonard Schapiro, 'The Role of the Jews in the Russian Revolutionary Movement', *Slavonic and East European Review*, Vol 40, No. 94 (December 1961), pp. 153–154.

in 1894.[178] But apostasy represented a public and explicit break with the community that could not be tolerated either by the communal leadership or the convert's neighbours. Working-class proselytes were placed under enormous social and psychological pressures from within the community.[179] For these reasons, evangelism amongst religious minorities in the East End involved only a small number of people, although its lack of success did not quell the hierarchies' anxieties over the issue.

In facilitating integration, in promoting religious instruction in schools, and in resisting outsider evangelism, the Church, the BoD, and the Jewish religious authorities followed very similar paths. The resemblances in the hierarchies' responses to challenges to their control, from whatever quarter, had its roots in the similar social origins and political inclinations of both leaderships. It also sprang from Catholicism and Judaism's shared continuing role into the late nineteenth century and beyond as ecclesiastical outsider groups in an English Protestant narrative. Given the similarities both in starting point and desired destination, it is perhaps surprising that the two leaderships did not make explicit common political cause more often. This was at least partly due to the resistance in British domestic politics to religious or ethnically based 'blocs' advancing minority interests, and the reluctance of both the Catholic and Jewish leaderships for the communities they had assumed the mantle of representing to vote *as* Jews or *as* Irish Catholics. Only during the education controversy did the hierarchies temporarily relax the prohibition on voting determined by religious identity. It should also be noted that fear of socialist radicalisation, even when not obviously apparent, was implicit in the concerns of the hierarchy that have been discussed in this chapter. Anglicisation, 'correct' religious instruction and a vigorous religious faith, safe from the temptations of outsider evangelism, would all strengthen working-class diasporic communities against the lures of the radical left. The adoption of an alternative faith, or indeed the wider secular culture of the metropolis, could easily, for the hierarchies, lead to socialism and subversion. In analysing the decisions and actions of the communal leaderships and drawing comparisons between the two, this narrative has strayed into the field of 'high' political history.

[178] B.L. Farjeon, *Aaron the Jew: A Novel*, Vol. 2 (London: Hutchinson and Co., 1894), pp. 194–195. See Rosalyn Livshin, 'The Other Self: Anglo-Jewish Fiction and the Representation of Jews in England, 1875–1905', in David Cesarani (ed.), *The Making of Modern Anglo-Jewry* (Oxford: Basil Blackwell, 1990), pp. 100–101. See also Israel Zangwill, 'English Judaism – A Criticism and a Clarification', *Jewish Quarterly Review*, Vol. 1, No. 4 (July 1889), pp. 389–390 and John Oswald Simon, 'Jews and Modern Thought', *Jewish Quarterly Review*, Vol. 11, No. 3 (April 1899), pp. 391–392 on the 'religious' and the 'secular' Jew. On the latter – 'They are Jews in spite of themselves, and in spite of their agnosticism.'

[179] Booth, *Life and Labour of the People in London, Religious Influences*, Vol. 2, pp. 231–232.

The focus will now return to the grass roots, analysing interactions on the ground between the East End Irish and Jewish communities and how belonging and difference functioned in physical, political, and cultural space in the period from 1889 to 1912.

# 5

# Grass-roots Interactions
# in the Diasporic East End

Having considered the agency and actions of outsiders, be they socialist organisers, communal leaderships, minority nationalists, or missionaries, this book will conclude by examining the interactions on the ground between the men and women who had migrated from Eastern Europe or Ireland to the East End and their descendants. This was the grass roots for whom and on whose behalf the protagonists of this study, whether revolutionary firebrands, trade union officials, or conservative religious leaders, claimed to be speaking and working. The Irish and Jewish diasporic working class were not mere passive receptacles as portrayed on occasion by both the socialist movement and the communal leaderships. Instead, they took an active part in defining the relationships formed with the city around them and with their neighbours in the streets and courts in which they lived. Radical politics provided one sphere in which these interactions could take place. In describing these interactions there is a difficult path to be navigated. It is necessary to avoid the rose-tinted narrative that stresses unproblematic inter-ethnic cooperation under the influence of a benevolent progressive movement, and an unbroken line of East End solidarity from the Dock Strike in 1889 to Cable Street in 1936. We must also be wary of the counter-argument, an account focusing only on ethnic tensions, racism, exclusion, and violence.[1] The reality lies somewhere in between, and it is on the complex and sometimes ambiguous personal relationships formed between individuals and communities that this chapter focuses. Violence and industrial unrest, as well as more peaceful facilitators of integration,

---

[1] See Tony Kushner, 'Jew and Non-Jew in the East End of London: Towards an Anthropology of "Everyday" Relations', in Geoffrey Alderman and Colin Holmes (eds), *Outsiders & Outcasts: Essays in Honour of William J. Fishman* (London: Gerald Duckworth and Co., 1993) for an extended overview of Jewish–Gentile social relations in East London that takes the discussion into the post-Second World War period.

could serve as a conduit for the creation of new East End identities, and shape Irish and Jewish communal and radical politics at a grass-roots level.

## The Roles of the Priest and the Rabbi in East London

The perceived power of the priest in the working-class Catholic communities of London throughout the nineteenth century, and the influence supposedly wielded by these communal leaders when compared with their Anglican or Nonconformist counterparts, was a source both of grudging admiration and suspicion for contemporary commentators. The degree to which many Catholic priests involved themselves in their flocks' day to day lives and shared in their hardships was compared favourably with the disconnection and indifference between those preaching and those being preached to felt by many in the Anglican Church. One Congregationalist minister commented to Charles Booth that 'The Romans ... are a real influence for good amongst the lowest class.'[2] The influence of the priesthood, particularly in Irish Catholic neighbourhoods, was proverbial. Jewish religious figures, whether the West End minister in Anglican apparel or the traditional East End *rav*, did not attract as much outside attention or even the sometimes benevolent jealousy of their Catholic counterparts that was displayed by Protestant clerics. However, within both Anglo-Jewry and the migrant populations of Stepney and Whitechapel the rabbi was a central figure in communal affairs. The position of priest and rabbi might appear on the surface to be radically different, but in the expectations of the neighbourhoods they ministered to similarities are evident, as was the complex reciprocal relationship at work between religious authorities and the diasporic communities.

The East End migrant rabbi in theory answered to the *Beth Din*, but many of the Jewish religious teachers in working-class areas simply ignored the ecclesiastical authorities, and even explicitly rejected their control.[3] The Catholic priest and leadership had a more formalised relationship. But within Catholic neighbourhoods the relationship between local religious leaders and their congregations was more nuanced than the contemporary narrative of the parish priest enjoying complete control over a submissive following of worshipers might suggest. In fact, both Catholic priests and Jewish religious leaders preaching and teaching in East London were involved in a system of give and take, with the religious and political messages being imparted as much shaped by their congregations as shaping

---

[2] Booth, *Life and Labour of the People in London*, Third Series, *Religious Influences*, Vol. 7, pp. 243–244.

[3] See Russell and Lewis, *The Jew in London*, pp. 97–99.

them. The grass-roots minority religious leaderships could lose the respect of or control over their parishioners as well as gain it, and religious leaders who transgressed the mores of migrant communities could find themselves ostracised in their parishes.

The main form of grass-roots Jewish religious worship in the late nineteenth-century and early twentieth-century East End took place in the *chevrot* – small places of worship, often in the back room of a house or a garret. These could be established with ease, requiring only a *minyan*, ten (male) worshippers, to function as a *shul* in Jewish religious law. The *chevrot* were places both of religious worship and discussion, and a support network for the worshippers. They formed an important chain in diasporic belonging, often named after the shtetl the migrants had travelled from, as well as a potential kernel for more explicit political organisation.[4]

In Booth's *Life and Labour* one *chevra*, visited by Beatrice Potter, is described thus:

> To reach the entrance you stumble over broken pavement and household debris … From the outside it appears a long wooden building surmounted by a skylight, very similar in construction to the ordinary sweater's workshop … From behind the trellis of the 'ladies gallery' you see at the far end of the room the richly curtained Ark of the Covenant, wherein are laid, attired by gorgeous vestments, the sacred scrolls of the Law.[5]

Potter goes on to mention the 'low, monotonous, but musical-toned recital of Hebrew prayers'. She concludes: 'you many imagine yourself in a far off eastern land'.[6] This was exactly the impression that the Anglo-Jewish leadership, ever anxious about how their East End co-religionists were perceived by wider society, wished to avoid. The *chevrot*, with their teachers often recent arrivals from Eastern Europe, seemed to some in the United Synagogue a relic of a Jewish past of ghettos, suspicion, persecution, and superstition. The Jewish establishment had an ambivalent attitude towards these places of worship and the influence of foreign rabbis. The *chevrot* were a bedrock of Jewish religious orthodoxy, and were usually hostile towards the doctrines of left-wing political movements.[7] However, they were also beyond the influence of the Anglo-Jewish leadership. Opposition to the independent or semi-independent *chevrot* in the Anglo-Jewish press was sometimes framed in practical rather than religious or political terms. An

---

[4] Gidley, 'Citizenship and Belonging', p. 131.

[5] Beatrice Potter, in Booth, *Life and Labour of the People in London*, First Series, *Poverty*, Vol. 3, p. 170.

[6] Beatrice Potter, in Booth, *Life and Labour of the People in London*, First Series, *Poverty*, Vol. 3, p. 170.

[7] C. Russell in Russell and Lewis, *The Jew in London*, pp. 127–128.

article in the *Jewish Chronicle* in March 1889, supporting the unification of the small-scale *chevrot*, stated the case thus:

> The scanty resources of too many *chevras* are frittered away in useless expenditure through an undue multiplication of these societies. It will thus also be possible to abolish those small *chevras* which meet in inconvenient, insanitary rooms, quite unsuitable, if not positively dangerous, as places of worship ... These *chevras* afford the surest foundation for raising the character and status of the Jewish working classes. If left severely alone their value as part of the organisation of the community is *nil*, but approached in a sympathetic spirit, attracted and attached to the main body, they become powerful potential elements of good and strength to the entire community.[8]

This is what Samuel Montagu attempted to achieve, with partial success, through the Federation of Synagogues. Montagu envisaged the Federation of Synagogues, whose primary aim was to bring a degree of unity to the Yiddish-speaking smaller *shuls* of the East End, as an umbrella organisation for the *chevrot* operating in the poorest parts of the capital. By Montagu's death in 1911 the membership of the Federation had surpassed that of the United Synagogue.[9] Crucially, Montagu also saw the Federation as a block against socialism and anarchism in the Jewish East End. In March 1889, Montagu stressed that 'One of the principal objects of the Federation was to endeavour to raise the social condition of the Jews in East London and prevent anything like anarchy and socialism.'[10] Montagu wished to bring order to the disorganisation of the *chevrot*, whilst accepting the use of Yiddish in synagogues and partially recognising the validity of the religious traditions brought over from Eastern Europe and the religious autonomy of worship in East London. The centralisation and control enjoyed by the Catholic Church, however, was never achieved, despite Montagu's efforts. In certain respects, there was common ground between what Samuel Montagu wanted to achieve with the Federation and the ambitions of Lily Montagu for Liberal Judaism in the first decade of the twentieth century. Both father and daughter wished to involve neglected elements of the Jewish East End proletariat that for whatever reason had fallen away from their religion, or felt marginalised from formal religious worship. The many differences between the Orthodox and Liberal conceptions of faith and worship, however, were profound, as evidenced by the bitterness of the Orthodox reaction to the formation of the JRU and the breakdown in filial relations within the Montagu family.

---

[8] *Jewish Chronicle* (8 March 1889).

[9] Alderman, *Modern British Jewry*, p. 154.

[10] Alderman, *Modern British Jewry*, pp. 166–167.

In a sermon preached at the Great Synagogue in 1891, Chief Rabbi Adler, discussing the East End Jewish community, commented: 'Granted that they [East End Jewry] may be inferior in refinement and culture to their wealthier brethren, yet do they not teach many a precious lesson of staunch, manly religious allegiance and of glad willingness to make heavy sacrifices for the sake of their faith?' He finished by appealing for 'the union of hearts [of East and West End Jewry] to continue and strengthen'.[11] Marriage was one key area where the religious autonomy of Orthodox Judaism in the East End collided with the legal framework of the wider society. Religious Jews, believing themselves divorced, as indeed they were under Jewish religious law, inadvertently committed what the state perceived as bigamy when remarrying. In Zangwill's *Children of the Ghetto*, one key sub-plot revolves around this disparity in what constituted marriage in 'English' and 'Jewish' legalistic terms. For the Jewish hierarchy this demonstrated the dangers of the fragmented nature of worship in Jewish East London, and the independence of 'foreign' rabbis beyond centralised control, disregarding both the strictures of the BoD and English law. Even by 1912, with the tailing off of the great migration of Jews from the Pale of Settlement, the autonomy of 'foreign' rabbis in the East End operating outside the control of the *Beth Din* and the civil statutes of wider English society caused the leadership much concern. In a statement to the Royal Commission on Divorce and Matrimonial Causes, the President of the BoD attacked the practice of Russian and Polish rabbis to solemnise Jewish marriages and to grant divorces (*gets*), with disregard to English civil law:

> [S]uch irregular proceedings on the part of these foreign Rabbis have been a constant source of trouble to the Board ... The position taken up by these Rabbis is, that it is their duty to administer the Jewish matrimonial law and that where the English law conflicts with the Jewish law the former must give way ... The misery caused in such cases [following a *get* and subsequent re-marriage] is entirely due to the action of the foreign Rabbis in this country.[12]

Catholic worship was centralised to a much greater degree than the multifaceted Jewish religious observance. The pious Catholic did not have to choose between multiple religious figures and bodies competing for loyalty, or between Orthodox, Reform, or Liberal affiliations. Catholic Modernism did not penetrate working-class Irish communities to any significant degree;

---

[11] Hermann Adler, *The Ideal Jewish Pastor: A Sermon Preached at the Great Synagogue* (London: Wertheimer, Lea and Co., 1891), pp. 16–17.

[12] Statement of the President of the BoD, 1912, Royal Commission on Divorce and Matrimonial Causes, in Englander, *A Documentary History of Jewish Immigrants*, pp. 55–56. See Feldman, *Englishmen and Jews*, pp. 296–297.

it was the preserve of middle-class intellectuals. However, in practical terms the Catholic Church at a grass-roots level was heavily reliant on the involvement of the Irish proletariat. The livelihood of the priest, the upkeep of buildings, and the maintenance of religious and educational instruction in the East End were all dependent upon the contributions, of both time and money, of working-class parishioners. The voluntary aid of the Catholic poor in fact extended to every facet of organised Catholicism in East London. The religious leadership acknowledged that the Catholic working class contributed proportionately more to the upkeep of churches than wealthy co-religionists. 'It is', wrote Cardinal Vaughan in an 1894 tract:

> chiefly the contributions of the industrious working classes that maintain our missions, they pay the burdensome and unproductive interest on capital debt, and are the steadfast supporters of the larger number of our churches. It is certain that a multitude of our missions would have to be closed were it not for the regular contributions of the poor, whose faith and zeal urge them to share their weekly wage with Christ Our Lord in the maintenance of His religion.[13]

*The Catholic Herald* frequently publicised the amounts raised by the Catholic poor to maintain their churches. In one article it proudly reported:

> In the course of the past seven years the poor people of Poplar have reduced the debt of the church [SS Mary and Joseph] to the extent of £3800, leaving £1000 still remaining. Considering the difficult circumstances of the case, the Catholics of Poplar may credit themselves with excellent work on behalf of their Church.[14]

Thus, whilst these churches in the East End did not enjoy the autonomy of the *chevrot*, the vital role played by the working classes in financing and maintaining missions gave Catholic worshipers a stake in the direction of their churches. This was coupled with an appreciation that without this support many Catholic missions would not have survived. This dependence by churches on the charity of parishioners again complicated the relationship between priest and congregation.

Clerics, of whatever denomination, shouldered a heavy weight of expectation from congregations when settling in an East End parish. In rural South-West Ireland and in the towns and villages of Poland and the Ukraine local religious leaderships commanded a significant degree of respect and deference. In poor rural communities it was often the priest or rabbi, as one of the rare figures in the community who was literate,

---

[13] Herbert Vaughan, *The Trinity Fund and the Material Condition of the Diocese* (London: Burns and Oates, 1894), p. 5.

[14] *Catholic Herald* (6 July 1900).

who transcribed letters to family who had emigrated, and read back their replies.[15] In the shtetls, the rabbi, as a respected figure in the community, would often take responsibility for dealing with the outside authorities. Disorientated migrants, often illiterate and in an urban environment for the first time, expected their religious leaders in the East End to continue to fulfil this role. In both communities during this period undertaking a religious vocation was seen as the highest honour that a (male) child could attempt to achieve.[16] In a humorous aside during an address by the Irish Nationalist politician John O'Connor to the Maccabaens, the MP noted: 'One of the things they [the Irish and the Jews] had in common was that the Irish people were very fond of making priests of their sons.'[17] The expectations of the communal hierarchies were no less great for prospective grass-roots religious leadership. In an editorial in the *Jewish Chronicle* of 31 January 1890, the 'ideal minister for the East End', it was suggested, would combine the following qualities:

> [He] must be neither a foreigner nor an Englishman ... He must be cosmopolitan. He must be foreign enough to be *en rapport* with the ideas and lives of his flock, and yet English enough to perceive and to resolutely oppose their undesirable characteristics. He must be at once on their level and immeasurably above them ... The mere fact that he is not of them, though he is among them, will suffice to hedge him with a dignity which will secure their respect and their trust.[18]

The language employed by the *Jewish Chronicle* suggested that for the English Jewish minister settling among and commanding the respect of immigrant East End Jewry was akin to taking up a position in some far outpost of the British Empire. The suspicion held by the Jewish establishment of Russian and Polish rabbinical teaching and preaching in the East End is also apparent. For the ideal minister, 'his freedom from narrow prejudice, his un-Russian way of looking at things, his broadminded, chivalrous mode of dealing with distress and misery – this must set him far above them'.[19] For

[15] See J.A. Jackson, *The Irish in Britain* (London: Routledge and Kegan Paul, 1963), p. 145 on the position of the rural Irish priest and Stampfer, *Families, Rabbis and Education* for discussion of the central role of Jewish religious leaders in the life of the community and its interactions with the outside world.

[16] Many of the leading Jewish and Irish socialists and nationalists in this period had in fact received in their youth an education intended to lead to a role as a priest or rabbi. See Rocker, *The London Years*, p. 72 for a description of the *Arbeter Fraynt* typesetter Narodiczky: 'He was an intelligent young man, who had received a good education, and had been studying to be a rabbi.'

[17] *The Jewish World* (9 March 1906).

[18] *Jewish Chronicle* (18 February 1898).

[19] *Jewish Chronicle* (18 February 1898).

the Anglo-Jewish hierarchy the ideal minister would combine the spiritual authority of a *rav* from the Pale of Settlement with the anglicised identity and values of a West End cleric. The supposed absence of an English rabbi of sufficient authority to 'protect' poor Jews from socialistic influences in East London was lamented in the *Jewish World*. 'Is it likely', the paper asked, 'that the Berner Street Club would have made any headway among the Jews of the East End if they had had to compete with a resident Rabbi of commanding authority?'[20] The desired qualities for those entering the Catholic clergy were no less demanding. In an article on the dangers facing Roman Catholic youth, *The Tablet* called for:

> More priests, living in their very midst, not jaded and worn out by the inevitable routine, but with time and energies to spare, to make friends of these young men, to spend their evenings with them, to know them personally and to take interest in them – this we may look forward to in the not far distant future.[21]

The power of the priest or rabbi in the diasporic East End communities cannot be doubted. However, both the influence enjoyed and the political leanings of the local religious leaders and teachers were by no means uniform. Elements of the metropolitan socialist and anarchist groups viewed the influence of the Catholic priest and Orthodox Jewish rabbi with suspicion. They regarded the grass-roots religious leadership as bastions and enforcers of that communal control so desired by the hierarchies. The sermons preached in church or synagogue were viewed as a means of furthering and cementing this control, and there was some truth in this. In the Catholic Church the West End leadership encouraged the parish priest both to monitor and to discourage radical and subversive activities in their neighbourhoods. In triennial visitation returns sent out by the Diocese of Westminster to priests of the different metropolitan parishes in 1911, among other questions on the state of the church building, marriages, and deaths, was the query: 'Have secret societies, spiritualism, or socialism obtained any footing among your people?'[22] In other words, priests were being encouraged to spy upon, or at least to scrutinise closely, their parishioners. But, in practice, within the confines of the hierarchy, Catholic priests had a certain amount of independence, both in expressing their own political preferences and in shaping their sermons to suit the opinions of their congregations. Indeed, a minority actively espoused

---

[20] *The Jewish World* (22 March 1889).

[21] *The Tablet* (14 May 1892).

[22] See Westminster Diocesan Archives Third Triennial Visitation Returns, 1911. Most correspondents replied curtly in the negative.

socialistic ideas, although, it must be emphasised, not with the approval of the hierarchy.[23]

Attitudes of parish priests towards the political activities of parishioners also varied according to the cultural and national background of the clerics. In her history of the Parish of St. Anne's Underwood Road in Whitechapel, Jean Olwen Maynard discusses the attitudes of East End priests from Poland, Lithuania, and Central Europe, coming from backgrounds 'where "socialism" was liable to mean something far more extreme than it did in Britain; most of the other East End priests didn't see it as a problem'.[24] In essence this reflected the position put forward by Robert Dell prior to his disillusionment with organised Catholicism. This stressed a fundamental divide between violent revolutionary socialist ideology on the continent and the form of gradualist, peaceful socialism prevalent in the United Kingdom, and that when the Papacy condemned 'socialism' it was the former that they were referring to. The attitudes of the East End priesthood towards grass-roots radical activity could range from committed socialism through various degrees of toleration to outright condemnation.

Attitudes towards the ethnic identity of the East End Catholic congregations also varied in the different parishes. The Church hierarchy from the 1840s onwards had strongly discouraged the maintenance of a separate Irish Catholic identity on English soil. But well into the twentieth century the rooting of Catholic faith in Irish identity continued to be a fixture in many East London parishes. The movement back to the use of Irish Gaelic may have originated with the educated professional London Irish middle class, but minority nationalism had strong and durable roots in the East End Irish working class. It was that demographic, after all, whose parents or grandparents had left Ireland in the most traumatic circumstances. It was among Irish East-Enders that resentment against both British colonial rule in Ireland and class exploitation in London was most potent. Irish priests and English priests with large Irish congregations tailored sermon and ritual to suit nationalist sensibilities – one priest in Bermondsey in South London 'forgetting' prayers for the monarch at the end of the service.[25] The testimonial given to one Catholic priest, Father William O'Connor of Lincoln's Inn Fields, born in Ireland but resident in the capital for many years, emphasised the continuing centrality of Gaelic identity for the London Irish in the Edwardian period. The Irish Nationalist MP Joseph Devlin, speaking at the testimonial, reminisced that O'Connor had once

---

[23] *The Labour Leader* (31 January 1908).

[24] Westminster Diocesan Archives, AAW/BOX LE, Jean Olwen Maynard, 'History of the Parish of St. Anne's Underwood Road, Vol. IV, 1911–1938'.

[25] Fielding, *Class and Ethnicity*, p. 41.

stated: 'No matter where the young priests went they should be faithful to the interests of the old country as well as to the interests of the faith.'[26]

O'Connor was the picture of the stereotypical rural Irish priest, commanding both fear and respect, transported to the backstreets of inner-city London. He achieved a degree of local notoriety in Wapping for his habit of chasing up miscreants and dragging them out of the local pubs, occasionally administering a beating in the street.[27] Father Lawless of Poplar also achieved a good deal of local fame, again prepared physically to chastise his flock, and held in 'absolute awe' by his parishioners.[28] Following Dean Lawless's death in 1902, the *Catholic Herald* reported at the funeral that 'a visitor to Poplar and Bow districts could easily imagine himself in a Catholic country. At the Poplar Liberal Club in the East India Rd, and at all the public buildings and churches in the neighbourhood flags were flying at half-mast, nearly all the shops were closed, and everywhere were to be signs of mourning.'[29]

But respect could be lost as well as gained, and whilst clerics did enjoy a great degree of influence over the political loyalties of their congregations, automatic adhesion to the politics of the individual priest was by no means guaranteed. Areas such as the Isle of Dogs and Wapping, neighbourhoods with large Irish Catholic populations mainly employed in dock work, achieved a degree of local fame for the independence displayed by these workers from priestly influence.[30] 'Poor Fr Egglemeers on the Isle of Dogs had nothing like that sort of influence [that Catholic priests usually enjoyed]. He had completely given up on his parishioners, whom he saw as having turned against the Church because they thought Cardinal Vaughan too conservative in his politics, and told the interviewer "I let them go to hell!".'[31]

Jewish and Irish Catholic migrants carried over from the rural communities they had left a tradition of deference, respect, even fear of clerics. Parallel to this there was also a subversive tradition of mocking and subtly undermining religious leaders, and of jokes directed at the priest or rabbi. One classic figure in the popular culture of the Irish countryside was the miserly priest who 'never put his hand in his pockets' and was always 'stood' a drink. Both

[26] *The Catholic Weekly* (8 July 1904).

[27] Westminster Diocesan Archives, AAW/BOX KV, Jean Olwen Maynard, 'History of the Parish of Guardian Angels, Mile End, Vol. I, 1868–1903'.

[28] Westminster Diocesan Archives, AAW/BOX KV, Jean Olwen Maynard, 'History of the Parish of Guardian Angels, Mile End, Vol. I, 1868–1903'.

[29] *The Catholic Herald* (24 October 1902).

[30] Brodie, *Politics of the Poor*, p. 194.

[31] Westminster Diocesan Archives, AAW/BOX KV, Jean Olwen Maynard, 'History of the Parish of Guardian Angels, Mile End, Vol. I, 1868–1903'.

priest and rabbi could be the subject of rather ribald humour as well. The strictness of the religious instruction of Catholic and Jewish children, and the noted propensity for instructors to resort to corporal punishment, also created a legacy of low-grade hostility that survived into adulthood.[32] The East End communist Hymie Fagan, recalling his religious instruction as a child, commented: 'Our teacher, the "Malamud" [instructor] was an evil tempered man, who slashed at us with his cane at the slightest provocation.' For Fagan, the beatings suffered as a boy continued to colour his views on organised religion as a grown man.[33]

The relationship between the cleric and the congregation was a reciprocal process, and if the politics of the local religious leadership at a parish level were substantially different from those of the worshippers, alienation and loss of influence could follow. When a religious leader was perceived to have transgressed the mores of the diasporic community, outright hostility and ostracism could be the result. Such was the case for Michael Wechster, reader at the Great Garden Street Synagogue in Whitechapel. Wechster had apparently reported a Jewish immigrant to the Metropolitan Police on a charge of vagrancy outside the synagogue. It soon transpired that the man was in fact a deserter from the Russian army, and having served his initial sentence of one month's hard labour would be deported back to Russia, where it was likely that he would be shot.[34]

The case aroused a good deal of anger amongst the Jewish community in Whitechapel, and the Home Secretary was petitioned. Wechster meanwhile found himself the target of widespread resentment and hostility among the congregation of the synagogue, and was ultimately stripped of his position as reader, and advised that he should 'leave London' as soon as possible. Wechster took his case against the synagogue to the *Beth Din*, and, when they ruled against him, to the Whitechapel County Court. J. Anthony Hawke, representing the synagogue, at one point asked the plaintiff: 'Would it not be regarded as a disgraceful thing for a minister of the Jewish faith to give in charge a beggar who asked for alms?'[35] The case is an interesting one. Wechster had broken no laws in turning the Russian beggar over to the police for vagrancy; in fact, he had every legal right to do so. But he had transgressed the conventions and practice of the community he was employed to minister to. Refusing to bestow charity to someone in need, and turning a co-religionist over to the police to face a custodial sentence and

---

[32] See Berrol, *East Side/East End*, p. 4.

[33] Manchester People's History Museum, CP/IND/FAG/1/5, Childhood memories of Hymie Fagan, pp. 10–11.

[34] *Pall Mall Gazette* (19 October 1906).

[35] *Pall Mall Gazette* (19 October 1906).

most likely deportation, Wechster had offended the values brought over with
the diaspora from Eastern Europe. Having committed this transgression,
the congregation responded by demanding and succeeding in obtaining his
dismissal.

This case illustrates the importance of popular opinion amongst the
diasporic communities concerning local ecclesiastical figures. In both
the Jewish and Catholic populations clerics were expected to observe the
custom of settling problems and transgressions *within* the community
or neighbourhood rather than resorting to the outside forces of law and
order, whilst consistently urging their flocks to abstain from breaking
the law. One example of this was the role many Catholic priests adopted
in deprived urban areas from the mid-nineteenth century as unofficial
policemen, going into areas where the police could not safely enter,
and admonishing and chastening offenders without resorting to legal
sanction.[36] The structures that Jewish and Catholic clerics were part of
were radically different, with the Jewish *rav* enjoying a far greater degree
of explicit autonomy and independence than the Catholic priest. But
the expectations of both communities about the role a religious leader
should assume, and what were considered affirmations or transgressions
of communal mores were similar.

Catholicism had traditionally stressed the doctrine of 'Holy Poverty' –
that the poor, by the very nature of their suffering and want, were closer
to God and godliness; that poverty 'was not a sin, but God's will, part of
the natural order of life'.[37] Joseph Keating, an Irish migrant to London
(by way of Wales) who later published recollections of his experiences in
*My Struggle for Life* (1916), expressed his own views on the spiritual and
social nature of extreme want: 'We were poor. There was nothing else
the matter with us. We were poor and they were rich. That was the only
difference between us. I saw that landowners, employers, and all rich
men and women were social criminals.'[38] Nevertheless, part of the power
and influence of the priest in poor immigrant communities sprang from
the fact that the clergy were largely perceived as *sharing* the poverty of
the congregation.[39] 'Holy Poverty' aside, much of the East End Catholic
clergy was appalled by the levels of deprivation they encountered in their

---

[36] Raphael Samuel, 'The Roman Catholic Church and the Irish Poor', in Swift and Gilley,
*The Irish in the Victorian City*, p. 277.

[37] See Lees, *Exiles of Erin*, p. 194 and Sheridan Gilley, 'Vulgar Piety and the Brompton
Oratory, 1850–1860', in Swift and Gilley, *The Irish in the Victorian City*, p. 256.

[38] Joseph Keating, *My Struggle for Life* (Dublin: University College Dublin Press, 1916),
pp. 292–293.

[39] Raphael Samuel, 'The Roman Catholic Church and the Irish Poor', in Swift and Gilley,
*The Irish in the Victorian City*, p. 275.

parishes, and attempted to draw the attention of the outside world towards it. In an 1893 letter, the famous Father Lawless of Polar wrote to *The Tablet* that much of his congregation, a few weeks before Christmas, existed on the brink of starvation:

> The main part of our people are in a chronic state of poverty, and the sad decrease of work in our docks makes things each winter more critical. The old people and the women and children suffer most ... The local workhouse is simply crowded, and the sad thing is to see so many young men and women among its inmates, and that without any fault of their own, but simply because they cannot get any work ... I will not weary you by speaking of individual cases of misery, but I could show you some homes utterly desolate through want, and men and women dying without the smallest alleviation in their sufferings. Many others, once comfortably off, and thoroughly sober, honest and respectable, are now starving, though they suffer in silence and try to hide their terrible position. For God's sake, plead for us before Christmas Day comes, that we may be able to cheer some of them on that glorious feast.[40]

Central to the Jewish religious tradition was the concept of *tzedakah*, 'social justice as distributive equality' and the bestowing of charity as a religious duty.[41] At a grass-roots level, religious charity in the Jewish East End could be a financial contribution or take the form of an invitation back to a rabbi's home to celebrate a religious festival. In *Children of the Ghetto*, Zangwill describes one such occasion:

> [O]n the other side of Reb Shemuel walked Eliphaz Chowchoski, a miserable-looking Pole, whom Reb Shemuel was taking home to supper. In those days Reb Shemuel was not alone in taking to his hearth 'the Sabbath guest' – some forlorn starveling or other – to sit at the table in like honour with the master. It was an object-lesson in Equality and Fraternity for the children of many a well-to-do household, nor did it fail altogether in the homes of the poor. 'All Israel are brothers,' and how better honour the Sabbath than by making the lip-babble a reality?[42]

For both Jewish and Gentile radicals, however, such goodwill and hospitality by grass-roots religious leaders and communal figures was but a drop in an ocean of poverty, if it was not accompanied by redistribution of wealth.

---

[40] Westminster Diocesan Archives, AAW/BOX ET, Jean Olwen Maynard, 'History of the Parish of St. Mary and Joseph Poplars, Vol. 2, 1881–1894'.

[41] See Rozin, *The Rich and the Poor* for a detailed discussion of *tzedakah* in the nineteenth century and Black, *The Social Politics of Anglo-Jewry* for Anglo-Jewish philanthropy in the East End.

[42] Zangwill, *Children of the Ghetto*, pp. 236–237.

Robert Blatchford, describing the charitable efforts of the Catholic Church in poor areas of the country, wrote: 'I find the Pope speaking of the valuable services of the Church in relieving poverty. But why *relief*? Why all this costly machinery for the purpose of making the wronged industrious poor into paupers? Why *relieve* poverty? Why not *abolish* poverty?'[43]

In religious Judaism there was no idealisation of 'Holy Poverty' as a state nearer to salvation as was to be found in the pronouncements of the Church leadership when discussing the material wants of the poor.[44] For both the Anglo-Jewish leadership and East End immigrant Jewry, poverty, if not exactly shameful, was not something to be celebrated or fetishised.[45] The Anglo-Jewish leadership, and in particular the Jewish Board of Guardians, established in 1859, made great efforts to ensure that Jewish poverty and its alleviation remained a communal affair. Essentially, the Board aimed to ensure that destitute Jews would be provided for by Jewish charities. It was recognised at an early stage that it was almost impossible for the workhouses established under the New Poor Law of 1834 to cater sufficiently for observant Jewish dietary and religious needs.[46] The successful efforts of the Board of Guardians and other organisations to ensure that Jewish poverty was addressed by Jewish charity and provision, in close cooperation with the Poor Law authorities, is reflected in statistics on pauperism in the East London area. The 1903 Royal Commission on Alien Immigration reported that whilst the London-wide proportion of men and women classified as paupers was recorded at 7.9 per cent, amongst 'aliens' it was 2.4 per cent. In Stepney, the overall figure was again 7.9 per cent of the population, with 'alien' pauperism estimated at 3.7 per cent.[47]

By comparison, the Church was content for poor Catholics to fall back on the provisions of the state in times of want. From the wave of migration following the Famine, Irish transients, particularly seasonal labourers, had sought shelter in the casual wards of workhouses, and whole family units in the workhouse proper.[48] In spite of, or perhaps because of, this widespread use of the workhouse system, the Irish Catholic relationship with the New Poor Law was a traumatic one.[49] From the early nineteenth

[43] Blatchford, *Socialism*, p. 11 (original emphasis).

[44] Jerry Z. Muller, *Capitalism and the Jews* (Princeton, NJ: Princeton University Press, 2010), p. 84.

[45] Muller, *Capitalism and the Jews*.

[46] V.D. Lipman, *A Century of Social Service, 1859–1959: The Jewish Board of Guardians* (London: Routledge and Kegan Paul, 1959), p. 11.

[47] Jones, *Immigration and Social Policy in Britain*, p. 89.

[48] M.A. Crowther, *The Workhouse System, 1834–129: The History of an English Social Institution* (London: Methuen and Co. Ltd, 1983), pp. 248–249.

[49] See Lynn H. Lees, 'Patterns of Lower-Class Life: Irish Slum Communities in

century and up to the 1870s and beyond, the Poor Law was used by local authorities forcibly to repatriate Irish immigrants, and at the high point of the immigration 'crisis' of the mid-nineteenth century several thousand Irish paupers were being deported every year. After 1846, the law was modified to allow Irish migrants who had been settled in a particular area for over five years to seek relief in the parish in which they were resident. However, in many cases this merely stoked the determination of local authorities to repatriate Irish immigrants before the five-year cut-off point had been reached.[50] The workhouse boards of the mid-nineteenth century were also widely viewed in Irish communities as being prejudiced against the Catholic faith, and unwilling to allow provision for Catholic worship or the attentions of a Catholic priest.[51] Thus, whilst Jewish poverty was internalised to some degree, kept concealed under the cloak of communal provision and communal control, Irish pauperism in the East End was highly visible and public. The Board of Guardians, by adopting the role of the fulcrum of communal charity within East End Jewry, also complicated class relations in poor Jewish neighbourhoods. The Guardians inspired a complex mix of gratitude and resentment among those unfortunate enough to require recourse to charity, internalising social tensions within East End Jewry.[52] The Irish relationship with the workhouse and the casual ward, on the other hand, a relationship from which the Church had effectively detached itself, did not affect the nature of the interactions between working-class Catholics and their communal leaderships to the same degree.[53]

## The East End Neighbourhood and Spatial Separation

In turn of the century London, a great deal of importance was placed by both East-Enders and outside observers on the 'character' of particular neighbourhoods. Certain areas of the metropolis appeared to be in a

---

Nineteenth Century London', in Stephan Thernstrom and Richard Sennett, *Nineteenth-Century Cities: Essays in the New Urban History* (New Haven, Conn.: Yale University Press, 1969), p. 361 for discussion of the negative inferences drawn by wider society by Irish recourse to charity.

[50] Michael E. Rose, 'Settlement, Removal and the New Poor Law', in Derek Fraser, *The New Poor Law in the Nineteenth Century* (London: Macmillan, 1976), pp. 38–39.

[51] Crowther, *The Workhouse System*, pp. 129–130 and Hickman, *Religion, Class and Identity*, p. 184.

[52] See Rozin, *The Rich and the Poor* and White, *Rothschild Buildings*.

[53] See David Feldman, 'Migrants, Immigrants and Welfare from the Old Poor Law to the Welfare State', *Transactions of the Royal Historical Society*, Vol. 13 (2003) for an overview of diasporic minorities and their interactions with systems of charitable relief.

constant state of social flux, gaining and losing 'respectability' as rooms were sublet, slums torn down, social housing erected, and rents increased.[54] In parts of East London something akin to a war of attrition, fought street by street, seemed to be waged between the 'respectable' working class and a highly mobile underclass. At the beginning of Jack London's *People of the Abyss* the writer discusses the situation with his landlady. 'This street', the women informs him, after a query about subletting, 'is the very last. All the other streets were like this eight or ten years ago, and all the people were very respectable. But the others have driven our kind out ... The others, the foreigners and lower-class people, can get five or six families into this house, where we can only get one.'[55] Charles Booth described in *Life and Labour* how 'buildings' acquired a certain character:

> Jews' Buildings, rowdy Buildings, genteel Buildings etc., all being estimated as such by public opinion. And public criticism, it may be added, resting on strong prejudices, may be trusted to define sharply and to perpetuate the distinctions between the tenants of different Buildings. Racial prejudices keep the Christians apart from the Jews.[56]

This territorialism and how neighbourhoods were popularly perceived was strongly linked to the supposed ethnic character of streets or areas of the city. The 'Fenian barracks' of the mid-nineteenth century may have disappeared, but at the beginning of the twentieth century areas across London were still popularly perceived as 'Irish' in character.[57] In the Jewish case, with a different alphabet and language and different places of worship, the feeling of a cultural 'shift' in the character of certain districts was even more pronounced. In George R. Sims's popular 1906 work *Living London*, the various articles about different facets of London life have headings such as 'Russia in East London', 'Oriental London', 'Italy in London', 'Scottish, Irish and Welsh London'.[58] It was received wisdom that space in London was ethnically demarcated to a significant degree. In reality, ethnic demarcation in London was significantly less pronounced than in the large American

---

[54] Between 1880 and 1900 rent in the East London boroughs increased by 25.3 per cent, as compared with 11.7 per cent in the North London boroughs, 11.4 per cent in the West London boroughs and 10.4 per cent in the South London boroughs – an increase blamed in some quarters on (Jewish) immigration into the area. From Board of Trade, British and Foreign Trade and Industrial Condition Figures, quoted in Laura Vaughan, 'A Study of the Spatial Characteristics of the Jews in London, 1695 and 1895' (MSc thesis, University College London, 1994), p. 22.

[55] London, *The People of the Abyss*, p. 14.

[56] Booth, *Life and Labour of the People in London*, First Series, *Poverty*, Vol. 3, p. 37.

[57] Lees, *Exiles of Erin*, p. 63.

[58] See Sims, *Living London*.

cities such as New York.[59] In nearly all the London boroughs, even those perceived as having on some level a 'foreign' composition, foreign-born populations were in a minority. The minority presence on the electoral roll, whether through property or residence qualifications, was also smaller than the wider population.[60]

Nevertheless, any movement of immigrants, particularly Eastern European Jewish migrants, into an area was frequently framed in the language of invasion, of unwelcome change being forced upon reluctant communities. Tied in with this was a nostalgia for a previous period 'before the immigrants', for an ethnically and religiously homogenous East End. This evocation of a halcyon past, directed against Jewish settlement, ignored the ethnic tension between the local population and Irish arrivals that had existed a generation before, and which still occasionally flared up. 'I have had about sixteen years connection with the Whitechapel Union, and I never met among the Irish people so much coarseness as I have met among these [Jews]', said one East End midwife:

> Samuel Street ... used to be a street occupied by poor English and Irish people. In the afternoons you would see the steps inside cleaned and the women with clean white aprons sit in summer time inside the doors, perhaps at needlework with their little children about. Now it is a seething mass of refuse filth ... and the stench from the refuse and the filth is disgraceful.[61]

This visceral association of a migrant community with dirt and disease could have been taken word for word from Mayhew's description of the Irish underclass in the mid-nineteenth century, or Engels's descriptions of the Irish in Manchester at that time.[62] As Garrard writes, 'if things were bad because of the arrival of "them Jews", it followed that the period before they came was a veritable golden age, when life was not merely clean and pure, but uncomplicated: for anti-alien hostility was, after all, an attempt to comprehend complexity by simplification.'[63]

For the Catholic press, the demographic changes taking place in East London in the 1890s and 1900s were framed in terms of dwindling congregations, and of streets and buildings being abandoned to the new migrants. Again, the language employed in these reports, particularly in the *Catholic Herald* but also in *The Tablet*, is that of invasion, of Jews supplanting Catholics territorially in the East End:

[59] Riis, *How the Other Half Lives*, pp. 23–24.
[60] Thompson, *Socialists, Liberals and Labour*, p. 26.
[61] Jones, *Immigration and Social Policy in Britain*, p. 75.
[62] See Chapter 1 on the connection between minorities and perceived 'dirtiness'.
[63] Garrard, *The English and Immigration*, p. 51.

A few years ago the greengrocery trade was mainly in the hands of Catholics, but now they have entirely lost it and it is carried on by Jew shopkeepers, a fact made unmistakable by the number of Hebrew advertisements visible in the windows. The mission in Spitalfields ... has in consequence shrunk from ten thousand to something like three or four thousand.[64]

There is a very large Irish Catholic population in Wapping; and Fr Beckley is to be congratulated on having as yet escaped the foreign invasion by the continental undesirables.[65]

[D]uring the past few months many of the oldest residents of SS Mary and Michael's have been driven out to make way for the Jews. Some have settled down in the north portion of the parish, but the majority have gone to Forest Gate and East Ham.[66]

These fears of displacement partly explained the importance of the regular parades and processions organised by the Catholic Church on holy days in the Church calendar. These functioned as both a claim to and a reminder of the wider East End, Jewish and Gentile, of the continuing presence of the Catholic Church and Catholic communities in East London. The parades, replete with religious symbolism and tokens of Irish national identity, were much enjoyed and were a focus of interest for both believers taking part and spectators lining the routes. They were generally good-natured events, a brief change for both East End Catholics and the wider population from the usual humdrum state of affairs.[67] The cross-cultural component of these processions is clear from a description in the *Catholic Weekly* of one such event in Whitechapel:

The long procession troops slowly out of church and files down the little grey street paved with clumsy cobble-stones. The priests lead the way, bearing a statue of Our Lady, and the crowds follow in swift, orderly succession. Very charming are the Children of Mary in their white frocks and veils, blue ribbons, and graceful wreathes. The altar-boys, in vivid red, strike a note of brilliant colour. The grey draperies of a group of Tamil women ... excite considerable comment; they are not a common sight in the East End, and their dark, imperturbable faces, adorned with gold nose-rings, render them unusually striking among the sickly white pinched faces that surround them ... it is a typically East End crowd on its very best behaviour – orderly, sympathetic one would say, and above

[64] *The Tablet* (25 September 1897).

[65] *The Catholic Herald* (13 June 1902).

[66] *The Catholic Herald* (13 June 1902).

[67] Giulia Ni Dhulchaointigh, 'Irish Communities in East London and their Processions, 1900–1914', *Socialist History*, 45 (2014), pp. 51–55.

all things, reverent. All classes are represented: even the Jewish or Polish alien watches there in company with his swarthy wife and lean, dark children.[68]

This recounting of one religious parade in the East End vividly illustrates the multiple interactions taking place within the diaspora space of Edwardian East London, beyond binary definitions of white/black, English/Irish, or Jewish/Gentile. Catholics of different ethnic backgrounds came together to affirm their common faith, while non-Catholics participated in this affirmation, if only through enjoying the spectacle of the parade.

From the 1880s onwards, it was popularly held that once a neighbourhood or group of buildings had acquired a Jewish 'character', an exodus of Gentile residents would inevitably result, that the 'native' population would be displaced. Charles Booth wrote of the increase in the Jewish population of Whitechapel as 'like the slow rising of a flood. Street after street is occupied. No Gentile could live in the same houses as these foreign Jews'.[69] Contemporary descriptions of immigrant Jewish settlement in East London emphasise this supposed ethnic demarcation, and the division of the East End into Jewish and non-Jewish areas, often framed in the supposed prejudices of the local Irish communities in Wapping and St. George's-in-the-East.[70]

The ethnic character of territory in the East End was frequently depicted as a zero-sum game: that a certain street or area would be either *entirely* Jewish or *entirely* non-Jewish, with some streets where it would be 'impossible' for Jews to settle acting as 'barriers' between Jewish settlement and the rest of London. To quote Barnett:

> the division between Jew and Gentile is usually sharply defined ... Carmen, dockers etc. mainly Irish, who have no dealings with the Jews and will not live with them. Broken windows and other forcible arguments have not infrequently been used to convince the unlucky Jew, who has had the temerity to take up his abode in these streets, that for him at least, they are not desirable homes.[71]

As late as 1911, one landlord being interviewed during the Sidney Street enquiry commented on his properties: 'They cannot get our own English

---

[68] *Catholic Weekly* (15 September 1902).

[69] Booth, *Life and Labour of the People in London*, Third Series, *Religious Influences*, Vol. 2, p. 3.

[70] Samuel A. Barnett, 'Introduction', in Russell and Lewis, *The Jew in London*, pp. xlii–xliii.

[71] See Barnett, 'Introduction', *The Jew in London*, p. xxxix. See also Feldman, 'The Importance of Being English', p. 72: 'It was well known that there were few Jews in the south ward of St. George's because the largely Irish inhabitants would not let them settle.'

people to live with them. I should have the houses all empty, they are all aliens round here.'[72] This spatial separation was certainly a factor in some areas of the East End, particularly St. George's in the East, but the division into demarcated ethnic neighbourhoods was not a universal phenomenon, either in East London or in the wider metropolis.[73] Geographical division and territorialism formed one side of the grass-roots economic, social, and political interactions taking place within diaspora space, but was not the whole of the picture. Parallel to mutual hostility and incomprehension existed inter-ethnic cooperation, and links established between Jewish and Gentile charitable institutions.

## Economic and Social Interactions

If housing and accommodation was one arena for potential inter-ethnic interactions (or lack of the same) and inter-ethnic tension between Jewish and Catholic migrant communities, then the workplace, sites of leisure activities, and the school yard were additionally areas of inter-ethnic contact, cooperation, conflict, and demarcation in East London.

The East End public house played a central role in both economic and social interactions in the metropolis. The pub operated, particularly in the dockland areas of East and South London, as an unofficial labour exchange. For labourers on the docks and on the building sites, the pub was a location where employment could be secured, as well as a place of relaxation after the working day. It was also common to 'seal the deal' with the foreman taking on labour with a drink, and for wages to be paid in the pub.[74] East End Irish pubs, providing Irish food, Irish drink, and Irish music, formed a powerful bond with the homeland that had been left behind.[75] The pub was also a centre of Irish political activity, where meetings could be held, and collections for the Irish Nationalist movement taken up. Different public houses, according to the affiliations of landlord and clientele, took on different political hues. The East End pub also formed territory favourable to cultural interactions between Irish and English communities in London, an important facilitator in the formation of a common East End working-class culture.[76]

72  National Archives, HO/144/19780, Sidney Street Enquiry, 1911.

73  The St. George's and Wapping Liberal and Radical Association would gain widespread notoriety in 1903 when they explicitly rejected a candidate put forward by the local Labour Party organisation on the explicit grounds of his Jewish identity – Holmes, *Anti-Semitism in British Society*, p. 110.

74  Brodie, *Politics of the Poor*, p. 145.

75  Ni Dhulchaointigh, 'The Irish Population of London', p. 25.

76  Michael A. Smith, *The Public House, Leisure and Social Control* (Salford: University of

Yet the public house was also an area of ethnic exclusion and a source of inter-ethnic tension and conflict. In many pubs it was made clear that Jewish custom was not welcome.[77] In contemporary discussion on immigration into the East End and cultural tensions between communities, the differing attitudes towards leisure activities of Jews and their Gentile neighbours were frequently cited as a point of difference. In the religiously observant migrant Jewish community the synagogue, and religious institutions and spaces, rather than the public house or music hall, formed the centre of socialisation and relaxation as well as of worship.[78] For Orthodox East End Jewry the local synagogue was invested with a cultural and social significance, a centre of recreation as well as religious observance that was exceptional, even when compared with the role of the Church in the leisure-time activities of pious Catholics. It should also be noted that in Orthodox synagogues it was primarily a zone of *male* interaction. The degree of anti-religious polemic and rhetoric employed by some of the Jewish socialist and anarchist groups of the period was at least in part a reaction to the importance of the *shul* in the day-to-day lives of the immigrant Jewish working class.

In the Jewish communities of East London, alcohol was generally enjoyed at home amongst family and close friends, rather than in the public house. Fermin Rocker, recounting his childhood, wrote: 'The pub that stood across the street [from his relations] was a Gentile preserve, and the Jew who wandered into it was an exception indeed.'[79] For C. Russell in his contribution to *The Jew in London*, anglicisation was the key factor in the ways that East End Jewry spent their leisure hours, and consequentially how they were viewed by their Gentile neighbours. Russell draws a distinction between 'English' and 'foreign' Jews, and how they were perceived by the wider society: 'They [the English Jews] are pronounced to be good fellows, and "just like us Christians." They spend their money freely and "have the best of everything"; and command respect, especially amongst the habitués of the public house ... Foreigners, on the other hand, are for the most part, cordially disliked.'[80]

Despite this rather optimistic interpretation of the attitudes held by the wider East End working class towards Anglo-Jewry, many riverside East End pubs were certainly less than hospitable to Jewish clientele,

---

Salford Centre for Work and Leisure Studies, 1984), p. 21 for the role of the pub in facilitating urban working-class culture and pp. 35–38 for the relationship between the public house and hyper-masculinity.

[77] Feldman, *Englishmen and Jews*, p. 251.

[78] See White, *Rothschild Buildings*, pp. 87–88 and Kershen, *Strangers*, p. 88.

[79] Fermin Rocker, *The East End Years: A Stepney Childhood* (London: Freedom Press, 1998), pp. 55–56.

[80] Russell and Lewis, *The Jew in London*, p. 25.

whether 'English' or 'foreigners'. Being questioned during a sitting of the parliamentary Alien Immigration Committee, Mr Walmer, discussing Jewish–Gentile relations in the East End, responded to a question by Lord Rothschild on whether 'there was a feeling against Jews manifested in public houses' by replying that 'when you go into a public house, and the conversation turns on the subject, you find a general feeling against them', perhaps in part because, in Lord Rothschild's words, 'the majority of Jews don't go to a public house'. 'I admit', answered Mr Walmer, 'the Jews are a sober race.'[81] East End publicans were famous for the inclination of their politics towards the Conservative Party (the Liberals and later Labour were both seen as pro-temperance, whilst the Tories were viewed, rightly or wrongly, as supporting both the publican and the breweries).[82] The priest was not the only figure in East End Catholic life attempting to influence politically the immigrant communities.

This social demarcation also had consequences for economic interactions and divisions between the Jewish and non-Jewish communities. If Jewish drinkers were not welcome in, or not inclined to enter, the public houses where labour was recruited, it became less likely that Jews would find employment on the docks or on building sites. The absence of 'foreigners' on the docks, as compared with the other East London industries, was noted by Beatrice Potter in an 1887 article which concluded: 'Unfortunately the presence of the foreigner is the only unpleasant feature common to East London which is omitted from the composition of dock and waterside life.'[83]

A report in *The Times* on the eve of the 1889 dock strike estimated that only 2 per cent of the dock labourers were Jewish.[84] It was popularly supposed that even if Jewish workers succeeded in gaining employment on the docks they would speedily relinquish the work after suffering the chaff and antisemitic bullying of their English and Irish peers. As early as 1867, decades before the great migration from Eastern Europe, J.H. Stallard, in his *London Pauperism amongst Jews and Christians* (1867), wrote:

The occupations of the Jews are undoubtedly influenced, to a certain extent, by the prejudices which still prevent themselves from working on

[81] *Jewish Chronicle* (20 June 1902). See also G.S. Reaney, 'The Moral Aspect', in Arnold White, *The Destitute Alien in Great Britain* (London: Swan Sonneschein, 1892), p. 87 for discussion of ethnic politics and sobriety in the East End.

[82] See David M. Fahey, 'Temperance and the Liberal Party: Lord Peel's Report 1899', *Journal of British Studies*, Vol. 10, No. 2 (May 1971).

[83] LSE PASSFIELD 7/1/7 Beatrice Potter, 'London Dock Labour in 1887 (draft copy)', *Nineteenth Century*, No. 128 (October 1887).

[84] *The Times* (29 August 1889), in McCarthy, *The Great Dock Strike*, p. 32.

comfortable terms with the English and Irish labourers. If a Jew gets work at the Docks, he is so jeered and chaffed that he is obliged to give it up. He is not rough enough to retaliate, for the Dock labourers are the very lowest of their class; and for the same reasons day labour is impossible on railways and public works.[85]

This is an early example of a familiar stereotype that would become a feature of antisemitic literature in the late nineteenth and early twentieth centuries, that of Jews as 'effeminate' and physically weak. This trope was able to coalesce with the simultaneous belief that Jews were able to work longer hours and undertake heavier labour on less food than their non-Jewish competitors. It was widely held on the docks, by Ben Tillett amongst others, that many London Irish labourers had been 'forced out' of traditionally Irish East End trades by the Jewish influx. Interviewed by the Sweating Committee in 1890, Tillett said:

> If I were to go outside the London docks [i.e., where men were waiting to be hired] and ask the men there whether they had been brought up to any trade, I should find at least 25 per cent of them had been at some trade; and they were pretty well divided between the tailoring and the shoemaking; especially the Irish cockney whose parents were in tailoring; they have been driven to the docks.[86]

If Jewish workers were largely absent from employment in trades considered 'Irish', such as dock work, labour on building sites or the railways, or in the gasworks, trades considered 'Jewish', most notably tailoring work, boot-making, and cabinet-making, in fact employed a large non-Jewish workforce, both male and female.[87] Despite substantial cooperation between English, Irish, and Jewish workers in the industrial action of 1889 and 1911–1912, this amiability did not extend to welcoming Jewish workers to take up employment on the docks. Through into the inter-war period dockland work remained largely the preserve of English, Irish, and London Irish labourers, although from the 1890s onwards the demographic make-up of the East End docks was changing from a predominantly Irish and London Irish workforce to one drawing its labour from recent migrants from the British countryside.[88]

---

[85] J.H. Stallard, *London Pauperism among Jews and Christians* (London: J.E. Taylor and Co., 1867), p. 8.

[86] Stedman Jones, *Outcast London*, p. 110.

[87] See James A. Schmiechen, *Sweated Industries and Sweated Labor: The London Clothing Trade, 1860–1914* (London: Croom Helm, 1984) for discussion of the interactions of gender and ethnicity in the sweated garment trade in the late nineteenth and early twentieth centuries.

[88] Denvir, *The Irish in Britain*, pp. 394–395.

Economic and social interactions between Jewish families and their Irish neighbours in the East End also took place on a more informal level. The role of *shabbos goyahs*, a (female) Gentile acquaintance of a Jewish household who, for a financial consideration, would perform certain tasks for the family on the Sabbath, was often taken by Irish Catholic women.[89] These grass-roots economic interactions between Irish and Jewish women are frequently mentioned in the transcripts of the interviews carried out with Jewish men and women who had been children in the Edwardian period. 'Susie, an Irish woman, lived in one of the lodgings in Flower and Dean Street, and she used to do work for my mother. She used to clean up the flat and do little errands – mother was getting on ... Susie was very trustworthy, although she drank.'[90] 'Mother used to get a woman from there for 3d or 4d to come and clean the place out, and she'd give her a meal ... Once a week ... And she was glad to sit down and have a meal.'[91] They form an alternative narrative to that of exclusion that was apparent in the economic interactions around the docklands.

Coupled with these semi-formal economic interactions, existing somewhere between a job and a favour, was a more formalised relationship between middle- and lower middle-class Jewish families and Irish women in domestic service, still at this time the major occupation for young working-class women.[92] Bronwen Walter has discussed in detail the class context of these economic relationships between Jewish mistresses and Irish Catholic servants, identifying the class and ethnic tensions at work: 'At a very intimate scale Irish women were part of Jewish family life in a way that was not reciprocated. Whereas Irish women observed and took part in cleaning, cooking, child and elder care for Jewish families, Jewish people did not have this close relationship with Irish families.'[93] This non-reciprocal class relationship was at least partly due, of course, to the marked reluctance of young working-class Jewish women to enter domestic service.

Friendships formed between Jews and Catholics at the East End board schools sometimes led to significant inter-ethnic social interactions, including visits to children's homes, often the first time Jewish and Gentile neighbours had examined each other's domestic life at close quarters. These cultural interactions could be fraught with confusion:

We had a girl in my class called Nelly; she was a Christian [Irish] girl

---

[89]   See Zangwill, *Children of the Ghetto*, p. 97.

[90]   Interview in White, *Rothschild Buildings*, p. 141.

[91]   Interview in White, *Rothschild Buildings*, p. 140.

[92]   Walter, *Outsiders Inside*, p. 144.

[93]   Walter, 'Irish/Jewish Diasporic Intersections in the East End of London: Paradoxes and Shared Locations', in Prum, *La Place de l'autre*, pp. 59–60.

and I liked her very much. She used to come to school without shoes on her feet. I couldn't understand it; no shoes and stockings and its raining … I used to very often go home to her for tea; and I could smell a very nice welcoming smell – it was bacon. Although her mother offered it to me I had an idea I mustn't eat it. I told my mother what had happened and asked her 'Why mustn't I eat it?' … And mother said, 'Because it's not very healthy' and I said, 'But Nelly Conlan walks about with bare feet and she's never had a cold in her life!'[94]

Whilst voluntary schools catered for particular denominations, in the secular board schools a good deal of social interaction took place. In the absence of a Jewish voluntary school, Christian church schools took in Jewish children whilst the construction of a Jewish institution was taking place. Nellie Bugeja, a schoolgirl in the Edwardian East End, recalled Jewish classmates at St. Anne's, the Roman Catholic school she attended. 'Fr Murphy was friendly with their Rabbi. These Jewish children never forgot the Marist Priests and Nuns and visited them long after they left to attend their own Jewish school which had to be built. They [the Jewish children] even wore Shamrock on St Patrick's Day.'[95] Along with these positive examples of inter-ethnic interaction at school level, however, was an undercurrent of ethnic violence and intimidation between youths in the East End, which was frequently sparked by identifying an individual or group as belonging to a certain school, and thus a particular religious or ethnic group.

The most profound expression of positive interaction between the different migrant communities negotiating East End diaspora space was inter-marriage. To circumvent hostility from neighbours and religious leaderships, conversion by one party to the faith of the other was sometimes a precondition of formalised union, or when the couple began to have children. Both Catholic and Jewish religious authorities often required a commitment on behalf of the husband and wife that any children would be raised in the appropriate faith before sanctifying a marriage. An article in the *Jewish World* of October 1890 warned of the dire consequences of 'mixed' religious marriages without an explicit adoption of either the bride's or groom's religion at an early stage: 'For, when the children arrive at years of discretion, it generally happens that they are influenced by the religious opinions of one or another of their parents, and from this alone has resulted the hopeless ruin of many a home where a certain degree of happiness formerly existed.'[96]

---

[94] Interview in White, *Rothschild Buildings*, p. 143.

[95] Westminster Diocesan Archives, AAW BOX LE, Jean Olwen Maynard, 'History of the Parish of St Anne's, Underwood Road, Vol. IV, 1911–1938'.

[96] *The Jewish World* (3 October 1890).

C.J. Goldsmid-Montefiore, writing in 1935 and reflecting on the problems faced by the Jewish community in his lifetime, discussed perceptions of intermarriage before the First World War in the following terms:

> We were brought up to regard marriage with Christians as impermissible and wrong … The objection to intermarriage was purely religious. It had absolutely nothing to do with race or blood … As a tiny minority living amid big majorities, it is perfectly obvious, and is, indeed, borne out by facts, the tiny minority would, before long, be absorbed in the big majorities.[97]

The visitation returns from East End Catholic churches to the Westminster Diocese from 1905, 1908, and 1911 reveal that in almost every East End parish mixed marriages (that is marriages between Catholics and non-Catholics) were taking place on a regular basis. In St. Mary and Michael's Catholic church off the Commercial Road in 1911 the priest solemnised thirty-nine marriages between Catholics and fifteen between Catholics and non-Catholics, showing that almost 30 per cent of partnerships in the parish were 'mixed'. In St. Mary and Joseph in Poplar in 1905 there were fourteen marriages within the Catholic faith and eleven 'mixed'. In Guardian Angels in Mile End, the 1905 records show a *majority* of mixed marriages conducted in the church, eleven 'mixed' against six arranged between two Catholics. Only one church in the period, St. Casimir's, a Lithuanian church in St. George's-in-the-East, registered no mixed marriages.[98] In East End Irish Catholic communities inter-marriage, if not a day-to-day occurrence, happened fairly often. The visitation returns do not indicate the faith of the non-Catholic party, whether Protestant or Jewish. The mixed marriage was another expression of the fluidity of identity and religious and ethnic-based roles in working-class migrant communities, a potent mix of demarcated difference, rejection, and belonging, the discarding of old identities, or elements of old identities, and the assumption of new ones.[99]

---

[97] Special Collections, Hartley Library, University of Southampton, MS 108/4, 'A Die-Hard's Confession: Some Old Fashioned Opinions and Reflections about the Jews', 1935, p. 11–13.

[98] Dioceses of Westminster Visitation Returns, Box MQ, 1911, Dioceses Visitation Returns for SS Mary and Michael's Church, Commercial Road; Box ET, 1905 Dioceses Visitation Returns for SS Mary and Joseph, Poplar; Box KV, 1905 Dioceses Visitation Returns for Guardian Angels, Mile End; Box ZT, 1908, Dioceses Visitation Returns for St. Casimir's, St. George's-in-the East.

[99] In his 'Introduction' to *The Jew in London*, pp. xvi-xvii, Samuel Barnett writes that 'Intermarriage between Jews and Christians has already begun, even where each consort retains his or her religion … the practice of intermarriage is by far the most powerful solvent of racial distinctions where the two races live intermingled in the same city.'

Certain social organisations, both religious and secular, that would seem to be obviously ethnically or religiously demarcated, in fact catered for East-Enders of various religious or ethnic backgrounds. One example was the Catholic Seaman's Club in Wellclose Square, Mile End, run by Father Donnelly, which catered to Protestants and Jews as well as Catholics. The Jews who attended the club, according to Father Donnelly, looked upon the Irish Catholics as 'strange, inexplicable creatures', but were not unfriendly.[100] In *Life and Labour*, Booth describes in glowing terms a refuge of the [Catholic] Sisters of Mercy in the East End, 'where Protestants, Jews and Catholics have been received with equal kindness, and without a question asked to their religion; where the only requirements for their admission are that they should be poor, homeless, and deserving'. Moreover, hostels of various denominational affiliations in East London opened their doors to the homeless and destitute of all backgrounds.[101] Generally, there was cooperation and cordial relations between Jewish and Christian charitable concerns in the metropolis. In an article on antisemitism, the *Catholic Weekly* reminded its readers: 'The rich Jews of London are amongst the most generous and munificent supporters of Catholic charities. Not long ago a wealthy Jew left £20,000 to a home for aged and invalid Catholics. The poorer Jews are said to be kind and charitable to their Catholic neighbours.'[102]

Another Christian charity with strong links to the East End Jewish community was the Children's Dinners and Orphans' Aid Fund, established by the Christian philanthropists Mr and Mrs Breton. In recognition of the support given by Jewish friends of the Fund, the group laid on a party and meal for a hundred Jewish children in Whitechapel in early 1898, first offering the menu for the scrutiny of the Chief Rabbi, the event taking place at a kosher restaurant on Brick Lane. The *Jewish Chronicle* described the event as 'probably the first on which a body of Christian workers have entertained a party of Jewish children at a dinner for the sole purpose of giving testimony to the support that Jewish friends have given to a non-Jewish charity.'[103] This inter-ethnic cooperation between grass-roots religious and charitable institutions forms an alternative narrative to the sensationalist headlines featured in elements of the East End press, stressing conflict and discord, of 'Jerusalem on Thames' and the supposedly ever-brewing 'Judenhetz' (pogrom) in East London. These positive and negative diasporic

---

[100] Westminster Diocesan Archives, AAW BOX KV, Jean Olwen Maynard, 'History of the Parish of Guardian Angels, Mile End, Vol. I, 1868–1903'.

[101] Booth, *Life and Labour of the People in London*, Third Series, *Religious Influences*, Vol. 7, pp. 265–266.

[102] *The Catholic Weekly* (15 July 1904).

[103] *Jewish Chronicle* (18 February 1898).

interactions illustrate the point that the communities were not static in self-definition and attitudes towards others, but were in fact constantly negotiating political, economic, and social space with their neighbours. These negotiations and comparisons were not taking place solely within minority groups, isolated from the outside world, or between minorities and a dominant host society, but also between different minority groups, sharing a common outsider status and often a similar socio-economic position. The workplace, the public house, the school, and the family home were all arenas in which these negotiations and definitions were worked out. However, in a less benign manner, self-definitions were also arrived at on a street level through physical confrontation, and it is to ethnic, religious, and political violence in diaspora space that the chapter now turns.

## Inter-ethnic, Religious, and Political Violence in the East End

Provocative reports by the metropolitan press aside, London was relatively free of explicit political or ethnically motivated violence in the period under discussion. The East London pogrom did not take place. This was despite the dire warnings which local newspapers and anti-migrant commentators such as Arnold White and W.H. Wilkins had frequently made in the 1880s and early 1890s.[104] However, whilst inter-ethnic and religious violence was not as severe or as frequent in London as in other parts of the country, physical confrontation between different groups in the East End did inform the nature of grass-roots communal interactions and definitions of identity, a question of whom one defined oneself *against*.[105] Political violence, particularly during periods of industrial unrest, also had the potential to cause serious violence *within* minority communities. This was a division between those who supported strike action and those who did not, or who exploited the situation to undertake employment as what the bosses termed 'free labourers' and what the striking workers contemptuously labelled 'blacklegs'.

### Inter-ethnic Violence

Reports in the press of open, ethnically motivated violence in the period between adult Jews and Irish Catholics in East London are rare. The most frequently cited example of physical confrontation between the two groups was occasioned by a number of Jewish families attempting to

---

104 *Pall Mall Gazette* (February 1886). Reaney, 'The Moral Aspect', p. 88. See Donald L. Horowitz, *The Deadly Ethnic Riot* (Berkeley: University of California Press, 2001) for discussion of the preconditions and patterns of serious ethnic violence.

105 For an overview of violence in the capital, see Clive Bloom, *Violent London: 2000 Years of Riots, Rebels and Revolts* (London: Pan Books, 2003) (republished 2004).

settle in an Irish area of St. George's-in-the-East in 1902. A contemporary report described what followed: '[The] natives, some three or four hundred strong, made a rush for the van. The occupants beat a hasty retreat, while the crowd pulled the furniture out of the van, smashing it to pieces, and afterwards wrecked the van itself.'[106] Violence between Jewish and Irish working-class communities in the East End most frequently manifested itself in confrontations, and occasionally pitched battles, between groups of youths. Attendance at a certain school, and the wearing of a particular school uniform often served as a marker of ethnic and religious identity. On one level these rivalries were part of normal East End working-class life, as it was and would continue to be.[107] But oral history and interviews carried out with East-Enders who had grown up in the Edwardian period attest to the importance of ethnic tensions informing the nature of these hostilities among schoolchildren and teenagers. A generation before, tensions between East End Irish and Italian children had been initiated by the challenge 'Garibaldi or the Pope?', reflecting the Italian political situation of the 1860s, and obviously picked up by the local children.[108] Similarly, from the 1880s onwards, violence and physical confrontations between Jewish and Gentile youths was often preceded by antisemitic taunts and insults. Frequently this violence was occasioned by Jewish youngsters straying into 'non-Jewish' neighbourhoods in a distinctive school uniform. Areas such as Flower and Dean Street in Spitalfields that formed intersections between different neighbourhoods were flash points for confrontations in the period under consideration and beyond.[109] Nate Zamet remembered that:

> Outside our immediate street you could go through areas which were completely non-Jewish and for instance there was a street called Dean Street ... there was a school, a non-Jewish school, and if you walked through Dean Street by the school and there was a crowd there and they thought they recognised you as Jewish they would probably throw some nasty ... expletives at you, possibly try to start a fight
>
> ...
>
> [O]nce there was an attack on the Jewish girls from school going home. It was winter, in the snow, and snowballs with stones stuck inside them were thrown at the girls and ... we were all very angry about it ... we got together and several boys who had left the school but lived in Dean

---

[106] *East London Advertiser* (18 June 1902), in Brodie, *The Politics of the Poor*, p. 189.

[107] Clarence Rook, 'Hooligan London', in Sims, *Living London*, p. 231.

[108] Raphael Samuel, 'An Irish Religion', in *Patriotism*, Vol. 2, p. 101. See also Paz, *Popular Anti-Catholicism in Mid-Victorian England*, p. 252 for discussion of the Hyde Park 'Garibaldi Riots' of 1862.

[109] For violence between Irish and Jewish youths, see Fielding, *Class and Ethnicity*, p. 68 and Humphries, *Hooligans or Rebels*, p. 193.

Street and little alleyways there, we got together and we all walked, after the school time, round to these buildings. We threw stones and broke windows.[110]

One interviewee in *Rothschild Buildings* recalled: 'There was constant fighting between the Jews and the Christians. There were often street fights ... And we had to run the gauntlet in those days ... it was difficult to walk through [some] streets.'[111] Certain streets were to be avoided, and acquired a particular reputation for antisemitism and violence. Such incidents, apparently trivial, could be dismissed as mere playground scuffles. However, these territorial tensions between gangs of youths in the East End on occasion had serious and even fatal results. After one altercation between a group of Jewish and Gentile children in Spitalfields, a ten-year-old boy was stabbed to death, following what was described as a 'permanent feud' between the two gangs.[112] Following the tragedy, communal leaders moved swiftly to avert the further confrontations that appeared inevitable. The following article was published in the *Jewish Chronicle* in the week following the murder:

> The Rev. Mr Davies informs us that there is absolutely no enmity existing between Jewish and Christian adults. He himself is on the friendliest terms with the Jewish parishioners, going to their weddings, betrothals, etc. It appears that both Gentile and Jewish boys bear some sort of animosity against each other, which should be promptly suppressed ... He desires us to clearly state that there is no truth whatever in the statement which appeared in several newspapers, that there existed a feud between the Jews and Gentiles living in the district. They were living together on the most amicable terms. There was, it is true, a very small fraction of both denominations who evinced an intolerant spirit towards each other, but the inhabitants in general were quite otherwise disposed.[113]

It is significant that the majority of the violence between adolescents in the East End involved children and youths who had been *born* in London, rather than migrants who had travelled from another country. It was second- and third-generation Irish and Jewish adolescents who claimed physical ownership over the street or court they had been raised in, and were willing to contest it through violence. As with the social activities described above, physical confrontation was a means of defining one's position in often disorientating diaspora space. The Revd Davies, quoted above in the *Jewish*

---

110   Tape J.M./320, Interview with Nate Zamet, carried out by Debbie Seedburgh on behalf of the Jewish Museum, London (unknown date).

111   Interview in White, *Rothschild Buildings*, p. 135.

112   *Jewish Chronicle* (25 March 1898).

113   *Jewish Chronicle* (1 April 1898).

*Chronicle* report on communal violence between Jewish and Gentile children, was understandably eager to challenge these claims of general hostility between the Jewish and non-Jewish communities of the area. Explicit inter-ethnic violence between adults as opposed to youths was a rarity. The question Davies does not address is to what extent this ethnic hostility between youths was being incubated in the attitudes expressed by parents at home. Ethnic violence continued to manifest itself in certain avenues after school leaving age. One arena in which ethnic tension co-mingled with general antisocial behaviour was in the criminal gangs that flourished in East London, whose membership was often based on ethnicity or religion as well as geographical location. These organisations often maintained a separate 'Irish' or 'Jewish' identity into the inter-war period and beyond.[114]

## Religious Violence

If anti-Jewish sentiment had to some extent displaced anti-Irish feeling amongst the wider population in the late nineteenth century, tensions between Catholics and Protestants in the area, though generally dormant, could flare up on occasion.[115] Nationally, suspicion of 'Rome' and 'popish influence', though perhaps not as intense as it had been a generation before, was still widely felt. Edwardian Liverpool witnessed serious sectarian violence in 1909. In the northern mill towns and the docklands of Liverpool and Glasgow, economic and housing demarcations between the two religious affiliations were still a fact of everyday life.[116] Sectarianism and Protestant–Catholic violence in London, however, tended to occur sporadically, rather than, as was the case with Liverpool and Glasgow, forming a permanent underlying tension. This could manifest itself politically (as the negative reaction to the appointment of the Catholic Alderman Knill to the post of Lord Mayor of London in 1892 illustrated) or at a grass-roots street level.[117] Violence, when it did take place, was generally sparked by religious processions or outdoor religious meetings, although, as with tensions between Jewish and Gentile children, school affiliation could be a precipitate.[118] As with the inter-ethnic confrontations, issues of territory – the control of the neighbourhood and the

[114] See Humphries, *Hooligans or Rebels* for discussion of the inter-ethnic tensions involved in pre-Second World War urban gang culture.

[115] Hugh McLeod, *Religion and the Working Class in Nineteenth Century Britain* (London: Macmillan Publishers Ltd, 1984), p. 37.

[116] See Eric Taplin, *The Dockers' Union: A Study of the National Union of Dockworkers, 1889–1922* (Leicester: Leicester University Press, 1986), pp. 23–24 on the sectarian spatial separation present in the Liverpool docks.

[117] *The Clarion* (1 October 1892).

[118] Anna Davin, *Growing Up Poor: Home, School and Street in London, 1870–1914* (London: Rivers Oram Press, 1996), p. 109.

street, or the platform at a meeting by a particular group or denomination, if only for a few hours – were often the spark for sectarian violence. St Patrick's Day, with its numerous Catholic processions throughout the East End and its affirmations of Roman Catholic faith and Irish identity, often witnessed confrontations and minor acts of violence.[119]

Although these parades generally passed without serious trouble, and formed something of a spectacle and distraction for the wider population, religious tension was present under the surface. The events were heavily tied in with diasporic Irish identity:

> [A]t the 6.00 AM Mass there was a special exhortation to the parishioners on how to spend the day, and then the men all held up their shamrocks to be blessed … Afterwards they all marched out of the church, led by the priests wearing green rosettes and shamrocks, and proceeded through the streets to Wade Street.[120]

In Poplar, where 'certain streets … had a reputation for Protestant bigotry', the processions of the League of the Cross were stewarded by 'very burly Irish dockers', 'taking part … to deter opposition'.[121]

Sectarian violence in the capital was often sparked by deliberately provocative actions, purposely undertaken to incite violence or at least discord. To insult or manhandle a member of the Catholic clergy was viewed by working-class parishioners as a serious attack on both the community and the faith they held, to be responded to in kind. The anti-Italian violence of the 1860s had its roots in unsubstantiated claims that Italian radicals had assaulted Catholic priests and nuns.[122] In *Life and Labour*, Booth recounted an anecdote passed on to him by a dockland parish priest, two of whose congregation had seized a man said to have insulted the cleric, and were waiting on the counsel of the priest as to what to do with the unhappy malcontent.[123]

On occasion, however, sectarian tensions extended beyond disrespectful behaviour towards individual clerics. A series of meetings held in Hyde Park in February of 1896 led to clashes between Protestants and Irish Catholics on a scale and with a degree of bitterness rarely seen in religious interactions in

---

[119] See Humphries, *Hooligans or Rebels?*, pp. 189–190.

[120] Westminster Diocesan Archives, AAW BOX ET, Jean Olwen Maynard, 'History of the Parish of St Mary and St Joseph's Poplar, Vol. 2, 1881–1894'.

[121] Westminster Diocesan Archives, AAW BOX ET, Jean Olwen Maynard, 'History of the Parish of St Mary and St Joseph's Poplar, Vol. 2, 1881–1894'.

[122] Paz, *Popular Anti-Catholicism*, p. 264. This would be repeated in the inter-war period in reactions to events in Spain between 1936 and 1939.

[123] Booth, *Life and Labour of the People in London*, Third Series, *Religious Influences, Inner South London*, Vol. IV (London: Macmillan, 1903), p. 202.

the capital by the 1890s. An organisation called the Protestant Alliance had taken to holding meetings on Sunday afternoons at Speakers' Corner in the Park. During one of these meetings consecrated wafers and a rosary were produced by the speakers who, according to the police report on the meeting, 'ridiculed' these elements of Catholic religious tradition in such a way 'calculated to produce a breach of the peace'. The Alliance in its turn claimed that the rosary and wafers had been produced, 'by way of illustration'.[124] Whether intended as a provocation or not, the second meeting of the Protestant Alliance ended in fighting between Catholics and Protestants, with the police struggling to maintain order. Following the Hyde Park confrontation questions were asked by the leaders of the Irish Nationalist Party in the House of Commons over the violence, and the seeming inability of the police to prevent provocative addresses and actions: '[If] the police have no powers to stop the exhibition of sacred emblems', declared one Irish MP, 'the probabilities are very greatly in favour of Catholics in this country doing it themselves.'[125] The Protestant Alliance, meanwhile, in a letter to the Home Office, placed the blame on 'Roman Catholic toughs', claiming the violence had been initiated by Catholics intent on creating a 'disturbance'.[126]

Despite debate in the House of Commons, no prohibition on further such meetings was passed. The Hyde Park disturbances and the activities of the Protestant Alliance did not spill into communal violence on the streets of the East End between Catholics and Protestants. However, in the summer of 1896, further confrontations between Protestant speakers and a Catholic audience occurred, following an address in which a bottle of 'holy water' was produced and ridiculed. A general assault on the speakers was prevented only by the large police presence at the meeting. Two of the men addressing the meeting were arrested and subsequently charged with 'behaving in a disorderly manner by conducting an assembly of persons, other than in a decent and disorderly manner'. The lawyer representing one of the men, Frank Cable, claimed that his client was 'Not against the Catholics, but against Roman Catholic doctrines'.[127]

This was not the last occasion that working-class Catholics would clash with the Protestant Alliance in the capital. Following a Catholic procession through the East End in the summer of 1911, sectarian insults between marchers and spectators degenerated into a riot as the march made its way through Canning Town. There were no serious injuries, and the police swiftly intervened in the dispute, but it illustrates that even at the end

---

[124] National Archives, HO 45/10257/X5806A, Meeting at Hyde Park.
[125] *The Times* (21 February 1896).
[126] National Archives, HO 45/10257/X5806A/2, Meeting at Hyde Park.
[127] *The Advertiser* (9 June 1896).

of the period under discussion, sectarian tensions between Catholics and Protestants were present. The descent into violence during this particular religious procession was very much the exception to the rule. Parades were generally good-natured in character, whether because of the good humour and general benign curiosity of the non-Catholic onlookers or the efficiency and presence of the stewards. That this was not the case in Canning Town was blamed (by the Catholic priests present at the march, Father Fletcher and Father Filmer) on the activities of the Protestant Alliance in the neighbourhood prior to the procession: 'We were not altogether surprised that a disturbance broke out, for the Protestant Alliance has been conducting a campaign in the district, and indeed, some people have expressed their determination to come and wreck our procession.'[128] Blows were exchanged between marchers and spectators following 'a foul and grossly offensive remark' made by an onlooker as the procession went past. Both the police and the organisers of the parade were of the opinion that the violence was spontaneous in nature, a response to the efforts of the Protestant Alliance in the area but not an organised assault planned by that body. After order was restored:

> In the evening, to reassure the Catholics in the district who were seriously alarmed by the rumours flying about, we held another informal procession visiting all the shrines which had been erected on the route. A conclusive proof that the attack had not been organised was afforded by the reverent reception this second procession received.[129]

The activities of the Protestant Alliance illustrate the fallacy in the assertion that by the end of the nineteenth century Irish Catholics in the capital had ceased to be an ethnic and religious 'other' in anti-migrant discourse, wholly replaced as targets for popular opprobrium by newer arrivals. Catholicism, into the Edwardian period, remained a negative binary opposite to a certain English Protestant self-definition. The Protestant Alliance was a small minority, if a vocal one, but they were symptomatic of a persistent prejudice. What distinguished the activities of the Protestant Alliance in Poplar and other parts of London from contemporaneous sectarian violence in Liverpool and Glasgow was the absence of a significant working-class Irish Protestant community involved in the tension.[130] The violence in Poplar and Canning Town was not an overspill from communal tensions on the other side of the Irish Sea.

---

128 *Catholic Herald* (15 July 1911).

129 *Catholic Herald* (15 July 1911).

130 Sheridan Gilley, 'Roman Catholicism and the Irish in England', in MacRaild, *The Great Famine and Beyond*, p. 159.

There are comparisons to be drawn between the Protestant Alliance and that other belligerent turn-of-the-century pressure group, the British Brothers' League. The similarities between the organisations are striking. Both groups combined provocative demonstrations calculated to provoke the minorities on which they focused their vitriol, the Protestant Alliance in the ways described above, the BBL though marches, meetings, and inflammatory speeches in areas of East London with a large Jewish population, with a denial of ethnically based prejudice. The Protestant Alliance maintained that its actions were not directed against the Irish as an ethnic group per se, or indeed against Catholics, but against Roman 'doctrine'.[131] Similarly, the BBL denied any antisemitic intent, in official literature using the term 'alien' rather than 'Jew'.[132] Both attempted to gain the support of the English Protestant East End working class. The BBL courted media attention more skilfully than the Protestant Alliance, and was on the surface more successful; its primary campaigning point, legislative restriction of Jewish immigration, having been achieved in 1905. However, in areas where it could draw on a well of anti-Catholic resentment, not in East London but in cities such as Liverpool and Glasgow, the Protestant Alliance and its successor organisations would prove to have strong and durable roots. The BBL and the Protestant Alliance reinforced an unsettling truth for both Jewish and Irish diasporas in East London. At the end of the Edwardian period, among communities that had been resident in the East End for generations, organisations commanding at least a modicum of popular support contested their British identity and their right to work and worship freely as they chose. By virtue of ethnicity or religion, or both, the BBL and the Protestant Alliance stressed Jewish and Irish outsider status in a wider national narrative.

### Political Violence

Political violence against a common enemy in the East End could potentially bring together disparate communities and bridge communal divisions. At the same time it could act as a divisive force amongst and between minority communities. The 'blackleg', the 'scab', the worker who crossed the picket line during a strike, was prominent in the demonology of the turn-of-the-century labour movement. The 'blackleg' was not only a class enemy, but a class traitor. For the late nineteenth-century socialist press, no invective was too strong to be employed against 'blackleg' labour. During the 1889 strikes, lauded in both the radical and mainstream press for the general good-feeling and lack of violence involved, attacks on 'scabs' were reported in some socialist publications with something approaching a bitter satisfaction.

---

[131] *The Advertiser* (9 June 1896).
[132] Glover, *Literature, Immigration and Diaspora*, p. 102.

An article in the *Commonweal* of 31 August 1889, whilst the dock strike was at its height, is typical:

> Unfortunate individuals afflicted with this detestable disease [i.e., 'blacklegging'] have, according to common reports, been treated to water cure by a ducking in the docks, their heads have been punched without mercy, and they are always certain of a good drubbing and kicking if their amateur doctors can lay hold of them ... Even the roughest of strikers are very peaceful in their large processions; but woe to any scab upon whom an isolated party of them lay hands on after working hours. A friend of mine saw one of them kicked into a state of insensibility.[133]

An article in the same journal the next month concluded: 'No wonder the blacklegs are departing, filled with the sad conviction that their lives are not secure in the neighbourhood of the docks.'[134] The violence was not all one-sided. Certain 'free labourers' working at the Wapping wharf during an 1891 strike armed themselves with revolvers and threatened the pickets outside the docks, unimpeded, apparently, by the local police force.[135]

While the strikes of 1889 were perceived as heralding a (fragile) labour alliance in the capital that reached across different industries and different ethnicities, the issue of 'blacklegging' served to divide minority communities, in both the docking and tailoring industries. There was much discussion of strike-breakers being 'shipped in' from Germany, Belgium, or indeed from the British countryside, but on occasion 'blacklegs' were in fact the neighbours of strikers, sometimes from the same family network, increasing the bitterness of these disputes.[136] In the East End Jewish community in particular during 1889, the split between those on strike and those willing to work led to tensions and physical confrontations within East London Jewry. This did not reflect the class divide existing between the solidly middle-class BoD and the working-class neighbourhoods of Whitechapel and Stepney. Neither was it symptomatic of the religious tensions between Orthodox Jewish believers and atheistic socialists and anarchists. The 1889 strike and subsequent disputes in the East End pitted elements of the same class and religious demographic, men and women often living on the same street, against each other.

A Home Office report issued during the dock and tailoring strikes, detailing cases of assault and intimidation believed to be related to strike

---

133  *Commonweal* (31 August 1889).
134  *Commonweal* (28 September 1889).
135  Tsuzuki, *Tom Mann*, p. 80.
136  See *East London Observer* (24 August 1889): '[There were rumours that] between 2000 and 3000 Germans were to arrive in the river in the morning ... "German sausages more likely" was one man's remark when he heard this.'

action, illustrates the divisions within the Jewish community at this time. In Whitechapel, Isaac Jubbinsky was arrested for attempting to intimidate Jane Konigsberg, while in St.-George's-in-the-East, Aster Cohen was charged with assault and intimidation against Emanuel Jacob, and Louis Barbisky was on the same charge against Abraham Moritz. At Great Prescott Street, Lewis Levy was charged with threatening Hermain Manhein.[137] Sometimes the aggravation between strikers and strike-breakers went beyond intimidation. One Jewish woman growing up in the East End recalled the tensions between her brother and a Jewish dock worker (one of the few employed in this industry), on strike during the period of industrial unrest, who occupied the flat above them in their housing block:

> And he [the other man] used to wait on him and he wanted to give him a good hiding one night – the one that worked at the docks cos he was on strike and my brother was doing his job ... he got paid well for it, and my brother had to avoid him ... cos he would have murdered him. As he came home they used to throw bricks through the train windows ... Course my brother was glad of the job.[138]

The tensions implicit in fraught industrial relations could set neighbours against each other. Strike-breakers from outside the community, although co-religionists, could also be the target of the accumulated anger and suspicion that accompanied industrial action. One case reported by the local press concerned an unfortunate group of Polish Jewish workers, some fifteen in number, who had responded to advertisements placed by employers in the continental press calling for workers in the tailoring industry during the strike period. Arriving in Whitechapel and swiftly being identified as 'blacklegs', the bedraggled 'greeners' struggled in vain to find lodgings as they traversed the area, whilst also attracting the attention and opprobrium of the locals: '[It] was not until they had got clear of the tailoring district that they were able to secure accommodation', reported the *Echo*.[139]

The East End Jewish bakers' strike of 1904 produced further examples of communal solidarity during social upheaval, with 'immigrant housewives' refusing to buy bread that was not stamped with the union label, so that 'the grocers were left with so much unsold bread that they immediately switched to union-based suppliers'.[140] The treatment of Jewish 'blacklegs' from within the Jewish community illustrates the multifaceted nature of

---

[137] National Archives, HO 144/227/A50732, Dock Strike, Cases of intimidation which have come to the knowledge of the police since the commencement of the dock strike, 21 September 1889.

[138] Interview in White, *Rothschild Buildings*, p. 94.

[139] *The Echo* (12 October 1889).

[140] Fishman, *East End Jewish Radicals*, p. 253.

diasporic identity and definitions. 'Us' and 'them', 'insiders' and 'outsiders', could, in times of severe industrial tension, be formulated not along religious or ethnic lines, but in terms of who was 'with' the union and who was not. The nature of these inter-communal tensions in the Jewish communities of the East End also puts into sharp perspective the difficulties apparent in contemporary trade union discourse on the role taken by ethnic and religious minorities during strike action. In these narratives communities were depicted *en masse* as being for or against industrial action, discounting the complex processes by which individuals chose either to support the trade unions or to continue to work.

During the 1911–1912 wave of industrial action, these socio-political tensions occasioned by the strikes within East End Jewry were less apparent. Jewish trade unionism in the capital was more firmly rooted by this point, with regular and less fluctuating memberships. The great wave of migration from the Pale of Settlement that had begun in 1881 was reaching its end. There had been renewed migration following the pogroms of 1903, military conscription during the Russo-Japanese War, and the backlash following the Russian Revolution of 1905. However, the age of the 'greener', at least in terms of Jewish immigration, was coming to a conclusion, which facilitated a more stable and successful Jewish trade union movement. This was a movement that had begun to achieve concrete results in terms of wages and hours of employment in the tailoring and associated trades. Anne Kershen identified a number of key factors explaining the increased strength of metropolitan Jewish trade unionism in the years immediately before the First World War. This included a greater degree of anglicisation of Jewish workers by the end of the decade, and in economic terms the integration of the levels of production in the tailoring industry. It was also due to the quality of leadership and the practical skills of Rudolph Rocker and Philip Kaplan, who had guided the unions through the strike.[141] In general, however, the metropolitan strikes of 1911–1912 had an undercurrent of violence, a sense of dread, and a fear of possible social conflagration that were not present in the disputes of 1889. The years following the end of the Edwardian period witnessed an upsurge of domestic political violence and partisan division generally, and labour relations reflected this. The docking and tailoring strikes of 1911–1912 gained little of the cross-political support that had greeted the strikes of 1889 or editorials in newspapers such as *The Times* expressing sympathy for the strikers.

The Home Office documents of the period, detailing correspondence between Winston Churchill, the Home Secretary, and London-based businesses during the strikes, point to an atmosphere of near hysteria in

---

[141] Kershen, *Uniting the Tailors*, p. 156.

the capital during the dock strikes of 1911. A telegram from H.L. Raphael's Refinery to the Home Office gives a flavour of the general feeling of the time, of the possibility of a rapidly escalating and perhaps armed confrontation between strikers and employers. 'I think it right to inform you', the telegram read, 'that I have made complete preparations against any attack on this place [by strikers], that our men are fully armed, and that we shall not sit still and watch our property being looted.'[142] A letter from the Millwall docks, an area of heavy Irish settlement, known for its political radicalism, to the Home Office read:

> The situation in the Isle of Dogs is so serious that a vast amount of property, and possibly the lives of many workers, will be in danger. Although our workpeople wish to remain at work, they are unable to do so, owing to the threats and angry crowds in the streets, which the police at present seem powerless to disperse.[143]

Increasingly, both strikers and strike-breakers were armed, sometimes with pistols, and in areas of the East End widespread intimidation took place.[144] The failure of the dockers to achieve their goals in the protracted struggle of 1911–1912 only increased the malign atmosphere of distrust and frustration surrounding the aftermath of the strikes. As in 1889, propensity towards strike action or 'blacklegging' was framed in contemporary journals in ethnic terms, the militancy and activism of trade unionists from particular backgrounds reflecting on the wider minority community.

The successfully concluded tailoring strike in some senses 'redeemed' East End Jewish trade unions in the eyes of the wider movement. Meanwhile, the press portrayed other communities in the capital, especially Asian workers, as natural strike-breakers.[145] The anti-Jewish polemic of the 1890s stressed the Smilesian economic qualities, the supposed ability and willingness to work impossibly long hours in terrible conditions for little money and less food, of the Jewish worker. By the end of the Edwardian period these tropes were being recycled and directed at the (still numerically marginal) Chinese communities of East London.[146] The framing of this depiction of

---

[142] National Archives, HO 144/1157/212342/28, Letter to Home Office from H.L. Raphael's Refinery, 9 August 1911.

[143] National Archives, HO 144/1157/212342/91, Letter to Home Office from Millwall Docks, 10 August 1911. See Brodie, *Politics of the Poor*, p. 194.

[144] Holton, *British Syndicalism*, p. 123. Ross M. Martin, *TUC: The Growth of a Pressure Group, 1868–1976* (Oxford: Oxford University Press, 1980), pp. 103–104.

[145] See Benton and Gomez, *The Chinese in Britain*, p. 311 for discussion of Irish–Chinese relations in dockland areas of Britain.

[146] See Benton and Gomez, *The Chinese in Britain*, pp. 262–268 for discussion of Chinese trade unionism in the United Kingdom, especially the activities of the Nautical Progress Society –

strike-making and strike-breaking in the language of nationality is evident from an article from a 'Special Daily War Edition' of the socialist journal the *Journeyman*:

> It is with regret – sincere and undisguised regret – that we have to record the breaking at last of the magnificent solidarity [during the 1912 dockers' strike] of the Scandinavians ... it is no light thing for any individual, however big they are, to play traitor to a race, easy though it may seem to do so for a trade.[147]

The behaviour of workers in a context such as 1889 or 1911–1912 was, as discussed above, taken by revolutionary journals to be representative of the wider nationality to which the workers belonged, and thus where they fitted in the struggle between capital and labour.

Conflicts between strikers and 'blacklegs' in the diasporic East End were, by definition, sporadic and occasional in nature, occurring during industrial disputes, although strike-breaking did leave a legacy of bitterness in communities that could last for many years. Of a more permanent and day-to-day nature were the difficult relations between the radical migrant organisations and the Metropolitan Police, the representatives of state power on the streets of the East End. The relationship between the Irish community and the police in the nineteenth century has been discussed in detail by historians.[148] It was frequently posited in the mid-nineteenth century that there were certain areas of East and South London with large Irish populations where it was unsafe for the police to venture, back streets where the writ of the law effectively did not run. Whether this was true or not, the difficult and even violent relations between Irish communities and the police were still being asserted when Charles Booth and his volunteers were collecting data in the 1890s.[149] The East End Jewish community was generally perceived to have a better relationship with the forces of law and

---

an organisation much neglected by historians. See also Tabili, *We Ask for British Justice*, p. 92 and Daniel Renshaw, 'Prejudice and Paranoia: A Comparative Study of Antisemitism and Sinophobia in Edwardian Britain', *Patterns of Prejudice*, Vol. 50, Issue 1 (2016).

[147] *Journeyman* (30 May 1912).

[148] See, among others, Roger Swift, 'Heroes or Villains?: The Irish, Crime and Disorder in Victorian England', *Albion: A Quarterly Journal Concerned with British Studies*, Vol. 29, No. 3 (Autumn 1997), pp. 399–421 and J.M. Feheny, 'Delinquency among Irish Catholic Children in Victorian London', *Irish Historical Studies*, Vol. 23, No. 92 (November 1983), pp. 319–329. Jennifer Davis's 'From "Rookeries" to "Communities": Race, Poverty and Policing in London, 1850–1985', *History Workshop*, No. 27 (Spring 1989), pp. 66–85 discusses police relations with immigrant communities from the post-Famine influx up to the Broadwater Farm riots of 1985.

[149] Booth, *Life and Labour of the People in London*, Third Series, *Religious Influences*, Vol. 1, *London North of the Thames: The Outer Ring* (London: Macmillan, 1902), p. 47 and Samuel 'The Roman Catholic Church and the Irish Poor', p. 278.

order.[150] The police, from interviews conducted by Charles Booth and others, seemed to regard East End Jewry as generally law-abiding, or at least non-violent, but also as 'clannish' and secretive, and (that old East London stereotype) prone to gambling.[151] One police constable claimed that 'the Jews are not men enough to be rough'.[152] On the question of police antisemitism, Nate Zamet responded: 'Not at all, not at all. I wasn't aware of any anti-Semitism … the police force were quite content with having [a] peaceful life.'[153] Despite the good relations that the Jewish hierarchy claimed characterised relationships between the community and the police, Hymie Fagan had far from positive memories of the role of the policeman in East End minority communities:

> They [the police] were hated … When patrolling Petticoat Lane, they would stop at any fruit stall and help themselves to whatever fruit took their fancy, without so much as a by your leave. There was never an objection by the fruit-stall owner, not if he was wise. The police had many ways of making his life uncomfortable … the police were a law unto themselves in the East End. What was the word of an immigrant shop-keeper, or stall-holder or ordinary citizen against the word of a policeman?[154]

This low-level working-class hostility towards what was perceived, certainly not solely in immigrant communities, as a partial and partially corrupt police force in the East End was apt to flare up at times of political agitation. This was particularly the case during strike action, when the police were often called upon to protect premises and safeguard 'blackleg' labour. During the 1889 dockers' strike, the Metropolitan Police had won widespread praise for the low-key, relaxed approach generally taken by the force during the dispute, which was credited with helping to prevent large-scale disruption. It must be noted that this was not wholly appreciated by the dock employers, who suspected police sympathy with the strikers.[155] But even during the events of 1889 there were allegations in the socialist

---

[150] See Susan L. Tananbaum, '"Morally Depraved and Abnormally Criminal": Jews and Crime in London and New York, 1880–1940', in Michael Berkowitz, Susan L. Tananbaum and Sam W. Bloom (eds), *Forging Modern Jewish Identities: Public Faces and Private Struggles* (London: Vallentine Mitchell, 2003).

[151] David Englander, 'Booth's Jews: The Presentation of Jews and Judaism in Life and Labour of the People in London', p. 306.

[152] Feldman, *Englishmen and Jews*, p. 285.

[153] Tape J.M./320, Interview with Nate Zamet, carried out by Debbie Seedburgh on behalf of the Jewish Museum, London (unknown date).

[154] Manchester People's History Museum, CP/IND/FAG/1/5, Childhood memories of Hymie Fagan.

[155] Joan Ballhatchet, 'The Police and the London Dock Strike of 1889', *History Workshop*, No. 32 (Autumn 1991), pp. 59–62.

press of police brutality against old men, women, and children, and reports
of crowds attacking mounted police with paving stones in Silvertown.[156]
Shared hostility towards the police among working-class communities in
East London could occasionally bridge social and cultural divisions. During
the autumn of 1906, a strike by Jewish bakers in Spitalfields evolved into
a general confrontation between the wider community of Flower and
Dean Street and the Metropolitan Police.[157] The street was one of those
intersections in the East End which witnessed a significant degree of
tension between Jewish and Gentile populations, particularly gangs of
youths, but the presence of the police could serve to put a temporary halt
to such hostile sentiment, and unite disparate groups against a common
opponent. Again, as with industrial action, common class antagonism
towards the representatives on the ground of the British state could cut
across religious and ethnic stratifications. Alliances between and collective
action by groups of youths of different ethnic backgrounds uniting against
the police remained a feature of the urban 'riot' in Britain throughout the
twentieth century and into the twenty-first.[158]

Certainly, Jewish radicals in the East End perceived themselves as
unfairly targeted and monitored by the police, just as did Irish Nationalists
(the two groups would find themselves sharing cells after the implementation of the Defence of the Realm Act (DORA) in 1914).[159] Jewish
socialists who had fled the Russian Tsarist regime had also brought with
them an understandable distrust of and hostility towards the apparatus
of the state. Following the Aliens Act of 1905, the police were also
expected to enforce expulsion orders, which were sometimes coupled
with a term of imprisonment and corporal punishment.[160] The police, and
the Home Office, were also perceived by revolutionary socialists, rightly
or wrongly, to be working in collusion with the security services of the
continental regimes from which many East End socialists and anarchists
were refugees. These agents, particularly those of the Tsarist Okhrana,
were busy at work in the capital. Rocker, amongst others, believed that
secret police forces were involved in attempts to provoke acts of terrorism

---

156 National Archives, HO/144/227/A50732/99-100, Silvertown disturbances and police
reaction, 1889.

157 White, *Rothschild Buildings*, p. 127.

158 See Paul Gilroy, *There Ain't No Black in the Union Jack* (London: Routledge, 1987)
(republished 1992), chapter 6, 'Conclusion: Urban Social Movement, "Race" and Community',
for discussion of the interplay of ethnicity, generational politics, class, and community
involved in the modern urban 'riot'.

159 Alderman, *London Jewry and London Politics*, p. 84.

160 See National Archives, HO 144/1008/141734, Home Office Minutes, October 1911,
'Whipping for contravention of expulsion order'.

by young 'lone wolves' in the capital, the better to discredit the wider movement.[161] Certain socialist organisations in the East End, most notably the International Working Men's Club on Berner Street, were repeatedly targeted by a hostile police force. On one occasion in the summer of 1885 it was asserted that the police had in effect taken part in a riot against the club members, inciting the 'mob' with 'cries against the "bloody foreigners"', assaulting those present and ransacking the building.[162]

A further confrontation involving the Club occurred in March 1889, following a parade of the Jewish unemployed, and again the Metropolitan Police was accused by the socialists of provoking a violent situation, and subsequently brutally interrogating the men and women they had arrested. At the end of this report in *Commonweal*, the writer, Frank Kitz, warned: 'It would be well for all concerned to take note that there is not the slightest intention on the part either of English or foreign Socialists to allow such police outrages to be perpetrated without risk to the perpetrators in future.'[163] Despite this ominous warning, there was little organised violence by any of the socialist groups, migrant or otherwise, against the Metropolitan Police in the period. Low-level and sometimes explicit police harassment continued to occur sporadically, if not to such a degree as could be labelled an organised campaign of intimidation. Violence against the police, as occurred in Flower and Dean Street in 1906, tended to take the form of unorganised and spontaneous action during the heat of industrial disputes and confrontations.

Violence, then, served to shape identity and belonging in the East End of London, just as positive communal interactions such as joint charitable concerns, social activities, or marriage did. Identity is a product of how one defines oneself against opponents as much as how one identifies friends. In some of the cases described above, of tit-for-tat gang warfare between youths in the East End, or in response to the provocative actions of the Protestant Alliance, violence acted as a solidifier of existing ethnic or religious divides in minority communities, reinforcing oppositions and boundaries. But during outbreaks of political confrontation, between strikers and 'blacklegs', or revolutionaries and the police, violence could lead to the formation of new identities and loyalties, based around class or East End geographical location rather than religion or ethnicity.

---

[161] Rocker, *The London Years*, pp. 108–109. See National Archives, HO/144/587/B2840C/92, HO 144/587/B2840C/99 and HO 144/587/B2840C/101 for Home Office correspondence on the activities of continental security services active in London and their requests for aid from the British State in monitoring foreign radicals resident in the metropolis.

[162] *Commonweal* (June 1885).

[163] *Commonweal* (23 March 1889).

## Grass-roots Interactions within the Socialist Movement

Charitable organisations and religious missions located in the East End provided one framework for positive inter-ethnic and inter-religious interactions between the diasporic communities of the area. Another sphere of possible cooperation, and an area where migrant populations could make common cause with each other, were the labour and socialist groups located in East London. The trade union movement, as evidenced by the ill-tempered debates at the various TUC congresses of the second half of the 1890s, contained ambivalent attitudes towards migrant labour. It was temperamentally inclined to support the worker being exploited in the sweatshops, but was at the same time aware of the resentment within much of the trade union rank and file towards migrant groups seen as undercutting their labour. It was also commonly held that certain migrants, particularly Jews, were 'natural' 'blacklegs', thus the importance of the tailoring strikes of 1889 and 1912, which confirmed for the wider movement that Jewish-based trade unions could not only organise but declare a strike, wage a campaign and see it through to a satisfactory conclusion.[164] The final part of this chapter will consider how trade union activity and the campaigns of various left-wing organisations affected inter-ethnic interactions and formation of East End identity at a grass-roots level.

From the earliest stirrings of Jewish radicalism and trade unionism in the East End an international and cross-cultural component to organisation and action was envisaged. The Hebrew Socialist Union (HSU) had hoped for cross-communal political cooperation, an alliance of poor Jews with their equally poor English and Irish neighbours, against both Jewish and Gentile exploiters. For Aaron Lieberman, founder of the HSU, an initially Jewish movement could perhaps operate as a first stepping stone towards a general organisation of the East End proletariat.[165] The Union declared that its aim was to 'spread Socialism among Jews as well as non-Jews ... to support organisations recognised by it and to unite all workers in the fight against their oppressors ... to unite with workers' organisations from other nations.'[166] These initial attempts to combine Jewish and Gentile workers in East London were not a success. But by the mid-1880s, English, Irish, and Jewish socialists were holding joint meetings in shared premises and sharing resources and facilities. The International Working Men's Club on Berner Street was one example – established by Jewish socialists but playing host to a range of speakers, Jewish and Gentile, and frequented by activists of

---

164  Kershen, *Uniting the Tailors*, pp. 154–156.
165  Fishman, *East End Jewish Radicals*, pp. 103–109.
166  Kershen, *Uniting the Tailors*, pp. 127–128.

all nationalities and ethnic backgrounds. Some non-Jewish activists threw themselves wholeheartedly into the radical and communal struggles of the Jewish East End. Rudolph Rocker recalled the composition of the Club on Berner Street, which also served as the headquarters of the *Arbeter Fraynt*: 'It was also used by non-Jewish comrades, Russians, Poles, Germans and others ... The members of the Mile End branch of the English Socialist League used the club for their meetings.'[167] In Rocker's East End Jubilee Street Club, Gentile and Jewish activists, anarchists, and syndicalists socialised and theorised together. One East London socialist who frequently addressed the audiences at the club was Ted Leggatt, in Rocker's words 'a big, burly Cockney carman ... he was a man of the people, racy of speech, with a rich cockney humour ... a good fellow, and a good comrade, a frequent visitor among the Jewish comrades, who were always glad to see him.'[168] In Rocker's memoirs he recalled other English comrades in the transnational anarchist and socialist movements based in the East End, including Frank Kitz, John Turner, Edward Carpenter, and Tom Bell, as well as the Irish American anarchist Harry Kelly.

Louise Raw has drawn attention to the heavy Irish presence amongst the match-women, and the leading role played by Irish women in the strike action of 1888, dating the politicisation and trade union organisation of the East End Irish working class from that year rather than the following one.[169] The socialist, feminist, and author Clementina Black cut her teeth in the strike action undertaken by the match-women. Annie Besant was also involved in the organisation of the strikers, once the strike had commenced. Like Eleanor Marx, a close comrade of Black, both women embraced the industrial struggle being fought out by English and Irish workers at Bryant and May, and soon to spread to the rest of East London. During the match-women's strike Besant had published a pamphlet entitled 'White Slavery', the title simultaneously evocative of themes of colonial exploitation (including in Ireland), the inequities of British capitalism, and prostitution.[170] In the same year Besant was elected onto the London School Board for Tower Hamlets. As a forerunner of the trade union alliances of the following year, Besant won the vote primarily due to a combination of Irish and Jewish workers in the East End, the former disregarding the wishes of the Church and the latter those of the Anglo-Jewish hierarchy. The support of East London migrant Jewry was partly based around the tireless support and agitation

---

[167] Rocker, *The London Years*, p. 59.
[168] Rocker, *The London Years*, p. 101.
[169] Raw, *Striking a Light*, pp. 173–176.
[170] Anne Taylor, *Annie Besant: A Biography* (Oxford: Oxford University Press, 1992), pp. 207–208.

of the Jewish socialist Lewis Lyons on Besant's behalf during the election campaign.[171]

The dockers' and tailors' strikes that followed this action by the match-women were the first real test of the fragile inter-ethnic cooperation established between socialists and trade unionists from the various East End communities. This meant organising not just a handful of temperamentally similar and politically aware radicals, but thousands of largely non-unionised casual workers. The tailors' strike was not a direct response to the dockers' strike that preceded it. It was not a movement towards some sort of general strike in support of the dockers and stevedores, but the dockers' strike certainly acted as a model for the strikes in the garment industry that followed. It is unlikely that industrial action within the East End tailoring workshops would have taken place on such a large scale without the example of what was taking place on the wharves and docks. When the furriers and cap makers of East London, another trade employing many Jewish workers, came out on strike in August 1889 they were addressed at a rally in Victoria Park by Annie Besant, who stressed 'that the foreign Jews who had been accused of underselling English labour were now bravely standing out against low wages and long hours'.[172] A number of English trade unionists also addressed the crowd, 'on behalf of their "English brothers"'.[173] The Times of 4 September 1889 reported on the industrial unrest thus:

> The strike epidemic is now spreading to the Jewish quarter of the East End ... It is stated that about 6,000 tailors are now out on strike, and that many more will turn out before the end of the week if their demands are not granted ... In one thing they [the different groups of strikers] are unanimous, and that is the demand for a higher rate of wages.[174]

Separate events, with separate causes and varying demands, but taking place concurrently, the struggles of the tailors and the dockers in 1889 became linked, not just in the public perception and in press reports of the industrial unrest, but also in the eyes of the strikers themselves. By the autumn of 1889, it was widely felt in the docklands that victory would not be complete without a successful conclusion to the tailors' strike as well. Elements of the non-socialist Jewish press, normally cautious on trade union matters, welcomed the alliance between Jewish, Irish, and English workers during the strike action as heralding a new period in Jewish–Gentile relations, undermining accusations of Jewish 'separation and clannishness'.[175]

171  Taylor, *Annie Besant*, p. 217.
172  *East London Observer* (24 August 1889).
173  *East London Observer* (24 August 1889).
174  *The Times* (4 September 1889), quoted in McCarthy, *The Great Dock Strike 1889*, p. 146.
175  *Jewish World* (6 September 1889).

The strikes of 1889 also commanded significant support among usually non-politicised members of the diasporic communities, as the aforementioned hostile treatment meted out to the suspected 'blacklegs' looking for lodgings in Whitechapel illustrates. David Feldman writes of this (brief) spirit of inter-communal cooperation and solidarity: 'The tailors' strike ... was notable for the degree of unity established between immigrant and English workers, trade unionists and revolutionaries, the strikers and shopkeepers of the East End.'[176] The dock strike too witnessed inter-ethnic cooperation in other avenues, not least the refusal of Chinese seamen (often pilloried as inveterate 'blacklegs' in the socialist press) to coal their steamers during the industrial action, for which they were (illegally) held in an East End police station for some time.[177] *The Great Dock Strike*, published before the centenary of these events, in 1988, gives a perhaps rather romantic but still useful description of the alliances formed during the strikes of 1889:

> [The Jewish socialists were] eager to teach not only the politics of socialism and anarchism but the practicalities of literacy and organisation and were pleased to welcome the new recruits to the social institutions set up by the Jewish community in back rooms and halls and at the top of pubs. One can only conjecture what these Yiddish-speaking Jews from Poland, Russia and Eastern Europe thought of their new comrades in the classes ... Many of them had thick Irish accents. Many of the seamen and dockers were Lascars ... But this divergent group shared one thing in common and that was that they were all poor, underfed and badly clothed.[178]

One cross-cultural relationship within the East End socialist movement that would bear immediate political fruit was the friendship formed between Will Thorne and Eleanor Marx. Marx had been active in the metropolitan socialist movement from the mid-1880s onwards, and by the end of the decade was a key speaker at rallies and meetings in East London. Marx had met and discussed politics with many of the leading continental socialists of the period, and written on both the domestic and the international socialist movements. An SL member, she had taken an active role in coordinating the 1889 Dock Strike, helping to direct operations from the East End Irish public house which formed the strikers' base.[179] Eleanor had a less ambiguous attitude towards her Jewish background than her father. In her obituary, Eduard Bernstein wrote: 'At every opportunity she declared her

[176] Feldman, *Englishmen and Jews*, p. 221.

[177] Llewellyn Smith and Nash, *The Story of the Dockers Strike*, p. 105.

[178] McCarthy, *The Great Dock Strike 1889*, p. 78.

[179] Lynne Hapgood, '"Is This Friendship?" Eleanor Marx, Margaret Harkness and the Idea of Socialist Community', in John Stokes (ed.), *Eleanor Marx (1855–1898): Life, Work, Contacts* (Aldershot: Ashgate Publishing, 2000), pp. 132–133.

descent with a certain defiance. "I am a Jewess" – how often I heard her
... shout this with pride to the crowd from the rostrum. She felt herself
drawn to the Jewish proletarians of the East End with all the greater
sympathy.'[180] Marx commented to the German Jewish socialist Max Beer
that 'My happiest moments ... are when I am in the East End amidst Jewish
work people.'[181] Marx was also sympathetic towards Irish Nationalism,
particularly in its republican form. When James Connolly established the
Irish Socialist Republican Party in 1896, Marx was one of the first to send
a letter of congratulation to the Irish radical.[182]

At the beginning of 1889, Will Thorne, born in Birmingham of Irish
descent, a member of the SDF and working as a gasworker in East Ham,
began to organise his fellow-workers into a trade union. This effort brought
Thorne into contact with Marx, who not only advised Thorne on tactics,
and provided clerical assistance, but also taught hm to read and write.[183]
The union expanded rapidly, within four months of its formation boasting
a membership approaching some 20,000.[184] Marx's role in the gasworkers'
strike was recalled by Thorne in the following terms: 'An eloquent speaker,
fluent in several languages, she did good service both among the men and
women, and formed a women's branch of the union at Silvertown, of which
she became the secretary.'[185]

A speech given by Marx in October 1889 stressed that the working-class
unity being tested in the industrial struggle must cross gender as well as
ethnic and occupational lines:

> As the Dock Strike has taught them the great lesson that skilled and
> unskilled labour should work together, so the present strike should teach
> them the further great lesson, that they could only win by men and women
> working together.[186]

In his memoir, *My Life's Battles* (1925), Thorne paid tribute to Marx and
lamented her death by suicide: 'But for this tragedy I believe that Eleanor
would still have been living, and would have been a greater woman's leader

---

[180] Jacobs, *On Socialists and 'the Jewish Question' after Marx*, pp. 51–52.

[181] Tsuzuki, *The Life of Eleanor Marx*, p. 253.

[182] Tsuzuki, *The Life of Eleanor Marx*, p. 293.

[183] Will Thorne, *My Life's Battles* (London: George Newnes Ltd, 1925), p. 117.

[184] Pelling, *A History of British Trade Unionism*, p. 93.

[185] Thorne, *My Life's Battles*, p. 96. See also John Tully, *Silvertown: The Lost Story of a Strike that Shook London and Helped Launch the Modern Labor Movement* (New York: Monthly Review Press, 2014), pp. 122–127, for Marx's relationship with Thorne and the East End Irish community.

[186] *Borough of West Ham and Stratford Express* (9 October 1889), in Stokes, *Eleanor Marx*, 'Introduction', p. 7.

than the greatest of contemporary women.'[187] English-born but linked by her upbringing to the continental radical émigré milieu of earlier in the century, part of a metropolitan socialist intelligentsia and with a profound empathy for the English, Irish, and Jewish East End communities, Marx was a key intermediary figure in East London diaspora space.

The cross-communal actions of 1889 and the alliances formed during this period were put under considerable strain by the disappointments and mistakes that set back the trade union movement, both in London and nationally, over the course of the 1890s. A series of unofficial strikes in the East End clothing trades during 1891 were defeated by the employers, who locked out the workers and brought in 'blackleg' labour. There were also reports as early as 1890 of 'English' workers refusing to work in tailoring workshops with their Jewish co-workers.[188] It was not until the strikes of 1911–1912 that Jewish trade unionism and Jewish unionised labour would be considered on fully equal terms with its non-Jewish counterparts.[189]

Nevertheless, these periods of inter-ethnic cooperation occasioned by strike action, in both 1889 and 1911–1912, witnessed acts of grass-roots communal solidarity that had lasting and positive effects outside the arena of unionisation and political organisation. This was a system of cross-communal charity and support drawing on the help not only of local East End socialists but other secular and religious bodies as well. This support was in effect an expansion of the *Landsman* networks already present within the Jewish communities and similar networks present in other diasporic groups, ties of family and kinship carried over from the land left by migrants, or from the parents or grandparents of Jewish or Irish East-Enders. This charitable assistance, whether in the form of money, food, or a bed to sleep in, was a crucial part of immigrant settlement and survival in disorientating new conditions. Ian Mikardo, discussing the experiences of his father, wrote:

> If one of the newcomers ... walked into a synagogue on a Friday evening for Sabbath-eve prayers and looked at bit lost, there would always be a member of the congregation who would invite him home to break bread by the Sabbath candles ... And as a last resort, any door with a *mezuzah* on the doorpost had a Jewish family behind it, and nobody was ever turned away: nearly all of them poor, some very poor, but they were all ready to share what they had.[190]

---

[187] Thorne, *My Life's Battles*, pp. 148–149.

[188] Feldman, *Englishmen and Jews*, pp. 222–224; Pollins, *Economic History of the Jews of England*, p. 159.

[189] Kershen, *Uniting the Tailors*, pp. 154–156.

[190] Mikardo, *Backbencher*, pp. 8–9. A *mezuzah* is a parchment inscribed with verses from the Torah, traditionally affixed to the door frame in Jewish homes.

If the family breadwinner, male or female, fell ill or was otherwise incapacitated in the Jewish East End, neighbouring families would often provide childcare and make sure the family was fed and clothed for the duration.[191] During the periods of industrial unrest in the East End, the communal safety net was extended to provide for the families of striking workers, to provide shelter and food, particularly for the children of the men and women on strike. In 1889, relief for the families of striking dockers had involved the assistance of a wide range of often religiously based organisations. Protestant, Catholic, and Jewish bodies worked to this end in East London, setting up street kitchens and relief centres for the families of strikers.[192]

The support networks of 1911–1912 were more explicitly socialist in genesis and organisation. This assistance and hospitality transcended ethnic and religious boundaries – most notably during the strikes of 1912. After the tailoring strike had concluded successfully and the dock strike continued, without any prospect of immediate success, some 300 docker children, mainly from Catholic backgrounds, were clothed and fed by Jewish surrogate families in Stepney and Whitechapel. Rudolf Rocker and his anarcho-socialist circle were instrumental in placing the children of the striking dockers with sympathetic households.[193] Rocker described the process thus:

> We called a conference of the Jewish trade unions ... It was decided to ask Jewish families in the East End to take some of the dockers' children into their homes. Offers poured in. Unfortunately we couldn't accept them all. Members of the committee always went first to see the house and too often the family couldn't feed its own children properly. When we found a suitable home, Milly [Witkop, Rocker's lifetime partner] would go to the docks area with one or two other women to fetch the children. They were in a terribly undernourished state, barefoot, in rags ... Shopkeepers gave us shoes and clothing for them. Trade union leaders and social workers in the docks area spoke publicly of the kindness shown by the East End Jews. The docker parents used to come to the Jewish homes in Whitechapel and Stepney to see their children.[194]

Rocker and Milly Witkop took a couple of dockers' children into their own home during the prolonged industrial action, Rocker's son Fermin recalling his

> first glimpse of the little adoptees. I had trotted over to Jamaica Street one afternoon and on climbing up the stairs, met Milly on the landing

[191] White, *Rothschild Buildings*, pp. 97–98.

[192] Westminster Diocesan Archives, AAW/BOX ET, Jean Olwen Maynard, 'History of the Parish of St Mary and St Joseph's Poplar, Vol. II 1881–1894'.

[193] Colin Ward, 'Introduction', in Rocker, *The London Years*, pp. 2–3.

[194] Rocker, *The London Years*, p. 131.

holding a small child in her arms, while an older one was clinging to her skirt. Later I was told that these were children from a docker's family who were staying with Milly and Lazar because there was not enough for them to eat at home.[195]

During the strike Jewish bakers kept striking dockers and tailors and their families supplied with bread and other produce, sending out 600 loaves to families on a single day. Jewish families undertook to provide dockers with three hot meals for a week.[196] The relief and support offered by (often very poor) East End Jewish families under the aegis of Rocker and his comrades did not alter the course of the ultimately unsuccessful dock strike, but left a legacy of inter-ethnic cooperation that would grow in significance in the divisive inter-war years. The 1911–1912 period had been a time of exceptional hardship in the dockland areas of London, both English and Irish. At one point during the lockout a 'sensationalist weekly newspaper' had dispatched carts down to the East End where loaves of bread were thrown into the street for the men and women to scramble and fight for.[197] Unlike in 1889, the dockers undertook industrial action without enjoying widespread support outside of the labour movement, and as the strike wore on the prospect of victory receded. One East End clergyman, Father Ring, described the conditions in dockers' families as the industrial action continued:

> Landlords are fixing eviction orders on the houses, and this is driving the poor people almost mad. Not only is the East End racked with hunger, not only has every stick of furniture been pledged [i.e., pawned] in many instances, but a new horror is at hand … having parted with every stick of furniture, mothers have been unable to provide themselves with the nourishment necessary for the preservation of their own health and the lives of their infants.[198]

The hospitality offered to dockers' children by Jewish families during this time was a rare positive move during the bitterness of the nationwide confrontation between workers and employers on the docksides. The cooperation formed a notable example of beneficial grass-roots inter-ethnic interaction between Jews, Irish Catholics, and the English working class in this period. Rocker, who had helped coordinate the provision of the relief, became something of a folk hero in both Jewish and Gentile East End neighbourhoods. 'One day as I was walking along a narrow Whitechapel street with Milly an old Jew with a long white beard stopped me outside

---

[195] Rocker, *The East End Years*, pp. 93–94.
[196] Gidley, 'Citizenship and Belonging', pp. 34 and 87–88.
[197] Mess, *Casual Labour at the Docks*, pp. 53–54.
[198] *The Socialist Standard* (August 1912).

his house, and said: "May God bless you! You helped my children in their need. You are not a Jew, but you are a man!'"[199] The care of dockers' children by Jewish families in the strike period was echoed in a different context in 1914, when, after much publicity over their plight, Jewish families in the East End, as well as the Jews' Temporary Shelter in Whitechapel, took Belgian refugees temporarily into their homes.[200] These positive interactions between East End communities were recognition that both the Jewish and Gentile working classes of East London, during this period of industrial action, were suffering the same economic privation. The creation of an autonomous grass-roots 'safety-net' that was at certain times of hardship cross-communal in nature, forms an alternative narrative to that of spatial and cultural separation and inter-ethnic physical violence and tension. The impetus for this inter-ethnic support network that manifested itself during the months of industrial action came from the grass roots, the communities of East London themselves. In the years of war, economic hardship, and political extremism that followed the period documented in this book, often a time of apparent darkness, the hospitality offered to the children of the striking dockers in 1911–1912 left something of a legacy of hope in the diaspora space of the East End.

---

[199] Rocker, *The London Years*, p. 131.

[200] Westminster Diocesan Archives, AAW BOX LE, Jean Olwen Maynard, 'History of the Parish of St. Anne's Underwood Road, Vol. IV 1911–1938'.

# 6

# Conclusion

Socialist activity in the metropolis from the 1880s to 1912 was marked by an extraordinary degree of schism, ideological difference, and fratricidal conflict. This expressed itself in the lack of consistency in respect to concepts of difference and the practical labour organisation of Irish and Jewish communities. This state of affairs only began to change after the founding of the Labour Representation Committee in 1900. This in turn paved the way for the national electoral breakthrough of the Labour Party in the 1906 General Election, and the streamlining of and increased party discipline within mainstream socialist politics that followed.[1] The period 1889–1912 in a London-based context was characterised by the existence of a number of small, relatively weak, competing socialist groups, with attempts to arrive at a common platform or policy largely being frustrated. These groups had shifting memberships and often chaotic organisation. This differentiates the period from both from the radical politics preceding the emergence of new unionism in the 1880s and the progress of moderate socialism and Marxism after the First World War. Chartism in the 1830s and 1840s constituted a relatively ideologically cohesive movement with an explicit platform and policy endorsed by its members, even if the Chartist movement was split on the issue of the efficacy of violence to achieve political aims.[2] After 1918, metropolitan socialism was embodied in a Labour Party that had entered the mainstream and would soon govern nationally and a small but resilient

---

[1] Thompson, *Socialists, Liberals and Labour*, p. 225; Laybourn, *A History of British Trade Unionism*, p. 106; Fraser, *A History of British Trade Unionism*, p. 100.

[2] See E.C.K. Gonner, 'The Early History of Chartism, 1836–1839', *English Historical Review*, Vol. 4, No. 16 (October 1889), pp. 630–631 and John K. Walton, *Chartism* (London: Routledge, 1999), pp. 35–37 and 50–53. See also Edward Royle, *Chartism* (Harlow: Pearson Education, 1980) (republished 1996), chapter 6 for discussion of Chartist strategy and the division between proponents of 'moral force' and 'physical force'.

Communist Party of Great Britain (the CPGB). The mutual antipathy that existed between these two groups should not disguise the far more effective inner-party discipline that existed within both organisations as compared with their predecessors.[3] After 1918, it was easier for socialist parties to adopt a particular official 'line' on certain issues, antisemitism, Irish nationalism, and Catholicism included. This ensured that the official policy was adhered to both nationally and locally and that party members were bound by party discipline in public meetings and in print, with the ability effectively to punish members who publicly flouted official commitment to ethnic and religious tolerance.[4]

The years 1889 to 1912 was a period of atomisation for metropolitan socialism, confused and often chaotic, with matters of policy and ideology uncertain, constantly disputed, and up for debate. It was by no means clear, certainly in the 1890s, what form an electorally successful socialist party would take, or indeed whether socialism would succeed through the ballot box or through revolution.[5] Those elements of metropolitan socialism that favoured the electoral path positioned their revolutionary opponents as outside the native radical tradition, 'alien', to a greater or lesser degree. The disunited character of socialist politics in the 1889–1912 period is crucial in comprehending the ethnic demarcation of ideological positions within the London-based left. This manifested itself first in the labelling of certain strands of radicalism such as anarchism and syndicalism as intrinsically 'foreign', and more specifically in the former case, in an East End context, 'Jewish'. Secondly it expressed itself in the more general association of political violence with diasporic minorities. In a trade union context, during the prolonged and bitter strikes of the period, the designation of whole communities as being 'for' or 'against' industrial action, 'blacklegs' or 'good comrades', was predicated on ethnic identity. Such a conflation of ethnicity and politics was not apparent in Chartism, despite the involvement of a significant coterie of Irish radical leaders.[6] Neither was it present to the same degree in Labour and CPGB affairs in the inter-war period. Right-wing opponents of socialism might associate both Labour and the communists with Irish and Jewish minorities, not least the racist polemicist Joseph Banister. Banister, one of the leading antisemites of the Edwardian

---

[3] Matthew Worley, *Labour Inside the Gate: A History of the British Labour Party between the Wars* (London: I.B. Tauris and Co. Ltd, 2005), p. 217.

[4] Gisela C. Lebzelter, *Political Anti-Semitism in England, 1918–1939* (London: Macmillan, 1978), pp. 30–31.

[5] Bevir, *The Making of British Socialism*, pp. 101–104 and 267–269.

[6] See Connolly, *Labour in Ireland* for discussion of the Irish role in radicalism and early socialism on the British mainland prior to 1889. O'Higgins, 'The Irish Influence in the Chartist Movement', *Past and Present*, Vol. 20, No. 1 (November 1961).

period, was responsible for a typically vitriolic 1924 monograph whose (also typically) long-winded title ran, *Our Judaeo-Irish Labour Party: How the Interests of the British Working Man are Misrepresented and Betrayed by Politicians who are neither British nor Working Men.* However, such ethnic demarcations and characterisations (involving these two groups at least) were no longer being made to the same degree by socialists and trade unionists themselves.[7]

Ethnicity and ethnic difference played an important role for socialism and labour in the East End between 1889 and 1912 because of division, weakness, mutual suspicion, and uncertainty, and because ethnic difference was one means of distinguishing oneself from political opponents. With coalescence and increased confidence under the banner of Labour or the CPGB from the early 1920s, and the evolution of a more cohesive and streamlined trade union movement, ethnic divisions and demarcations within socialism in a Jewish or Irish context became less obvious. The relegation of anarchism, with its pre-First World War base in the Jewish East End, to the remote margins of radical politics after 1918, also undermined the conflation of that particular form of radical political activity with the Jewish diaspora.[8] In some respects, the CPGB would take on this mantle in the 1930s through an anti-fascist platform, Jewish areas of East London forming one of the key CPGB constituencies.[9] The CPGB enjoyed significant Jewish support, but was not viewed, on the left at least, as an explicitly Jewish organisation, or Jewish in character in the way that anarchism and nihilism were portrayed in the late-Victorian and Edwardian periods (although the fascist far-right constantly made this claim).

Did socialist attitudes towards Jewish and Irish diasporic groups evolve significantly between the waves of industrial militancy of 1889 and 1911–1912? An examination of the various socialist journals of the period reveals a peak in left-wing anti-Jewish sentiment during the Boer War and a decline after this point. The SDF resolution condemning antisemitism was necessitated by the increased volume of antisemitic speeches and articles from Hyndman and others that followed the outbreak of that conflict.[10] The Kishinev pogroms of 1903 occasioned renewed sympathy for Eastern European Jewry on the part of British socialism, as did, in a domestic context, the implementation

[7] Joseph Banister, *Our Judaeo-Irish Labour Party: How the Interests of the British Working Man are Misrepresented and Betrayed by Politicians who are neither British nor Working Men* (London: self-published, 1924). See also Kadish, *Bolsheviks and British Jews*, p. 36.

[8] Woodcock, *Anarchism*, pp. 452–453.

[9] Kevin Morgan, Gideon Cohen and Andrew Flinn, *Communists and British Society 1920–1991* (London: Rivers Oram Press, 2007), p. 188; Lebzelter, *Political Anti-Semitism in England*, p. 156.

[10] Kirk, *Comrades and Cousins*, pp. 192–193.

of the Aliens Act after 1905.[11] After the Boer War, portrayals of the stock antisemitic caricature of the 'big Jew', the sweater at home and the source of colonial oppression abroad, became less frequent in socialist literature. Nevertheless, as late as 1911, in connection with Samuel Montagu, *Justice* was still referring to 'Jew moneybags'.[12]

Contemporary attacks on Irish Catholics on ethnic grounds in the socialist press from 1889 onwards were rare, although anti-Irish stereotypes were very occasionally employed. More common were articles attacking the Catholic Church and in particular the Jesuits. Labour figures also stressed the divisive role of the Irish Nationalists in retarding working-class London Irish organisation under the Labour Party or other left-wing groups. Articles against the Church followed closely the Education Act controversies, whilst condemnations of the continuing loyalty of London Irish workers to the cause of Home Rule were particularly intense during election periods.[13] None of these sentiments had wholly disappeared by 1912, but their articulation was becoming somewhat rarer. For the trade union movement, which passed a number of resolutions calling for restriction of entry of aliens in the mid-1890s, and harboured a handful of explicit antisemites (Charles Freak being an example), successful mass unionisation of migrant communities changed attitudes towards the East End diasporas.[14]

By 1914, just under a quarter of the British labour force was organised into some kind of trade union.[15] The casual trades employing the majority of male working-class Irish Catholics in East London, above all those industries associated with the docklands, had become almost wholly unionised between 1889 and the First World War. Domestic servitude, still the major employer for Irish Catholic women, remained un-unionised, but this largely unrepresented demographic was on the whole ignored by male-dominated trade unionism in any case.[16] The Jewish route to mass working-class union representation within the sweatshops was a more tortuous affair. The successful tailors' strikes of 1911–1912 (involving both West End and East End tailors) witnessed the (eventual) arrival of a

[11] See Manchester People's History Museum, LRC/9/126/2, 'The International Kischinieff [*sic*] Massacre Protest Committee'. See Sam Johnson, *Pogroms, Peasants, Jews: Britain and Eastern Europe's 'Jewish Question', 1867–1925* (Basingstoke: Palgrave Macmillan, 2011), pp. 77–88 for discussion of British reactions to the pogrom.

[12] *Justice* (1 April 1911).

[13] Fielding, *Class and Ethnicity*, pp. 95–97 and 105.

[14] Warwick Modern Records Centre, MSS 292/PUB/4/1/2, Trade Union Congress Report, 1895, pp. 45–46.

[15] Hunt, *British Labour History*, p. 295; Laybourn, *A History of British Trade Unionism*, p. 106. National trade union membership grew from 2,477,000 in 1909 to 4,145,000 in 1914.

[16] Ebery and Preston, *Domestic Service*, p. 99.

mature Jewish trade unionism. This finally put to rest the categorisation of the Jewish proletariat as intrinsically unsuitable for unionisation that was frequently asserted by labour leaders in the 1890s.[17] Rudolph Rocker had written about the importance of the tailors' strike for Jewish involvement in the wider movement: 'If the West End strike collapsed, the Jewish workers would be blamed for it. The entire British trade union movement would become hostile to the Jews.'[18] Instead the Jewish trade unionists won out in the garment industry, although the striking dockers were defeated.

Ethnic demarcation of ideological difference, however, did not wholly disappear in the years preceding the First World War. Indeed, with the Houndsditch murders and the Sidney Street siege the conflation of 'foreigners' generally and Jews in particular with violent political action reached a peak.[19] By 1912, Irish Nationalist politics was also once again increasingly associated with violence, a conflation of Irish minorities with militant republicanism, now represented by the nascent Sinn Féin movement and the Irish Volunteers.[20] Increasingly, however, socialist and trade union discussion of ethnicity, and the framing of political involvement in ethnic terms, focused on Asian groups, and in particular Chinese workers in dockland areas and ports.

The prejudices examined in this book have largely been formulated by white groups and directed at other white groups, albeit with a recognition that both Irish and Jewish migrants at the end of the Victorian period were afforded only a conditional 'whiteness' in the late nineteenth-century racial stratification.[21] This study has not focused on prejudices, often framed in a colonial context, against peoples of colour between 1889 and 1912, except in specific relation to the overlap between attitudes to colonised nationalities and towards the Irish Catholic and Jewish diasporas. A distinction can be drawn between a 'colonial' prejudice against African and Asian 'othered' groups that in this period for most British men and women was largely abstract, and a 'domestic' prejudice against outsider groups such as Jews and Irish. This latter form of prejudice was centred in British inner-cities and sprang from issues such as housing, education, and employment, as well as political affiliations and religious faith. However, by the end of the Edwardian period, with an increasing settlement of black and Asian communities in dockland areas, a conflation of the two prejudices, 'domestic' and 'colonial', was taking

---

[17] Kershen, *Uniting the Tailors*, pp. 154–156.

[18] Rocker, *The London Years*, p. 127.

[19] German and Rees, *A People's History of London*, p. 167.

[20] Joseph E.A, O'Connell Jr, 'Arthur Griffith and the Development of Sinn Féin', *History Ireland*, Vol. 19, No. 4 (July/August 2011), p. 66.

[21] Lorimer, *Colour, Class and the Victorians*, pp. 14–16.

place. The black and Asian worker was increasingly viewed as an economic threat on both British ships and British soil.[22] In areas such as Limehouse in the East End, the Gorbals in Glasgow, and Tiger Bay in Cardiff, diaspora space was becoming more, not less complicated and multi-layered as the first decade of the twentieth century concluded. For the Webbs, this increasing cosmopolitanism, apparently on the model of the large American cities, was in itself a threat to socialism and progress. Writing in the *New Statesman* in 1913, the Webbs predicted that with:

> the races of Eastern or Southern Europe, the negroes, the Chinese [arriving in Britain] as already in parts of the United States, [would result] in such a heterogeneous and mongrel population that democratic self-government or even effective application of the policy of a national minimum of civilised life will become increasingly unobtainable.[23]

This in effect was a reprisal of the fears expressed in *Blackwood's Magazine* in 1901, of uncontrollable diasporic interactions taking place within the slums and ghettos of urban inner-cities and resulting in 'miscegenation' between various ethnic outsider groups, the final outcome of which would be a 'mongrel population'.[24]

The language and imagery of antisemitism and Sinophobia as expressed in the Edwardian period were remarkably similar.[25] So too was the sexual angst that surrounded attitudes towards Jews, Irish (tied up with Catholic faith and directed primarily against priests and nuns), and Chinese and black migrants. The Chinese worker, like the Jewish refugee, was both effeminised and portrayed as an insidious sexual threat – a source of corruption, involved in 'white slavery'. The black sailor, like the Irish migrant of the generation before, was both infantilised (in an explicitly colonial context) and viewed as uncontrollably aggressive and physically threatening.[26] Crucially, in the

---

[22] In particular, see the three journals, *The Dockers Record*, *Seafarer*, and *The Seaman*. See *Dockers Record* (June 1908); *Seafarer*, Vol. 1, No. 245 (12 July 1902), article entitled 'The Dusky Peril'; and back issues of *The Seaman* over the course of 1911 and 1912.

[23] Beatrice Webb and Sidney Webb, 'What is Socialism', *New Statesman* (30 August 1913), p. 654.

[24] Anon., 'Foreign Undesirables', *Blackwood's Magazine*, No. 1024 (February 1901), p. 289.

[25] Anon., 'Chinese and Aliens'.

[26] See Marek Kohn, *Dope Girls: The Birth of the British Drug Underground* (London: Granta Books, 1992), pp. 19–20; Benton and Gomez, *The Chinese in Britain*, pp. 301–302; Bristow, *Prostitution and Prejudice*. For an extreme dose of antisemitic sexual angst, see Banister, *Britain Under the Jews*. See Tabili, 'We Ask for British Justice', p. 51 for discussion of infantilisation of non-white sailors in popular literature. The stock figures used in racist portrayals of the Irish (male) in popular English journals of the mid-nineteenth century, Caliban, the gorilla, the Frankenstein Monster, were, significantly, simultaneously depicted as both child-like and rapists. As late as 1903, Charles Booth was describing the East End Irish as

context of left-wing attitudes towards difference, these 'othered' groups, like the Jews before them and the Irish before the Jews, were popularly viewed as being able to subsist on less food, in poorer living conditions, for lower wages. In 1919, areas of East London witnessed severe violence directed against peoples of colour, particularly black sailors keeping company with white women.[27] At no point in the period 1889 to 1912 was there organised violence against an ethnic minority in East London to this degree, even taking into account the activities of the BBL or the Protestant Alliance, or Irish–Jewish gang fights among youths. Anti-Jewish or anti-Irish racism continued to manifest itself post-1912, as the antisemitic activities of fascist groups in the East End in the 1930s, or economic and housing discrimination against Irish immigrants into the 1950s testify. The difference was that after the First World War these prejudices were no longer articulated by the organised left, or the trade unions, as they were in the 1889 to 1912 period. Polemic against black and Asian minorities was another matter, as far as the trade union movement was concerned.[28] What this manifestation of racism lacked was that religious component so important in late nineteenth-century anti-Irish or antisemitic prejudice. Catholicism or Judaism as binary opposites of a Protestant English national identity and narrative was a key part of the prejudices of both left and right that this book has examined. After this point ecclesiastical inclination ceded importance to skin colour.[29] The black and Asian diasporic 'others' settling in British cities were certainly more visible, even more so than their Irish or Jewish predecessors in the nineteenth century, and more vulnerable to overt racial discrimination and physical attack.[30]

How can we characterise East End Irish–Jewish relations and interactions in the 1889–1912 period? There was certainly latent hostility between the two populations, as evident both in gang fights between Jewish and Irish Catholic youth and in the way that newspapers such as the *Catholic Herald*

---

'unrestrained as children, and brutal when their passions are loosed'. Booth, *Life and Labour of the People in London*, Third Series, *Religious Influences*, Vol. 7, p. 37.

[27] Jacqueline Jenkinson, 'The 1919 Riots', in Panikos Panayi (ed.), *Racial Violence in Britain, 1840–1950* (Leicester: Leicester University Press, 1993), p. 95.

[28] Tabili, *'We Ask for British Justice'*, p. 88.

[29] In the early twenty-first century the conflation of religious and ethnic difference and 'otherness', and the idea of certain groups by virtue of religious faith standing outside the national narrative would re-emerge in anti-immigrant polemic on Muslim minorities in British cities. See Matti Bunzi, 'Between Anti-Semitism and Islamophobia: Some Thoughts on the New Europe', *American Ethnologist*, Vol. 32, No. 4 (November 2005) and Panayi, *An Immigration History of Britain*, p. 173.

[30] David Mason, *Race and Ethnicity in Modern Britain* (Oxford: Oxford University Press, 1995) (republished 2000), pp. 15–16. Hickman, *Religion, Class and Identity*, pp. 80 and 94.

reported on Jewish settlement in East London. There were also suspicions of a continuing antisemitic component in Church education of the young.[31] However, this did not translate into mass East End Irish support for far-right anti-immigrant organisations, or sustained serious violence between adults. Catholic–Jewish interactions also had a positive and mutually supportive component, apparent not only in the largely cordial relations between the hierarchies, but in friendships formed at school and comradeship in industrial disputes. There were also semi-formal economic interactions such as that of the *shabbas goyah*, and the formalised employment of domestic servants. Relationships between members of the two communities were partially predicated on faith and ethnicity, but not wholly; class, geographical location, and political inclination also determined relationships formed between Jews and Irish Catholics in East End diaspora space. Irish–Jewish interactions should not be romanticised, but neither should they be presented in an overly negative light.

Having compared the experiences of both the Irish and Jewish working classes and their communal religious and secular leaderships, what conclusions can be drawn on the fundamental similarities and differences in how radical and communal politics functioned in the two diasporic populations? Both communities shared a complex outsider status that combined ethnic and religious difference, and into the Edwardian period both were still at least partially excluded from a national narrative that was Protestant and Anglo-Saxon. As has been illustrated, this partial exclusion could affect conservative anglicised religious hierarchies as well as working-class migrants and their descendants. Both East End communities were poor, and the majority of Jewish and Irish men and women worked in difficult conditions for low pay, as did their English neighbours. One social characteristic that was shared by both the Irish and Jewish East End working class and the wider East London proletariat was a hyper-masculine culture with strictly demarcated gender roles, economic and social, and which placed a premium on the role of the male 'breadwinner'. Culturally and politically, certainly until the First World War, Jews and Irish Catholics remained separate from the wider East End proletariat. In both cases minority religion and the continuing strength of that religious faith differentiated Irish and Jewish workers from the majority of their English counterparts.

The continuing importance of Home Rule for London Irish communities and its predominance over labour politics in the period also distinguished the Irish working class from their English neighbours. In this period Zionism as a political force was only beginning to emerge – the movement would come into its own amongst London Jewry after the First World

---

31  See *Jewish Chronicle* (2 February 1906); Davin, *Growing Up Poor*, p. 203.

War.[32] Despite this partial removal from the politics of the wider working class and the difficulties discussed in organising minority workers into trade unions, men and women of Irish and Jewish descent played a disproportionate role in the leadership of the movement. Will Thorne, Ben Tillett, Jim Connell, Eleanor Marx, Woolf Wess, Lewis Lyons, and Theodore Rothstein all played key roles, and this is not an exhaustive list. The socialist splinter groups that emerged in the first decade of the twentieth century such as the SPGB, and the BSP, which the SDF evolved into at the end of the period, were both notable for the leading roles taken by Irish and Jewish socialists. The SPGB was led by an Irishman, Jack Fitzgerald, who had worked as a bricklayer and was, like Will Thorne, self-educated; the BSP included Rothstein, Zelda Kahan, and Jack Jones among its leading lights.[33] There were also important cultural mediators within socialism from outside the minority groups who immersed themselves in diasporic radical politics, Rudolph Rocker being the prime example. There were others who attempted to reconcile socialist beliefs and minority religion, such as Robert Dell. The former was extremely successful in his efforts, the latter ultimately frustrated and disillusioned in his attempt to bring together his Catholic faith and his socialist politics.

On education, on the promotion of the English language, in the positions adopted towards the three great threats to communal cohesion: socialism, secularism, and Protestant evangelism, the stances and policies of the metropolitan Catholic and Jewish hierarchies were, if not identical, strikingly similar. This remarkable confluence of agendas was located in a shared class background, a mutual inclination towards conservative and cautious politics, and a common recognition of the continued precariousness of the Catholic or Jewish social position in Protestant England. To a degree the Jewish leadership, addressing the arrival of Eastern European refugees after 1881, drew on the experiences of the Catholic hierarchy following the post-Famine Irish influx of the 1840s, particularly the Church campaign for cultural anglicisation and integration and the supplanting of Irish Gaelic by English among the Irish poor. Given the similarities in temperament, outlook, and agenda, it is perhaps strange that in the 1889 to 1912 period the two leaderships should make explicit political common cause only over Liberal amendments to the Education Act. Gordon's extremely successful campaign as an independent candidate in the LCC elections of 1904 showed

---

[32] Lucien Wolf, 'The Zionist Peril', *Jewish Quarterly Review*, Vol. 17, No. 1 (October 1904); Russell and Lewis, *The Jew in London*, p. 107; Alderman, *London Jewry and London Politics*, p. 79. See Stephan Wendehorst, *British Jewry, Zionism and the Jewish State, 1936–1956* (Oxford: Oxford University Press, 2012).

[33] Thompson, *Socialists, Liberals and Labour*, pp. 190 and 203.

the potential political power of a clear Catholic–Jewish alliance, at least in a specifically East End context.[34] The failure to build on this success is at least partly explained by the pronounced aversion of both hierarchies towards accusations, still potent in the Edwardian period, of Jewish or Catholic political 'cabals' attempting to influence wider British politics.

The 1902 Education Act controversy was the only point in this period at which nebulous shared interests coalesced into a concrete shared political platform. In some respects, the fears of the communal hierarchies were chimerical. Neither hierarchy was ultimately overthrown by atheistic revolutionaries emerging from the East End slums. Protestant evangelism made little impact in either community. The secular culture of the wider East London proletariat did not extinguish religious or cultural identity; instead, a compromise was reached in a new organic London Irish or Jewish identity. What did take place was a gradual demographic revolution, in the long term inevitable, the supplanting of the old leadership by the children and grandchildren of the migrant poor. This was a shift in the basis of communal power that came to fruition after the period on which this book has focused. However, even before 1912, Irish clerics were beginning to assume senior roles in the metropolitan Catholic Church, and the descendants of the Jewish refugee arrivals of the 1880s would have assumed the leadership of the BoD and the *Beth Din* by the end of the inter-war period.[35]

Irish and Jewish communities shared significant similarities in their relationship with radical and communal politics and with the host society. Some were inherent in the wider migrant experience of settling in Britain, while others were particular to the time period or the geographical location. There are also important contrasts evident when comparing the political and social dynamics at work in the Irish and Jewish diasporic populations settled in East London. These contrasts can be located in two fundamental points of divergence in the social structure of the two communities that would inform the shape of communal and radical politics throughout the 1889–1912 period. These would determine attitudes towards socialist activity from both within and outside the minority communities. The first point of divergence was the nature of communal authority within the immigrant neighbourhoods, the second, class relations within the community.

---

34  Alderman, *London Jewry and London Politics*, p. 49.

35  In 1903, Francis Bourne became the first Catholic cleric of Irish descent to become Archbishop of Westminster, although, like his predecessor Herbert Vaughan, he was unable to establish that almost instinctive bond Manning had shared with the Irish Catholic working class. See Sheridan Gilley, 'English Catholic Attitudes to Irish Catholics', p. 100. The changing of the guard in the Jewish communal leadership was confirmed when Selig Brodetsky assumed the leadership of the BoD in 1940, also confirming the respectability of Zionism by this point within Anglo-Jewry.

To examine this first point of divergence, authority in the Irish Catholic East End was *centralised* to a large degree, whilst authority in the Jewish East End was *fragmented*. The parish priest was not an automaton, and his parishioners did not blindly imbibe his sermons without question. Substantial financial support provided for the upkeep of churches and voluntary schools by the Catholic working class gave them a significant stake in the grass-roots instruments of Church authority. Irish women in particular played a key role in maintaining support for priest and parish infrastructure in local communities.[36] Each parish priest had their own views on socialism, trade unionism, and the use of the Irish language. Nevertheless, authority in Irish Catholic neighbourhoods was invested in one particularly body, the Church. Each parish would be ministered to by one particular priest, representing one physical church building, with religious education being imparted through a single source. The priest could occasionally lose control of his flock, but he would not have to be concerned with another Catholic priest attempting to usurp his authority. Certain areas of East London such as Millwall were famous for the radical inclination of Irish immigrants living in these neighbourhoods, but the position of the Church was not supplanted or replaced.[37] Behind this authority lay an international organisation with a strictly hierarchical structure. To quote Cardinal Vaughan again: 'The Church is governed by a hierarchy, not a House of Commons. Her constitution is divine, and not dependent like a political machine upon popular agitation and the see-saw of public opinion.'[38] Communal politics in Irish Catholic areas remained largely under the influence of the Church, and correspondingly because of this dominance socialist activity presented less of a threat to this secure communal control. Catholic trade unionists, as evidenced throughout the Edwardian education debates, were inclined to support the policy of the Church, rather than undermine it. The mainstream Irish Nationalist movement, still commanding significant support in Irish communities and knowing how to pick its battles, avoided conflict with the Church and partially encouraged the association of Catholicism and Irish national identity.[39] Disputes between Nationalists and the Church hierarchy, such as the 1908 Westminster controversy discussed in Chapter 4, were centred

[36] Vaughan, *The Trinity Fund and the Material Condition of the Diocese*, p. 5. See also back issues of *The Catholic Herald*.

[37] Brodie, *Politics of the Poor*, p. 194. Millwall was also, conversely, the base of the charismatic businessman and Tory politician F.A. Bullivant (see Chapter 2).

[38] Vaughan, *A Call on the Laity for Christian Work*, p. 14.

[39] Lawrence J. McCaffrey, 'Irish Nationalism and Irish Catholicism: A Study in Cultural Identity', *Church History*, Vol. 42, No. 4 (1973), pp. 527–528.

on issues such as the right to use Irish Gaelic in religious celebrations, but not the dominant position of the Church itself.

Jewish communal authority in East London, on the other hand, was divided and even chaotic when compared with its Catholic counterparts. There was no single seat of unimpeachable authority in East End Jewry. Within Ashkenazim there were different forms of religious Judaism – Orthodox, Reform, and Liberal. Within East End Orthodoxy, at least at the start of the 1890s, there were numerous rabbis and teachers, a variety of *chevrot* and synagogues, sometimes small in scale, and often competing with each other for members. In East London Jewry there were *multiple* and *competing* points of authority, rather than the one centralised authority present in migrant Catholicism. Samuel Montagu sought to address this fragmentation through his Federation of Synagogues, but the control of the BoD and the *Beth Din* was ultimately tenuous in East London; many immigrant rabbis did not recognise the religious authority of the West End leadership, or did so grudgingly.[40]

Certain elements of East End Jewish socialism in the period were more aggressive than their Irish counterparts, and more willing to attack explicitly both the hierarchies and organised religion. There was no East End Irish equivalent of the *Arbeter Fraynt*, aiming barbs and provocative language at the minority leadership. Consequently, in a purely domestic context, the Jewish leadership, compared with the Catholic Church, viewed socialism within the community as a more immediate challenge to its position. Unfortunately for Chief Rabbi Adler, the Jewish authorities had less means at their disposal to counter such challenges, as the comparison between the Jewish Orthodox ineffectual response to Liberal Judaism and the Catholic hierarchy's effective crushing of Modernism illustrates.

The second point of divergence, and inter-connected with the first, was the class dynamic at work within the two communities. In the East End in this period the majority of Jewish workers, men and women, labouring in the casual trades were employed by other Jews. Jewish tenants were also often paying rent to Jewish landlords.[41] Catholic workers, with the exception of some building firms, were not employed by other Irish Catholics to a significant extent. There was also the question of scale. Whilst Irish young women working as domestic servants might be employed in a small household, as was the case with Irish women employed in piece-work at home, Irish men employed on the docks and gasworks were operating in environments in which large numbers of workers were employed at any one time. The East End Jewish tailoring workshops on the other hand were often small in scale.

---

[40] See C. Russell, in Russell and Lewis, *The Jew in London*, pp. 97–99.
[41] Feldman, *Englishmen and Jews*, p. 174.

Thus, while class tensions in Irish Catholic East End communities were *externalised*, those within the Jewish population were *internalised*. Irish class resentment was projected outwards, directed at employers from outside the community and the English ruling class. Jewish working-class economic and social antipathy was largely directed at other Jews, whether small-scale employers or the BoD. The frequent employment of Jewish workers by kinsfolk also complicated class dynamics at work in the community.

In social terms, the Catholic Church assumed in inner-city areas with large Irish populations approximately the same position it enjoyed in rural Ireland from where the migrants had originated. It would be a great exaggeration to claim that the agrarian Irish communal dynamic, and the nature of Church authority, were wholly reproduced in East London. In religious terms, as has been noted, there were significant differences in approved practice and ritual between rural South-West Ireland and metropolitan London-based Catholicism, especially for the post-Famine wave of migrants of the 1840s and 1850s.[42] This taken into account, the communal relationship between the Church and people proceeded upon roughly familiar lines, albeit, under the influence of the hierarchy, primarily in English rather than in Irish. The Jewish migrant, on the other hand, had to negotiate an entirely new relationship with an Anglo-Jewish West End middle class that constituted the religious establishment in London, and for which there was no real parallel in the shtetls of the Pale of Settlement.[43] Working-class Irish Catholics had a difficult relationship with upper middle-class English or Old Catholics, the demographic stratum Cardinal Vaughan had come from and referred to in *Justice* (in reference to class origin) as 'Cawtholics'.[44] Ethnic tensions and racial prejudice between English and Irish Catholics were still factors into the 1890s, adding a dimension to Catholic interactions not present within metropolitan Jewry.[45] There was also an ambiguous attitude towards the thriving London Irish middle class that has largely been peripheral to this particular study.[46] But the West End/East End opposition that informed all facets of London Jewish communal politics was simply not present to the same extent.

Socialist organs such as *Justice* did not stress the dichotomy of the rich

[42] Gilley, 'Roman Catholicism and the Irish in England', p. 154.

[43] See Ben-Cion Pinchuk, 'Jewish Discourse and the Shtetl', *Jewish History*, Vol. 15, No. 2 (2001), pp. 173–174 and 177–178 for discussion of the tension and dislocation between shtetl life in the Pale of Settlement and in urbanised western society.

[44] *Justice* (22 July 1911).

[45] See 1895 advert placed in *The Tablet* by one 'Mrs B' offering employment to 'a Nurse, Catholic, not Irish', *The Tablet* (9 February 1895).

[46] See Ni Dhulchaointigh, 'The Irish Population of London', pp. 249–250 on middle-class London Irish attitudes towards the Irish proletariat.

Irish employer and the poor Irish labourer in an East End economic context as it did with the Jewish 'capitalist' and the Jewish 'greener'.[47] The equivalent figure in socialist literature was the Catholic priest. But this was spiritual control being posited by these journals, rather than economic.[48] Colonial history also externalised Irish class resentment against oppressive English power, with no real equivalent sentiment in the Jewish working class, for whom Britain had offered a sanctuary from Tsarist oppression. Again, in the Irish case, tensions were externalised rather than internalised. Jewish minority nationalism in this period aimed to *bolster* the British Empire. Zionism was seen by Zangwill among others as wholly compatible with the British imperial project.[49] These two divergent points of authority and class structure determined the differing paths that Jewish and Irish communal politics took between 1889 and 1912 and subsequently.

How do these interactions between left-wing politics and Irish and Jewish identity between 1889 and 1912 reflect on the wider history of the movement up to the twenty-first century? Throughout the late Victorian period and subsequently there was a constant tension between a desire to support and represent oppressed groups on the one hand and to defend the economic gains of the English working class on the other. In the 1890s, with TUC resolutions passed calling for entry restrictions for foreigners, it was by no means clear that socialism and in particular the Labour Party would become the 'natural' party of migrants and their descendants in urban areas. H. Snell, in a 1904 pamphlet generally attacking entry restrictions for migrants, ruminated: 'As a Labour Party we are not called upon to contend that all anti-alien feeling is necessarily immoral and unnecessary.'[50] Two years later, discussing the correct attitude of British socialism towards ethnic and religious minorities, E.B. Bax and Henry Quelch wrote:

> [Are] we to understand that socialism champions and aligns itself with every movement for class and race equality[?] ... This depends entirely upon the character of such movements. All which tend in the direction of socialism are encouraged and assisted by socialists. All which, no matter how reasonable or attractive they appear on the surface, are essentially antagonistic to socialism, socialists are bound to oppose as misleading and dangerous.[51]

[47] *Justice* (14 October 1899). See Snell, *The Foreigner in England*, p. 3.

[48] *Justice* (22 April 1893).

[49] Meri-Jane Rochelson, 'Zionism, Territorialism, Race, and Nation in the Thought and Politics of Israel Zangwill', in Bar-Yosef and Valman, *The 'Jew' in Late-Victorian and Edwardian Culture*, pp. 149–150.

[50] Snell, *The Foreigner in England*, p. 5.

[51] E. Belfort Bax and H. Quelch, *A New Catechism of Socialism* (London: Twentieth Century Press, 1906) (republished 1909), p. 39.

Julia Bush in *Behind the Lines* (1984) has charted the fortunes of the socialist movement and organised labour in the East End between 1914 and 1919, at the end of which the Labour Party had finally surmounted those formidable Liberal and Conservative party machines that had been operating in East London for a generation. It had also (eventually) become the 'natural' choice for both the Jewish and Irish (often newly enfranchised) working classes. In fact, Bush has argued that all of the factors behind the eventual Labour 'conquering' of East London were in fact present in 1914. Thirteen Labour MPs were elected in the area in 1924. The party had assumed control of *every* local council in the East End by 1925.[52] Although the war precipitated a split in British Marxism and the BSP on the question of support for the war effort, the London Labour Party and the East End trade unions emerged from the conflict ready to flex muscles developed in the period we have examined. These had been tempered in 1914–1918, and, when coupled with the Representation of the People Act in 1918, would result in long-term permanent political gains.[53] In the East End this led to the election of Jewish MPs and increased Irish Catholic involvement in local Labour politics. This was partly a result of the establishment of the Irish Free State in 1922 and the final irrelevancy of the Home Rule issue that had occasioned multi-generational support for Gladstonian Liberalism in East End Irish areas up to 1916.[54] By 1918, the older, factional, Yiddish-speaking trade unions were largely irrelevant in a new era of labour organisation, and by the mid-1920s the migrant socialist groups of the 1890s and 1900s had been swallowed up either by Labour or the CPGB.[55]

The explicit role of the left as the defender of oppressed or targeted minorities, however, only became wholly apparent in the anti-fascist resistance of the 1930s, although Labour had replaced the Liberal Party as the primary electoral representative of the Irish and Jewish working class by the early 1920s.[56] The Battle of Cable Street on 4 October 1936 would be subsequently celebrated as the high point of working-class Jewish–Irish cooperation (in an anti-fascist context) in East London, an epilogue of sorts to the communal solidarity of 1911–1912.[57] Once the left was explicitly opposed to legislative restrictions on entry into the United Kingdom in the early twentieth

[52] Julia Bush, *Behind the Lines: East London Labour, 1914–1919* (London: Merlin Press, 1984), pp. 20–21 and 234.

[53] Bush, *Behind the Lines*, p. 80. See Adelman, *The Decline of the Liberal Party*, p. 36.

[54] Bush, *Behind the Lines*, p. 220; Fielding, *Class and Ethnicity*, p. 105.

[55] Bush, *Behind the Lines*, p. 190.

[56] Alderman, *London Jewry and London Politics*, p. 80.

[57] Joe Jacobs, *Out of the Ghetto: My Youth in the East End, Communism and Fascism 1913–1939* (London: Simon, 1978), p. 257; Kershen, *Uniting the Tailors*, pp. 178–179. Fishman, 'Allies in the Promised Land', p. 48.

century, as the main socialist parties were by 1905, the movement stressed a British radical heritage that both defended the refugee from persecution and offered asylum to the political émigré.[58] In the Edwardian period, far-right groups, the BBL and the WDU, had emerged to make a bid for the support of the urban working class by attacking immigrant communities. This challenge would be repeated in the 1930s by the British Union of Fascists, in the late-1960s by the National Front, and in the early twenty-first century by the British National Party and the English Defence League. Labour and the left rose to meet these challenges, sometimes through peaceful means, and sometimes by meeting force with force. Nevertheless, there were moments, following the 'Rivers of Blood' speech of 1968, for instance, when significant support for an explicitly racist platform was evident in elements of the trade union movement and in the Labour-voting constituencies.[59] These moments of doubt have also posed the question about which sections of society a mass social-democratic organisation operating in a parliamentary democracy is there to represent. This is as relevant now as it was in 1906 when Joseph Foley wrote to Ramsay MacDonald demanding that the Labour Party support restriction of migration by both Jewish refugees and non-white dockers and sailors.[60]

After 1945 new diasporas would settle in the East End, as the old Irish and Jewish populations continued to migrate north and east. The concerns and struggles of these new 'others' were not far removed from those of the migrant groups of the 1890s and 1900s: housing, working conditions, discrimination, the presence of anti-immigrant organisations and interactions with the host society, with other migrant groups, and with their own communal hierarchies. As in the 1889–1912 period, the relationships formed between East End communities and the socialist and labour movements, and how these relationships were arrived at, were neither simple nor straightforward. This book has examined interactions and comparisons between two diasporic minorities settled in the eastern environs of London, but there are many other relationships formed within metropolitan diaspora space, historical and contemporary, waiting to be profitably explored by the historian and the sociologist. The kaleidoscope of diaspora space becomes more, not less, complex and multifaceted as it is interpreted and examined.

---

[58] Johnson, *Social Democratic Politics in Britain*, pp. 113–114; Snell, *The Foreigner in England*, p. 6.

[59] Amy Whipple, 'Revisiting the "Rivers of Blood" Controversy: Letters to Enoch Powell', *Journal of British Studies*, Vol. 48, No. 3 (July 2009), pp. 726–729.

[60] Manchester People's History Museum, LRC/19/397, Letter to J.R. MacDonald of the LRC from Joseph Foley of the British Sailors' and Firemen's Union, 19 January 1906.

# Bibliography

## Primary Sources

### Archival Sources
*Jewish Museum, Camden, London*
Tape J.M./320, Interview with Nate Zamet, carried out by Debbie Seedburgh on behalf of the Jewish Museum, London (unknown date)
Tape J.M./378, Interview with Jean Austin, carried out with Debbie Seedburgh on behalf of the Jewish Museum, London, 17 May 1994
Tape, J.M./381, Interview with Ivor Mairents, carried out by Cyril Silvertown on behalf of the Jewish Museum, London, 17 May 1994

*London Metropolitan Archives*
ACC/2712/GTS/366, Notices and circulars from various Jewish organisations
ACC/3121/A/015, Board of Deputies of British Jews, Minutes, Vol. 14
ACC/3121/E/03/028, Missionary Activities: Counter Action to Attempted Conversions, Report of the Mission Committee
ACC/3121/G/01/001/003, Board of Deputies of British Jews, Annual Report, April 1891
ACC/3121/G/01/001/004, Reports 1901–1905, April 1901: Jewish Lad in Dr Barnardo's Home

*London School of Economics Special Collections*
LSE/BOOTH/ B/224, pp. 150–157, Interview with Revd G. Martyold, Minister of the German Lutheran Church, Little Alie Street, 21 February 1898
LSE DELL 6/1, Correspondence and papers of Robert Dell
LSE DELL 6/2, Correspondence and papers of Robert Dell (continued)
LSE ILP/5, Pamphlets and leaflets
LSE ILP/8, Socialist and labour thought
LSE ILP/13, Pamphlets and leaflets of the Social Democratic Federation and the British Socialist Party

LSE PASSFIELD 7, Printed, typescript and manuscript copies of books, articles, essays, reviews and published letters by the Webbs, with related papers

### Manchester People's History Museum
CP/IND/FAG/1/5, Childhood memories of Hymie Fagan
LPGC/22/68, Letter from the Trade Union Section of the Catholic Federation to the Executive Committee of the Labour Party
LRC/9/126/2, 'The International Kischinieff Massacre Protest Committee'
LRC/19/397, Letter to J.R. MacDonald of the LRC from Joseph Foley of the British Sailors' and Firemen's Union, 19 January 1906

### National Archives
HO 45/10257/X5806A, Meeting at Hyde Park
HO 45/10257/X5806A/2, Meeting at Hyde Park
HO 45/10315/125890, Proposal to hang Czar of Russia in effigy, 1905
HO 144/227/A50732, Dock Strike, Cases of intimidation which have come to the knowledge of the police since the commencement of the dock strike, 21 September 1889
HO/144/227/A50732/99-100, Silvertown disturbances and police reaction, 1889
HO/144/587/B2840C/92-101, Home Office correspondence concerning foreign intelligence agencies
HO 144/1008/141734, Home Office Minutes, October 1911, 'Whipping for contravention of expulsion order'
HO 144/1157/212342/28, Letter to Home Office from H.L. Raphael's Refinery, 9 August 1911
HO 144/1157/212342/91, Letter to Home Office from Millwall Docks, 10 August 1911
HO/144/19780, Sidney Street Enquiry

### Special Collections, Hartley Library, University of Southampton
MS 108/4, C.J. Goldsmid-Montefiore, 'A Die-Hard's Confession: Some Old Fashioned Opinions and Reflections about the Jews', 1935
MS 147, Papers of D. Mellows, Report of the Sub-Committee of the Special Committee of the United Synagogue, 14 April 1897

### Warwick Modern Records Centre
MSS 240/W/3/2, Balance Sheet of the Great Strike of East London Tailors
MSS 240/W/3/11, William Wess correspondence
MSS 240/W/3/29, Speech by John Burns at meeting held at the Washington Music Hall, Battersea, 21 September 1890
MSS 292/PUB/4/1/1, Trade Union Congress Report, 1894
MSS 292/PUB/4/1/2, Trade Union Congress Report, 1895

MSS 292/PUB/4/1/3, Trade Union Congress Report, 1903
MSS 292/PUB/4/1/5, Trade Union Congress Report, 1905
MSS 292/PUB/4/1/7, Trade Union Congress Report, 1907
MSS 292/PUB/4/1/8, Trade Union Congress Report, 1908
MSS 292/PUB/4/1/10, Trade Union Congress Report, 1910
MSS 292/PUB/4/1/11, Trade Union Congress Report, 1911

*Westminster Diocesan Archives*
AAW/ Box 5/83g, Gaelic League Correspondence
AAW/BOX ET, 1905 Dioceses of Westminster Visitation Returns for SS Mary
    and Joseph, Poplar
AAW/BOX ET, Jean Olwen Maynard, 'History of the Parish of St. Mary and
    Joseph Poplars, Vol. II, 1881–1894'
AAW/BOX KV, 1905 Dioceses of Westminster Visitation Returns for Guardian
    Angels, Mile End
AAW BOX KV, Jean Olwen Maynard, 'History of the Parish of Guardian
    Angels, Mile End, Vol. I, 1868–1903'
AAW/BOX KV, Jean Olwen Maynard, 'History of the Parish of Guardian
    Angels, Mile End, Vol. II, 1903–1918'
AAW/BOX LE, Jean Olwen Maynard, 'History of the Parish of St. Anne's
    Underwood Road, Volume IV, 1911–1938'
AAW/Box MQ, 1911 Dioceses of Westminster Visitation Returns for SS Mary
    and Michael's Church, Commercial Road
AAW/BOX ZT, 1908 Dioceses of Westminster Visitation Returns for St.
    Casimir's, St. George's-in-the East
AAW/Third Triennial Visitation Returns, 1911
AAW/V, Correspondence of Cardinal Vaughan

Newspapers
*The Advertiser*
*Alarm – Anarchist Weekly for the Workers*
*Catholic Herald*
*The Catholic Weekly*
*The Clarion*
*Commonweal*
*Daily Chronicle*
*Daily Graphic*
*Daily News*
*East London Observer*
*The Echo*
*Freeman's Journal*
*ILP News*
*Industrial Syndicalist*

*Jewish Chronicle*
*Jewish Standard*
*Jewish World*
*The Journeyman*
*Justice*
*Labour Leader*
*Manchester Courier*
*Pall Mall Gazette*
*Socialist Standard*
*The Tablet*
*The Times*
*To-Day*
*WDU Notes*
*Weekly Times and Echo*

## Pamphlets

Norman Angel, *War and the Workers* (London: National Labour Press, 1912).

Anon., *Alien Immigration, Issued by the Conservative Central Office, Report of the Royal Commission on Alien Immigration, Extracts from the Evidence Given before Royal Commission and from the Commissionaires Report* (London: Conservative Central Office, undated).

—— *The Aliens Act Made Useless – Following Liberal Amendments to the 1905 Aliens Act* (London: Conservative Publication Department, 1906).

—— *Chinese and Aliens* (London: Conservative Publication Department, c.1904–1906).

—— *In Memoriam, The British Empire, Died March 26th 1902* (1902).

—— *'What is the Primrose League?'* (London: Primrose League, 1905).

E. Belfort Bax and H. Quelch, *A New Catechism of Socialism* (London: Twentieth Century Press, 1906) (republished 1909).

T.D. Benson, *A Socialist's View of the Reformation* (Manchester: National Labour Press, 1902).

Annie Besant, *Why I Am a Socialist* (London: self-published, 1886).

Kenelm Digby Best, *Why No Good Catholic Can be a Socialist* (London: Burns and Oates Ltd, 1890).

Robert Blatchford, *Socialism: A Reply to the Pope's Encyclical* (London: Clarion Press, 1895).

George E. Boxall, *The Anglo-Saxon: A Study in Evolution* (London: T. Unwin, 1906).

John Burns, *Bondage for Black, Slavery for Yellow Labour* (London: Kent and Matthews Ltd, 1904).

Jim Connell, *Brothers at Last – A Centenary Appeal to Celt and Saxon* (London: Labour Leader, 1898).

J. Connell, *Socialism and the Survival of the Fittest* (London: Twentieth Century Press, 1903).

Daniel De Leon, *Socialism Versus Anarchism – An Address by Daniel De Leon* (Edinburgh: Socialist Labour Press, 1908).

Frederick Harrison, *The Boer War: Letters from Frederick Harrison* (reprinted from the *Daily News*, 30 May–29 June 1901).

Revd Stewart D. Headlam, *The Guild of St. Matthew – What it is and Who Should Join it* (London: Guild of St. Matthew, 1895) (reprinted 1906).

J. Ernest Jones, *The Case for Progressive Imperialism (Demand for a Socialist Imperialist Party)* (Chester: Socialist Party, April 1903).

Karl Kautsky, *The Proletariat* (London: Twentieth Century Press, 1908).

James Leatham, *What is to be Done with the Anarchists?: A Lecture by James Leatham* (London: Twentieth Century Press, 1901).

H.W. Lee, *The First of May: The International Labour Day* (London: First of May Celebration Committee, SDF Office, 1907).

Conrad Noel, *Socialism and the Kingdom of God (Jewish Scriptures and Gospels)* (London: Church Socialist League, 1904).

Joseph Rickaby, *The Creed of Socialism* (London: Anti-Socialist Union Publication Department, 1910).

H. Snell, *The Foreigner in England – An Examination of the Problem of Alien Immigration* (London: Independent Labour Party, 1904).

C.B. Stanton, *Why We Should Agitate* (Aberdare: Haylings and Co., 1903).

Alex M. Thompson, *Towards Conscription* (London: Clarion Press, 1898).

Ben Tillett, *A Brief History of the Dockers Union* (London: Twentieth Century Press, 1910).

—— *Ben Tillett: Fighter and Pioneer* (London: Blanford Press, 1943).

Herbert Vaughan, *Catholics and their Civic Duties* (London: Burns and Oakes, 1894).

—— *The Trinity Fund and the Material Condition of the Diocese* (London: Burns and Oates, 1894).

—— *A Key to the Social Problem: An Appeal to the Laity* (London: Burns and Oates, 1895).

—— *A Crusade of Rescue for the Orphans* (London: Burns and Oates, 1899).

—— *A Call on the Laity for Christian Work* (London: Burns and Oates, 1900).

Sidney Webb, *The Decline of the Birth Rate* (London: Fabian Society, 1907).

Revd J.J. Welch, *Socialism, Individualism and Catholicism* (London: Sands and Co., 1910).

J. Stitt Wilson, *Moses, The Greatest of Labour Leaders* (Huddersfield: Social Crusade Book Depot, 1909).

—— *The Hebrew Prophets and the Social Revolution* (Huddersfield: Social Crusade Book Depot, 1909).

## Contemporary Monographs and Articles

Hermann Adler, *The Ideal Jewish Pastor: A Sermon Preached at the Great Synagogue* (London: Wertheimer, Lea and Co., 1891).

Anon., 'Foreign Undesirables', *Blackwood's Magazine*, No. 1024 (London: William Blackwood and Sons, February 1901).

—— 'The London Irish', *Blackwood's Edinburgh Magazine*, Vol. 170, No. 1029 (London: William Blackwood and Sons, July 1901).

Joseph Banister, *England Under the Jews* (London: self-published, 1901).

—— *Our Judaeo-Irish Labour Party: How the Interests of the British Working Man are Misrepresented and Betrayed by Politicians who are neither British nor Working Men* (London: self-published, 1924).

Hilaire Belloc, *The Church and Socialism* (London: Catholic Truth Society, 1909).

Annie Besant, *The Evolution of Society* (London: Freethought Publishing Company, 1886).

Walter Besant, *East London* (London: Chatto & Windus, 1902).

F.G. Bettany, *Stewart Headlam: A Biography* (London: John Murray, 1926).

Robert Blatchford, *Merrie England: A Plain Exposition of Socialism (American Edition)* (New York: Commonwealth Company, 1895).

—— *Dismal England* (London: Walter Scott Ltd, 1899).

—— *Britain for the British* (London: Clarion Press, 1902).

Charles Booth, *Life and Labour of the People in London*, First Series, *Poverty*, Vol. 1, *East, Central and South London* (London: Macmillan, 1902).

—— *Life and Labour of the People in London*, First Series, *Poverty*, Vol. 3, *Blocks of Buildings, Schools and Immigration* (London: Macmillan, 1902).

—— *Life and Labour of the People in London*, Third Series, *Religious Influences*, Vol. 1, *London North of the Thames: The Outer Ring* (London: Macmillan, 1902).

—— *Life and Labour of the People in London*, Third Series, *Religious Influences*, Vol. 2, *London North of the Thames: The Inner Ring* (London: Macmillan, 1902).

—— *Life and Labour of the People in London*, Third Series, *Religious Influences*, *Inner South London*, Vol. 4 (London: Macmillan, 1903).

—— *Life and Labour of the People in London*, Third Series, *Religious Influences*, Vol. 7, *Summary* (London: Macmillan, 1903).

—— *Life and Labour of the People in London, Notes on Social Influences and Conclusion* (London: Macmillan, 1903).

—— *On the City: Physical Patterns and Social Structure* (Chicago: University of Chicago Press, 1967).

William Booth, *In Darkest England and the Way Out* (London: McCorquodale & Co. Ltd, 1890).

Hilaire Bourdon, *The Church and the Future* (Edinburgh: Turnbull and Spears, 1903).

Edward Carpenter, *Boer and Briton* (Labour Press: Manchester, 1900).

William Cobbett, *Good Friday: The Murder of Jesus Christ by the Jews* (London: self-published, 1830).

Patrick Colquhoun, *A treatise on the police of the metropolis; containing a detail of the various crimes and misdemeanors by which public and private property and security are, at present, injured and endangered, and suggesting remedies for their prevention* (London: H. Fry, 1797).

James Connolly, *Labour in Ireland: Labour in Irish History, the Re-Conquest of Ireland* (Dublin: Maunsel and Company Ltd, 1917).

Michael Davitt, *Within the Pale: The True Story of Anti-Semitic Persecutions in Russia* (London: Hurst and Blackett Ltd, 1903).

Robert Dell, *The Catholic Church and the Social Question* (London: Catholic Press Company, 1899).

—— 'The Papal Attack on France', *The Nineteenth Century and After* (April 1906).

John Denvir, *The Irish in Britain* (London: Trench, Trubner and Co., Ltd, 1894).

G.C. Duggan, *The Stage Irishman: A History of the Irish Play and Stage Character from the Earliest Times* (London: Longmans, Green and Co., 1937).

Pierce Egan, *Boxiana; or Sketches of Ancient and Modern Pugilism: From the Days of the Renowned Broughton and Slack, to the Heroes of the Present Milling Era!* (London: G. Smeeton, 1812).

Friedrich Engels, *The Condition of the Working Class in England* (Oxford: Oxford University Press, 1993) (originally published 1844).

William Evans Gordon, *The Alien Immigrant* (London: William Heinemann, 1903).

Thomas G. Eyges, *Beyond the Horizon: The Story of a Radical Emigrant* (Boston: Group Free Society, 1944).

B.L. Farjeon, *Aaron the Jew: A Novel*, Vol. 2 (London: Hutchinson and Co., 1894).

W.T. Gidney, *The Jews and their Evangelisation* (London: Student Volunteer Missionary Union, 1899).

W. Gordon Gorman, *Converts to Rome: A Biographical List of the More Notable Converts to the Catholic Church in the United Kingdom During the Last Sixty Years* (London: Sands & Co., 1910).

Frederick J. Gould, *Hyndman as Prophet of Socialism* (London: Twentieth Century Press, 1924).

J.A. Hobson, *The Psychology of Jingoism* (London: Grant Richards, 1901).

John Hollingshead, *Ragged London in 1861* (London: J.M. Dent & Sons Ltd, 1986) (originally published 1861).

E.G. Howarth and M. Wilson, *West Ham: A Struggle in Social and Industrial Problems* (London: J.M. Dent and Company, 1907).

H.M. Hyndman, *The Historical Basis of Socialism in England* (London: Kegan Paul, Trench and Co., 1883).

S.H. Jeyes, *The Life of Sir Howard Vincent* (London: George Allen and Co., 1912).

Joseph Keating, *My Struggle for Life* (Dublin: University College Dublin Press, 1916).

V.I. Lenin, *On Britain* (Moscow: Progress Publishers, 1959) (republished 1979).

Amy Levy, *Reuben Sachs: A Sketch* (London: Macmillan and Co., 1889).

H. Llewellyn Smith, 'The Migration of Labour', in J.H. Levy (ed.), *The National Liberal Club Political Economy Circle, Transactions*, Vol. 1 (London: P.S. King and Son, 1891).

H. Llewellyn Smith and Vaughan Nash, *The Story of the Dockers Strike* (London: T. Fisher Unwin, 1890).

Jack London, *The People of the Abyss* (Teddington: Echo Library, 2007) (originally published 1903).

J. Ramsay MacDonald, *Syndicalism: A Critical Examination* (London: Constable and Co. Ltd, 1912).

Georgiana Putnam McEntee, *The Social Catholic Movement in Great Britain* (New York: The Macmillan Company, 1927).

F.A. McKenzie, *Famishing London – A Study of the Unemployed and Unemployable* (London, Hodder and Stoughton, 1903).

Henry Mayhew, *London Labour and the London Poor* (Harmondsworth: Penguin Books, 1985) (originally published 1861).

H.A. Mess, *Casual Labour at the Docks* (London: G. Bell and Sons Ltd, 1916).

Arthur Morrison, *A Child of the Jago* (Chicago, Academy Chicago Publishers, 1995) (originally published 1896).

L.A. Pooler, 'The Socialist Movement', *Irish Church Quarterly*, Vol. 5, No. 2 (October 1912).

Beatrice Potter, 'London Dock Labour in 1887 (draft copy)', *Nineteenth Century*, No. 128 (October 1887).

—— 'The Lords and the Sweating System', *Nineteenth Century*, No. 160 (June 1890).

Jacob Riis, *How the Other Half Lives* (New York: Penguin Books, 1997) (originally published 1890).

Rudolph Rocker, *The London Years* (Nottingham: Five Leaves Publications, 2005) (originally published 1956).

C. Russell and H.S. Lewis, *The Jew in London: A Study of Racial Character and Present-Day Conditions* (London: T. Fisher Unwin, 1900).

John Oswald Simon, 'Jews and Modern Thought', *Jewish Quarterly Review*, Vol. 11, No. 3 (April 1899).

George R. Sims (ed.), *Living London* (London: Cassell & Company Ltd, 1906).

J.H. Stallard, *London Pauperism among Jews and Christians* (London: J.E. Taylor and Co., 1867).

Will Thorne, *My Life's Battles* (London: George Newnes Ltd, 1925).

Edgar Wallace, *The Council of Justice* (London: Ward Lock and Co. Ltd, 1908).

Beatrice Webb and Sidney Webb, *Problems of Modern Industry* (London: Longman, Green and Co., 1898).

—— 'What is Socialism? XXI The Great Alternative (1) The Answer of Pessimism', *New Statesman* (30 August 1913).

Arnold White, *The Destitute Alien in Great Britain* (London: Swan Sonneschein, 1892).

—— *The Modern Jew* (London: William Heinemann, 1899).

W.H. Wilkins, *The Alien Invasion* (London: Methuen and Co., 1892).

Lucien Wolf, 'The Zionist Peril', *Jewish Quarterly Review*, Vol. 17, No. 1 (October 1904).

Israel Zangwill, 'English Judaism – A Criticism and a Clarification' *Jewish Quarterly Review*, Vol. 1, No. 4 (July 1889).

—— *Children of the Ghetto* (London: J.M. Dent and Sons Ltd, 1892) (republished 1909).

## Secondary Sources

### Monographs and Articles

Peter Ackroyd, *London: The Biography* (London: Vintage, 2001).

Paul Adelman, *The Decline of the Liberal Party, 1910–1931* (Harlow: Longman Group Ltd, 1981).

Nazneen Ahmed, with Jane Garnett, Ben Gidley, Alana Harris and Michael Keith, 'Historicising Diaspora Spaces: Performing Faith, Race, and Place in London's East End', in Jane Garnett and Sondra L. Hausner (eds), *Religion in Diaspora: Cultures of Citizenship* (Basingstoke: Palgrave Macmillan, 2015).

Geoffrey Alderman, *The Jewish Community in British Politics* (Oxford: Clarendon Press, 1983).

—— *London Jewry and London Politics, 1889–1986* (London: Routledge, 1989).

—— *Modern British Jewry* (Oxford: Oxford University Press, 1992).

Geoffrey Alderman and Colin Holmes (eds), *Outsiders & Outcasts: Essays in Honour of William J. Fishman* (London: Gerald Duckworth and Co., 1993).

Peter Alexander and Rick Halpern (eds), *Racializing Class, Classifying Race: Labour and Difference in Britain, the USA and Africa* (Basingstoke: Macmillan, 2000).

Joan Allen, 'Uneasy Transitions: Irish Nationalism, the Rise of Labour and the *Catholic Herald*, 1888–1918', in Lawrence Marley (ed.), *The British Labour Party and Twentieth Century Ireland* (Manchester: Manchester University Press, 2016).

Sascha Auerbach, *Race, Law and the 'Chinese Puzzle' in Imperial Britain* (New York: Palgrave Macmillan, 2009).

Joan Ballhatchet, 'The Police and the London Dock Strike of 1889', *History Workshop*, No. 32 (Autumn 1991).

Constance Bantman, *The French Anarchists in London: Exile and Transnationalism in the First Globalisation* (Liverpool: Liverpool University Press, 2013).

Eitan Bar-Yosef and Nadia Valman (eds), *The 'Jew' in Late-Victorian and*

*Edwardian Culture: Between the East End and East Africa* (Basingstoke: Palgrave Macmillan, 2009).

Ronald H. Bayor, *Neighbors in Conflict: The Irish, Germans, Jews and Italians of New York City, 1929–1941* (Baltimore, Md.: Johns Hopkins University Press, 1978).

Geoffrey Bell, *Troublesome Business: The Labour Party and the Irish Question* (London: Pluto Press Ltd, 1982).

Gregor Benton and Edmund Gomez, *The Chinese in Britain, 1800–Present: Economy, Transnationalism, Identity* (Basingstoke: Palgrave Macmillan, 2008).

Stefan Berger, 'Guest Editorial', 'International and Comparative History', *Socialist History*, 17 (London: Rivers Oram Press, 2000).

Stefan Berger and Chris Lorenz (eds), *The Contested Nation: Ethnicity, Class, Religion and Gender in National Histories* (Basingstoke: Palgrave Macmillan, 2008).

Michael Berkowitz, Susan L. Tananbaum and Sam W. Bloom (eds), *Forging Modern Jewish Identities: Public Faces and Private Struggles* (London: Vallentine Mitchell, 2003).

Chaim Bermant, *Point of Arrival: A Study of London's East End* (London: Eyre Methuen, 1975).

Selma Berrol, *East Side/East End: Eastern European Jews in London and New York, 1870–1920* (Westport, Conn.: Praeger Publishers, 1994).

Mark Bevir, *The Making of British Socialism* (Princeton, NJ: Princeton University Press, 2011).

Eugenio F. Biagini, *British Democracy and Irish Nationalism, 1876–1906* (Cambridge: Cambridge University Press, 2007).

Eugenio F. Biagini and Alastair J. Reid (eds), *Currents of Radicalism: Organised Labour and Party Politics in Britain, 1850–1914* (Cambridge: Cambridge University Press, 1991).

Andy Bielenberg (ed.), *The Irish Diaspora* (Harlow: Pearson Education, 2000).

Eugene C. Black, *The Social Politics of Anglo-Jewry, 1880–1920* (Oxford: Basil Blackwell, 1988).

Clive Bloom, *Violent London: 2000 Years of Riots, Rebels and Revolts* (London: Pan Books, 2003 (republished 2004).

Florence Boos (ed.), *William Morris's Socialist Diary* (London: Journeyman, 1985).

Florence Boos and William Boos, 'The Utopian Communism of William Morris', *History of Political Thought*, Vol. 7, No. 3 (Winter 1986).

George Bornstein, *The Colors of Zion: Blacks, Jews and Irish from 1845 to 1945* (Cambridge, Mass.: Harvard University Press, 2011).

Joanna Bourke, *Working Class Cultures in Britain, 1890–1960* (London: Routledge, 1994).

L.W. Brady, *T.P. O'Connor and the Liverpool Irish* (London: Royal Historical Society, 1983).

Avtar Brah, *Cartographies of Diaspora: Contesting Identities* (Oxford: Routledge, 1996).

Michael Brenner, Rainer Liedtke and David Rechter (eds), *Two Nations: British and German Jews in Comparative Perspective* (London: Leo Baeck Institute, 1999).

Tobias Brinkmann, *Points of Passage: Jewish Transmigrants from Eastern Europe to Scandinavia, Germany and Britain, 1880–1914* (New York: Berghahn Books, 2013).

Edward J. Bristow, *Prostitution and Prejudice: The Jewish Fight against White Slavery, 1870–1939* (Oxford: Clarendon Press, 1982).

Marc Brodie, *The Politics of the Poor: The East End of London, 1885–1914* (Oxford: Clarendon Press, 2004).

Matti Bunzi, 'Between Anti-Semitism and Islamophobia: Some Thoughts on the New Europe', *American Ethnologist*, Vol. 32, No. 4 (November 2005).

Kathy Burrell and Panikos Panayi (eds), *Histories and Memories: Migrants and their History in Britain* (London: Tauris Academic Studies, 2006).

Julia Bush, *Behind the Lines: East London Labour, 1914–1919* (London: Merlin Press, 1984).

Mervyn Busteed, 'Resistance and Respectability: Dilemmas of Irish Migrant Politics in Victorian Britain', *Immigrants and Minorities*, Vol. 27, Nos. 2–3 (2009).

J.S. Butcher, *Greyfriars School: A Prospectus* (London: Cassell, 1965).

Alex Butterworth, *The World That Never Was: A True Story of Dreamers, Schemers, Anarchists and Secret Agents* (London: Vintage Books, 2011).

Claudia Carlen, *The Papal Encyclicals, 1740–1878* (Wilmington, NC: McGrath Publishing Company, 1981).

Vicki Caron, 'Catholic Political Mobilization and Anti-Semitic Violence in Fin-de-Siècle France: The Case of the Union Nationale', *Journal of Modern History*, Vol. 81, No. 2 (June 2009).

David Cesarani (ed.), *The Making of Modern Anglo-Jewry* (Oxford: Basil Blackwell, 1990).

David Cesarani and Gemma Romain (eds), *Jews and Port Cities, 1590–1990: Commerce, Community and Cosmopolitanism* (London: Vallentine Mitchell, 2006).

Bryan Cheyette, *Constructions of 'the Jew' in English Literature and Society: Racial Representations, 1875–1945* (Cambridge: Cambridge University Press, 1993) (republished 1995).

Charles Chinn, *They Worked All Their Lives: Women of the Urban Poor in England, 1880–1939* (Manchester: Manchester University Press, 1988).

Nathan Cohen, 'The Yiddish Press and Yiddish Literature: A Fertile but Complex Relationship', *Modern Judaism*, Vol. 28, No. 2 (May 2008).

Ultan Cowley, *The Men Who Built Britain: A History of the Irish Navvy* (Dublin: Wolfhound Press, 2001) (republished 2004).

Clyde F. Crews, *English Catholic Modernism: Maude Petre's Way of Faith* (Tunbridge Wells: University of Notre Dame Press, 1984).

M.A. Crowther, *The Workhouse System, 1834–129: The History of an English Social Institution* (London: Methuen and Co. Ltd, 1983).

Fintan Cullen and R.F. Foster, *'Conquering England': Ireland in Victorian London* (London: National Portrait Gallery Publications, 2005).

L.P. Curtis, *Apes and Angels: The Irishman in Victorian Caricature* (Newton Abbot: David & Charles Ltd, 1971).

Gabriel Daly, 'Some Reflections on the Character of George Tyrrell', *Heythrop Journal: A Quarterly Review of Philosophy and Theology*, Vol. 10, No. 3 (July 1969).

Mary E. Daly, 'Irish Women and the Diaspora: Why They Matter', in D.A.J. MacPherson and Mary J. Hickman (eds), *Women and Irish Diaspora Identities: Theories, Concepts and New Perspectives* (Manchester: Manchester University Press, 2014).

A.J. Davies, *To Build a New Jerusalem: The British Labour Movement from the 1880s to the 1990s* (London: Michael Joseph, 1992).

Anna Davin, *Growing Up Poor: Home, School and Street in London, 1870–1914* (London: Rivers Oram Press, 1996).

Colin Davis, 'The Elusive Irishman: Ethnicity and the Post-War World of New York City and London Dockers', in Peter Alexander and Rick Halpern (eds), *Racializing Class, Classifying Race: Labour and Difference in Britain, the USA and Africa* (Basingstoke: Macmillan, 2000).

Jennifer Davis, 'From "Rookeries" to "Communities": Race, Poverty and Policing in London, 1850–1985', *History Workshop*, Vol. 27 (Spring 1989).

John W. Derry, *The Radical Tradition: Tom Paine to Lloyd George* (London: Macmillan and Company Ltd, 1967).

David Dutton, *A History of the Liberal Party since 1900* (Basingstoke: Palgrave Macmillan, 2004 (republished 2013).

Mark Ebery and Brian Preston, *Domestic Service in Late Victorian and Edwardian England* (Reading: University of Reading, 1976).

Benjamin J. Elton, *Britain's Chief Rabbis and the Religious Character of Anglo-Jewry, 1880–1970* (Manchester: Manchester University Press, 2009).

Todd M. Endelman, *Radical Assimilation in English Jewish History, 1656–1945* (Indianapolis: Indiana University Press, 1990).

—— *The Jews of Britain: 1656–2000* (Berkeley: University of California Press, 2002).

David Englander (ed.), *A Documentary History of Jewish Immigrants in Britain, 1840–1920* (London: Leicester University Press, 1994).

—— 'Booth's Jews: The Presentation of Jews and Judaism in *Life and Labour of the People in London*', in David Englander and Rosemary O'Day (eds), *Retrieved Riches: Social Investigation in Britain, 1840–1914* (Aldershot: Scolar Press, 1995).

David Englander and Rosemary O'Day (eds), *Retrieved Riches: Social Investigation in Britain, 1840–1914* (Aldershot: Scolar Press, 1995).

Neil Evans, 'Debate: British History: Past, Present – and Future', *Past and Present*, Vol. 119, Issue 1 (1988).

David M. Fahey, 'Temperance and the Liberal Party: Lord Peel's Report 1899', *Journal of British Studies*, Vol. 10, No. 2 (May 1971).

J.M. Feheny, 'Delinquency among Irish Catholic Children in Victorian London', *Irish Historical Studies*, Vol. 23, No. 92 (November 1983).

David Feldman, 'The Importance of Being English: Jewish Immigration and the Decay of Liberal England', in David Feldman and Gareth Stedman Jones (eds), *Metropolis London: Histories and Representations since 1800* (Oxford: Routledge, 1989).

—— 'Jews in London, 1880–1914', in Raphael Samuel (ed.), *Patriotism: The Making and Unmaking of British National Identity*, Vol. 2, *Minorities and Outsiders* (London: Routledge, 1989).

—— *Englishmen and Jews: Social Relations and Political Culture* (New Haven, Conn.: Yale University Press, 1994).

—— 'Migrants, Immigrants and Welfare from the Old Poor Law to the Welfare State', *Transactions of the Royal Historical Society*, Vol. 13 (2003).

—— 'Jews and the British Empire, c.1900', *History Workshop Journal*, No. 63 (Spring 2007).

—— '"Jews in the East End, Jews in the Polity": The Jew in the Text', *Interdisciplinary Studies in the Long Nineteenth Century*, No. 13 (2011).

David Feldman and Gareth Stedman Jones (eds), *Metropolis London: Histories and Representations since 1800* (Oxford: Routledge, 1989).

Frank Felsenstein, *Anti-Semitic Stereotypes: A Paradigm of Otherness in English Popular Culture, 1660–1830* (Baltimore, Md.: Johns Hopkins University Press, 1995).

Steven Fielding, *Class and Ethnicity: Irish Catholics in England, 1880–1939* (Buckingham: Open University Press, 1993).

William J. Fishman, *East End Jewish Radicals, 1875–1914* (London: Gerald Duckworth and Co. Ltd, 1975).

—— *East End 1888* (Nottingham: Five Leaves Publications, 2005) (first published by Gerald Duckworth & Co. Ltd, 1988).

—— 'Allies in the Promised Land: Reflections on the Jews and Irish in the East End' in Anne J. Kershen (ed.), *London: The Promised Land. The Migrant Experience in a Capital City* (Aldershot: Centre of Migration Studies, 1997).

K.H. Flynn, 'The Limerick Pogrom 1904', *History Ireland*, Vol. 12, No. 2 (Summer 2004).

Derek Fraser (ed.), *The New Poor Law in the Nineteenth Century* (London: Macmillan, 1976).

W. Hamish Fraser, *A History of British Trade Unionism, 1700–1998* (Basingstoke: Macmillan, 1999).

Christopher Frayling, 'The House that Jack Built', in Alexandra Warwick and Martin Willis, *Jack the Ripper: Media, Culture, History* (Manchester: Manchester University Press, 2007).

Sabine Freitag (ed.), *Exiles from European Revolutions: Refugees in Mid-Victorian London* (London: Berghahn Books, 2003).

Bernard Gainer, *The Alien Invasion: The Origins of the Aliens Act of 1905* (London: Heinemann, 1972).

Jane Garnett and Sondra L. Hausner (eds), *Religion in Diaspora: Cultures of Citizenship* (Basingstoke: Palgrave Macmillan, 2015).

John A. Garrard, *The English and Immigration, 1880–1910* (London: Oxford University Press, 1971).

Lindsey German and John Rees, *A People's History of London* (London: Verso, 2012).

Ben Gidley, *The Proletarian Other: Charles Booth and the Politics of Representation* (London: Goldsmiths College University of London, 2000).

Sheridan Gilley, 'Vulgar Piety and the Brompton Oratory, 1850–1860', in Roger Swift and Sheridan Gilley (eds), *The Irish in the Victorian City* (Beckenham: Croom Helm, 1985).

—— 'Catholics and Socialists in Scotland, 1900–1930', in Roger Swift and Sheridan Gilley (eds), *The Irish in Britain, 1815–1939* (London: Pinter Publishers Ltd, 1989).

—— 'Roman Catholicism and the Irish in England', in Donald M. MacRaild (ed.), *The Great Famine and Beyond: Irish Migrants in Britain in the Nineteenth and Twentieth Centuries* (Dublin: Irish Academic Press, 2000).

—— 'English Catholic Attitudes to Irish Catholics', in Roger Swift and Sheridan Gilley (eds), *Irish Identities in Victorian Britain* (Abingdon: Routledge, 2011).

Paul Gilroy, *There Ain't No Black in the Union Jack* (London: Routledge, 1987) (republished 1992).

David T. Gleeson (ed.), *The Irish in the Atlantic World* (Columbia: University of South Carolina Press, 2010).

David Glover, *Literature, Immigration, and Diaspora in Fin-de-Siècle England: A Cultural History of the 1905 Aliens Act* (Cambridge: Cambridge University Press, 2012).

Andrew Godley, *Jewish Immigrant Entrepreneurship in New York and London, 1880–1914: Enterprise and Culture* (Basingstoke: Palgrave, 2001).

David Goodway, *Anarchist Seeds beneath the Snow: Left-Libertarian Thought and British Writers from William Morris to Colin Ward* (Liverpool: Liverpool University Press, 2006).

Nancy L. Green, 'The Comparative Method and Poststructural Structuralism: New Perspectives for Migration Studies', *Journal of American Ethnic History*, Vol. 13, No. 4 (Summer 1994).

N.R. Gullifer, 'Opposition to the 1902 Education Act', *Oxford Review of Education*, Vol. 8, No. 1 (1982), p. 93.

Daniel Gutwein, *The Divided Elite: Economics, Politics and Anglo-Jewry, 1882–1917* (Leiden: E.J. Brill, 1992).

June Hannam and Karen Hunt, *Socialist Women: Britain, 1880s to 1920s* (London, Routledge, 2002).

Lynne Hapgood, "'Is This Friendship?' Eleanor Marx, Margaret Harkness and the Idea of Socialist Community', in John Stokes (ed.), *Eleanor Marx (1855–1898): Life, Work, Contacts* (Aldershot: Ashgate Publishing, 2000).

Philip Henderson (ed.), *The Letters of William Morris to his Family and Friends* (London: Longmans, Green and Co. Ltd, 1950).

Arthur Herman, *The Idea of Decline in Western History* (New York: The Free Press, 1997).

Mary J. Hickman, *Religion, Class and Identity: The State, the Catholic Church and the Education of the Irish in Britain* (Aldershot: Avebury, 1995).

Claire Hirshfield, 'The Anglo-Boer War and the Issue of Jewish Culpability', *Journal of Contemporary History*, Vol. 15, No. 4 (October 1980).

—— 'The British Left and the "Jewish Conspiracy": A Case Study of Modern Antisemitism', *Jewish Social Studies*, Vol. 43, No. 2 (Spring 1981).

Eric J. Hobsbawm, 'The "New Unionism" Reconsidered', in Wolfgang J. Mommsen and Hans-Gerhard Husung, *The Development of Trade Unionism in Great Britain and Germany, 1880–1914* (London: George Allen & Unwin, 1985).

Karin Hofmeester, *Jewish Workers and the Labour Movement: A Comparative Study of Amsterdam, London and Paris, 1870–1914* (Aldershot: Ashgate Publishing, 2004).

Colin Holmes, *Anti-Semitism in British Society, 1876–1939* (London: Edward Arnold, 1979).

—— *John Bull's Island: Immigration and British Society* (Basingstoke: Macmillan, 1988).

Rachael Holmes, *Eleanor Marx: A Life* (London: Bloomsbury, 2014).

Jenny Holt, *Public School Literature, Civic Education and the Politics of Male Adolescence* (Farnham: Ashgate Publishing, 2008).

Bob Holton, *British Syndicalism 1900–1914* (London: Pluto Press, 1976).

Pamela Horn, *The Rise and Fall of the Victorian Servant* (Dublin: Gill and Macmillan, 1975) (republished by Sutton Publishing Ltd, 2004).

Donald L. Horowitz, *The Deadly Ethnic Riot* (Berkeley: University of California Press, 2001).

Stephen Humphries, *Hooligans or Rebels? An Oral History of Working-Class Childhood and Youth, 1889–1939* (Oxford: Blackwell, 1995).

E.H. Hunt, *British Labour History, 1815–1914* (London: Weidenfeld & Nicolson, 1981).

Michael Hurley, 'George Tyrrell: Some post-Vatican II Impressions', *Heythrop Journal: A Quarterly Review of Philosophy and Theology*, Vol. 10, No. 3 (July 1969).

John Hutchinson, *The Dynamics of Cultural Nationalism: The Gaelic Revival and the Creation of the Irish Nation State* (London: Allen & Unwin, 1987).

—— 'Diaspora Dilemmas and Shifting Allegiances: The Irish in London between Nationalism, Catholicism and Labourism, 1900 to 1922', *Studies in Ethnicity and Nationalism*, Vol. 10, No. 1 (2010).

J.A. Jackson, *The Irish in Britain* (London: Routledge and Kegan Paul, 1963).

Jack Jacobs, *On Socialists and 'the Jewish Question' after Marx* (New York: New York University Press, 1992).

Joe Jacobs, *Out of the Ghetto: My Youth in the East End, Communism and Fascism, 1913–1939* (London: Simon, 1978).

Matthew Frye Jacobson, *Whiteness of a Different Color: European Immigrants and the Alchemy of Race* (Cambridge, Mass.: Harvard University Press, 1998).

Jacqueline Jenkinson, 'The 1919 Riots', in Panikos Panayi (ed.), *Racial Violence in Britain, 1840–1950* (Leicester: Leicester University Press, 1993).

Graham Johnson, *Social Democratic Politics in Britain, 1881–1911* (New York: The Edwin Mellen Press, 2002).

Sam Johnson, *Pogroms, Peasants, Jews: Britain and Eastern Europe's 'Jewish Question', 1867–1925* (Basingstoke: Palgrave Macmillan, 2011).

Catherine Jones, *Immigration and Social Policy in Britain* (Cambridge: Tavistock Publications, 1977).

Greta Jones, *Social Darwinism and English Thought: The Interaction between Biological and Social Theory* (Chichester: Harvester Press, 1980).

Tony Judge, *Tory Socialist: Robert Blatchford and Merrie England* (Dublin: Mentor Books, 2013).

Anthony Julius, *Trials of the Diaspora: A History of Anti-Semitism in England* (Oxford: Oxford University Press, 2010).

Preben Kaarsholm, 'Pro-Boers', in Raphael Samuel (ed.), *Patriotism: The Making and Unmaking of British National Identity*, Vol. 1, *History and Politics* (London: Routledge, 1989).

Sharman Kadish, *Bolsheviks and British Jews: The Anglo-Jewish Community, Britain and the Russian Revolution* (London: Frank Cass, 1992).

—— 'A Good Jew and a Good Englishman': *The Jewish Lads' & Girls' Brigade, 1895–1995* (London: Valentine Mitchell, 1995).

Norman Kelvin (ed.), *The Collected Letters of William Morris*, Vol. 4 (Princeton, NJ: Princeton University Press, 1996).

William Kenefick, 'Jewish and Catholic Irish Relations: The Glasgow Waterfront', in David Cesarani and Gemma Romain (eds), *Jews and Port Cities, 1590–1990: Commerce, Community and Cosmopolitanism* (London: Vallentine Mitchell, 2006).

Dermot Keogh and Andrew McCarthy, *Limerick Boycott of 1904: Anti-Semitism in Ireland* (Cork: Mercier Press, 2005).

Anne J. Kershen, *Uniting the Tailors: Trade Unionism among the Tailors of London and Leeds, 1870–1939* (Ilford: Frank Cass, 1995).

—— (ed.), *London: The Promised Land. The Migrant Experience in a Capital City* (Aldershot: Centre of Migration Studies, 1997).

—— *Strangers, Aliens and Asians: Huguenots, Jews and Bangladeshis in Spitalfields, 1660–2000* (Abingdon: Routledge, 2005).

—— 'The Migrant at Home in Spitalfields: Memory, Myth and Reality', in Kathy Burrell and Panikos Panayi (eds), *Histories and Memories: Migrants and their History in Britain* (London: Tauris Academic Studies, 2006).

Neville Kirk, *Change, Continuity and Class: Labour in British Society, 1850–1920* (Manchester: Manchester University Press, 1998).

—— *Comrades and Cousins: Globalisation, Workers and Labour Movements in Britain, the USA and Australia from the 1880s to 1914* (London: Merlin Press, 2003).

Marek Kohn, *Dope Girls: The Birth of the British Drug Underground* (London: Granta Books, 1992).

Seth Koven, *Slumming: Sexual and Social Politics in Victorian London* (Princeton, NJ: Princeton University Press, 2004).

Paul Kriwaczek, *Yiddish Civilisation: The Rise and Fall of a Forgotten Nation* (London: Phoenix, 2005) (republished 2006).

Tony Kushner (ed.), *The Jewish Heritage in British History: Englishness and Jewishness* (London: Frank Cass, 1992).

—— 'Jew and Non-Jew in the East End of London: Towards an Anthropology of "Everyday" Relations', in Geoffrey Alderman and Colin Holmes (eds), *Outsiders & Outcasts: Essays in Honour of William J. Fishman* (London: Gerald Duckworth and Co., 1993).

Vivi Lachs, 'The Yiddish *Veker* in London: Morris Winchevsky, Building a Broad Left Through Poetry, 1884–1894', *Socialist History*, 45 (2014).

Fintan Lane, 'William Morris and Irish Politics', *History Ireland*, Vol. 8, No. 1 (Spring 2000).

Keith Laybourn, *A History of British Trade Unionism* (Stroud: Alan Sutton Publishing, 1992) (republished 1997).

Gisela C. Lebzelter, *Political Anti-Semitism in England, 1918–1939* (London: Macmillan, 1978).

Alan J. Lee, 'Conservatism, Traditionalism and the British Working Class', in David E. Martin and David Rubinstein (eds), *Ideology and the Labour Movement: Essays Presented to John Saville* (London: Croom Helm, 1979).

—— 'Aspects of the Working-Class Response to the Jews in Britain, 1880–1914', in Kenneth Lunn (ed.), *Hosts, Immigrants and Minorities: Historical Responses to Newcomers in British Society 1870–1914* (Folkstone: W.M. Dawson and Sons, 1980).

Lynn H. Lees, 'Patterns of Lower-Class Life: Irish Slum Communities in Nineteenth Century London', in Stephan Thernstrom and Richard Sennett, *Nineteenth-Century Cities: Essays in the New Urban History* (New Haven, Conn.: Yale University Press, 1969).

—— *Exiles of Erin: Irish Migrants in Victorian Britain* (Manchester: Manchester University Press, 1979).

Nora Levin, *Jewish Socialist Movements, 1871–1917: While Messiah Tarried* (London: Routledge and Kegan Paul, 1978).

Thomas Linehan, *Modernism and British Socialism* (Basingstoke: Palgrave Macmillan, 2012).

V.D. Lipman, *A Century of Social Service, 1859–1959: The Jewish Board of Guardians* (London: Routledge and Kegan Paul, 1959).

—— *A History of the Jews in Britain since 1858* (Leicester: Leicester University Press, 1990).

Rosalyn Livshin, 'The Other Self: Anglo-Jewish Fiction and the Representation of Jews in England, 1875–1905', in David Cesarani (ed.), *The Making of Modern Anglo-Jewry* (Oxford: Basil Blackwell, 1990).

Douglas A. Lorimer, *Colour, Class and the Victorians* (Leicester: Leicester University Press, 1978).

—— 'Race, Science and Culture', in Shearer West (ed.), *The Victorians and Race* (Aldershot: Ashgate Publishing, 1996).

Kenneth Lunn (ed.), *Hosts, Immigrants and Minorities: Historical Responses to Newcomers in British Society 1870–1914* (Folkstone: W.M. Dawson and Sons, 1980).

Lawrence J. McCaffrey, 'Irish Nationalism and Irish Catholicism: A Study in Cultural Identity', *Church History*, Vol. 42, No. 4 (1973).

Terry McCarthy (ed.), *The Great Dock Strike 1889* (London: Weidenfeld & Nicolson, 1988).

Vincent Alan McCelland, *Cardinal Manning: His Public Life and Influence, 1865–1892* (London: Oxford University Press, 1962).

John M. MacKenzie, *Propaganda and Empire: The Manipulation of British Public Opinion* (Manchester: Manchester University Press, 1984) (republished 1988).

Hugh McLeod, 'Working-Class Religion in Late-Victorian London: Booth's "Religious Influences" Revisited', in David Englander and Rosemary O'Day (eds), *Retrieved Riches: Social Investigation in Britain, 1840–1914* (Aldershot: Scolar Press, 1995).

D.A.J. MacPherson and Mary J. Hickman (eds), *Women and Irish Diaspora Identities: Theories, Concepts and New Perspectives* (Manchester: Manchester University Press, 2014).

Donald M. MacRaild, *Irish Migrants in Modern Britain, 1750–1922* (Basingstoke: Macmillan, 1999).

—— 'Crossing Migrant Frontiers: Comparative Reflections on Irish Migrants in Britain and the United States in the Nineteenth Century', in Donald M. MacRaild (ed.), *The Great Famine and Beyond: Irish Migrants in Britain in the Nineteenth and Twentieth Centuries* (Dublin: Irish Academic Press, 2000).

—— (ed.), *The Great Famine and Beyond: Irish Migrants in Britain in the Nineteenth and Twentieth Centuries* (Dublin: Irish Academic Press, 2000).

—— *The Irish Diaspora in Britain, 1750–1939* (Basingstoke: Palgrave Macmillan, 2011).

J.A. Mangan, and James Walvin (eds), *Manliness and Morality: Middle-Class Masculinity in Britain and America, 1800–1940* (Manchester: Manchester University Press, 1987).

Kevin Manton, *Socialism and Education in Britain, 1893–1902* (London: Woburn Press, 2001).

Lara Marks, *Working Wives and Working Mothers: A Comparative Study of Irish and Eastern European Jewish Married Women's Work and Motherhood in East London, 1870–1914* (London: PNL Press, 1990).

—— '"The Luckless Waifs and Strays of Humanity": Irish and Jewish Immigrant Unwed Mothers in London, 1870–1939', *Twentieth Century British History*, Vol. 3, No. 2 (1992).

Lawrence Marley (ed.), *The British Labour Party and Twentieth Century Ireland* (Manchester: Manchester University Press, 2016).

John Marriott, *Beyond the Tower: A History of East London* (New Haven, Conn.: Yale University Press, 2012).

David E. Martin, *Labour in British Society, 1830–1914* (Basingstoke: Macmillan, 2000).

David E. Martin and David Rubinstein (eds), *Ideology and the Labour Movement: Essays Presented to John Saville* (London: Croom Helm, 1979).

Ross M. Martin, *TUC: The Growth of a Pressure Group, 1868–1976* (Oxford: Oxford University Press, 1980).

David Mason, *Race and Ethnicity in Modern Britain* (Oxford: Oxford University Press, 1995) (republished 2000).

Ian Mikardo, *Ian Mikardo: Back-Bencher* (London: Weidenfeld & Nicolson, 1988).

David Miller, *Anarchism* (London: J.M. Dent & Sons Ltd, 1984).

Martin A. Miller, *Kropotkin* (Chicago: University of Chicago Press, 1976).

Wolfgang J. Mommsen and Hans-Gerhard Husung, *The Development of Trade Unionism in Great Britain and Germany, 1880–1914* (London: George Allen & Unwin, 1985).

Kevin Morgan, Gideon Cohen and Andrew Flinn, *Communists and British Society 1920–1991* (London: Rivers Oram Press, 2007).

Jerry Z. Muller, *Capitalism and the Jews* (Princeton, NJ: Princeton University Press, 2010).

Deborah Mutch, 'The Merry England Triptych, Robert Blatchford, Edward Fay and the Didactic Use of Clarion Fiction', *Victorian Periodicals Review*, Vol. 38, No. 1 (Spring 2005).

Paul Newland, *The Cultural Construction of London's East End: Urban Iconography, Modernity and the Spacialisation of Englishness* (Amsterdam: Rodopi, 2008).

John Newsinger, *Fenianism in Mid-Victorian Britain* (London: Pluto Press, 1994).

Giulia Ni Dhulchaointigh, 'Irish Communities in East London and their Processions, 1900–1914', *Socialist History*, 45 (2014).

E.H. Norman, *Anti-Catholicism in Victorian England* (London: George Allen & Unwin, 1968).

Joseph E.A. O'Connell Jr, 'Arthur Griffith and the Development of Sinn Féin', *History Ireland*, Vol. 19, No. 4 (July/August 2011).

Alan O'Day, *The English Face of Irish Nationalism: Parnellite Involvement in British Politics, 1880–86* (Dublin: Gill and Macmillan Ltd, 1977).

Edward T. O'Donnell, 'Hibernians versus Hebrews? A New Look at the 1902 Jacob Joseph Funeral Riot', *Journal of the Gilded Age and Progressive Era*, Vol. 6, No. 2 (April 2007).

Rachel O'Higgins, 'The Irish Influence in the Chartist Movement', *Past and Present*, Vol. 20, No. 1 (November 1961).

Irving Osborne, *Jewish Junior County Awards in East London Schools, 1893–1914, An Interim Report and Guide to Sources*, East London Research Papers, Centre for East London Studies, Queen Mary College, University of London, 1988.

Gearoid O'Tuathaigh, 'A Tangled Legacy: The Irish "Inheritance" of British Labour', in Lawrence Marley (ed.), *The British Labour Party and Twentieth Century Ireland* (Manchester: Manchester University Press, 2016).

M.A.G. O'Tuathaigh, 'The Irish in Nineteenth Century Britain: Problems of Integration', in Roger Swift and Sheridan Gilley (eds), *The Irish in the Victorian City* (Beckenham: Croom Helm, 1985).

Alan Palmer, *The East End: Four Centuries of London Life* (London: John Murray, 1989).

Panikos Panayi (ed.), *Racial Violence in Britain, 1840–1950* (Leicester: Leicester University Press, 1993).

—— *Immigration, Ethnicity and Racism, 1815–1945* (Manchester: Manchester University Press, 1994).

—— *An Immigration History of Britain: Multicultural Racism since 1800* (Harlow: Pearson Education, 2010).

D.G. Paz, *Popular Anti-Catholicism in Mid-Victorian England* (Stanford, Calif.: Stanford University Press, 1992).

Geoffrey Pearson, *Hooligan: A History of Respectable Fears* (Basingstoke: Macmillan, 1983).

Jill Pellew, 'The Home Office and the Aliens Act, 1905', *Historical Journal*, Vol. 32, Issue 2 (1989).

Henry Pelling, *A History of British Trade Unionism* (Basingstoke: Macmillan, 1963) (republished 1987).

—— *Origins of the Labour Party, 1880–1900* (Oxford: Oxford University Press, 1965) (republished 1979).

Susan D. Pennybacker, *A Vision for London, 1889–1914: Labour, Everyday Life and the LCC Experiment* (London: Routledge, 1993).

Ben-Cion Pinchuk, 'Jewish Discourse and the Shtetl', *Jewish History*, Vol. 15, No. 2 (2001).

Leon Poliakov, *The Aryan Myth: A History of Racist and Nationalist Ideas in Europe* (London: Sussex University Press, 1974).

Harold Pollins, *Economic History of the Jews in England* (East Brunswick, NJ: Associated University Press, 1982).

Liviu Popoviciu, Chris Haywood and Máirtín Mac an Ghaill, 'Migrating Masculinities: The Irish Diaspora in Britain', *Irish Studies Review*, Vol. 14, No. 2 (May 2006).

Bernard Porter, *Critics of Empire: British Radical Attitudes to Colonialism in Africa, 1895–1914* (London: Macmillan, 1968).

Leonard Prager, 'A Bibliography of Yiddish Periodicals in Great Britain (1867–1967)', in *Studies in Bibliography and Booklore*, Vol. 9, No. 1 (Spring 1969).

—— *Yiddish Culture in Britain: A Guide* (Frankfurt am Main: Peter Lang, 1990).

Martin Pugh, *'Hurrah for the Blackshirts!': Fascists and Fascism in Britain between the Wars* (London: Pimlico, 2006).

Louise Raw, *Striking A Light: The Bryant and May Matchwomen and their Place in History* (London: Continuum International Publishing Group, 2009).

Daniel Renshaw, 'Control, Cohesion and Faith', *Socialist History*, 45 (2014).

—— 'Prejudice and Paranoia: A Comparative Study of Antisemitism and Sinophobia in Edwardian Britain', *Patterns of Prejudice*, Vol. 50, Issue 1 (2016).

Paul B. Rich, *Race and Empire in British Politics* (Cambridge: University of Cambridge, 1986) (republished 1990).

Colin Richmond, 'Englishness and Medieval Anglo-Jewry', in Tony Kushner (ed.), *The Jewish Heritage in British History: Englishness and Jewishness* (London: Frank Cass, 1992).

Lawrence Rigal and Rosita Rosenberg, *Liberal Judaism: The First Hundred Years* (London: Union of Liberal and Progressive Synagogues, 2004).

Keith Robbins, 'Ethnicity, Religion, Class and Gender and the "Island Story/ ies": Great Britain and Ireland', in Stefan Berger and Chris Lorenz (eds), *The Contested Nation: Ethnicity, Class, Religion and Gender in National Histories* (Basingstoke: Palgrave Macmillan, 2008).

Elizabeth Roberts, *Women's Work, 1840–1940* (Basingstoke: Macmillan, 1988).

T.W.E. Roche, *The Key in the Lock: A History of Immigration Control in England from 1066 to the Present Day* (London: John Murray, 1969).

Meri-Jane Rochelson, 'Zionism, Territorialism, Race, and Nation in the Thought and Politics of Israel Zangwill', in Eitan Bar-Yosef and Nadia Valman (eds), *The 'Jew' in Late-Victorian and Edwardian Culture: Between the East End and East Africa* (Basingstoke: Palgrave Macmillan, 2009).

Fermin Rocker, *The East End Years: A Stepney Childhood* (London: Freedom Press, 1998).

Michael E. Rose, 'Settlement, Removal and the New Poor Law', in Derek Fraser (ed.), *The New Poor Law in the Nineteenth Century* (London: Macmillan, 1976).

Sonya O. Rose, *Limited Livelihoods: Gender and Class in Nineteenth Century England* (Berkeley: University of California Press, 1992).

Lulla Adler Rosenfeld, *The Yiddish Theatre and Jacob P. Adler* (New York: Shapolsky Publishers Inc., 1977) (republished 1988).

Ellen Ross, 'Fierce Questions and Taunts: Married Life in Working-Class London, 1870–1914', in David Feldman and Gareth Stedman Jones (eds), *Metropolis London: Histories and Representations since 1800* (Oxford: Routledge, 1989).

Edward Royle, *Chartism* (Harlow: Pearson Education, 1980) (republished 1996).

Mordechai Rozin, *The Rich and the Poor: Jewish Philanthropy and Social Control in Nineteenth Century London* (Brighton: Sussex Academic Press, 1999).

William D. Rubinstein, *A History of the Jews of the English-Speaking World: Great Britain* (Basingstoke: Macmillan, 1996).

William D. Rubinstein and Hilary L. Rubinstein, *Philosemitism: Admiration and Support in the English-speaking World for Jews, 1840–1939* (Basingstoke: Macmillan, 1999).

Raphael Samuel, 'The Roman Catholic Church and the Irish Poor', in Roger Swift and Sheridan Gilley (eds), *The Irish in the Victorian City* (Beckenham: Croom Helm, 1985).

—— (ed.), *Patriotism: The Making and Unmaking of British National Identity*, Vol. 1, *History and Politics* (London: Routledge, 1989).

—— (ed.), *Patriotism: The Making and Unmaking of British National Identity*, Vol. 2, *Minorities and Outsiders* (London: Routledge, 1989).

—— 'An Irish Religion', in Raphael Samuel (ed.), *Patriotism: The Making and Unmaking of British National Identity*, Vol. 2, *Minorities and Outsiders* (London: Routledge, 1989).

John Saville, *The Labour Movement in Britain* (London: Faber and Faber, 1988).

Leonard Schapiro, 'The Role of the Jews in the Russian Revolutionary Movement', *Slavonic and East European Review*, Vol 40, No. 94 (December 1961).

James A. Schmiechen, *Sweated Industries and Sweated Labor: The London Clothing Trade, 1860–1914* (London: Croom Helm, 1984).

Jonathan Schneer, *Ben Tillett: Portrait of a Labour Leader* (Beckenham: Croom Helm, 1982).

Laura Schwartz, '"What We Feel is Needed is a Union for Domestics Such as the Miners Have": The Domestic Workers' Union of Great Britain and Ireland, 1908–1914', *Twentieth-Century British History*, Vol. 25, No. 2 (2014).

Nigel Scotland, *Squires in the Slums: Settlements and Missions in Late-Victorian Britain* (London: I.B. Tauris, 2006).

Dennis Sewell, *Catholics: Britain's Largest Minority* (London: Viking, 2001).

Rob Sewell, *In the Cause of Labour: A History of British Trade Unionism* (London: Wellred Books, 2003).

John Shepherd 'Labour and Parliament: The Lib.-Labs. As the First Working Class MPs, 1885–1906', in Eugenio F. Biagini and Alastair J. Reid (eds), *Currents of Radicalism: Organised Labour and Party Politics in Britain, 1850–1914* (Cambridge: Cambridge University Press, 1991).

Haia Shpayer-Makov, 'Anarchism in British Public Opinion, 1880–1914', *Victorian Studies*, Vol. 31, No. 4 (Summer 1988).

Brian Simon, *Education and the Labour Movement, 1870–1920* (London: Lawrence and Wishart, 1965).

Michael A. Smith, *The Public House, Leisure and Social Control* (Salford: University of Salford Centre for Work and Leisure Studies, 1984).

Lucio Sponza, *Italian Immigrants in Nineteenth-Century Britain: Realities and Images* (Leicester: Leicester University Press, 1988).

—— 'Italian Immigrants in Britain: Perspectives and Self-Perceptions', in Kathy Burrell and Panikos Panayi (eds), *Histories and Memories: Migrants and their History in Britain* (London: Tauris Academic Studies, 2006).

John Springhall, Brian Fraser and Michael Hoare, *Sure & Steadfast: A History of the Boys' Brigade, 1883 to 1983* (London: Collins, 1983).

—— 'Building Character in the British Boy: The Attempt to Extend Christian Manliness to Working Class Adolescents, 1880–1914', in J.A. Mangan and James Walvin (eds), *Manliness and Morality: Middle-class Masculinity in Britain and America, 1800–1940* (Manchester: Manchester University Press, 1987).

Henry Felix Srebrnik, *London Jews and British Communism, 1935–1945* (Ilford: Vallentine Mitchell, 1995).

David Stack, *The First Darwinian Left: Socialism and Darwinism, 1859–1914* (Cheltenham: New Clarion Press, 2003).

Shaul Stampfer, *Families, Rabbis and Education: Traditional Jewish Society in Nineteenth-Century Eastern Europe* (Portland, Oreg.: Litman Library of Jewish Civilization, 2014).

Gareth Stedman Jones, *Outcast London: A Study in the Relationship between Classes in Victorian Society* (Harmondsworth: Penguin Books, 1971).

—— 'The Cockney and the Nation', in David Feldman and Gareth Stedman Jones (eds), *Metropolis London: Histories and Representations since 1800* (Oxford: Routledge, 1989).

John Stokes (ed.), *Eleanor Marx (1855–1898): Life, Work, Contacts* (Aldershot: Ashgate Publishing, 2000).

Roger Swift, 'Crime and the Irish in Nineteenth Century Britain', in Roger Swift and Sheridan Gilley (eds), *The Irish in Britain, 1815–1939* (London: Pinter Publishers Ltd, 1989).

—— 'Heroes or Villains?: The Irish, Crime and Disorder in Victorian England', in *Albion: A Quarterly Journal Concerned with British Studies*, Vol. 29, No. 3 (Autumn 1997).

—— (ed.), *Irish Migrants in Britain, 1815–1914: A Documentary History* (Cork: Cork University Press), 2002.

—— *Behaving Badly? Irish Migrants and Crime in the Victorian City: An Inaugural Lecture Delivered at Chester College of Higher Education* (Chester: Chester Academic Press, 2006).

Roger Swift and Sheridan Gilley (eds), *The Irish in the Victorian City* (Beckenham: Croom Helm, 1985).

—— (eds), *The Irish in Britain, 1815–1939* (London: Pinter Publishers Ltd, 1989).

—— *Irish Identities in Victorian Britain* (Abingdon: Routledge, 2011).

Alan Sykes, 'Radical Conservatism and the Working Classes in Edwardian England: The Case of the Workers Defence Union', *English Historical Review*, Vol. 113, No. 545 (November 1988).

Laura Tabili, *'We Ask for British Justice': Workers and Racial Difference in Late Imperial Britain* (Ithaca, NY: Cornell University Press, 1994).

Susan L. Tananbaum, 'Jewish Feminist Organisations in Britain and Germany at the Turn of the Century', in Michael Brenner, Rainer Liedtke and David Rechter (eds), *Two Nations: British and German Jews in Comparative Perspective* (London: Leo Baeck Institute, 1999).

—— '"Morally Depraved and Abnormally Criminal": Jews and Crime in London and New York, 1880–1940', in Michael Berkowitz, Susan L. Tananbaum and Sam W. Bloom (eds), *Forging Modern Jewish Identities: Public Faces and Private Struggles* (London: Vallentine Mitchell, 2003).

—— *Jewish Immigrants in London, 1880–1939* (London: Pickering and Chatto, 2014).

Eric Taplin, *The Dockers Union: A Study of the National Union of Dockworkers, 1889–1922* (Leicester: Leicester University Press, 1986).

Anne Taylor, *Annie Besant: A Biography* (Oxford: Oxford University Press, 1992).

Tony Taylor, *The Politics of Reaction: The Ideology of the Cecils and the Challenge of Secular Education, 1889–1902* (Leeds: University of Leeds Educational Administration and History Monographs, 1997).

Eric G. Tenbus, *English Catholics and the Education of the Poor, 1847–1902* (London: Pickering and Chatto, 2010).

Stephan Thernstrom and Richard Sennett, *Nineteenth-Century Cities: Essays in the New Urban History* (New Haven, Conn.: Yale University Press, 1969).

Deborah Thom, 'Free from Chains? The Image of Women's Labour in London, 1900–1920', in David Feldman and Gareth Stedman Jones (eds), *Metropolis London: Histories and Representations since 1800* (Oxford: Routledge, 1989).

Paul Thompson, *Socialists, Liberals and Labour: The Struggle for London, 1885–1914* (London: Routledge and Kegan Paul, 1967).

Pat Thorne, 'Labour and Local Politics: Radicalism, Democracy and Social Reform, 1880–1914', in Eugenio F. Biagini and Alastair J. Reid (eds), *Currents of Radicalism: Organised Labour and Party Politics in Britain, 1850–1914* (Cambridge: Cambridge University Press, 1991).

Richard Thurlow, *Fascism in Britain: A History, 1918–1985* (Oxford: Basil Blackwell, 1987).

Lara Trubowitz, 'Acting like an Alien: "Civil" Antisemitism, the Rhetoricized Jew, and Early Twentieth-Century British Immigration Law', in Eitan Bar-Yosef and Nadia Valman (eds), *The 'Jew' in Late-Victorian and Edwardian Culture: Between the East End and East Africa* (Basingstoke: Palgrave Macmillan, 2009).

Annelise Truninger, *Paddy and the Paycock: A Study of the Stage Irishman from Shakespeare to O'Casey* (Berne: Francke Verlag, 1976).

Chushichi Tsuzuki, *H.M. Hyndman and British Socialism* (Oxford: Oxford University Press, 1961).

—— *The Life of Eleanor Marx, 1855–1898: A Socialist Tragedy* (Oxford: Clarendon Press, 1967).

—— *Tom Mann, 1856–1941: The Challenges of Labour* (Oxford: Clarendon Press, 1991).

Barbara W. Tuchman, *The Proud Tower: A Portrait of the World before the War, 1890–1914* (London: Hamish Hamilton, 1966).

John Tully, *Silvertown: The Lost Story of a Strike that Shook London and Helped Launch the Modern Labor Movement* (New York: Monthly Review Press, 2014).

Ellen M., Umansky, *Lily Montagu and the Advancement of Liberal Judaism: From Vision to Vocation* (New York: The Edwin Mellen Press, 1983).

W.E. Vaughan (ed.), *A New History of Ireland*, Vol. 6, *Ireland Under the Union, II: 1870–1921* (Oxford: Oxford University Press, 2010).

Satnam Virdee, *Racism, Class and the Racialized Outsider* (Basingstoke: Palgrave Macmillan, 2014).

John Wain (ed.), *The Oxford Anthology of English Poetry*, Vol. 2 (Oxford: Oxford University Press, 1986) (republished 2003).

Marcus Waithe, *William Morris's Utopia of Strangers: Victorian Medievalism and the Ideal of Hospitality* (Cambridge: D.S. Brewer, 2006).

—— 'The Laws of Hospitality: Liberty, Generosity and the Limits of Dissent in William Morris's "The Tables Turned" and "News from Nowhere"', *Yearbook of English Studies*, Vol. 36, No. 2 (2006).

Judith Walkowitz, *City of Dreadful Delight* (London: Virago Press, 1992).

Bronwen Walter, *Outsiders Inside: Whiteness, Place and Irish Women* (London: Routledge, 2001).

—— 'Irish/Jewish Diasporic Intersections in the East End of London: Paradoxes and Shared Locations', in M. Prum (ed.), *La Place de l'autre* (Paris: L'Harmattan, 2010).

—— 'Strangers on the Inside: Irish Women Servants in England, 1881', in Roger Swift and Sheridan Gilley, *Irish Identities in Victorian Britain* (Abingdon: Routledge, 2011).

—— 'Placing Irish Women Within and Beyond the British Empire: Contexts and Comparisons', in D.A.J. MacPherson and Mary J. Hickman (eds), *Women and Irish Diaspora Identities: Theories, Concepts and New Perspectives* (Manchester: Manchester University Press, 2014).

John K. Walton, *Chartism* (London: Routledge, 1999).

James Walvin, *Passage to Britain* (Harmondsworth: Penguin Books, 1984).

Paul Ward, *Red Flag and Union Jack: Englishness, Patriotism and the British Left, 1881–1924* (Martlesham: Boydell Press, 1998).

—— *Britishness Since 1970* (Oxford: Routledge, 2004).

Alexandra Warwick and Martin Willis, *Jack the Ripper: Media, Culture, History* (Manchester: Manchester University Press, 2007).

Stephan Wendehorst, *British Jewry, Zionism and the Jewish State, 1936–1956* (Oxford: Oxford University Press, 2012).

Shearer West (ed.), *The Victorians and Race* (Aldershot: Ashgate Publishing, 1996).

Amy Whipple, 'Revisiting the "Rivers of Blood" Controversy: Letters to Enoch Powell', *Journal of British Studies*, Vol. 48, No. 3 (July 2009).

Jerry White, *Rothschild Buildings: Life in an East End Tenement Block, 1887–1920* (London: Routledge and Kegan Paul, 1980).

—— *London in the 19th Century* (London: Vintage, 2008).

J.M. Winter, 'The Webbs and the Non-White World: A Case of Socialist Racialism', *Journal of Contemporary History*, Vol. 9, No. 1 (January 1974).

Sarah Wise, *The Blackest Streets: The Life and Death of a Victorian Slum* (London: Vintage, 2009).

George Woodcock, *Anarchism: A History of Libertarian Ideas and Movements* (Harmondsworth: Penguin Books, 1962).

Matthew Worley, *Labour Inside the Gate: A History of the British Labour Party between the Wars* (London: I.B. Tauris and Co. Ltd, 2005).

Ken Young, *Local Politics and the Rise of Party: The London Municipal Society and the Conservative Intervention in Local Elections, 1894–1963* (Leicester: Leicester University Press, 1975).

## Unpublished Theses

Ben Gidley, 'Citizenship and Belonging: East London Jewish Radicals 1903–1918' (PhD, Goldsmiths, University of London, 2003).

L.V. Marks, 'Irish and Jewish Women's Experience of Childbirth and Infant Care in East London, 1870–1939 (DPhil, University of Oxford, 1990).

J.E.B. Munson, 'A Study of Nonconformity in Edwardian England as Revealed by the Passive Resistance Movement against the 1902 Education Act' (DPhil, University of Oxford, 1973).

Giulia Ni Dhulchaointigh, 'The Irish Population of London, 1900–14: Connections and Disconnections' (PhD, Trinity College Dublin, 2013).

Laura Vaughan, 'A Study of the Spatial Characteristics of the Jews in London, 1695 and 1895' (MSc, University College London, 1994).

# Index